T0340121

Health Insurance Systems: An International Comparison

Health Insurance Systems: An International Comparison

Thomas Rice

Distinguished Professor, Department of Health Policy and Management,
UCLA Fielding School of Public Health, Los Angeles, CA, United States

ELSEVIER

ACADEMIC PRESS

An imprint of Elsevier

Academic Press is an imprint of Elsevier
125 London Wall, London EC2Y 5AS, United Kingdom
525 B Street, Suite 1650, San Diego, CA 92101, United States
50 Hampshire Street, 5th Floor, Cambridge, MA 02139, United States
The Boulevard, Langford Lane, Kidlington, Oxford OX5 1GB, United Kingdom

Notices
Knowledge and best practice in this field are constantly changing. As new research and experience broaden our understanding, changes in research methods, professional practices, or medical treatment may become necessary.

Practitioners and researchers must always rely on their own experience and knowledge in evaluating and using any information, methods, compounds, or experiments described herein. In using such information or methods they should be mindful of their own safety and the safety of others, including parties for whom they have a professional responsibility.

To the fullest extent of the law, neither the Publisher nor the authors, contributors, or editors, assume any liability for any injury and/or damage to persons or property as a matter of products liability, negligence or otherwise, or from any use or operation of any methods, products, instructions, or ideas contained in the material herein.

Library of Congress Cataloging-in-Publication Data
A catalog record for this book is available from the Library of Congress

British Library Cataloguing-in-Publication Data
A catalogue record for this book is available from the British Library

ISBN 978-0-12-816072-5

For information on all Academic Press publications
visit our website at https://www.elsevier.com/books-and-journals

Publisher: Brian Romer
Editorial Project Manager: Lindsay Lawrence
Production Project Manager: Niranjan Bhaskaran
Cover Designer: Greg Harris

Typeset by SPi Global, India

Working together
to grow libraries in
developing countries

www.elsevier.com • www.bookaid.org

In memory of Uwe Reinhardt

Contents

Part II
The countries

Section A
Universal coverage systems with a single insurer

Section C
Universal coverage systems with competing insurers

Section D
Systems without universal coverage

Part III
Cross-country comparisons

About the author

Thomas Rice is Distinguished Professor of
Health Policy and Management at the UCLA
Fielding School of Public Health. A health
economist, his areas of interest include
international healthcare systems, health
insurance, competition and regulation, and
behavioral economics. He has also written
books on health economics, the behavioral
economics of health, and the US healthcare
system. Dr. Rice was previously editor of the
journal *Medical Care Research and Review*
and is an elected member of the National
Academy of Medicine. He has served as chair
of the Board of Directors of AcademyHealth,

the leading US organization focused on the health services and health policy
research, and has chaired its Board of Directors and directed its Annual
Research Meeting.

Part I

Overview

Chapter 1

Introduction

The purpose of this book is to describe key facets of health insurance systems in 10 high-income countries, with dual aims of providing an understanding of the different ways in which nations organize their systems and evaluating their successes and failures. By explaining many components of each system and providing comparative data on performance across countries, the book highlights "best practices" that the countries have developed.

All countries face the challenge of providing access to high-quality health care while not "breaking the bank." Generally, their health policy communities identify problems impeding these goals and rely on their own countries' experiences to craft improvements. Increasingly, though, policy makers have been open to examining the experiences in other countries that face similar challenges. An example from some time ago was changing the way that hospitals were paid after the United States successfully implemented a system called diagnosis-related groups (DRGs) into its Medicare program in 1983. DRGs represented a move away from paying a separate fee for each day a patient was hospitalized, to one where a single fee was paid for an entire stay, providing a strong financial incentive to shorten the time in the hospital. The use of DRGs diffused rapidly in Europe [1] and beyond and is now the most common way of paying for hospital care in high-income countries.

A second example of international diffusion centers on pharmaceutical payment. In 1992, Australia was the first country to require that new pharmaceutical products be subject to rigorous cost-effectiveness analyses before being included in the list of covered benefits [2, 3]. More recently, most European countries have begun to adopt two distinct but interrelated strategies to control drug spending: internal and external reference pricing. Under internal reference pricing, if consumers want to choose a drug that costs more than others on the market but which research shows does not provide additional medical benefits, they must pay for the difference out of pocket. External reference pricing limits how much a country will pay for particular drugs by setting as a maximum amount paid by other countries. Both of these techniques have now disseminated to a large majority of European countries [4] and to other regions as well.

These are just two examples that demonstrate the enormous potential available when countries closely track what others are doing and work together to solve common problems. The individual country chapters in this book highlight

Health Insurance Systems: An International Comparison. https://doi.org/10.1016/B978-0-12-816072-5.00017-1

3

innovations such as these, while the comparison chapters provide evidence of the success of these and many other policy strategies.

The 10 countries

Ten countries are included in the book: Australia, Canada, France, Germany, Japan, the Netherlands, Sweden, Switzerland, the United Kingdom, and the United States. Except for the last chapter of this book, which focuses somewhat more on lessons for the United States, each of the 10 countries receives equal attention.

I have been studying these particular countries for almost 20 years and included them in the second edition of a health economics book I wrote in 2003 to illustrate the role of government in health policy, worldwide [5].[a] These countries are, and have been for at least two decades, among those most often identified as having healthcare systems worth learning from. They also account for half of the world's 20 wealthiest countries with at least 5 million people. The reason that I did not originally include any middle- or low-income countries was that their health insurance systems are different enough that I did not think they could provide as many lessons for the United States.

Then, as now, these 10 countries are of particular policy interest. That is true of other countries as well, but the selected countries provide enough breadth and diversity to represent the major extant health insurance systems.[b] The 10 countries encompass different ways of organizing health insurance, ranging from those with government-heavy single-payer systems to others that focus more on competition between competing health insurance plans. If I were to pick just one or two things that have intrigued me about each country over the years, they are the following:

Australia has a single-payer public health insurance system providing basic coverage to everyone, but also gives strong financial incentives to its citizenry to purchase private coverage, allowing many wealthier people to avoid long waits for receiving hospital care and to choose hospital-based specialists.

Canada is often pointed to by those on the left as a model that the United States could emulate, with strong government involvement in health insurance and much lower spending than the United States. However, its benefit package is more limited than other countries, leading to potential access problems, and there are continuing concerns about waiting to receive certain types of care.

---

a. The fourth edition of the book, with Lynn Unruh as a coauthor, was published in 2016 [6], and a fifth edition is scheduled to be published in 2021, with Andrew Barnes as another coauthor.
b. One country not included here whose health insurance has received a great deal of attention is Singapore, whose system is based in part on tax-favored individual savings accounts used to pay for certain care coupled with a separate system covering potentially catastrophic expenses. Both brief [7, 8] and book-length [9, 10] treatments of the system are available.

France provides an intriguing hybrid; although it is nominally a country with multiple insurers, there is no choice among them and the government is considerably more involved in regulating health technology and determining provider fees.

Germany developed the first health insurance system in the late 1800s and still is the prototype for "**Bismarck**-style" social insurance systems, a key characteristic of which is that government plays a relatively small role in health insurance, with most decisions devolving to "corporatist" organizations representing the interests of insurers and providers. Unlike the other countries, it also has a parallel private health insurance system used by about one-tenth of the population.

Japan is intriguing in several ways: it has the longest life expectancies, the oldest population, perhaps the highest assortment of high-tech medicine and equipment, its people use more services than those in nearly all other countries, and government sets physician fees at very low levels by international standards.

The *Netherlands*, more than any other country except perhaps the United States, bases its system on competition between health insurers—so-called "regulated" or "managed" competition—with a national system quite like the individual insurance marketplaces in the United States. Unlike the USA, it has achieved universal coverage with excellent performance on a number of outcome measures coupled with relatively low spending.

Sweden's system embodies the Scandinavian social welfare ethic of ensuring that people's needs, including health care, are fairly met, through a government system basing power in regional rather than national hands.

Switzerland, like the Netherlands, has an insurance system based on regulated competition but unlike other wealthy countries, its financing system relies heavily on patient out-of-pocket spending, raising concerns about financial access to care.

The *United Kingdom* provides the prototype for a national health service based on strong national government control, with one intriguing feature being that new services and drugs are generally covered only if they meet strict cost-effectiveness criteria. Spending is also low by international standards such that there have been complaints for decades about underfunding and waiting to receive some services.

The *United States* is the only one of the ten countries that does not guarantee coverage for its residents and has several parallel insurance systems (rather than a single national health insurance plan) serving different segments of the population. It spends far more on health care than the other countries, but shows poor performance both in financial access to care and various health outcomes.

Purpose and organization of the book

The book focuses on health insurance rather than the delivery of services. This reflects both my training as a health economist and lack of training in medicine.

Moreover, it would be difficult to cover both financing and delivery of so many countries in a single book. Each country would deserve its own book, and indeed, such books are available on each of the 10 countries. The most ambitious effort to write country-specific books is carried out by the European Observatory on Health Systems and Policies, a partnership of the World Health Organization/ Europe, the European Community, the World Bank, and several countries, regions, and universities [11]. One set of products offered by the Observatory, and available free on the Internet, are full-length books on the healthcare systems of dozens of countries, not just in Europe but also in North America and Asia. Since 2010, over 40 countries have had new or updated volumes published. My involvement in the European Observatory began with being asked to put together a team to write the first book about the US system (2013) [12], with a second edition published in 2020 [13].

The current book is intended for multiple audiences. One is the classroom, and in particular, courses on comparative health systems and health policy. Because no background is necessary to understand the material, it is appropriate for both undergraduate and graduate students. The second audience is the worldwide health policy community. It is hoped that by providing both compact descriptions of each country's health insurance system, as well as data from numerous sources comparing those systems and their performance, it will allow policy analysts to better understand the features of different systems that either improve or impede excellent performance. A third audience is the general reader who wishes to learn about this critical aspect of health policy: how countries protect their populations from the consequences of illness.

There is one substantive component of health insurance that is not included: coverage for long-term care. Long-term care is typically regulated and financed differently from acute care—often being the responsibility of localities—and thus can vary greatly even within countries, making it difficult to summarize.

The book is organized into three main parts. The remainder of Part I provides an overview of the main aspects of health insurance systems, including a brief historical description; an overview of how health insurance is organized, governed, and financed across the countries; what services are covered and to what extent; the role of private health insurance that often supplements the public system; choice of insurer and provider; provider payment; and issues countries face with respect to access, equity, and controlling expenditures.

The 10 chapters that constitute Part II of the book (Chapter 3 through 12) summarize each of the health insurance system components mentioned above for each country. The chapters are divided into four groups. The first three groups include the nine countries that provide universal health insurance coverage. Section A discusses the countries with a single public insurer: the United Kingdom, Canada, Sweden, and Australia. Section B contains chapters on France and Japan, which have multiple insurers but do not offer consumers a choice of insurer. Section C examines three countries that do offer such a choice: Germany, Switzerland, and the Netherlands. Section D, on systems that do not provide universal coverage, contains only one country: the United States.

In Part III of the book (Chapters 13 through 16), we compare the 10 systems' characteristics along with equity and efficiency and finally draw some insights about comparative performance and tentative lessons from the country discussions and comparative data.

Acknowledgments

Over the 3 years I have spent researching and writing this book, I have received extraordinary help from friends and colleagues and have also relied on the kindness of (many) strangers—experts about their countries' health insurance systems whose writings I had admired. My greatest thanks are to my wife, Katherine Desmond, who read and commented on every chapter, vastly improving both the content and readability. She also created the tables and figures that appear in the final part of the book. Kanon Mori, a UCLA student, did an outstanding job in creating the endnote files upon which each chapter's bibliography is based. I would also like to give special thanks to Roosa Tikkanen, who provided invaluable comments on nearly half of the chapters and who helped guide me through the use of the Commonwealth Fund's data.

This book would not have been possible without a bevy of country experts who provided critiques of my drafts of each of the country-specific chapters. In particular, I am indebted to the following people:

Australia: Fran Collyer, Stephen Duckett, Jeffrey Richardson, Roosa Tikkanen, and Sharon Willcox
Canada: Sara Allin, Michel Grignon, Noah Ivers, Gregory Marchildon, Danielle Martin, Karen Palmer, and Carolyn Tuohy
France: Paul Dourgnon, Zeynep Or, Victor Rodwin, and Monika Steffen
Germany: Miriam Blumel, Reinhard Busse, Bernard Gibis, and Konrad Obermann
Japan: Naoki Ikegami, Ryu Niki, Reo Takaku, and Yusuke Tsugawa
Netherlands: Ewout van Ginneken, Madelon Kroneman, Erik Schut, and Wynand van de Ven
Sweden: Anders Anell, Anna Glenngard, and Nils Janlov
Switzerland: Luca Crivelli, Monika Diebold, Alberto Holly, Wilm Quentin, and Roosa Tikkkanen
The *United Kingdom*: Jonathan Cylus, Mark Dayan, Martin McKee, and Adam Oliver
The *United States*: Andrew Barnes, Jon Gabel, and Gerald Kominski

I am equally indebted to several people who read and commented on some or all of the cross-country comparisons that constitute Part III of the book: Sara Allin, Gerard Anderson, Ewout van Ginneken, Richard Kronick, Corrina Moucheraud, Dimitra Panteli, and Roosa Tikkanen.

Finally, I express my deep appreciation to the Rockefeller Foundation's Bellagio Center in Italy, which provided a residency where I began the drafting of the book.

Needless to say, any errors or misinterpretations are entirely my own.

References

[1] Wiley M. From the origins of DRGs to their implementation in Europe. In: Busse R, Geissler A, Quentin W, Wiley M, editors. Diagnosis-related groups in Europe by the European Observatory on Health Systems and Policies series. Berkshire: McGraw-Hill; 2011.
[2] Freund DA. Initial development of the Australian Guidelines. Med Care 1996;34(12 Suppl):DS211–215.

[3] Healy J, Sharman E, Lokuge B. Australia: health system review. In: Healy J, editor. Health systems in transition. 5th ed, vol. 8. Copenhagen: The European Observatory on Health Systems and Policies; 2006.

[4] Hoagland GW, Parekh A, Hamm N, Cassling K, Fernekes C. Examining two approaches to U.S. drug pricing: International prices and therapeutic equivalency. Bipartisan Policy Center; 2019.

[5] Rice T. The economics of health reconsidered. 2nd ed. Chicago: Health Administration Press; 2003.

[6] Rice T, Unruh L. The economics of health reconsidered. 4th ed. Health Administration Press; 2016.

[7] Klein E. Is Singapore's "miracle" health care system the answer for America? Vox; 2017. [Internet]. [Accessed 27 November 2020]. Available from: https://www.vox.com/policy-and-politics/2017/4/25/15356118/singapore-health-care-system-explained.

[8] Earn LC. In: Tikkanen R, Osborn R, Mossialos E, Djordjevic A, Wharton GA, editors. Singapore. International health care system profiles. The Commonwealth Fund; 2020. [Internet]. [Accessed 27 November 2020]. Available from: https://www.commonwealthfund.org/international-health-policy-center/countries/singapore.

[9] Lim J. Myth or magic—The Singapore healthcare system. Singapore: Select Publishing; 2013.

[10] Haseltine WA. Affordable excellence: The Singapore healthcare story. Singapore & Washington, DC: Ridge Books & Brookings Institution Press; 2013.

[11] About us. The European Observatory on Health Systems and Policies [Internet]. [Accessed 27 November 2020]. Available from: https://www.euro.who.int/en/about-us/partners/observatory/about-us.

[12] Rice T, Rosenau P, Unruh LY, Barnes AJ, Saltman RB, van Ginneken E. United States of America: health system review. Health Syst Transit 2013;15(3):1–431.

[13] Rice T, Rosenau P, Unruh LY, Barnes AJ, van Ginneken E. United States of America: health system review. Health Syst Transit 2020;22(4):i–441.

Chapter 2

Key components of national health insurance systems

This chapter describes some of the key decisions countries must make when designing and implementing health insurance systems, setting the stage for the descriptions of the individual countries' systems in Part II of this book. Even though health insurance is only one part of a country's overall health care system, judgments in just this one area must be made on a staggering number of issues, including: How much of a country's resources should be devoted to health care? Is health care coverage universal? Is this achieved mainly through public or private insurance? What services are covered? How are premiums set, and how much do people have to pay out-of-pocket for services? How much regulation is there and how it is carried out? When there is private insurance, what is its role—who has it, how is it obtained, what does it cover, and who pays? Are for-profit entities allowed, and in what sectors? How are providers paid, and what types of incentives are they given to increase quality and control spending? Do people have free choice of hospitals and specialists? How are costs to be contained? What rationing mechanisms are in place and toward whom are they oriented—suppliers of services or users?

This chapter discusses the most important of these decisions. While specific countries are mentioned, a detailed discussion is left to the chapters on each country. Before proceeding, however, it is useful to present research that has been done on categorizing the different ways in which national health systems have been organized.

Categorizing health insurance systems

As in other fields, the study of comparative health systems has sought to develop typologies to classify and therefore help one understand the similarities and differences between health care systems across the world. There are a number of good reviews of alternative categorizations of health systems [1–3].

Bismarck and Beveridge

This classic distinction, now somewhat out of favor, divides systems into three categories, two named after historical figures: **Bismarck** vs **Beveridge** vs private insurance [1]. Otto von Bismarck served as the first German chancellor,

Health Insurance Systems: An International Comparison. https://doi.org/10.1016/B978-0-12-816072-5.00004-3

from 1871 to 1890. He is thought by many as the founder of what is often called "social insurance" in the Western World. Under his leadership, Germany enacted sickness, accident, and old-age insurance. Most accounts do not attribute this to his progressive ideas so much as trying to provide something tangible that would keep workers from joining the competing socialist movement. These insurance programs do not look very much like what we see today, but one element does stand out: employers and workers shared in contributing to the cost of the programs, with government playing more of a background role. To this day, payroll assessments are key sources of funds for several of the countries reviewed in this book. Perhaps because of the close association between Bismarck and Germany, the German system is still considered the prototypical social insurance system.

Unlike Bismarck, William Beveridge was a social scientist, although he did serve in British Parliament briefly. He was the architect of a 1942 report that was later instrumental in implementing various welfare programs in the United Kingdom after World War II, particularly the founding of the National Health Service (NHS). Unlike the Bismarck model, the NHS is a nationalized health care system based largely on strong national oversight as well as tax revenues rather than payroll assessments from the workplace. Again, with Beveridge coming from the United Kingdom, its system is often considered the prototype "national" system. Box 2.1 lists a number of distinctions between the textbook models of the two systems.

BOX 2.1 Characteristics of Bismarck vs Beveridge health care systems.

Bismarck	Beveridge
Social insurance	National health system
Membership based on contributions	Membership based on citizenship/residency
Funded mainly by payroll taxes or premiums	Funded mainly by tax revenues
Multiple insurers or sickness funds	Single insurer or payer
Revenue often earmarked for health care	Revenue competes with other budget items
Run by corporatist organizations	Run by national or/or local government
Providers often private entities	Providers often government employees or publicly contracted

(Source: Based in part on: Kutzin J. Bismarck vs. Beveridge: Is there increasing convergence between health financing systems. World Health Organizations; November 21-22, 2011. https://www.oecd.org/gov/budgeting/49095378.pdf.)

The third model, private insurance, forms the basis of only one of the countries covered in this book: the United States. Its exceptionalism in this regard is exemplified by a 2013 study by Bohm and colleagues, which listed it as the only one out of 27 OECD countries relying mainly on private regulation, financing, *and* provision of services [4]. Nevertheless, all countries reviewed here have a private insurance component, mainly for the sale of additional insurance benefits beyond those covered under national programs.

Categorizing health care systems as being either Bismarckian- or Beveridge-style has become less common recently with the onset of two developments: the convergence of various health care system elements across countries and the establishment of a newer health system model based on "managed competition," which is essentially a system of competing insurers. France provides an example of convergence. Traditionally, it has been viewed as social insurance system, with employers and employees jointly contributing to mandatory mutual benefit associations as early as the 1930s. Over time, however, the government began to play a larger role. In some ways, it is now difficult to come up with substantive differences, other than sources of financing, between France's system and those with nationalized health service systems: residents are not given a choice of insurer, and government enforces strong regulation and establishes the fees that providers are paid. Japan, too, shares these characteristics: there are thousands of insurers but no choice, and government exercises a strong control by setting a fee schedule that applies to all services and prescription drugs.

The other factor making the Bismarck-Beveridge breakdown less relevant today is emergence of more health care systems that rely on the consumer choice of competing private (usually nonprofit) insurance companies. The theoretical underpinnings of such systems are based on the writings of US economist Alain Enthoven from the late 1970s [5, 6]. Enthoven's "Consumer Choice Health Plan" was built upon the notion of insurance companies vying against each other for customers. The basis of competition was value: insurers that provided more benefits and quality per dollar of **premium**, it was theorized, would drive less-efficient insurers out of the marketplace. Insurers, in turn, would choose only those providers who themselves were cost-effective, creating competition in the hospital and physician markets as well. To make all of this work, Enthoven and colleagues designed a system that would allow for fair competition, which included open enrollment with equal premiums for everyone within a given insurance plan regardless of health status, standardized benefits to allow for easy comparison between competing insurers, a choice of insurers, and subsidies for those who would otherwise be unable to afford coverage. The United States and the Netherlands have, more than any other countries in the world, embraced many (but not all) of the tenets of managed competition. Two other countries included here, Germany and Switzerland, also rely on regulated competition among insurers as key components of their own systems.

Who controls regulation, financing, and service provision?

Katharina Bohm and colleagues developed a more complex categorization of health systems based on a 3×3 matrix [4]. One axis included the three "core dimensions" of health care systems: regulation, financing, and service provision. Within each of these, there are three possible responsible entities: state, societal, and private. "Societal" means that nongovernmental entities are responsible for making key decisions in the health care sector. These are often called "**corporatist**" organizations. Germany offers an example of this, where decisions about such issues of what services are covered and how much they are reimbursed are jointly made by consortia or insurers and providers negotiating with each other, with only minimal government involvement.

Only 10 of the possible 27 combinations were deemed to be plausible by the authors; for example, it does not make sense that regulation would be in private hands at the same time that financing would be in public hands. Out of these 10 plausible arrangements, just 5 of them were used by the 27 OECD countries examined by the authors, listed below along with examples from our 10 countries.

Type 1: a *national health service* with state control of regulation, financing, and provision (Sweden, United Kingdom)

Type 2: a *national health insurance* system with state control of regulation and financing, but private control of provision (Australia, Canada)

Type 3: a ***social health insurance*** system with societal control of regulation and financing, and private control of provision (Germany, Switzerland)

Type 4: a *state-run social health insurance* system, with state control of regulation, societal control of financing, and private control of provision (France, Japan, the Netherlands)

Type 5: a *private health insurance* system, with private control of regulation, financing, and provision (United States)

A problem recognized by Bohm and colleagues is that nearly all countries exhibit multiple entities that are involved in regulation, financing, and provision. For example, employers and employees may share in the payment of insurance premiums, but governments often augment these with tax revenues. To deal with complexities like these, the authors note that they "have concentrated on the system(s) with the greatest population coverage" [4, p. 262], noting, for example, that even though the United States is classified as employing private funding, in fact the public share of health care expenditures exceeds the private share of total health care expenditures under certain methods of accounting.[a]

---

[a] Whether the public or private share of health care spending is larger in the United States depends on how private spending is defined. As shown in Table 13.2, government paid for 45% of health expenditures, private insurance 35%, and out-of-pocket 12% (with other spending accounting for the remaining 8%). If one defines OOP spending as being "private," then the private share of spending would exceed the public share by a small amount.

Another problem, discussed next, is that countries with quite different health insurance systems end up in the same category.

Categories used in this book

This book uses four categories to classify the 10 countries. They are:

- Universal coverage systems with a single primary insurer
- Universal coverage systems with multiple primary insurers but no choice
- Universal coverage systems with competing primary insurers
- Systems without universal coverage

The term "primary insurer" represents the insurance that forms the basis of universal coverage, which we also sometimes call "statutory insurance." In most of the countries covered, people do have a choice of insurance plans when seeking additional coverage; insurance that provides this additional coverage is called voluntary health insurance (VHI).

There are several reasons why this simple classification system is employed here. As noted, the Bismarck/Beveridge distinction does not capture the ways in which health system characteristics have converged over the last few decades. Moreover, Bohm and colleagues' classification combines very different systems into a single type. Health insurance in the Netherlands (type 4) is based mainly on consumer choice of competing insurers, that is, managed competition. France and Japan, with which it is categorized, do not provide individuals a choice of insurance.[b]

This book is about health insurance, and arguably, the main attribute that distinguishes countries now is whether people are assigned their particular insurer or if they are able to freely choose among them. In 4 of the 10 countries (Australia, Canada, Sweden, and the United Kingdom), there is not public or mandatory health insurance per se, but rather health care coverage provided by the government. In that sense, there is no "choice" of insurer. Two countries (France and Japan) have multiple insurers but individuals are assigned coverage, and thus, they are similar to these other countries in that consumer choice is not driving competition for insurance.

In the other four countries (Germany, the Netherlands, Switzerland, and the United States), consumer choices are driving key components of the health care system, but the way in which they do so varies. In Germany, premium differences play a relatively minor role in that there is relatively little dispersion in the premiums charged by alternative plans. Premium differences are important in plan choice in the Netherlands, Switzerland, and the United States, but in the latter two countries, consumers generally also choose whether and which managed care plan to join; such plans restrict the particular providers they can see.

---

[b] Most researchers of comparative health systems would likely say that the Netherlands shares more system characteristics with Germany and Switzerland than it does with France and Japan.

In the four-group categorization, the United States is singled out: it is the only country not grouped with others because it does not offer universal coverage. There are many reasons besides lacking universal coverage that could justify the United States being by itself in a category: employment being the basis of most people's coverage, unusually large reliance on for-profit insurance, lack of uniform benefits across insurers, a parallel "safety-net" coverage system, and its outlier status in how much it spends—the list goes on. Nevertheless, it is the lack of universal coverage that drives several of these unique features.

The shortcoming of this classification system is that it does not explicitly consider other key system features that more complex categorizations do, such as choice of providers. This is not a major concern, however, because other relevant system features are explicitly discussed in this chapter on each country.

Key system components

Part II of this book presents chapters on each of the 10 countries, divided according to the 4 system types just presented. Each chapter has two sections: The Big Picture and Details. Under Details, the text is divided into 11 subtopics:

History
Overview of the health insurance system
Governance
Financing
Coverage
Voluntary health insurance
Choice
Providers' payment
Assuring access and equity
Controlling expenditures
Key policy issues

The remainder of this chapter explains most of these concepts (the 3rd through the 10th) and provides examples across the 10 countries. Several of these dimensions are revisited in Chapters 13 through 15 in cross-country comparison tables and figures.

Governance

The governance of national health care systems depends on a variety of factors including the type of health care system, historical events, and of course, politics.

Health system type determines, to some degree, governance structures. Systems most aligned with a Beveridge model tend to strongly rely on government to carry out and regulate health system activities. What varies most is the level of government at which these activities predominantly take place.

In the United Kingdom, governance is more centered at the national level—albeit largely separately for English, Scotland, Wales, and Northern Ireland. In contrast, Sweden vests nearly all governing powers in regional and local authorities. Similarly, Canadian authority rests mainly in the provinces.

Strong government involvement is also true in systems with multiple insurers that do not offer consumers the choice of insurer. National government has particularly important roles in France and Japan. The role of government, while significant, is smaller in the countries that allow patients a choice of insurer. In Germany and Switzerland in particular, corporatist bodies—mainly consortia of payers and consortia of providers—negotiate with each other over such things as provider fees. It is difficult to generalize too much about the United States because the source of coverage is fairly evenly divided between the private sector (mainly employers) and the government sector (mainly Medicare and Medicaid).

Historical events can play a strong role in governance as well. In Switzerland, most power is concentrated at the regional level because the Swiss constitution states that the national government has authority only in areas that are explicitly noted in the constitution. The same was true in Australia until after World War II, when its constitution was amended to allow the national government authority in the areas of sickness and hospital benefits, and medical and dental services. The United States provides a good example of the importance of historical happenstance. Reliance on employment as the source of health insurance coverage dates back to World War II. Because of a labor shortage, wage and price controls were instituted to control how much firms could pay for scarce labor. That induced companies to provide additional compensation in the form of nonwage benefits—mainly health insurance. The courts eventually ruled that such "fringe benefits" were not part of employees' taxable income, which in turn provided a strong economic incentive for health insurance to be provided through the workplace.

Politics, of course, plays a major role in shaping health care governance in all countries. A classic example is from the United Kingdom, where the conservative government of Margaret Thatcher tried to inject a strong dose of competition into the National Health System by introducing "internal markets" into the existing, government-heavy hospital system.

While further generalizations are risky, there are a few consistent patterns across countries. National government generally is responsible for:

- Health system planning and policy
- Setting health care benefit packages and cost-sharing requirements
- Assessing new technologies and pharmaceuticals for inclusion in benefit packages
- Directly providing subsidies for those with low incomes, or providing funding to regional governments to do so
- Setting health care budgets (among countries that do)

- Regulating private/voluntary health insurance
- Overseeing, subsidizing, and sometimes providing care so such groups as military, veterans, and indigenous populations as well as prisoners.

In many countries, regional government is responsible for overseeing, and often directly providing, hospital care. Long-term care (a topic not covered in this book) is often overseen and sometimes provided by local governments. Both regional and local governments typically are involved in preventive activities such as immunizations as well as public health and community services.

Financing

This discussion is divided into two parts: the different sources of revenue that are used to fund health care services, and the progressivity or regressivity of these different sources of revenue.

Sources of revenue

Fully understanding how individual countries finance their health care systems is difficult, in part because some revenue comes from general government sources (e.g., income taxes, consumption taxes such as a value-added tax (VAT)), while others may be collected specifically for the health care system (e.g., public and private insurance premiums). The US Medicare program provides an example. Part A of Medicare, which funds inpatient hospital care for seniors and the disabled, is paid for mainly through an earmarked payroll tax on all Americans' wages. It has a trust fund that, in effect, acts as a bank account, the solvency of which is closely watched. (The most recent estimate is that it will go into deficit in 2024 unless either spending is reduced or taxes raised.) In contrast, Part B, which covers physician care, is primarily funded through general government tax revenues. This is also true of Part D, prescription drug coverage. For the latter two programs, about 75% of revenue comes from taxes; the remaining 25%, from beneficiary premium contributions.

Countries with national health systems tend to rely more on different forms of tax funding, while those with **sickness funds**/insurance companies raise most revenues through earmarked payroll taxes, typically levied on both employers and employees. All countries, of course, use a variety of sources to fund their health care systems (Tables 13.2 and 13.3). The particular sources employed have varying implications. One concerns political pressure on health care budgets. Countries with national health systems, which rely more on general tax revenue as opposed to payroll taxes, must explicitly weigh spending on health care against other national and regional priorities, including education, social programs, long-term care, transportation, national defense, and interest payments on the national debt. Because of these and other competing priorities, health care spending may be subject to more political pressure than in countries relying on payroll taxes. As stated by Naoki Ikegami and colleagues in the context of Japan, an important advantage of social insurance "is that the benefit package is defined as an entitlement and is financed by contributions that are earmarked for health care." They go on to say that a key weakness of social insurance, compared with tax-based systems, "is that solidarity is limited to people enrolled in the same plan [so that] plans that have enrollees with high average income and low risk will oppose any national equalisation because this process would lead to increased contribution rates" [7, p. 1106].

Evidence supporting these can be found from the Commonwealth Fund's 2016 survey of adults in 11 countries, 9 of which are included in this book. (Data from the survey appear in Table 15.13.) Regarding Ikegami's hypothesis that national health systems are more likely to be underfunded, the survey results provide the percentage of the adult population seeking care who indicated that they had to wait (a) 2 or more months for a specialist appointment, and (b) 4 or more months for elective surgery [8, Appendix 3]. In both instances, the four countries with national health systems (Australia, Canada, Sweden, and the United Kingdom) showed longer waiting times. While it is difficult to reject all alternative hypotheses, it would seem reasonable to expect that countries relying on payroll taxes to fund their budgets are somewhat more insulated from policy decisions involving competing government resources. In this case, that could translate into shorter waiting lists. His second hypothesis—that social insurance (as opposed to tax-funded) systems would show less social solidarity— is also partly supported by the data. In examining the equity of the 11 systems, the United Kingdom and Sweden ranked the first and the third, respectively. Interestingly, the Netherlands, a country that relies heavily on markets albeit undergirded by strong protection mechanisms, ranked the second.

Progressivity and regressivity

To understand this aspect of financing, some concepts first need to be defined. If a financial system is vertically equitable, it means that those with higher income or wealth pay a greater proportion of it toward financing. Or, quoting Gavin Mooney, **vertical equity** is "the unequal, but equitable, treatment of unequals" [9, p. 80].

The concepts of vertical equity and progressivity go hand in hand. Financing systems such as **progressive** income taxes, where wealthier people pay a larger proportion of their income, are vertically equitable. For example, a tax would be progressive if, on average, millionaires paid 30% of income, while lower-middle class persons paid 10%. If these numbers were reversed, with the lower-middle class person paying 30% and the wealthier person 10%, the tax would be **regressive**. If, on the other hand, each paid an average of 20%, the tax is called *proportional*. While it is obviously a matter of opinion which system is superior, most wealthy countries promote the belief that health care services should be provided to all those who need it regardless of ability to pay. This is strongly consistent with the notion of vertical equity as poorer persons are less able to afford care. Under a vertically equitable system, they will pay a lower proportion of income to receive a given set of services.

There is a second term of note, **horizontal equity**, defined as the equal treatment of equals. In particular, in a horizontally equitable system, people with similar resources would pay similar tax rates or premiums. Japan is an example of a system lacking in horizontal equity. Japanese receiving coverage from any of 1400 or so large employers pay different premiums based on the risk profile of employees, and those in 50 regions—mainly the self-employed, unemployed, and senior citizens below the age of 75—have premiums that vary 4-fold, based again on risk profile as well as on how generous their regions are in making premium contributions on behalf of the insured [7].

Returning to vertical equity, what types of health care financing revenues are progressive or regressive? It is difficult to generalize as it depends on a number of factors. Income taxes, for example, may be levied at national or subnational levels, so their overall impact on income distribution is unclear. In the United States, for example, there is a progressive federal income tax, but some states have no income taxes of their own and instead collect revenues through more regressive methods. Others are highly progressive: the wealthiest Californians, for example, pay 13.3% of income above a threshold in addition to all federal taxes paid. Overall, though, researchers have found that countries that finance more of their health care through income taxes have more progressive overall financing systems [10].

Not all general tax revenues are progressive, however. Examples include those on the purchase of goods and property. Sales or VAT taxes are financially harder on those with lower incomes as any given purchase will have associated with it a fixed tax that is a greater proportion of a poorer person's income. As a result, certain necessities, such as groceries, are often exempted or taxed at a lower rate In general, however, consumption taxes are generally recognized as regressive. While it might seem that property taxes would be progressive because property owners tend to be wealthier, the opposite generally is true because renters bear the financial repercussions of the taxes paid by property owners. In sum, the extent to which tax financing of health care is progressive or regressive depends on many factors, including the type of taxes levied, the progressivity of tax rates, and the exclusion of particular goods from consumption taxes.

Countries with multiple insurers rely more on insurance premiums to pay for health care, and these are often split between employers and employees. Sometimes, however, the amount is capped at a certain income level, making these premium payments regressive rather than proportional. Germany is an example. Both employers and employees share payment of 14.6% of wages for health care coverage, but contributions are capped, with no payroll taxes levied on wages over 54,450 euros in 2019. This makes them somewhat regressive; people with incomes above this threshold pay a lower percentage of their income toward the taxes than others.

There are two other sources of health care funding: voluntary health insurance (VHI) premiums and out-of-pocket (OOP) spending. We will defer the discussion of VHI until later, except to say that these premiums are generally regressive both because they constitute a larger part of income for those who are less well off, and because they are often subsidized by employers. Those in the labor market tend to be better off, so such subsidies make VHI premiums even more regressive. Out-of-pocket (OOP) spending on **deductibles, copayments**, and **coinsurance** are (except for the very poor) the same irrespective of a person's income, are therefore highly regressive: they take a bigger bite out of the incomes of the poor and near poor in all countries.

Previous researchers have been able to aggregate and quantify some of these distinctions. The work of Adam Wagstaff, Eddy van Doorslaer, and colleagues is especially pertinent [10]. Unfortunately, the research does not appear to have been replicated and is largely based on the health systems in place 20-plus years ago.[c] The study is still relevant, however, because there is little reason to believe that the system characteristics associated with progressivity would have changed very much. Rather, it is the health systems themselves that have changed (e.g., Switzerland moving away from private insurance sold by for-profit companies).

Using data from consumer expenditure surveys in individual countries, the authors calculated the progressivity/regressivity of the components of financing (direct taxes, indirect taxes, social insurance premiums, private insurance premiums, and direct payments including OOP spending and payment for uncovered services). They found that direct (e.g., income) taxes were progressive in all 13 countries that they studied, but that indirect (e.g., sales, VAT) taxes were regressive. Premiums for social insurance, normally paid through the workplace, tended to be fairly progressive except in countries where people could opt of the public system, as in Germany. Generally, private insurance premiums were regressive, especially in countries where it is the main source of coverage, as in the US. OOP payments were also found to be highly regressive [10].

Coverage[d]

For a user of health care, one of the most important elements of a country's health care system is what services are—and are not—covered, and to what extent. Costs that are not covered either must be paid OOP, or through VHI, which may entail an additional premium payment. (Sometimes, as is the case in France, government subsidizes VHI for poor persons.) Fig. 2.1 provides a useful schematic [11].

---

[c] Eddy van Doorslaer, personal communication, October 26, 2018.
[d] Long-term care (LTC) systems are not covered in this book. LTC is almost always financed differently from acute care, and moreover, LTC financing often varies greatly within countries in part because it is often administered by local governments.

Note the two cubes. The smaller one represents total spending by the public or statutory insurance system; for convenience, it is labeled as "public spending." The larger cube shows total spending in the country. The difference between the two cubes is what is left for the user to pay, which, as noted, may be partly covered by VHI. There are three parts to this user liability: spending by those who lack insurance coverage (lack of "breadth"), spending on services not covered by the public systems (lack of "scope"), and cost-sharing for publicly funded services (lack of "depth").

Breadth of coverage

Beginning with breadth (that is, moving on the X-axis in the figure from right to left), all countries covered in this book other than Germany and the United States have near universal coverage for their citizenry, either through public systems or through a mandate that everyone obtains coverage. This coverage may be provided directly by the government, or when people are required to purchase coverage from an array of insurers. The latter is the case in the public insurance sector of Germany, the Netherlands, and Switzerland, each of which strongly enforces the mandate [12]. Germany also has universal coverage, but about 11% of the population, including those with the highest income, as well as some civil servants and self-employed individuals, obtain their coverage through private insurance.

Breadth of coverage in the United States differs from the other countries because there is not a national or regional universal health insurance program. About 9% of the US population is uninsured, so coverage is therefore narrower than in the other nine countries. The inner cube in Fig. 2.1 is best thought of as spending on the Medicare and Medicaid programs: Medicare covers Americans aged 65 and older and some disabled persons, and Medicaid covers some but not all poor and near-poor persons as well as some disabled persons, depending on their state of residence. The rest of the population chooses whether or not to purchase coverage, with a large majority receiving it through employment. For a short period, 2014–18, coverage for most other persons was required as part of an individual mandate but that requirement was repealed, effective in 2019. It is difficult to summarize the scope and depth of coverage in the United States as that varies by insurance program and type of service.

Scope of coverage

Regarding scope (moving from front to back in the figure on the Z-axis), all countries tend to cover inpatient hospital services and physician services. Beyond that, the benefits vary considerably by country and even within country. Typical exclusions from public coverage are adult dental care, eye and hearing care, medical appliances, physical and other therapies, complementary and alternative medicine, and cosmetic procedures. Pharmaceuticals generally are covered except in Canada, where there is considerable variability by province.

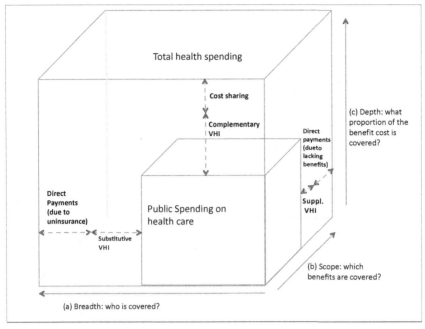

FIG. 2.1 The components of health insurance coverage.*(Sources: Busse R, Schlette S. Health policy developments issue 7/8 focus on prevention, health and ageing and human resources. Gütersloh: Verlag Bertelsmann Stiftung; 2007; Rice T, Quentin W, Anell A, Barnes AJ, Rosenau P, Unruh LY, et al. Revisiting out-of-pocket requirements: trends in spending, financial access barriers, and policy in ten high-income countries. BMC Health Serv Res 2018;18(1):371.)*

In Canadian provinces, drugs purchased by seniors, those with long-term chronic illnesses, and the poor are often covered [13].

Depth of coverage

Finally, regarding depth (moving from bottom to top on the Y-axis), cost-sharing requirements are common in all countries. Box 2.2 defines the different mechanisms, which include deductibles, coinsurance, and copayments. Which are used depends not only on country but also on the type of service and individual (e.g., children are often excluded). Another element, not shown in the figure, relates to maximum liabilities. It is common for countries to establish a maximum OOP threshold per year, after which point there is no further patient cost-sharing. To illustrate, although the Swiss face far higher annual per-capita OOP spending than Americans, they are protected against experiencing the most serious financial consequences of illness because there is an annual cap on OOP spending. Adults there pay a maximum of about $1100 per year (about $400 for children). In 2019, Americans with employer-sponsored coverage faced a maximum averaging about $4000 [14], and individual insurance sold on the ACA exchanges had maximums of no more than $8150 in 2020 [15].

BOX 2.2   Different types of patient cost-sharing requirements.

The term "cost-sharing" refers to payments that patients may be required to make when they receive health care services. These are paid out-of-pocket or by voluntary health insurance policies that they may own. There are three major types of cost-sharing requirements and one other related term.

Deductibles are an amount of money that has to be paid by or on behalf of the patient during a specified time period before insurance benefits are paid out. Deductibles usually but do not always apply to a calendar year. For example, people with a $2000 annual deductible will pay the full amount for the first $2000 of medical fees incurred during the year. Once the deductible is met, they may still be subject to paying coinsurance and/or copayments on spending above the deductible. In some instances, certain services (e.g., preventive care) are not subject to the deductible so as to encourage more people to use those services.

Coinsurance is the percentage of a medical bill that has to be paid by or on behalf of the patient. A 20% coinsurance rate on a $100 service means that the patient must pay $20, with the insurer paying the remaining $80.

Copayments are a monetary (e.g., dollar) amount that must be paid by or on behalf of the patient when receiving a service, e.g., a $20 copayment for each night spend in a hospital or a $10 copayment for a prescription medicine.

Out-of-Pocket Maximum is the most a patient is required to pay in cost-sharing requirements during a time period (usually a year). After reaching that expenditure level, insurance pays all remaining costs. While usually unrelated to income, in Germany it is set at 2% of household income, or 1% for these with a serious chronic illness.

Voluntary health insurance

The concept of voluntary private insurance is relevant to all of the countries except Japan and the United States. In the other countries, a portion of residents supplement their public insurance with private coverage. There is a great variation among these countries, however. Only about 10% of those in Sweden and the United Kingdom own VHI, whereas 96% of the French have it (Table 13.4). They are sold both by for-profit and by nonprofit companies. While laws vary, sometimes issuing insurance companies are allowed to deny coverage to those they do not want to cover, or charge sicker people more.

There are three types of VHI: substitutive, supplementary, and complementary (see Fig. 2.1). These are represented on the three axes of the larger cube. Persons not covered by public insurance purchase *substitutive VHI*; this is what the 11% of Germans do who opt out of public coverage. Substitutive coverage is not relevant to the other countries, where public or statutorily required insurance covers nearly all citizens.

Supplementary VHI deals with a lack of scope because not all types of services are covered by public insurance. Dental care is perhaps the most common example but it also can cover any of a number of other things as well such as eyeglasses and contact lenses, eye care, physiotherapy, and alternative medicines. Another common benefit is access to private rooms in hospitals. Supplementary coverage sometimes provides policyholders with more choice in provider selection or in helping to "jump the queue" to receive specialist care or elective procedures more quickly, such as in Australia.

Finally, *complementary VHI* generally pays for the remaining costs of services that are only partly paid for by public or statutory systems. Coverage of cost-sharing for prescription drugs is oftentimes the most important benefit, but it also may include help with hospital and physician services when they are not provided free of charge, and sometimes provides a host of other benefits. While sometimes complementary VHI covers all remaining costs, it may only cover a portion of them, e.g., in the case of prescription drugs. Complementary VHI is essential in some countries, such as France, where nominal coinsurance rates are very high: 20% for hospital care, 30% for physician visits, and even more for some prescription drugs. (It is now possessed by almost everyone in France and premiums are subsidized for the poor.)

VHI is different in Japan than in the other countries. It does not cover additional services or coinsurance. Rather, it is used as income replacement when a person becomes ill and therefore compensates for lost income when a person is unable to work. Nor does the concept of VHI translate well to the United States, but for different reasons. For those with employer-sponsored coverage, the majority of Americans, generally there is no VHI market. This is also the case for those with coverage through the ACA marketplaces. In both cases, if people incur medical expenses, they pay for any gaps in coverage OOP. Those with Medicaid coverage do not need VHI because care is free or costs very little. The only real market for VHI in the United States is for Medicare beneficiaries, where it is used to supplement the considerable gaps in Medicare's payment structure. Approximately 30% of Medicare beneficiaries purchase "Medigap" policies that provide this coverage [16].

Choice

We have already discussed one choice: that of insurance plan. Part II of this book categorizes the countries based on this criterion. In Australia, Canada, Sweden, and the United Kingdom, there is not health insurance per se so much as a public health coverage program; by definition, there is no choice. In France and Japan, there are multiple insurers, although of a very different magnitude: a handful in France versus over 1500 in Japan. The individual cannot choose and instead is assigned an insurer based on such factors as employment status and place of residency, and in Japan, age as well. Three European countries (Germany, the Netherlands, and Switzerland) provide consumers a choice among competing insurers, some of which involve using a restricted network of providers, which may reduce premiums. This is also true in the United States for much, but not all of the population. In the United States, almost all large employers offer a choice of plans but smaller ones often do not. Medicare beneficiaries who choose to join a managed care (Part C) plan have a choice of insurers. Similarly, there is a choice among prescription drug plans (Part D). Those with Medicaid may or may not have a choice among managed care plans, depending on the state in which they live.

In all of the countries, individuals can choose their primary care physician. The main exceptions are when a person enrolls in a managed care plan with a limited network of physicians, or when practices choose not to accept new patients. Restrictions through managed care plans occur most commonly in the United States and Switzerland. Countries do vary regarding the choice of hospital and specialist. Some countries allow patients free choice of either or both without getting a referral from a primary care doctor. Those that require referrals have what is known as a "**gatekeeping**" system, where primary care physicians must provide a referral for the service to be covered or, if it is covered, to obtain the lowest cost-sharing requirements.

Provider payment

We examine the three aspects of provider payment: hospitals, physicians, and pharmaceuticals.

Hospital payment

Hospital payment methods have evolved considerably over the years, gravitating from systems where hospitals received more by keeping patients longer, to ones in which payments are based on the hospital stay, usually irrespective of length. **Diagnosis-related groups**, or DRGs, are now used (albeit sometimes with different names) in most countries as the primary method of paying for inpatient hospital care. They were first developed in the United States to pay hospitals under the Medicare program (covering seniors and some of the disabled population), beginning in 1983. Patients who come into the hospital with similar diagnoses and expected treatment regimens are categorized into a particular DRG. The hospital receives a fixed fee for a patient in a particular DRG irrespective of how long the patient stays and how many resources are used.[e] In the US Medicare program, there are over 700 DRGs, each with a different payment rate. To provide an example, Medicare DRG 234 is for a coronary bypass operation with cardiac catheterization for patients who do not have a major comorbidity or complication. DRGs provide strong financial incentives

---

[e] For very long stays, hospitals may be compensated more. In the US Medicare program, these are called "outlier" payments. They are necessary not only to promote fairness to hospitals, but also so as to not discourage hospitals from admitting patients with comorbidities that may increase the expected intensity and cost of care.

for hospitals not to keep patients too long, both reducing expenses and exposure to infections. The potential negative impact is if hospitals discharge patients too soon. One way to try to reduce the latter is by penalizing hospitals (for example, through no additional payment) if a patient is re-hospitalized for the same condition within a certain period of time such as 1 month.

Other methods can also be employed to pay hospitals. Canadian provinces pay hospitals largely through global budgets. This is a fixed amount of money per year provided to a specific hospital to cover all of its operating costs excepting physician fees and the purchase of capital equipment; amounts typically are negotiated annually between provincial health officials and each hospital. Global budgets provide a strong incentive for hospitals to control spending, because spending beyond the negotiated amount is likely to result in losses. It also allows the provinces to leverage their bargaining power and keep to a budget. The main potential downside is that hospitals may skimp on hiring personnel, which could impair the quality of inpatient care provided.

Physician payment

There are three overarching systems of paying physicians: fee-for-service (FFS), salary, and **capitation**. With the exception of the Netherlands, Sweden, and the United Kingdom, the majority of physicians in the other countries examined here are paid by FFS. The terms "FFS" and "salary" are self-explanatory. Under capitation payment, a physician (usually primary care) receives a fixed amount of money per time unit (often per year) for each person under his or her care. These payment methods, which typically are adjusted to account for the health risk and therefore expected intensity of care that a patient is likely to receive, are explained further in Box. 2.3.

Each payment method has its advantages and disadvantages. The latter are summarized by James Robinson [17, p. 149].

Fee-for-service rewards the provision of inappropriate services, the fraudulent upcoding of visits and procedures, and the churning of "ping-pong" referrals among specialists. Capitation rewards the denial of appropriate services, the dumping of the chronically ill, and a narrow scope of practice that refers out every time-consuming patient. Salary undermines productivity, condones on-the-job leisure, and fosters a bureaucratic mentality in which every procedure is someone else's problem.

Robinson dubbed these the three "worst" ways to pay physicians. While somewhat tongue-in-cheek, since they are the *only* real payment options, his point was that each of these methods needs to be modified to align physicians' incentives correctly. Most methods of doing so fall in the category of "pay-for-performance," or P4P. The majority of countries discussed here are beginning to explore P4P. The two countries using it the most, and with the most experience, are the United Kingdom and the United States.

BOX 2.3 Paying physicians: Fee-for-service, capitation, salary, and pay-for-performance.

Fee-for-Service (FFS) is the most common way of paying for physicians' services, worldwide. The physician is paid a separate fee for each service provided. On the one hand, it can be argued that this system creates an ethical bond between the patient and the physician as the patient has purchased the time and skill of the physician so as to do everything possible for the patient. On the other hand, FFS can provide an incentive to provide unnecessary services, thereby increasing health care spending. Insurers may deal with this by monitoring the number and types of services provided, or enacting a budget whereby the provision of more services will result in lower fees for each service provided.

In a world without insurance, FFS would be a simple matter: physicians would charge an amount that the patient would be responsible for paying. Insurance complicates this arrangement by putting a third party into the equation. Insurers do not want to pay whatever a physician charges so they need to come up with some sort of payment mechanism. These are called "fee schedules," listing the thousands of different procedures and the amount to be paid. Fee schedules can be established unilaterally by the insurer, be it government or private, or can be negotiated by groups representing insurers with groups representing physicians. Insurers often also establish utilization review systems to help ensure that the services provided are medically appropriate and/or of sufficiently high quality.

In some health care systems, physicians can charge patients more than the fee schedule amounts. This is called "**balance billing**" or "extra billing."

Capitation payment usually occurs in the primary care area. Under capitation, the physician receives a fixed payment for each patient under his or her care. This fee is often calculated on an annual basis. If a capitated physician had 1500 patients under her care and the capitation rate were $1000 per patient per year, she would earn $150,000.

The inherent incentives of capitation are the opposite of FFS. From a purely pecuniary standpoint, the incentive is to have a large panel of patients but to underprovide services because the provision of an extra service provides no additional income. There are obviously limits on this: patients may get sick and require *more* care, or they may become dissatisfied and move to another physician. Capitation systems are often coupled with bonuses or penalties to help promote the provision of high-quality care.

Salary is a fixed payment for all work done in a particular time period such as a year. It is often used when physicians are employees of the government or of a hospital. There are advantages and disadvantages to the economic incentives of salary. On the positive side, it provides incentives neither to overprovide, like FFS, nor to underprovide, like capitation. On the negative side, there is little economic incentive to work hard since harder work does not result in more pay, nor does excelling in one's practice. Because of this, salary systems are often coupled with incentives to be productive such as treating a certain number of patients per day.

Pay-for-Performance (P4P) is the term that encompasses financial rewards or penalties that provide incentives for providers to perform in the way that a public or private insurer desires. It applies to both hospital and physician payment. Examples of the types of performance that may be targeted by P4P programs to physicians include providing preventive care (e.g., immunizations, cancer screening), achieving high patient satisfaction levels as determined through surveys, and using electronic medical records. Examples targeted to hospitals include abiding by recognized practices (e.g., giving aspirin or beta blockers to heart attack victims), providing safe care (e.g., reducing infections), and lowering readmission rates.

Pharmaceutical payment

Pharmaceutical expenditures are of policy concern in all countries examined here. Most countries use a variety of methods to encourage the use of lower-priced generic medicines although some are more successful than others (Table 15.16). In some countries, like Japan, fees generally are set and updated by government, albeit with input from interest groups and with an eye on the market [18]. Another common method is the use of **"reference pricing"** to determine payment rates for drugs. There are two types of reference pricing systems. The first, *external* reference pricing, applies to large numbers of drugs. In this scheme, a country examines how much other countries pay for particular drugs and sets its payment rates accordingly. One source reports a World Health Organization study that found 36 of 41 European countries employed external reference pricing for at least some drugs, and 26 used it as the only mechanism to control prices [19]. Most countries use fewer than 10 other countries to develop their price indices, typically picking other countries based on similarities in wealth [20].

The other type of reference pricing is *internal*. The idea here is to base insurer coverage on the price of domestically available substitutes. Typically, the insurer will only cover the cheapest alternatives, which are often generic, and the patient is responsible for the some of the cost-sharing, providing even more of economic incentive to choose the cheaper drug. Germany provides a good example. If a new drug only provides minimal additional therapeutic benefits over alternatives already on the market, the sickness funds (insurers) will only reimburse the price it pays for the alternative. The manufacturer is free to set its own price, but the difference between that price and the reference price must be paid OOP by the patient. In contrast, when a new drug offers significant additional therapeutic alternatives, then negotiations take place between the manufacturer and the consortia for sickness funds [21].

Assuring access and equity

Wealthy countries generally espouse the belief that health care services should be provided to all those who need it regardless of ability to pay. But this philosophy can go even farther, for example, as described by Richard Saltman: "every individual regardless of income or social standing has the same services delivered by the same health care providers and with the same clinical outcome" [22, p. 1]. The term **"solidarity"** is often used, especially in Europe, to encompass concepts such as these. Saltman makes it clear, though, that the concept has been and is applied flexibly, "adapting to and reflecting the changing historical, economic, political and social environment around it" [22, p. 2]—for example, increasing patient OOP payments in the wake of the great recession.

Germany, which has provided social insurance longer than any other country, employs the term, *Sozialgesetzbuch*, or social code, the idea being that people's health needs should determine what care they are entitled to, but how much they have to pay for it depends on their ability to do so [23]. Sweden strives to go beyond equality of access, striving for everyone to attain equal health [24]. In France, solidarity encompasses equal access for all of those who are ill [25]. Japan's Ministry of Health's vision for its health care system in 2035 is based in part on "solidarity built on autonomy," "a health care system that supports individuals to actively participate in their community; and a system that, rather than asking people to face challenges alone, provides an adequate safety net, and encourages proactive approaches in health care to ensure that each person has access to the benefits of wellness" [26].

Actions speak louder than words, of course. Saltman argues that European solidarity was shaken by the financial crises around 2008. Lawrence Brown and David Chinitz, in commenting on Saltman, believe that there is still "a solid core" but with "blurred edges," with three core elements of solidarity still operational: universality of coverage and access, redistribution from the healthier/wealthier to sicker/poorer, and uniform access to the health care system on equal terms so that "care should be allocated solely on the basis of medical need" [27, p. 2]. Chapter 14 focuses on the extent to which countries are now succeeding in manifesting the concept of solidarity through their achievement of equity in both health care access and health care outcomes.

There are many ways in which countries strive to assure access and equity [11]. Examples include subsidizing premiums and cost-sharing payments for those with lower incomes; setting maximum amounts people have to spend on health care; providing or subsidizing the purchase of VHI; providing economic protections to groups such as children, seniors, and people with chronic conditions; helping to improve access to those living in rural populations; working to reduce racial, ethnic, and gender disparities in access and use of services; and devoting resources to help native populations.

There is another aspect of access and equity that is not further discussed in this book: health care services for undocumented immigrants. As many countries have faced burgeoning immigration crises, there has been, of late, more attention devoted to the issue. In spite of this, there has been little research published on the topic, in part because of the obvious difficulty in collecting information from people who are undocumented.,

In general, undocumented individuals do not have access to the universal health care systems in any country. A study of European countries from 2012 concluded that most only guarantee emergency care, while some are more generous [28, p. 1]. In France, for example, those in the country for three or more months who are in poverty receive free medical care [29, p. 71]. Each of the four non-European countries also has its own policies. For example, Canadian provinces do not provide entry into the provincial health plans, although like the European countries, they do provide a limited service coverage such as emergency hospital services [30]. Coverage is limited in the United States as well, with some states providing services to undocumented pregnant women and children. In 2019, California became the first state to offer subsidized health benefits up to the age of 25 for undocumented immigrants with low incomes under its Medicaid program [31].

Controlling expenditures

In his classic book, *Who Shall Live?*, the health economist Victor Fuchs asserts that the economic way of thinking entails three axioms: (a) resources are scarce in relation to human wants, (b) these resources have alternative uses, and (c) different people want different things [32]. He dubs those who deny proposition (a) as having a "romantic" view of the world, and those who deny (b) and (c), a "monotechnic" viewpoint. Fuchs views neither sympathetically.

In fact, health care, like any resource, needs to be rationed. This position is often criticized, particularly in the United States, where discussion of increased government involvement in the health care market has even devolved into accusations of turning decision-making over to bureaucrats overseeing "death panels" [33]. Every country rations health care and always has done so. It is not a matter of *whether* it happens, but *how* it happens. There are two overall categories of health care rationing: on the demand side of the market and on the supply side. Every country uses both but to different degrees. The extent to which a country is successful in controlling its health care expenditures depends, in large measure, on which of these particular tools are used and how successful they are in the context of that particular country's history and political circumstances.

Demand-side rationing

In a competitive marketplace, economists often espouse demand-side methods. In an ideal marketplace, the alternatives before the consumer are clear, as is information about relative benefits and costs of each option. Price is then used as the method to ration care. Consumers not willing to pay the price of a particular service or prescription drug are essentially saying that they would get more out of spending their money on other things. Government has little place in such a marketplace; explicitly limiting the availability of services subverts free choice and will result in an allocation of goods not in people's best interests.

Demand-side rationing is commonly used but more so in the United States than in the other countries. In the United States, where coverage is not universal, premiums are one mechanism that limits who has coverage. The other countries considered here all have universal coverage but employ methods that come into effect when a person seeks care. Some use deductibles, and most use coinsurance and/or copayments for covered services. Except for exempted groups (e.g., children, seniors, those with certain diseases), patient cost-sharing for prescription drugs is common in all of the countries.

Moreover, no country covers every single health care service, and some services are covered by public programs only rarely. Adult dental care is an example. In the countries examined in this book, only Germany, Japan, and the United Kingdom provide a broad coverage for adults, albeit in some cases with substantial patient cost-sharing. As a result, most people either pay for dental care OOP or use VHI.

Demand-side rationing can be successful in controlling expenditures in that under most circumstances, it will have a dampening effect on demand for services: if people have to pay more, generally they will use less. (This isn't always true: for example, once inside a hospital, patients have little say on what services they will receive irrespective of the costs they are required to pay.) Nevertheless, it can have also adverse consequences, in two ways. The first concerns its impact on equity. When services are rationed on price, those with less ability to pay are doubly disadvantaged: if they use a service, it will consume more of their resources, but if they cannot afford the service, their health can suffer. While all countries account for this to some degree by making health care cheaper for the poor, in most countries those with lower incomes are more likely to forgo medical and dental care (Figs. 14.1 and 14.4) and are also more likely to spend a large percentage of their income on medical care (Figs. 14.9 and 14.10).

The second problem goes back to the assumption about good consumer information. There is a great deal of research showing that consumers facing cost-sharing will not only choose to reduce their use of marginally effective products and services, but will also cut back just as much on necessary care [34]. In recent years, there is a burgeoning literature showing that higher prescription drug copayments have had a sharp dampening effect on the purchase of medically necessary medications for those with chronic illnesses [35, 36]. While difficult to ascertain, it is plausible that many of those cutting back do not recognize the severity of the health risks entailed in doing so.

Supply-side rationing

Supply-side rationing mechanisms are more varied in scope. Broadly speaking, four commonly used devices are as follows: (a) controlling the supply or use of personnel or capital; (b) choosing not to cover all services; (c) regulating health care prices charged or paid; and (d) directly regulating total expenditures (global budgets). These mechanisms are used in all countries but to different degrees. Economists, particularly in the United States, worry that such mechanisms are arbitrary and may lead to resource allocations that are not aligned with what people want.

There are numerous examples of (a), including controlling: medical school enrollment, the distribution of residency spots in particular specialties, hospital construction, the number of hospital beds, which equipment can be used in particular hospitals, and the equipment used in outpatient settings. Perhaps the most notable example of (b) is the NICE—the National Institute for Health and Care Excellence in the United Kingdom. Whenever possible, new services proposed for inclusion as a covered benefit in the National Health Service need to be assessed by a cost-effectiveness analysis. With some exceptions, only those services considered to be cost-effective as defined by costing less than 30,000 British pounds per quality-adjusted life year attained are included.

With regard to (c), governments in many of the countries discussed in this book set prices throughout the health care sector, including how much hospitals are paid, physician fee levels, and prescription drug prices. In Japan, for example, the Central Government's Ministry of Health develops and updates a fee schedule that applies to nearly all services and drugs—fees that are generally considered low by international standards. Sometimes, however, these fees are not set by government but rather negotiated between consortia of insurers and providers (Germany) or through negotiations between competing insurers and provider networks (the United States). In the case of pharmaceutical prices, the use of reference pricing also provides a good example (see earlier discussion under pharmaceutical payment).

Public budgeting provides an example of (d). Such budgets are set or negotiated in all countries. Sometimes they cover most of a country's health expenditures (e.g., in the United Kingdom, they are distributed from central government to local administrative bodies overseen by general practitioners), or by sector (e.g., for seniors and the disabled in the United States under the Medicare program), or via global budgets for individual hospitals (e.g., Canada), or through individual physician budgets (e.g., Germany).

With this background in mind, Part II of this book will describe each of the above features of the health insurance systems in Australia, Canada, France, Germany, Japan, the Netherlands, Sweden, Switzerland, the United Kingdom, and the United States, along with providing system overviews, history, and discussion of key policy issues.

References

[1] Burau V, Blank RH. Comparing health policy: an assessment of typologies of health systems. J Comp Policy Anal Res Pract 2006;8(1):63–76.

[2] Wendt C. Changing healthcare system types. Soc Policy Adm 2014;48(7):864–82.

[3] Ferreira PL, Tavares AI, Quintal C, Santana P. EU health systems classification: a new proposal from EURO-HEALTHY. BMC Health Serv Res 2018;18(1):511.

[4] Bohm K, Schmid A, Gotze R, Landwehr C, Rothgang H. Five types of OECD healthcare systems: empirical results of a deductive classification. Health Policy 2013;113(3):258–69.

[5] Enthoven AC. Consumer-choice health plan (first of two parts). Inflation and inequity in health care today: alternatives for cost control and an analysis of proposals for national health insurance. N Engl J Med 1978;298(12):650–8.

[6] Enthoven AC. Health plan: The practical solution to the soaring cost of medical care. 1st ed. Washington, DC: Beard Books; 1980.

[7] Ikegami N, Yoo BK, Hashimoto H, Matsumoto M, Ogata H, Babazono A, et al. Japanese universal health coverage: evolution, achievements, and challenges. Lancet 2011;378(9796):1106–15.

[8] Schneider EC, Sarnak DO, Squires D, Shah A, Doty MM. Mirror, mirror 2017: International comparison reflects flaws and opportunities for better U.S. health care. Mirror, Mirror: The Commonwealth Fund; 2017.

[9] Mooney G, Jan S. Vertical equity: weighting outcomes? or establishing procedures? Health Policy 1997;39(1):79–87.

[10] Wagstaff A, Van Doorslaer E. Equity in health care finance and delivery. In: Culyer AJ, Newhouse JP, editors. Handbook of health economics. 1st ed, vol. 1B. Amsterdam, North Holland: Elsevier; 2000. p. 893–1910.

[11] Rice T, Quentin W, Anell A, Barnes AJ, Rosenau P, Unruh LY, et al. Revisiting out-of-pocket requirements: trends in spending, financial access barriers, and policy in ten high-income countries. BMC Health Serv Res 2018;18(1):371.

[12] Van Ginneken E, Rice T. Enforcing enrollment in health insurance exchanges: evidence from the Netherlands, Switzerland, and Germany. Med Care Res Rev 2015;72(4):496–509.

[13] Provincial and Territorial Public Drug Benefit Programs. Government of Canada [Internet]. [Accessed 23 September 2020]. Available from: https://www.canada.ca/en/health-canada/services/health-care-system/pharmaceuticals/access-insurance-coverage-prescription-medicines/provincial-territorial-public-drug-benefit-programs.html.Provincial and Territorial Public Drug Benefit Programs. Government of Canada [Internet]. [Accessed 23 September 2020]. Available from: https://www.canada.ca/en/health-canada/services/health-care-system/pharmaceuticals/access-insurance-coverage-prescription-medicines/provincial-territorial-public-drug-benefit-programs.html.

[14] Claxton G, Rae M, Damico A, Young G, McDermott D, Whitmore H. Employer health benefits. San Francisco, CA: Henry J. Kaiser Family Foundation; 2019.[15]HealthCare.gov. Out-of-pocket maximum/limit. U.S. Centers for Medicare & Medicaid Services [Internet]. [Accessed 23 September 2020]. Available from: https://www.healthcare.gov/glossary/out-of-pocket-maximum-limit/#:~:text=For%20the%202020%20plan%20year,and%20%2415%2C800%20for%20a%20family.HealthCare.gov. Out-of-pocket maximum/limit. U.S. Centers for Medicare & Medicaid Services [Internet]. [Accessed 23 September 2020]. Available from: https://www.healthcare.gov/glossary/out-of-pocket-maximum-limit/#:~:text=For%20the%202020%20plan%20year,and%20%2415%2C800%20for%20a%20family.

[16] Anon. An overview of medicare. Medicare. Kaiser Family Foundation; 2019. [Internet]. [Accessed 21 September 2020]. Available from: https://www.kff.org/medicare/issue-brief/an-overview-of-medicare/.

[17] Robinson JC. Theory and practice in the design of physician payment incentives. Milbank Q 2001;79(2):149–77. III.

[18] Ikegami N. Controlling health expenditures by revisions to the fee schedule in Japan. In: Ikegami N, editor. Universal health coverage for inclusive and sustainable development lessons from Japan. Washington, DC: World Bank; 2014 [chapter 5].

[19] LaPointe J. Exploring international reference pricing for pharmaceuticals. Policy and regulation news. Xtelligent Healthcare Media, LLC; 2019. [Internet]. [Accessed 23 September 2020]. Available from: https://pharmanewsintel.com/news/exploring-international-reference-pricing-for-pharmaceuticals.

[20] Leopold C, Vogler S, Mantel-Teeuwisse AK, de Joncheere K, Leufkens HG, Laing R. Differences in external price referencing in Europe: a descriptive overview. Health Policy 2012;104(1):50–60.

[21] Robinson JC, Panteli C, Ex P. Reference pricing in Germany: Implications for U.S. pharmaceutical purchasing. The Commonwealth Fund; 2019.

[22] Saltman RB. Health sector solidarity: a core European value but with broadly varying content. Isr J Health Policy Res 2015;4:5.

[23] Pfaff M, Wassener D. Germany. J Health Polit Policy Law 2000;25(5):907–14.

[24] Anell A. Swedish healthcare under pressure. Health Econ 2005;14(Suppl. 1):S237–54.

[25] Bellanger MM, Mosse PR. The search for the Holy Grail: combining decentralised planning and contracting mechanisms in the French health care system. Health Econ 2005;14(Suppl. 1):S119–32.

[26] Anon. The Japan vision: Health care 2035. Health Care 2035 Advisory Panel; 2015.

[27] Brown LD, Chinitz DP. Saltman on solidarity. Isr J Health Policy Res 2015;4:27.

[28] Gray BH, van Ginneken E. Health care for undocumented migrants: European approaches. Issue Brief (Commonw Fund) 2012;33:1–12.

[29] Chevreul K, Brigham KB, Durand-Zaleski I, Hernández-Quevedo C. In: Hernández-Quevedo C, Nolte E, Van Ginneken E, editors. France: Health system review. Health systems in transition, vol. 17. Copenhagen: The European Observatory on Health Systems and Policies; 2015.

[30] Allin S, Marchildon G, Peckham A. In: Tikkanen R, Osborn R, Mossialos E, Djordjevic A, Wharton GA, editors. Canada. International health care system profiles. The Commonwealth Fund; 2020. [Internet]. [Accessed 15 September 2020]. Available from: https://www.commonwealthfund.org/international-health-policy-center/countries/canada.

[31] Bollag S, Ashton A. Undocumented immigrants to get health care in Gavin Newsom's California budget deal. The Sacramento Bee; 2019. [Internet]. [Accessed 23 September 2020]. Available from: https://www.sacbee.com/news/politics-government/capitol-alert/article231310348.html.

[32] Fuchs VR. Who shall live? Health, economics and social choice. 2nd ed. World Scientific Publishing Company; 2011.

[33] Span P. A quiet end to the 'death panels' debate. The New York Times; 2015. [Internet]. [Accessed 23 September 2020]. Available from: https://www.nytimes.com/2015/11/24/health/end-of-death-panels-myth-brings-new-end-of-life-challenges.html?login=email&auth=login-email.

[34] Rice T, Unruh L. The economics of health reconsidered. 4th ed. Health Administration Press; 2015.

[35] Agarwal R, Mazurenko O, Menachemi N. High-deductible health plans reduce health care cost and utilization, including use of needed preventive services. Health Aff (Millwood) 2017;36(10):1762–8.

[36] Brot-Goldberg ZC, Chandra A, Handel BR, Kolstad JT. What does a deductible do? The impact of cost-sharing on health care prices, quantities, and spending dynamics. Q J Econ 2017;132(3):1261–318.

Part II

The countries

Section A

Universal coverage systems with a single insurer

Chapter 3

United Kingdom

The big picture

The four countries that constitute the United Kingdom—England, Scotland, Wales, and Northern Ireland—each has its own version of the National Health System (NHS). With many shared characteristics, they provide a prototype of one way to organize a healthcare system, with heavy government involvement in both the financing and, to varying degrees, delivery of care. The system is funded primarily from general taxes rather than employment-based premiums, private insurance, or user fees. As discussed in Chapter 2, it was initiated after World War II following a 1942 report by social scientist William Beveridge; systems like these have often been classified as **Beveridge**-style.[a] According to Clive Smee, from the beginning it had "the aim of providing health care that was universal, comprehensive, and free at the point of delivery. … Arguably, the distinguishing feature of the NHS is its combination of equity of access, underpinned by universal coverage and very little cost sharing, and tight expenditure control" [1, p. 947]. T.R. Reid puts it this way: "People go their entire lives without ever paying a doctor or hospital bill; in Britain, this is considered normal" [2, p. 104]. Studies have shown it to be the most equitable among high-income countries [3], and along with Australia, it ranks lowest in expenditures among the countries covered in this book (Table 15.3) [4].

These low expenditures are a product of how the system is set up. Government establishes a global budget. Most of this budget is distributed to local areas through **capitation** payments, overseen by local administrative bodies, called clinical commissioning groups (CCGs)s, that are governed by boards whose members are local general practitioners (GPs). CCGs have responsibility for ensuring that patients in their local areas receive appropriate care, including hospitalizations. There is an emphasis on primary rather than specialty care and most physician payments are by capitation and salary with incentives to improve quality, although there is still some fee-for-service (FFS). Moreover, there is an influential advisory group reporting to the government on which new

---

[a] The other country in the book whose healthcare system is most closely aligned with the Beveridge model is Sweden.

Health Insurance Systems: An International Comparison. https://doi.org/10.1016/B978-0-12-816072-5.00010-9

procedures and pharmaceuticals are considered to be cost-effective; generally, new services that are deemed to be cost-ineffective are not covered, although many services have never been assessed.[b]

A hallmark of the NHS is the use of cost-effectiveness analyses to determine which new technologies and medicines will be covered as well as how much to pay for them. Most other countries employ health technology assessment, but the United Kingdom is unusual in employing a cost-effectiveness threshold. In England, the government agency that makes these decisions, the National Institute of Health and Care Effectiveness, or NICE, has been doing so since 1999. Generally, new technologies and drugs must be able to achieve, on average, an additional quality-adjusted life year (QALY) for every 20,000 to 30,000 British pounds (approximately $27,000 to $40,000 US) or else they will not be covered; this also provides a useful negotiating power for government in its negotiations with industry.

One of the biggest complaints about the NHS over the years has been that it is underfunded [5], spending far less than many other European countries. The result was crowding, long waiting lists, and complaints about the quality of care. As one example of the latter, the United Kingdom ranks next to poorest, only above the United States among our 10 countries, in keeping down **mortality amenable to health care**, a measure of deaths that should not occur in a well-functioning healthcare system [6].

Over the decades, these issues have brought political pressure to invest more in the NHS. There was a substantial increase in spending in 1999 that was ultimately associated with improvements in amenable mortality in England compared with the other nations that comprise the United Kingdom [7]. Since 2010, however, the rate of increase in spending has declined. Over the longer term, changes in spending have ebbed and flowed, partly based on the state of the economy and partly on which party was in power, and with it, the length of waiting lists and perceptions of quality. At the time of writing, the government has committed to invest more with the hopes of restraining problems such as these, although whether this will come to pass, given the severe consequences of both COVID-19 pandemic and **Brexit** are difficult to predict.

It is difficult to generalize too much, however. Over the past 20 years, the healthcare systems of the four countries that constitute the United Kingdom have diverged as a result of "devolution," which provided a great deal of autonomy to each. England has continued to rely more on market forces between purchasers and providers of health care as well as on consumer choice of GP and hospital. Scotland, in contrast, has moved more to a system that integrates the payers and providers with less of an emphasis on patient choice [8, p. 37].

---

[b] Adam Oliver, personal communication, July 27, 2020.

The details

History

There was little in the way of formal healthcare coverage provided by the central government in the United Kingdom through the 19th century, with most expenses either paid out-of-pocket or through charity with local government bodies providing basic care for the poor. That changed in the early 20th century with the growth of the medical profession and pressure from the labor movement, resulting in the passage of the Health Insurance Act of 1911. The Act provided workers with compulsory coverage for sick pay and physicians' (but not hospital) services. Because those not in the labor force (including dependents) were ineligible, only about one-third of the population was covered [9 (p. 25), 10]. It was funded by employees (who paid 4 pence a week), employers (3 pence), and government (2 pence). David Lloyd George, the chief sponsor, campaigned for the system with the slogan, "ninepence for fourpence" [11]. This early legislation has bearing on the way the system subsequently evolved as care was provided free of charge and doctors were paid on a capitated basis.

Subsequently, and until the end of World War II, there was a patchwork of programs to help pay the costs of medical care, with a mix of public, private, and charity care. Medical care was concentrated in hospitals and largely funded by charity. Local government continued to provide some care for the poor as well as for mothers, children, and those with infectious diseases. Many in the working class continued to have coverage through the Health Insurance Act noted earlier [12]. The middle class, however, was largely excluded from hospital coverage provided by the patchwork mentioned earlier. They often had to use costly private doctors, providing an additional political impetus for comprehensive reform [13].

Prior to World War II, the inequities of a system that had spotty coverage and left many financially vulnerable led to calls for change, particularly by those on the left. While fundamental reform could not be implemented during the war, the stage was set by the publication of a report in 1942 commissioned by the wartime coalition government, entitled, "Social Insurance and Allied Services," authored by William Beveridge. Its most important component was calling for the establishment of government-administered national health system [14]. After the war, the Labour party took power and passed legislation establishing the NHS, which became operational in 1948. Incremental changes to the NHS were made over the next several decades, mainly related to modernizing facilities and technologies [8, p. 14]. A critical change was the introduction of patient copayments for prescription drugs, dental care, and eyeglasses in 1952 to quell burgeoning demand and contain spending [15].

Fundamental changes occurred near the end of Margaret Thatcher's 11 years as prime minister. With the Conservative Party in power, the National Health Service and Community Care Act of 1990 initiated various procompetitive components into the NHS in England, most notably, the introduction of "internal markets." Prior to that, the government was both primary purchaser and main provider of healthcare services. With internal markets, these responsibilities were separated, with the stated purposes of increasing efficiency and responsiveness to consumer demands, including shortening long waiting lists to receive services. On one side were the purchasers, mainly district health authorities and "GP fundholders." The district health authorities contracted with providers to deliver services needed by people in that district, while the GP fundholders were primary care organizations [9, p. 27]. These organizations or practices were required to have a minimum of 11,000 patients. They could apply for their own budgets from the NHS, using this funding not only to provide primary care services to their patients, but also to purchase hospital, specialty, community, and mental health services [8, p. 16]. On the other side of the market, hospitals became trusts that competed against each other to receive contracts for their services [1].

Over the next two decades, the names of the purchasing and provider groups would change (the main ones now used in England, respectively, are clinical commissioning groups and foundation trusts) but the responsibilities, while evolved, have not altered dramatically. Thus, the internal market system established under Margaret Thatcher was still largely intact until only a few years ago, albeit with different names given to the purchasers and providers of services—at least in England.

There is much debate about whether the internal market system was largely successful or unsuccessful, but it did not last intact through the end of the decade, as the Labour party came into power in 1997 and made significant changes. But subsequent conservative governments attempted to reinstill competition among providers. One such piece of legislation was the Health and Social Care Act of 2012, about which Adam Oliver wrote, can "legitimately be viewed, somewhat generously, as messy and complex, and the political process that produced it a fiasco" [16, p. 235]. More recently, there has been something of a retreat from some of the ideas in the 2012 Act, especially the role of the market, and movement toward integrated care systems that encourage cooperation between key governing and delivering bodies. These more integrated systems have existed in the other three countries for many years. Summing things up, Scott Greer has stated, "The English NHS has been so constantly, and consistently, reformed that it is difficult to pick out individual reforms that mattered most" [17, p. 20].

One other piece of history is critical: devolution. In the late 1990s, a formal process of devolution took place with a great bearing on the NHS: Scotland, Wales, and Northern Ireland each voted to assume more power to govern themselves. At this point, the healthcare systems began to diverge, with England relying more on the split between purchasers and providers to drive efficiency, and the other countries more on a model relying on central planning [17].

Overview of the health insurance system

The four UK countries' health systems share many characteristics, including universal coverage funded largely through taxes, strong roles for GPs including **gatekeeping** responsibilities for specialty and hospital care, salaried inpatient physicians, and the use of cost-effectiveness analysis to control price growth and prioritize new treatments and drugs. There are some significant differences in the systems in each of the countries, however. They are grouped together here in part because cross-national data on performance, the focus of the last section of the book, provide comparisons between the United Kingdom as a whole and other countries. Nevertheless, the focus here will be on the English system, as it covers 84% of the total UK population.[c] Some key differences between England and the other countries are noted throughout.

The United Kingdom's NHS provides access to care (rather than insurance) to its population, largely free from user charges except for drugs and dental care, and is mainly funded through tax revenues. Enrollment is automatic although registration with a GP is required. In England, the NHS Constitution stipulates seven principles, including coverage of comprehensive health services for everyone, access based on clinical need rather than an ability to pay, patient-centeredness, and providing the best value for taxpayers' money [18]. Most hospital beds are public, and most physicians receive much of their income from the NHS. There is only a small voluntary health insurance sector that provides better access (shorter waits, more amenities) to those who enroll, primarily for nonurgent treatment, although some individuals also self-pay.

A key component of the NHS in England is the CCGs. All GPs and GP practices are required to be members of their local CCGs, which serve, on average, about one quarter of a million people. They receive budgets from NHS England and are responsible for both planning for the care of their populations and contracting out ("commissioning") other services, including elective hospital, maternity, mental health, and community care. The budgets they receive are based on the number of enrollees but adjusted for such factors as age, input costs, the socioeconomic status of enrollees, and some measures of health [8, p. 51]. In 2016, there were 211 CCGs in England [19]. About two-thirds of the NHS England service budget is allotted to the CCGs, with most of the remainder going to services that NHS England commissions directly including primary care and specialty services [20].[d] The United Kingdom is unusual among countries in giving GPs so much authority in its healthcare system through the power they wield through the CCGs, although in reality they have somewhat limited discretion given constraints in capacity in most areas.[e]

---

[c] Of the remaining 16%, 8% live in Scotland, 5% in Wales, and 3% in Northern Ireland.

[d] Primary care services are commissioned directly by NHS England to avoid conflict of interest within CCGs, which provide some of those services. Primary care, however, is often "co-commissioned" between the NHS and CCGs.

[e] Martin McKee, personal communication, September 10, 2020.

Another purchasing entity involves the trusts, which provide hospital care and some other patient services. They are mainly hospitals (and mostly public) and must abide by all NHS rules, including deriving no more than 49% of their revenues from private sources. There are also trusts providing community, mental health, and ambulance care. One stated aim of establishing trusts was to allow local communities to have more influence over the care they receive rather than having it determined centrally by the NHS, but some argue that there is little evidence that this has happened.[e] All trusts, and especially foundation trusts, have a degree of autonomy with regard to their internal operations, such as how they allocate the budgets they receive from purchasers of care and other sources, such as funds for supporting the education of health professionals and research [8, p. 83].

One feature that has received a great deal of international attention is how ineffective or marginally effective care is discouraged. NHS services are rationed. Most new services and drugs are covered only if they pass a strict cost-effectiveness test, although as noted this also provides a very useful price-negotiating tactic for the government. Another feature is that physician payments are based more on capitation and salary rather than FFS.

Governance

There are health departments in each of the four governments of the countries constituting the United Kingdom. In England, it sets national health policy, although since the Health and Social Care Act of 2012, the department no longer is responsible for the delivery of services under the NHS. Instead, NHS England now has that responsibility [8, p. 18]. NHS England, working with leadership from seven regional systems, oversees the implementation of national health policy, provides resources to CCGs, and purchases some services directly [8 (p. 18), 21]. There are similar bodies in the other three UK countries although their responsibilities vary. One of the most significant ways is that the purchaser-provider split, began under the Thatcher government, now exists only in England and, to a lesser extent, Northern Ireland and is quickly being replaced by a system focused on integrated care [8, p. 17]. Scotland, in particular, had moved away from the competition-based model based on the purchaser-provider split to one of "cooperation and integration" several years earlier [8, p. 17].

A component of the NHS that has received worldwide attention is NICE. It is an independent organization accountable to England's Department of Health and Social Care and covering England and Wales. Separate bodies exist in Scotland and Northern Ireland. NICE advises on which new services, health technologies, and drugs are to be covered. It also issues practice guidelines on how certain conditions should be treated.

Financing

Government financing of total health expenditures is relatively high in the United Kingdom—77% in 2018. In contrast, voluntary health insurance (VHI) covers just 3% of expenditures, and out-of-pocket (OOP) spending, about 16% [4]. A considerable portion of out-of-pocket (OOP) spending is for the health component of long-term care, which is not covered in this book.

In the past, the UK system was often viewed as underfunded, and compared to other countries, it was. In 2000, it spent just 6.0% of GDP on health, considerably lower than the other countries considered here. Japan, at 7.2%, was the second-lowest spender. By 2010, however, UK spending jumped to 8.4% of GDP, proportionally a 40% increase. By then, its spending was comparable to both Australia and Japan [4]. This increase was intentional; there had been widespread complaints about waiting lists (reportedly as long as 18 months) and quality [22]. The Labour government, which was in power during that decade after Conservative rule during the previous 20 years, committed itself to bring its spending to levels more consistent with other European nations [8, p. 41]. This included addressing a large maintenance backlog and augmentation of capital equipment such as MRI and CT scanners [8, p. 63]. Since then, however, expenditures have fallen again compared to the other countries as a result of the economic crisis that began in the late 2000s as well as the election of Conservative-led governments since 2010.[f]

Funding for healthcare and other social services allocated to the four countries is based on the Barnett formula. Under the formula, the UK treasury department sets spending levels for England. The other three UK countries receive block grants to carry out their activities proportional to their population sizes, although they can decide what proportion of the monies in the block grant they wish to spend on health.[g] Increases or decreases in England's budget are reflected by proportional changes in the block grant sizes. The formula, much criticized for decades in part because it does not consider the respective population needs of the four countries—no adjustments are made for factors such as poverty rates and population age—continues to be used [8, p. 52].

The main source of revenue for government funding is taxes, including income taxes, value-added taxes (VAT), corporate tax, and taxes on consumables such as gasoline, tobacco, and alcohol. There is also an assessment on employers and employees called that National Insurance Contribution (NIC). When collected, revenue is not earmarked to health but rather goes into the general coffers [8, p. 51]. Of total UK revenues, over 60% is from the three largest sources: income taxes (25%), NIC (19%), and VAT (18%) [23].

Income taxes are progressive, and it has been estimated that the top 1% of earners provide one-third of income tax revenue, and over 40% of the population pays no income taxes [24]. In contrast, the VAT is regressive because consumption goods constitute a larger portion of total income for those with

---

[f] Jon Cylus, personal communication, August 12, 2020, and Martin McKee, personal communication, September 10, 2020.
[g] Mark Dayan, personal communication, February 17, 2020.

lower incomes. The VAT rate is 20% of the items bought by consumers, with exceptions for food and some other items. For people in most job categories, NIC rates are largely proportional at 12% of payroll earnings, but they become regressive for those with higher incomes, as the rate drops to 2% for incomes above about £50,000 per year. Overall, the financing system appears to be mildly progressive [9, p. 87].

Coverage

Breadth

Coverage is universal and automatic for the vast majority of residents, although as noted it is necessary to register with a GP. Those with refugee status also have free access to primary healthcare services. For others, such as temporary visitors, emergency care and services for specific communicable diseases are covered. Increasingly, those who do not have valid visas (e.g., have stayed longer than permitted) are billed in advance to receive care [25]. This intentional effort to create a "hostile environment" for undocumented individuals, which began in 2012, is discussed later, under Assuring Access and Equity.

Scope

NHS benefits are broad, covering nearly all services. Unlike most counties, basic dental care is covered for the entire population but with substantial patient cost sharing. Basic vision care such as eyeglasses and contact lenses is not covered except for certain population groups.

Depth

While most services are covered free of charge, there are cost-sharing requirements for some services, particularly in England. In 2019, there was a £9 charge for each prescription filled but those who anticipate using prescriptions regularly can prepay £104 annually, which covers all costs. Most who require regular prescriptions are excluded from paying anything: children and students age 18 and younger, adults age 60 and older, pregnant women and new mothers, some poor and disabled persons, and those with particular diseases. As a result, in 2016, 89% of English prescriptions were provided free of charge [26]. For dental care, there are three **copayment** levels depending on type of service: either £23, £62, or £269. Like drugs, certain groups are excluded from paying but not as many (e.g., medical conditions and old age do not exempt a person) [27]. Free eye tests and optical vouchers to help pay for eyeglasses or contact lenses are provided largely to the same people who can receive free prescription drugs [28].

The other UK countries have their own cost-sharing structures. The most important difference compared to England is that in Scotland, Wales, and Northern Ireland, there are no copayments for prescription drugs.

Voluntary health insurance

Private or voluntary health insurance (VHI) pays a relatively small role in the United Kingdom, accounting for only 3% of total expenditures and covering about one-tenth of the population [29]. An estimated 82% obtain coverage through their employers [30, p. 91]. Its role may be more important than it first appears, however, serving as "a safety valve for the wealthy disaffected"—those who find that waits are too long or amenities lacking [31].

Chapter 2 discusses different kinds of VHI, the two most common being policies that provide supplemental coverage and those providing complementary coverage. In the United Kingdom, it plays both roles. Its main supplementary role is providing potentially quicker access to specialty services as well as choice of either a private wing in a public hospital or a private hospital. Some specialists give priority to patients with VHI because it can lead to increased income. All specialists are free to work extra to see private patients at more lucrative FFS rates so long as they meet their NHS commitments.[b] One estimate is that the average specialist increases his or her income by about 50% through seeing private patients, although this varies from very little (in rural areas where few have this coverage) to doubling or tripling salaries (in some London practices). This, in turn, could increase waiting time for the remainder of the NHS population, but some argue that it also takes some pressure off the NHS, as those who use private services still pay their taxes to support the public system but use fewer of its resources [31].

Some VHI policies provide coverage for things not covered by the NHS such as complementary and alternative medicine. Complementary VHI coverage, in turn, covers the cost-sharing component of items not fully covered by the NHS, especially dental services and, in England, prescription drugs. Premiums vary according to age and health status at the time of enrollment [29].

Choice

There is no choice of public insurer in the United Kingdom as everyone is covered under the NHS. The only role of private health insurance companies is to provide VHI.

Patients can choose any GP they wish although many practices report that they are full and not accepting new patients [26]. This is also true of hospitals; even though there is choice, in practice, it may be difficult to obtain a timely appointment, except in an emergency.[h] Patient choice appears to be a greater political priority in England than in the other three UK countries, which, unlike England, do not rely on it as a key method of improving their systems [8 (p. 37), 32].

---

[h] Jon Cylus, personal communication, August 12, 2020.

Provider payment

Hospitals

There are both public and private hospitals in the United Kingdom. In England, the larger hospitals tend to be public and treat a large majority of cases. There are also private hospitals that tend to focus on non-NHS-covered services (e.g., bariatric surgery and fertility treatment) but not intensive or emergency care. They are often used when public hospital waiting lists are long, and the care provided there is often paid for by the NHS at NHS rates [30, p. 96]. Less than 10% of NHS hospital spending in England is at private hospitals, however [26]. Moreover, only about one percentage of beds in NHS-England hospitals are devoted to private-pay patients [33].

Most of the hospital payment, about 60% in England, is provided by CCGs to hospital trusts through a **diagnosis-related group** (DRG)-type system called Payment by Results (PBR). Other sectors, such as emergency care, also employ this system. Ezekiel Emanuel reports that "PBR has increasingly been criticized for its fee-for-service model, which incentivizes volume over quality and value. In response, commissioning of health care services in the UK is moving towards greater use of capitation and other alternative payment arrangements" [30, p. 96].

Payment rates are set by the NHS at the national level. Much of the remaining hospital payment is for services like emergency and mental health. Payment by individuals and private insurers to private hospitals for care not covered by the NHS is not regulated, although the major insurers have strict tariffs as well as referral criteria.[e] The other countries use different hospital payment systems. Scotland, for example, pays hospitals mainly on the basis of global budgets [34].

Physicians

Most primary care physicians and physician groups in general practice are independent contractors rather than government employees even though the vast majority of their payments are from the NHS. GP practices are paid primarily by a combination of capitation rates, some FFS for preventive services like vaccinations, and performance bonuses. These bonuses, in turn, are based to a large degree on adhering to practice guidelines deemed by the government to be consistent with best practices in coordinating the care of patients with chronic diseases. Individual GPs, however, are often paid a salary from their group [8 (p. 58), 26].

Along with the United States, the United Kingdom (particularly England) relies more on pay-for-performance than any other country. In England, performance bonuses can constitute a significant (although declining) part of GP incomes, which are high by the standards of most other countries [35]. In 2013, the maximum was reduced from 25% to 15% [36]. It was estimated that in 2017–18, quality payments constituted as average of 8% of GP incomes [37]. Nevertheless, by paying their GPs well and providing them with so much authority through their central role in CCGs, the United Kingdom has demonstrated an unusually strong focus on primary care [2].

Specialists are usually hospital employees paid on a salary basis. They can augment their salaries through clinical excellence awards and by engaging in private practice, and sometimes this occurs in public hospitals [38]. A little more than half do augment their income through private clinical work.

Pharmaceuticals

The United Kingdom has the highest generic pharmaceutical penetration of any European nation. 85% of prescriptions are generic, constituting 38% of outpatient drug spending. This is due, in part, to practice guidelines provided to GPs. As a result, pharmaceutical expenditures are lower than in most of Europe [25]. Another way in which England controls these costs is through the Voluntary Pricing Access Scheme, an agreement between the NHS and pharmaceutical companies that allows the companies to set prices for new drug but limits the increase in annual spending on NHS-covered branded pharmaceuticals to 2% per year [39]. The purpose of the scheme is to balance the need for pharmaceutical companies to embark on research with the NHS's need to control spending.

NICE also plays a role in keeping pharmaceutical spending under control. As noted earlier, it tends not to recommend new drugs as cost-effective if they exceed 20,000–30,000 British pounds per QALY. It is noteworthy that certain cancer drugs in England are subject to higher thresholds through the Cancer Drug Fund [40, 41].

Assuring access and equity

In many ways, access is outstanding in the United Kingdom, unsurprisingly, given that there is universal coverage and most care is free at the point of service. International comparisons, shown in detail in Chapter 14, attest to this. Among nine countries considered in this book (all except Japan), the Commonwealth Fund's 2016 population surveys of each country found that people in the United Kingdom reported the fewest of these problems:

- Had a cost-related access problem in the past year (5.5%),
- Had serious problem or unable to pay medical bills (4%), and
- Skipped dental care or a checkup due to cost in past year (9.5%).

More significantly from an equity standpoint, these reported problems were lowest among the nine countries for those in the bottom half of the income distribution [3]. Other data, from the World Bank, show a similar pattern: only 2% of those in the United Kingdom's lowest income quintile reported spending 2% or more of their income OOP, also the lowest among the countries, although data were not available for Germany and the Netherlands [42].

There are three primary access problems that have received a great deal of attention. Two are by design but the other is not. One of the formers regards an access to services or drugs that NICE does not deem cost-effective. Those wanting to use them have to pay OOP. This is intentional; one of the principles in the

NHS constitution is that it "is committed to providing best value for taxpayers' money" [18].

The second intentional one is the creation of the hostile environment for undocumented immigrants. This policy began in 2012 under future prime minister Theresa May, who was Home Secretary at the time. At the time May stated that "The aim is to create, here in Britain, a really hostile environment for illegal immigrants" [43].[e] Since that time, the NHS has been sharing nonclinical data with the Home Office, which among other things is in charge of "securing the UK border and controlling immigration" [44]. One consequence is that some residents who are entitled to NHS care have been deterred from seeking it [45].

The unintentional access problem, waiting lists, has historically been a big problem in the United Kingdom. The Commonwealth Fund surveys find that residents of the United Kingdom (along with Swedes) wait longer for surgical appointments and elective survey than all of the other countries except Canada [3]. Policy makers have confronted this issue over the decades. Major inroads were made in the early 2000s with a large infusion into the NHS budget, mainly to deal with this problem as well as provide more flexibility for physicians to "moonlight" by treating private-pay patients. Nevertheless, the problem has since grown. Waiting times increased at least through 2018 both for emergency care and elective surgery, as demand has outstripped the workforce available—a problem that could intensify under Brexit, given the loss of health professionals from the European Union as well as the possible economic consequences it may cause [25]. Irene Papanicolas and colleagues note, "As the migration of healthcare professionals has decreased since 2015, as evidenced by an 87% drop in new nurses coming from the EU to work in the UK from 2016–17 to 2017–18, the existing staffing challenges facing the NHS will clearly be further exacerbated"—citing fewer training stipends and "uncertainty about the status of immigrant workers in the light of the Brexit referendum…" [46, p. 11].

Since 2004, the NHS constitution has provided residents with the right to wait no longer than fixed amounts of time. These maximum waits vary by country but generally are 18 weeks to see a specialist; in the case of cancer, it is 2 weeks (with treatment within 62 days). There is also a pledge (not a right) to receive emergency care within 4 hours, from the time spent in the emergency department until the patient is discharged or transferred. A 2018 House of Commons report found that England had not met its target (which was set at meeting the above thresholds 92% of the time) in any year since 2015. Wales has not met its target for elective surgery since 2009, Scotland since 2014, nor has Northern Ireland been meeting its targets. There were originally supposed to be financial penalties exacted from providers with longer waiting lists but these were deemed to be counterproductive and therefore are not being enforced [47]. In 2019, England began to impose fines of 2500 British pounds on providers and commissioners for each patient having to wait more than a year from referral to treatment, although they were suspended during the COVID-19 crisis [47].

Controlling expenditures

Compared to the other countries in the book, UK spending on health care is very low. In 2019, it was estimated to be third lowest to Australia and the Netherlands in terms of GDP devoted to health and the lowest of the 10 countries in per capita spending. It spent about 4% less per capita than Japan, the second-lowest country, and 40% less than Switzerland, the highest European country. The US per capita spending was 2.4 times as great as in the United Kingdom (see Table 15.3) [25].

There are pluses and minuses reflected in these low spending figures. One plus is that it may be a marker of efficiency, and indeed, the United Kingdom ranks first among 11 countries on administrative efficiency by the Commonwealth Fund [3].[i] Another is that more resources are potentially available for other societal priorities, although in actuality public social spending as a proportion of GDP is around the median for the countries in this book [48]. But there are disadvantages as well, particularly with regard to waiting a long time to receive services and potential quality problems. The same Commonwealth Fund study found the United Kingdom ranking 10th of 11 countries in healthcare outcomes based on several measures of mortality, disability, and cancer survival [3].

There are a number of ways in which the United Kingdom has held down health expenses.

- There is a global budget for health care [26], including an explicit limit on how much is spent on brand-name drugs, with spending above that amount being the financial responsibility of the pharmaceutical companies. Similarly, GPs are expected to prescribe generic rather than brand-name drugs and there are limits on how much drug manufacturers can earn in profits on NHS-approved medications [8, p. 35].
- The finances of CCGs are closely monitored by the national government to ensure that they do not run into deficit in any given year [26].
- There is an emphasis on primary care and gatekeeping. CCGs, which emphasize primary care, are fiscally responsible for much of the nonprimary care provided in their geographic areas. Moreover, most physicians are paid on a capitation or salary basis, removing much of the inflationary pressure of FFS medicine.
- While several other countries base coverage decisions for pharmaceuticals on cost-effectiveness criteria, the United Kingdom, through the work of NICE, applies these criteria to most new clinical services and diagnostic

---

[i] This was based on a composite of seven indicators gathered from surveys of both doctors and patients, including how much time doctors spent on insurance or claims, obtaining prescriptions for their patients, and providing quality data; and whether patients had to go to an emergency department because a regular doctor was not available, tests results were not available when needed, the doctor ordered a test the patient thought was unnecessary because it had done in the past 2 years, and spending too much time on paperwork or disputing medical bills.

testing as well. Moreover, NICE uses an explicit threshold (in terms of the cost of additional QALY) to make recommendations regarding whether new drugs are to be included in the NHS benefits package, which in turn augments its negotiating power with industry.

- Expenditures on major capital are lower than in any of the other countries in this book. It is estimated that in 2017, the United Kingdom spent 3.2% of its total health expenditures on capital; high spenders, like Germany and Japan, spent around 10% (and moreover, these percentages were from a larger base level per capita spending). Similarly, the United Kingdom has the lowest level of MRIs and CT scanners per capita, just one-third of the average among 35 OECD countries [49].

Key policy issues

In the decade between 2010 and 2020, the NHS suffered from major funding deficiencies despite faster increases in demand and costs of providing services, difficulties with providers staying within their budgets, and severe workforce shortages. Regarding the latter, one estimate is that there were 100,000 hospital staff vacancies, 40,000 of which were nurses [50]. As noted, this has implications for both quality and waiting times. An even more immediate problem is a shortage of primary care doctors, who play a key gatekeeping role for the entire system. There have been calls for more funding in general [48], training more primary care physicians and nurses, but in the meantime, allied professions such as therapists, physicians assistants, and pharmacists are being employed to perform tasks previously conducted by physicians and nurses [51].

These problems cannot be dealt with solely through regulatory reform. In 2018, the prime minister announced that NHS-England funding would be increased by an average of 3.4% annually (adjusted for inflation) through 2024, far more than the one percentage average annual increases in recent years. To receive this funding augmentation, England's NHS was to develop long-term plans [50]. Most of the recommendations related to the delivery of care and enhancement of the size of the workforce. However, given the combined impact of COVID-19 and Brexit, it is uncertain whether this commitment will be upheld.[e]

An immediate goal is to improve hospital finances through collaboration between the NHS and the hospital trusts along with an infusion of new monies. The plan also includes moving from activity-based (e.g., DRG funding) for hospital care to capitation payments, providing hospitals an incentive to coordinate with community care providers—a clear movement away from the tradition of internal markets, where competition rather than cooperation is the engine for improving value. This movement is consistent with a larger goal of reducing health inequalities in part through more emphasis on community and mental health services. In return for augmented funding and a commitment to help hospital funds that are in deficit, there is an expectation that providers (as well as the NHS and CCGs) increase productivity growth by 1.1% per year over a five-year period [50]. With the new infusion of funding, along with a myriad of planned delivery system changes, it is hoped that quality measures will improve and waiting lists will become shorter.

References

[1] Smee C. United Kingdom. J Health Polit Policy Law 2000;25(5):945–51.

[2] Reid TR. The healing of America: A global quest for better, cheaper, and fairer health care. New York: Penguin Press; 2009.

[3] Schneider EC, Sarnak DO, Squires D, Shah A, Doty MM. Mirror, mirror 2017: International comparison reflects flaws and opportunities for better U.S. health care. Mirror, Mirror: The Commonwealth Fund; 2017.

[4] Anon. OECD health statistics 2020. OECD; 2020. [Online Database]. [Accessed 26 August 2020]. Available from: http://www.oecd.org/els/health-systems/health-data.htm.

[5] Klein E. In the UK's health system, rationing isn't a dirty word. Vox; 2020. [Internet]. [Accessed 18 October 2020]. Available from: https://www.vox.com/2020/1/28/21074386/health-care-rationing-britain-nhs-nice-medicare-for-all.

[6] Karanikolos M, editor. Mortality amenable to health care (deaths per 100,000 population), 2016. International health care system profiles. The Commonwealth Fund; 2019. (European Observatory on Health Systems and Policies 2019). [Internet]. [Accessed 2 September 2020]. Available from: https://www.commonwealthfund.org/international-health-policy-center/system-stats/mortality-amenable.

[7] Desai M, Nolte E, Karanikolos M, Khoshaba B, McKee M. Measuring NHS performance 1990–2009 using amenable mortality: interpret with care. J R Soc Med 2011;104(9):370–9.

[8] Cylus J, Richardson E, Findley L, Longley M, O'Neill C, Stee D. United Kingdom: health system review. Health Syst Transit 2015;17(5):1–125.

[9] Boyle S. United Kingdom (England): health system review. Health Syst Transit 2011;13(1):1–486.

[10] View all themes. The Cabinet Papers. The National Archives [Web archive]. [Accessed 18 October 2020]. Available from: https://www.nationalarchives.gov.uk/cabinetpapers/themes/browse-by-theme.htm?WT.ac=View%20all%20themes.

[11] Leach R. No convergence. Taxation; 2012 [4353].

[12] Gorsky M. The NHS in Britain: any lesson from history for universal health coverage? In: Medcalf A, Bhattacharya S, Momen H, Saavedra M, Jones M, editors. Health for all: The journey of universal health coverage. Hyderabad: Orient Blackswan; 2015 [chapter 7].

[13] Doyle B, Cresswell R. What was healthcare like before the NHS? The Conversation; 2018. [Internet]. [Accessed 18 October 2020]. Available from: https://theconversation.com/what-was-healthcare-like-before-the-nhs-99055.

[14] The welfare state. Citizenship. The National Archives [Internet]. [Accessed 18 October 2020]. Available from: http://www.nationalarchives.gov.uk/pathways/citizenship/brave_new_world/welfare.htm.

[15] Triggle N. The history of the NHS in charts. BBC; 2018. [News]. [Accessed 18 October 2020]. Available from: https://www.bbc.com/news/health-44560590.

[16] Oliver A. Reflecting on the UK government's health and social care act 2012: introduction. Health Econ Policy Law 2013;8(2):235–6.

[17] Greer SL. Devolution and health in the UK: policy and its lessons since 1998. Br Med Bull 2016;118(1):16–24.

[18] Anon. The NHS Constitution for England. National Health Service. Department of Health and Social Care; 2015. [Internet]. [Accessed 18 October 2020]. Available from: https://www.gov.uk/government/publications/the-nhs-constitution-for-england/the-nhs-constitution-for-england.

[19] Henderson R. Clinical commissioning groups. Patient; 2016. [Internet]. [Accessed 18 October 2020]. Available from: https://patient.info/doctor/clinical-commissioning-groups-ccgs.

[20] NHS England. NHS [Internet]. [Accessed 18 October 2020]. Available from: https://www.england.nhs.uk/commissioning/who-commissions-nhs-services/nhs-england/.

[21] About us. NHS [Internet]. [Accessed 18 October 2020]. Available from: https://www.england.nhs.uk/about/.

[22] Brown H. Tony Blair's legacy for the UK's National Health Service. Lancet 2007;369(9574):1679–82.

[23] Miller H, Roantree B. Tax revenues: Where does the money come from and what are the next government's challenges? The Institute for Fiscal Studies; 2017.

[24] Elliott L. Top 1% of earners in UK account for more than a third of income tax. The Guardian; 2019. [Internet]. [Accessed 18 October 2020]. Available from: https://www.theguardian.com/business/2019/nov/13/richest-britain-income-tax-revenues-institute-fiscal-studies.

[25] OECD and European Observatory on Health Systems and Policies. United Kingdom: Country health profile 2019. State of health in the EU. Paris: OECD Publishing; 2019.

[26] Thorlby R. In: Tikkanen R, Osborn R, Mossialos E, Djordjevic A, Wharton GA, editors. England. International health care system profiles. The Commonwealth Fund; 2020. [Internet]. [Accessed 18 October 2020]. Available from: https://www.commonwealthfund.org/international-health-policy-center/countries/england.

[27] When you need to pay towards NHS care. NHS [Internet]. [Accessed 18 October 2020]. Available from: https://www.nhs.uk/using-the-nhs/help-with-health-costs/when-you-need-to-pay-towards-nhs-care/.

[28] Free NHS eye tests and optical vouchers. NHS [Internet]. [Accessed 18 October 2020]. Available from: https://www.nhs.uk/using-the-nhs/help-with-health-costs/free-nhs-eye-tests-and-optical-vouchers/.

[29] Sagan A, Thomson S. Voluntary health insurance in Europe. vol. 1. United Kingdom: WHO Regional Office for Europe; 2016.

[30] Emanuel EJ. Which country has the world's best health care? New York: PublicAffairs; 2020.

[31] Wachter B. The awkward world of private insurance in the UK. The Health Care Blog; 2012. [Blog]. [Accessed 18 October 2020]. Available from: https://thehealthcareblog.com/blog/2012/01/16/the-awkward-world-of-private-insurance-in-the-uk/.

[32] Kaehne A. One NHS, or many? The national health service under devolution. Political Insight 2014;5(2):30–3.

[33] Ewbank L, Thompson J, McKenna H, Anandaciva S. NHS hospital bed numbers: Past, present, future. The King's Fund; 2020 [2].

[34] Scottish hospital reimbursement system. Med Tech Reimbursement Consulting [Online course]. [Accessed 18 October 2020]. Available from: https://www.a-marketaccess.com/scotland.

[35] Laugesen MJ, Glied SA. Higher fees paid to US physicians drive higher spending for physician services compared to other countries. Health Aff (Millwood) 2011;30(9):1647–56.

[36] Roland M, Guthrie B. Quality and outcomes framework: what have we learnt? BMJ 2016;354:i4060.

[37] Moberly T, Stahl-Timmins W. QOF now accounts for less than 10% of GP practice income. BMJ 2019;365:l1489.

[38] Leys C. Treating private patients in NHS hospitals—Benefit or cost? Center for Health and the Public Interest; 2018. [Blog]. [Accessed 18 October 2020]. Available from: https://chpi.org.uk/blog/treating-private-patients-in-nhs-hospitals-benefit-or-cost/.

[39] Heads of Agreement Summary. Houses of Parliament [Dataset]. [Accessed 18 October 2020]. Available from: http://data.parliament.uk/DepositedPapers/Files/DEP2018-1160/HoA_Summary.pdf.

[40] Leigh S, Granby P. A tale of two thresholds: a framework for prioritization within the cancer drugs fund. Value Health 2016;19(5):567–76.

[41] NHS England. Appraisal and funding of cancer drugs from July 2016 (including the new Cancer Drugs Fund)—A new deal for patients, taxpayers and industry. vol. 1.0. London: NHS England Cancer Drugs Fund Team; 2016.

[42] Wagstaff A, Eozenou P, Neelsen S, Smitz M. The 2019 update of the health equity and financial protection indicators database: An overview. World Bank; 2019 [8879].

[43] Anon. The hostile environment for immigrants. Global Justice Now; 2018. [Briefing]. [Accessed 23 October 2020]. Available from: https://www.globaljustice.org.uk/resources/hostile-environment-immigrants.

[44] About Us. Home Office. Gov.UK [Internet]. [Accessed 23 October 2020]. Available from: https://www.gov.uk/government/organisations/home-office/about.

[45] Hiam L, Steele S, McKee M. Creating a 'hostile environment for migrants': the British government's use of health service data to restrict immigration is a very bad idea. Health Econ Policy Law 2018;13(2):107–17.

[46] Papanicolas I, Mossialos E, Gundersen A, Woskie L, Jha AK. Performance of UK National Health Service compared with other high income countries: observational study. BMJ 2019;367:l6326.

[47] Parkin E. NHS maximum waiting time standards. Commons Library Briefing; 2020 [CBP08846].

[48] Papanicolas I, Woskie LR, Jha AK. Health care spending in the United States and other high-income countries. JAMA 2018;319(10):1024–39.

[49] OECD. Health at a glance 2019. Paris: OECD Publishing; 2019.

[50] Charles A, Ewbank L, McKenna H, Wenzel L. The NHS long-term plan explained. The King's Fund; 2019.

[51] Beech J, Bottery S, Charlesworth A, Evans H, Gershlick B, Hemmings N, et al. Full table of recommendations. In: Closing the gap. The King's Fund; 2019 [chapter 10].

Chapter 4

Canada

The big picture

Canada has received worldwide recognition for the achievements of its "**single-payer**" healthcare system. In what is not really one system but rather 13——one for each of the 10 provinces and three territories[a]—patients are guaranteed access, free at point of service, to hospital, physician, and associated diagnostic services, as well as inpatient drug therapies. Many health outcome measures are excellent [1][b] and public spending has been contained in large part due to provinces taking advantage of their strong bargaining power in their negotiations with hospitals and physicians, and through provincial governments' control over public hospitals. Administrative costs, moreover, are very low because the financing and provider payment systems are much simpler than those in many other countries, and because nearly all hospitals operate on a nonprofit basis. Indeed, Canada provided the model upon which the Taiwanese health insurance system is based [2] and is often used as an example by US researchers and policy advocates as a model to reform the US system [3, 4]. It is also a source of national pride [5].

Through the late 1940s, the Canadian health insurance system was not radically different from that of the United States, relying mainly on private coverage [6, 7]. Gradually, and province-by-province, it transformed itself into an entirely different model, with universal coverage for hospital care being enacted by the provinces at different times in the 1950s, and for physician care, mainly in the 1960s. Private insurance for services covered by the systems in each province was all but eliminated. By 1971 all provinces provided universal coverage for inpatient hospital and coverage for physician services funded largely by tax revenues. Economist Robert Evans writes of this "quasi-controlled experiment," noting historic similarities between the United States and Canada in

---

[a] For simplicity, the chapter refers to provinces, but most of the material applies to the territories as well, which constitute 0.3% percent of the nation's population.

[b] For example, Canada is tied for 10th among 195 countries in the Healthcare Access and Quality (HAQ) index, which is discussed further in Chapter 15. Among the 10 countries covered in this book, it is tied for 5th highest.

Health Insurance Systems: An International Comparison. https://doi.org/10.1016/B978-0-12-816072-5.00008-0
57

culture, language, geography, and even healthcare delivery—but with one sharp difference:

> *[S]tarting in the 1950s, their ways of reimbursing health care began to diverge sharply. By 1971, Canada had universal coverage of hospital and medical care for all of its citizens, within provincially based, government-run plans financed from tax revenue, and with no parallel private system of either insurance or delivery. The United States, in contrast, chose to rely on a patchwork of public and private plans, with a level of direct patient payment which is easily the highest in the developed world [8, p. 110].*[c]

Until the mid-1960s, Canada devoted a greater proportion of national income to health care than the United States [5, 10]. Evans points out that Canada not only achieved universal coverage by the early 1970s, but, by 1987, was spending 2.6 percentage points less of **gross domestic product** (GDP) on health care. By 2019, those differences had ballooned to 6.2% points (10.8% vs 17.0%) [11].

The Canadian system also has notable shortcomings. Two that have received a great deal of attention are financial barriers to accessing treatment beyond hospital and physicians' services, and long average waiting times for receiving certain types of services in some jurisdictions. Canada's public financing system has been described as "narrow but deep" [12, p. 20]. Hospital and physician services are paid for in full by the provincial health plans because additional billing beyond the provincial fee is effectively prohibited, but many others are not covered or covered only partly. Outpatient pharmaceuticals are the most obvious example, as Canada is the only country in this book with universal coverage that does not provide a universal pharmaceutical benefit. Rather, public and private coverage and out-of-pocket (OOP) expenditures for pharmaceuticals vary both by province, and within province, creating substantial access problems for some [2]. It is estimated that in 2016, 14% of Canadians had no pharmaceutical coverage through either public or private sources [2]. Other services with little or no publicly funded coverage are dentistry, psychologists' and nonphysician-provided mental health care, vision products and services, and outpatient rehabilitation therapies. Instead, people pay with private voluntary health insurance (VHI) or OOP, both of which are more burdensome on low-income individuals and families.

Over the last several decades, waits to see some specialists and for some elective surgeries have been problematic. When the Commonwealth Fund surveyed the population of five countries in 2002, Canada had the longest self-reported waits [13]. It still had the longest waits in 2016 when 11 countries were surveyed [14], with some variation across jurisdictions and particular procedures. Long waiting lists are common among tax-funded systems; citizens of Australia, Sweden, and the United Kingdom also grapple with waiting

---

[c] For a book-length analysis of this natural experiment, see Ref. [9].

times, but on average, the problem appears to be greater in Canada than elsewhere. To provide a single example, the Commonwealth Fund's 2016 national population surveys of 9 of the 10 countries considered here (all but Japan) show that among those saying they needed specialist care in the past 2 years, 30% of Canadians report waiting 2 months or more for a specialist appointment, higher than in the United Kingdom (23%) and Sweden (19%). In contrast, figures for France, the Netherlands, and the United States were 6% or less [14]. If one examines administrative rather than patient survey data, waiting times to obtain various types of elective surgery tend to be higher in Canada than in the Netherlands, Sweden, and the United Kingdom, but lower than those in Australia [15].

A more subtle problem appears to be stasis in the form of slow adaptation to changes in both treatment coverage and innovations in service financing [16].[d] This is exemplified by such things as the lack of comprehensive drug coverage and heavy reliance on **fee-for-service** (FFS) payment methods. Danielle Martin and colleagues write:

> [U]niversal coverage is an aspiration, not a destination. ... In Canada, the necessary work has not been done for more than 40 years. The Canadian experience thus offers a cautionary tale on incrementalism. In the absence of bold political vision and courage, coverage expansion can be very difficult to achieve, with the result that the Canadian version of universal health coverage is at risk of becoming outdated. ... [R]eform requires a willingness on part of government to pursue change, rather than simply managing the status quo. Clear mechanisms are lacking to consistently realign resources to meet population needs, promote evidence-based medicine, reduce variation, and contain costs [5, p. 1731].

Noah Ivers and colleagues reach a similar conclusion, stating that the "organization of Canada's healthcare system seems to be frozen in time" because, "Fundamentally, medicine has changed, but the structure of Canadian Medicare has not" [2, p. 1252]. Their explanation, in brief, is that the system "works just well enough for those who need it and vote." Entrenched interests among the provinces, providers, and even patient groups have made the political cost of fundamental change too high.

Things are beginning to change, however. An example discussed later in the chapter involves the province of Ontario, which has adopted some innovative models of delivery primary care with the aim of improving quality through better care coordination, lowering costs, and encouraging physicians to choose primary over specialty care. In the province, most primary care physicians are now paid by a combination of **capitation**, salary, and performance-based reimbursement systems rather than FFS [17].

---

[d] A thorough discussion and list of recommendations for "unleashing innovation" in the Canadian healthcare system was prepared by a government-commissioned panel in 2015, sometimes referred to as the Naylor report.

The details

History

Like the United States, Canada did not have much of a history of health insurance until well into the 20th century. Wealthier people paid OOP for their care, and poorer people often received charity care from hospitals financed by municipalities, philanthropic organizations, or churches—or forwent services altogether. While there was much discussion during the 1930s and 1940s about greater government involvement, this was strongly opposed by provincial medical organizations. Following an example set in the United States, hospitals in some provinces sold prepaid care akin to Blue Cross as a way of deriving necessary revenues during and after the Great Depression. But it was not until after World War II that government provision of healthcare coverage began in earnest [18]. Great Britain provided one model, a National Health Service, which began in 1948. Such a centralized system, however, faced strong opposition not only from organized medicine, but also from the provinces, which had constitutional jurisdiction over most hospital care since the founding of the country in 1867 [18, 19].

In 1947, the province of Saskatchewan was the first to provide universal coverage for hospital care and was followed by two other western provinces, British Columbia and Alberta, in 1948 and 1950, respectively. In 1957, the federal government passed legislation that stipulated the conditions needing to be met for provinces to receive federal subsidies, and by 1961, all the provinces had joined. During the 1960s, medical care outside of the hospital was added in spite of strong opposition by physician groups, which went on strike for 23 days in Saskatchewan in 1962—the day that the province implemented its universal program. The dispute was resolved, with universal coverage for both hospitals and physicians in Saskatchewan retained after an agreement was reached that physicians would be autonomous, paid mainly on a FFS basis, and could choose not to enroll in Medicare [12 (p. 20), 20].

Further federal action followed in the mid-1960s, with subsidies to the provinces tied to their enacting programs of universal hospital and physician coverage that met four conditions: universality, public administration, comprehensiveness, and portability. All provinces had joined by the early 1970s, creating the system now called Medicare [12, pp. 19–21].

The current system was consolidated in 1984 with the passage of the Canada Health Act. One of the main provisions of the Act was giving provinces 3 years to eliminate any patient's cost sharing for hospital and physician services and prohibit physicians from using "extra" or "**balance billing**" for fees in excess of each province's fee schedule [18]. It thus made more explicit the condition of accessible care that had been part of the original Medicare legislation by specifying financial penalties for provinces not meeting the condition.[e]

---

[e] Carolyn Tuohy, personal communication, July 29, 2020.

Overview of the health insurance system

Canada does not provide health insurance per se; rather, residents are covered by a universal health insurance program in their provinces that provides payment for nearly all hospital and physician services, and sometimes more. Enrollment is required for new arrivals to a province.

Each of the 13 provinces and territories administers its own system for providing healthcare coverage to its population; it is therefore inaccurate to talk about a single "Canadian" healthcare system. Provinces are bound, however, to conform to the Canada Health Act and its five conditions if they are to receive federal subsidies [12 (p. 20), 21]:

- Universality: Provincial health plans must provide all qualified residents with medically necessary hospital, physician, and diagnostic services.
- Public administration: Provincial health plans must be run on a nonprofit basis by a public authority. (This does not in any way prohibit for-profit medicine on the provider side.)
- Comprehensiveness: Coverage of all medically necessary services must be provided by hospitals and physicians, with other types of services covered at the discretion of provinces. (As noted elsewhere, Canada defines "comprehensiveness" in a more limited fashion than other high-income countries, particularly in the area of prescription medications.)
- Portability: Provinces must provide coverage to all new residents within 3 months and cover the cost of care (at the province's own reimbursement rates) when Canadians travel to other provinces or outside of the country.
- Accessibility: There cannot be any patient cost sharing for hospital and physician services, and physicians are not permitted to bill patients any additional amounts [18, 22].[f]

Provincial health plans differ from each other in a number of ways. First, beyond the basket of guaranteed universal health coverage services, they cover different additional services, and to different extents. Second, for services not fully covered, the provinces can choose segments of the population to subsidize—e.g., elders, the poor. Third, in negotiations with the provincial medical associations, each province devises its own reimbursement rates for hospitals and physicians. Fourth, they are free to use different sources of revenue to fund their systems.

Unlike the other countries reviewed in this book, in Canada there is no private insurance coverage for hospital and physician services that are provided for

---

[f] This guarantee of accessibility does not preclude waiting for services, although some mild guarantees were promised through 2007 legislation, whereby provinces agreed to implement a Patient Waiting Time Guarantee. The federal government put over $1 billion (Can.) into the initiative, but provinces only had to enforce one clinical area (e.g., cardiac care, cancer radiation therapy, and cataract surgery), with some choosing particular metrics because those had already been meeting the waiting time target.

by the provincial plans. Instead, private insurance, which is usually purchased by employers, provides benefits for services where provincial plans' benefits are limited (e.g., pharmaceuticals) or for those that are uncovered for most people (e.g., dental care).

Governance

Most of the authority over health care lies with the provinces. Subject to the federal stipulation contained in the Canada Health Act that requires provinces to cover all medically necessary services, provinces (each of which has a ministry of health) specify the services they will cover and negotiate with the medical association in each province over payment rates. By and large, provinces cover similar hospital and physician services. Services excluded from coverage are, according to Carolyn Tuohy, "heavily concentrated in areas related to aesthetic services, reproductive technology, and some psychologically related services—similar to the range of services outside the core of physician and hospital services in other jurisdictions, such as the U.K." [23, p. 475].

To different degrees, provinces delegate planning and sometimes administration of the provincial hospital and institutional services to their own regional health authorities (HAs) and province-wide HAs. HAs usually are responsible for assuring the provision or purchase of services as well as population planning for these services [12, pp. 24–28]. The degree of regional power has varied over time, with a movement toward greater decentralization in the 1990s. After mixed and sometimes disappointing results, more recently there has been a movement in some provinces toward centralizing authority that in some instances has meant that such decisions are made at the provincial level rather than by HAs [24, 25].

The federal government also has important responsibilities, its overriding one being to ensure that the provinces are meeting their responsibilities under the Canada Health Act and other national legislative mandates. Some other responsibilities include: providing supplemental health benefits (e.g., prescriptions and dental and vision care) to eligible Indigenous peoples; coverage for serving members of the military, eligible veterans, some inmates, and some groups of refugee claimants; overseeing a number of public health activities including drug safety; funding of information technology initiatives; and funding research primarily through the Canadian Institutes of Health Research [12, pp. 23–25, 29–31].

Financing

Government sources make up 70% of total health expenditures mostly through the income tax system, with the remaining 30% almost evenly split between VHI and OOP [11]. This is a lower percentage for government/statutory coverage than any of the European countries covered in this book except Switzerland.

Japan is much higher than Canada, Australia a little lower, and the United States, far lower [11]. Here we focus on government spending, with VHI and OOP discussed later.

Nearly all (93%) of government expenditures are made by the provinces and territories, but about one-fourth of this is recouped by contributions from the federal government. The sources of both provincial and federal spending are tax revenues [12, p. 68]. The transfer of funds from the federal government to the provinces is called the Canada Health Transfer [25]. Prior to 2014, provinces with lower per capita tax revenues received greater per capita federal transfers, but now these transfers are based only on the number of people in the province; they are not adjusted for average health status in the provinces [12 (p. 71), 26, 27].[g] From 2004 to 2017, the federal government raised the amount it paid the provinces by 6% per year. This annual increase has since been lowered to about 3% per year or by growth in GDP, whichever is larger [28]. It is noteworthy that provinces are fully at risk for spending above the fixed federal transfer. This means that health care must compete against all other provincial spending priorities.

As noted, the bulk of healthcare funding comes from the provinces. On average, 50% of provincial revenues are derived from income and corporate taxes, 40% from sales taxes, and 10% from payroll taxes. About 80% of the federal revenues from which the transfer is taken are from income and corporate taxes and the remainder from sales taxes [12, p. 58]. Overall, the mixture of revenues leans somewhat toward progressive sources although more regressive sales taxes are a substantial component. The conclusion that the system is somewhat progressive overall is supported by research that indicated that the wealthiest 20% of Canadians are responsible for 50% of tax revenue used to fund health services, but use fewer than 20% of those services [12, p. 151].

Coverage

Breadth

Coverage in Canada is universal for legal residents. For those who are not legal residents, it varies, with temporary coverage for refugees seeking asylum, but no guaranteed coverage other than emergency hospital services for undocumented people. Some of these requirements for refugees have changed as a result of COVID-19 [12, p. 64].[h]

---

[g] There is one federal transfer payment that is based on the wealth of the province: revenue from natural resources and taxes. Only provinces with low levels of wealth relative to others receive these payments, but their use is not confined to health care; they can be used for such things as education and social services. In 2018–19, six provinces received these equalization payments, with a majority of the monies going to Quebec.

[h] Karen Palmer, personal communication, July 3, 2020.

Scope

Under each provincial plan, all people living in Canada are provided with coverage for all hospital, physician, and diagnostic services. Beyond that, the scope of coverage varies by province and is generally considered more meager than in other high-income countries with universal coverage. The most notable example is for pharmaceuticals. All provinces provide some pharmaceutical coverage for low-income individuals and most cover senior citizens, but other groups often lack coverage. Most of the provinces do provide catastrophic coverage for large prescription drug expenditures.[i] Ontario provides one example. For those who are without VHI that pays all of their drug costs, the province provides coverage more than 4400 different drugs for $2 (Can.) per prescription after household spending on drugs exceeds 4% of income [29]. British Columbia provides a second example, where there is an annual maximum on family OOP spending based on income—even for those who are relatively wealthy. In 2020, the maximums for families with $50,000 (Can.), $100,000, and $250,000 in annual incomes were $1500, $3000, and $7000, respectively [30]. (At the time of writing, the Canadian dollar was worth 0.79 the value of the US dollar.)

There is also limited coverage for dental care, vision care, medical devices, and mental health care provided by nonphysicians, depending on province [12, p. 65].

Depth

Hospital, physician, diagnostic services, and inpatient drug therapies are covered in full by provincial health plans, as required by the Canada Health Act. There are no deductibles or cost-sharing requirements.

As noted, publicly funded prescription drug coverage varies by province but generally includes some or all seniors and all poorer persons. Ontario again provides an example. The province's drug benefit program includes coverage for those age 65 and older, younger persons living in a facility or who are disabled, as well as individuals age 24 and younger who are not covered by private insurance. How much seniors pay OOP depends on their incomes. Other provinces, like British Columbia, only cover low-income seniors.

Voluntary health insurance

VHI plays a larger role in Canada than in any of the nine countries with universal coverage discussed in this book, covering about 15% of national health expenditures in 2018 [11]. It is possessed by about two-thirds of Canadians [12 (p. 74), 25],[j] and sold by around 130 companies, 80% of which operate on a

---

[i] Sara Allin, personal communication, January 4, 2020.
[j] While it pays for about the same percentage of total health expenditures as in France, VHI coverage there is now effectively mandatory.

for-profit basis [31, p. 63]. In Canada, most provinces prohibit private insurance from covering services that are included in the provincial health plan benefit packages. In others, while private insurance is permitted to cover hospital and physician services, no such market exists. This is because physicians must opt out of the public system, their main source of income, and thus, the duplicative insurance market is too small to be profitable.

As a result, the main role of VHI is to provide reimbursement for uncovered services as well as pay the cost-sharing requirements for services that are sometimes partially covered, particularly pharmaceuticals. It does not provide faster access to services [12, p. 74]. VHI coverage is not evenly distributed among the population. Because 90% is paid for through employment group contracts or similar arrangements, those who are in permanent, full-time employed positions are much more likely to have such coverage [12, p. 74]. Persons likely to be uncovered are the self-employed, unemployed, retirees, women, young people, and those with lower incomes [5].

About three-fourths of VHI expenses are for prescription drugs (40%), dental care (28%), and private rooms in hospitals (6%) [12, p. 74]. The remainder is for a miscellany of services including nonphysician professional services and vision care. The specific benefits provided by VHI are difficult to summarize because they are designed to fill gaps in provincial coverage, which vary across the provinces. Moreover, benefits may vary across companies or across different types of plans within companies. The two most common are "extended health" plans and dental plans. In the extended benefit plans, generally there are cost-sharing requirements. Annual deductibles [usually less than $40 (US)] are typical as are **coinsurance** rates of 10% or 20%. Dental plans often have higher cost sharing, e.g., 50% for orthodontia and major restorative services. Finally, there are often annual maximum payouts for eyeglasses, orthodontia, and other services [32].

Choice

All legal residents are covered by their provincial health plans. Private duplicative insurance is essentially prohibited for hospital, physician, and diagnostic services. Canadians are free to choose any hospital or physician they wish in the province. General practitioners (GPs) act as **gatekeepers** in most provinces, and usually patients being referred to specialist care can choose the specialist they wish to see by requesting a referral to that individual [12, p. 49].

Provider payment

Hospitals

Public or private not-for-profit hospitals provide nearly all acute care in Canada [12, p. 100]. In Ontario, which has 38% of the population, most hospitals are private not-for-profit institutions that receive the bulk of their budgets through a public funder, whether it is the Ministry of Health directly or a provincial or regional HA. In Quebec, the second largest province, local rather than regional bodies own and operate the hospitals [33, p. 423]. In the other provinces, the HAs own and operate the hospitals [12, p. 77].

Most hospital payments in the Canadian system are from annual global budgets, which in the case of private nonprofit hospitals are determined by negotiation between the province and each hospital. Generally, these portions of budgets are based in large part on historical trends [12, p. 77]. They are popular among the provinces in part because they make it easy to monitor and control spending [31, 67]. There is a small amount of activity-based funding (e.g., targeted funding and incentive pay; **diagnosis-related groups**), and this is increasing, though it is not predominant in any of the provinces [12, p. 77]. Hospitals that exceed their budgets and cannot justify it are generally at financial risk for the excess. Budgets generally do not include major capital equipment, which is negotiated separately.

Physicians

In most provinces, primary care physicians are paid on a FFS basis, comprising an estimated 70% of total payments nationally [31, p. 68]. There is some experimentation with **pay for performance** (P4P) incentives for meeting specific treatment goals, and with capitation and other forms of non-FFS payment for primary care physicians. FFS is also the dominant method of paying specialists, but some provinces are using alternatives in a minority of cases. Rates are set in negotiation between the provinces and the provincial medical associations [12, pp. 23–25].

Ontario provides the clearest example of experimentation with payment. Since the early 2000s, the province has adopted some innovative primary care models with the aim of achieving better service coordination, improved quality, lower costs, and, at the same time, encouraging new physicians to choose primary over specialty care. The percentage of primary care physicians paid on a purely FFS basis fell from 94% in 2002 to less than 25% in 2015—and half of that reduced number were providing more specialized services. For primary care physicians, total reliance on FFS was replaced by a combination of capitation, salary, and performance-based reimbursement systems with some incentive to control volumes [17].

Pharmaceuticals

Canada spends more than most other countries on pharmaceuticals, ranking after the United States and Switzerland among all OECD countries. Generic uptake is high, around 74%, but unit prices are high as well [12, p. 118]. In 1987, Canada established the Patented Medicine Prices Review Board (PMPRB) with a mandate to "protect the interests of Canadian consumers by ensuring that the prices of patented medicines sold in Canada are not 'excessive'." The Board reviews the prices charged by pharmaceutical manufacturers for new patented drugs and has the authority to reduce those prices if they are deemed excessive. These determinations are based on such factors as the prices and medical benefits of other drugs in that same class [31, p. 75], the prices paid in other countries, and general inflation rates [34]. More specifically, according to Greg Marchildon and colleagues, the PMPRB "regulates the price of newly patented drugs in Canada by setting the maximum price at the median of the listed price across several countries … France, Germany, Italy, Sweden, Switzerland, the UK and the USA. … [Provinces] then negotiate confidential price discounts through the Pan-Canadian Pharmaceutical Alliance" [12, p. 117]. Provinces, however, are not bound by the Board's recommendations and are free to negotiate separately with manufacturers.[k]

There have also been some modest efforts to control generic prices paid by provincial drug plans through this Alliance. By combining purchasing power across the provinces, it attempts to bring down both brand-name and generic drug prices. In 2018, it negotiated agreements for 67 popular generic drugs, pricing them at 10%–18% of the brand-name drug price [35].

Assuring access and equity

Access to care in Canada depends, in large measure, on the types of services being considered. For services that are required to be fully covered by provinces—hospital, physician, and diagnostic services—there are no direct financial barriers. Care is free at point of service with no **deductibles** or other cost-sharing requirements. Moreover, the revenue sources to pay for this are mainly **progressive**, coming from taxes. One access problem is there are very remote parts of Canada where there are few providers, so patients must travel long distances.

Canada is the only country discussed in this book with universal coverage that does not provide a guaranteed pharmaceutical benefit although there is much discussion about changing this. Provinces do provide some coverage in varying degrees but for most people it is necessary to have VHI coverage to enjoy financial protection in case of illness requiring outpatient medications. This is even more the case for services where there is very little or no public coverage: dental care, mental health services provided by nonphysicians, vision care, and physical therapy. VHI is possessed by two-thirds of the population—generally those people who work for employers offering it and their families. As noted, certain people are less likely to have VHI coverage: self-employed, unemployed, retirees, women, young people, and those with lower incomes. As a result, the Commonwealth Fund population surveys of the countries considered in this book (all but Japan) show that in 2016, self-reported access to dental care was the lowest after the United States, with 41% of Canadians in the bottom half

---

[k] Michel Grignon, personal communication, October 16, 2020.

of the income distribution stating that they skipped dental care or a checkup in the past year due to costs [14].

The other concern is waiting times. Data from the Commonwealth Fund surveys, which are based on population surveys rather than administrative data, show that Canadians have the longest waits on a number of measures of any of the countries considered here: seeing a doctor or nurse, the same or next day the last time they needed medical care, waiting two or more months for a specialist appointment, waiting four or more months for elective surgery, and waiting two or more hours in the emergency room. To illustrate how much of an outlier Canada is, its figure from the Commonwealth surveys for waiting two or more months for a specialist appointment was 30%. The next highest of our countries was 19%, with five being less than 10%, and two (France and Germany) less than 5% [14].

In contrast, data from the OECD are based on medical records—specifically, the time between when a specialist puts a patient on a waiting list and the time they receive the treatment. Measured this way, waiting times are lower than in Australia, comparable to those in the United Kingdom, but higher than in two other countries considered here: the Netherlands and Sweden [36, Figure 5.17].

Controlling expenditures

Canada's total expenditures devoted to health care are moderate; at 10.8% of GDP in 2019, they are 7th among the 10 countries covered here. This was almost the same percentage it spent in 2010. Canada holds a similar ranking with regard to per capita spending (see Table 15.3) [11]. One particular area in which Canadian costs appear to be lower than other countries is administrative spending. In the area of hospital spending, a study of several countries in 2010 found that hospital administrative costs comprised just 12% of hospital costs, compared to 15% in the England, 20% in the Netherlands, and 25% in the United States [37] Another measure, the administrative costs of governing and financing the health system, is 3.1% of total healthcare spending in Canada, which ranks 4th lowest among the 10 countries (Table 15.3) [11].

In addition to low administrative costs, Canada has been successful in controlling expenditures in large part through the **monopsony** power held by the provinces: they are the nearly exclusive purchaser of hospital, physician, and diagnostic services, which provides them tremendous bargaining leverage. Provinces, of course, have many other funding responsibilities beyond health care. Ontario, for example, spent 60% of its 2019–20 budget on items other than health and long-term care [38]. When one combines this need to control spending with the ability to do so, it is understandable that Canada's spending is lower than most of the other countries examined in this book. Another mechanism for cost control is rationing the supply of physicians and hospital beds, which are also on the low side compared to other countries but comparable to the United States (see Table 15.6).

The federal government helps provinces in expenditure control through carrying out research and advisory activities or working with intergovernmental nonprofit organizations engaged in such tasks. Important among these are national organizations that provide research and recommendations on medical technologies and pharmaceuticals. One is the Canadian Agency for Drugs and Technology in Health, which carries out health technology assessments on medical devices and drugs to help the provinces and other payers make informed decisions about what technologies to cover and how much to pay for them [12, p. 43]. Other such agencies, including the Patented Medicine Prices Review Board and the Pan-Canadian Pharmaceutical Alliance, provide information about the appropriate prices of new and generic drugs. It is unlikely, however, that more substantial control of drug prices will occur in the absence of a national pharmaceutical drug benefit.

Key policy issues

In spite of most Canadians' pride in their healthcare system, they would like to see improvements. In a 2016 survey, only 35% agreed with the statement that "The system works pretty well and only minor changes are necessary to make it work better." This was third lowest among our countries (excepting Japan), exceeding only Sweden (31%) and the United States (19%) but lagging far behind Germany (60%) and Switzerland (58%) [39].

Three issues are of particular importance. The first is the universal health coverage package, whose scope is narrower than in other countries. The uneven prescription drug coverage between provinces and among different groups of people within provinces has resulted in a great deal of debate on augmenting the pan-Canadian benefits package to include prescription drugs. In 2016, a national citizens panel recommended a national Pharmacare program [40]. In 2019, the federally created Advisory Council on the Implementation of National Pharmacare also recommended a single-payer program administered by the provinces to help entice provinces that do not want to cede power in their jurisdiction over health care. Provincial programs would have to meet or exceed federal standards; a national formulary would be established; and unlike in current Medicare, there would be OOP costs but people would be protected by a cap that private insurers would be allowed to supplement [41, 42]. Previous surveys show that about 90% of the Canadian population supports a national pharmaceutical benefits program [43]. However, one could view the support as "soft" in that the majority of Canadians also oppose funding if a new drug benefit would require additional premiums or higher taxes [44].

The second issue is Canada's long waiting times to receive some services in some jurisdictions. This problem has persisted over the decades and progress in addressing it successfully has been slow despite considerable efforts in some provinces. Wait times span many parts of the healthcare system, including receiving specialist appointments and elective surgery, in the emergency department, and in seeing a primary care provider on a timely basis [12, p. 132].

Even seemingly unambitious targets, such as providing hip and knee replacements within half a year, were met only about 70% of the time in 2019 [45]. The reasons behind these persistent problems are difficult to fully explain. One possibility is that provinces, which are at financial risk for healthcare spending given that federal contributions are fixed, are under great pressure to contain healthcare spending in the context of competing priorities. But because wait times have been a problem during both times of economic growth and recession, other factors may be responsible, including organizational issues such as no centralized list to manage waits and system inefficiencies.[1] Many partial remedies have been suggested. One example is the wider use of virtual consultations between primary care and specialty physicians to provide the former with more guidance to treat patients who can be treated without the need for a specialist consult, a trend obviously accelerated by COVID-19, with many patients unwilling to seek care outside of their homes [46].

Waiting lists have been a complaint in Canada for decades. Andreas Laupacis writes, "There will be no easy fixes – the solution will likely require a combination of an increase in the number of some specialists, more access to existing operating rooms, a change in how wait lists are managed, greater use of non-physicians where appropriate, more complete data to measure our progress and the innovative use of technology" [47].

A third issue is that Canada has been slow to adopt effective policies that have been long part of some other countries' systems. Two mentioned at the beginning of the chapter were the lack of a national prescription drug benefit and lack of innovation in both financing and delivery. With the exception of Ontario, Canada does not often employ methods to pay hospitals and physicians in ways that some believe will foster efficiency. Instead, the current FFS system results in the overprovision of services and global budgets, the deemphasis of quality of care. Moreover, according to Greg Marchildon and colleagues, "physicians continue to be independent, with few mechanisms for holding them accountable for the costs incurred by their patients in the system, the quality of the care they provide or the health outcomes of their patients. In part, poor integration reflects the limited sharing and use of clinical information across providers and overall lack of province-wide interoperable [electronic medical records]" [12, p. 165].

In many other countries, there has been a movement toward more market-oriented healthcare systems, but Canada has not gone in that direction—and applauded by some for not doing so. Nevertheless, there are small but strong interest groups, especially in two western provinces of British Columbia and Alberta, advocating for Canada to allow for more private financing, particularly by allowing private insurance for services that would duplicate those covered in provincial medical plans. The main argument made by these interest groups is that this could provide a way of ameliorating waiting lists.

---

[1] Sara Allin, personal communication, November 20, 2019.

At the time of writing, the British Columbia Supreme Court is deliberating on a case directly relevant to the issue of the role of markets in Canada. The trial, which took over 3 years, pits a physician, Brian Day, against the provincial government. Day, an orthopedic surgeon, operated a private clinic whose practices violated the British Columbia's Medical Services Plan, the public system responsible for providing all hospital and physician care. His suit asks the court to overturn the current system to: (a) allow physicians to charge amounts in excess of the provincial fee schedule; (b) allow physicians to bill private insurance, ownership of which would provide faster access to care—so-called queue jumping; and (c) allow physicians to participate in both the provincial health plan and private insurance simultaneously. Currently, physicians can charge patients directly only if they treat all of their patients in private clinics, and as a result, there is not an active private insurance market that competes against the provinces. Opponents fear that these changes could lead to longer waits for those who do not have private coverage as well as greater financial barriers to receiving timely care [48]. Whatever the court rules, the case is likely end up at the Supreme Court of Canada, so the outcome is relevant to the entire Canadian system.

References

[1] G.B.D. Healthcare Access and Quality Collaborators. Measuring performance on the Healthcare Access and Quality Index for 195 countries and territories and selected subnational locations: a systematic analysis from the Global Burden of Disease Study 2016. Lancet 2018;391(10136):2236–71.

[2] Ivers N, Brown AD, Detsky AS. Lessons from the Canadian experience with single-payer health insurance: just comfortable enough with the status quo. JAMA Intern Med 2018;178(9):1250–5.

[3] Lasser KE, Himmelstein DU, Woolhandler S. Access to care, health status, and health disparities in the United States and Canada: results of a cross-national population-based survey. Am J Public Health 2006;96(7):1300–7.

[4] Bernie ES. Sanders went to Canada, and a dream of 'Medicare for all' flourished. The New York Times; 2019. [News]. (Accessed 15 September 2020). Available from: https://www.nytimes.com/2019/09/09/us/politics/bernie-sanders-health-care.html?auth=login-google.

[5] Martin D, Miller AP, Quesnel-Vallee A, Caron NR, Vissandjee B, Marchildon GP. Canada's universal health-care system: achieving its potential. Lancet 2018;391(10131):1718–35.

[6] Evans RG. Health care in Canada: patterns of funding and regulation. J Health Polit Policy Law 1983;8(1):1–43.

[7] Tuohy C. Icon and taboo: single-payer politics in Canada and the US. J Int Comp Soc Policy 2019;35(1):5–24.

[8] Evans RG. Tension, compression, and shear: directions, stresses, and outcomes of health care cost control. J Health Polit Policy Law 1990;15(1):101–28.

[9] Maioni A. Parting at the crossroads: The emergence of health insurance in the United States and Canada. Princeton University Press; 1998.

[10] Anderson GF, Reinhardt UE, Hussey PS, Petrosyan V. It's the prices, stupid: why the United States is so different from other countries. Health Aff (Millwood) 2003;22(3):89–105.

[11] OECD.Stat. OECD [Web browser]. [Accessed 3 September 2020]. Available from: https://stats.oecd.org/Index.aspx?ThemeTreeId=9.

[12] Marchildon GP, Allin S, Merkur S. Canada: health system review. Health Syst Transit 2020;22(3):i–194.

[13] Schoenbaum S, Doty M, Schoen C, Audet A, Davis K. Mirror, mirror on the wall: Looking at the quality of American health care through the patient's lens. Mirror, Mirror: The Commonwealth Fund; 2004.

[14] Schneider EC, Sarnak DO, Squires D, Shah A, Doty MM. Mirror, mirror 2017: International comparison reflects flaws and opportunities for better U.S. health care. Mirror, Mirror: The Commonwealth Fund; 2017.

[15] OECD. Figure 2.3 Waiting times for common surgery vary from less than a month to over a year. Waiting Times for Health Services: Next in Line. OECD Health Policy Studies. Paris: OECD Publishing; 2020.

[16] Anon. Unleashing innovation: Excellent healthcare for Canada. Report of the Advisory Panel on Healthcare Innovation. Ottawa: Minister of Health, Canada; 2015.

[17] Marchildon GP, Hutchison B. Primary care in Ontario, Canada: new proposals after 15 years of reform. Health Policy 2016;120(7):732–8.

[18] MacDougall H, Pope F, Tarasoff T. Making medicare: The history of health in Canada, 1914-2007. Canadian Museum of History; 2010. [Online exhibit]. (Accessed 15 September 2020). Available from: https://www.historymuseum.ca/cmc/exhibitions/hist/medicare/medic00e.html.

[19] Butler M, Tiedemann M. The federal role in health and health care. Library of Parliament, Parliament of Canada; 2011.

[20] Kliff S. The doctor's strike that nearly killed Canada's medicare-for-all plan, explained. Vox; 2019. [Internet]. (Accessed 15 September 2020). Available from: https://www.vox.com/policy-and-politics/2019/3/29/18265530/medicare-canada-saskatchewan-doctor-strike.

[21] Flood C, Choudhry S. Strengthening the foundations: Modernizing the Canada Health Act. vol. 13. Royal Commission on the Future of Health Care in Canada; 2002. Discussion Paper.

[22] Anon. Patient wait times guarantees. Wait times for health services. Government of Canada; 2012. [Internet]. [Accessed 15 September 2020]. Available from: https://www.canada.ca/en/health-canada/services/quality-care/wait-times/patient-wait-times-guarantees.html.

[23] Tuohy CH. Single payers, multiple systems: the scope and limits of subnational variation under a federal health policy framework. J Health Polit Policy Law 2009;34(4):453–96.

[24] Marchildon GP. The crisis of regionalization. Healthc Manage Forum 2015;28(6):236–8.

[25] Allin S, Marchildon G, Peckham A. In: Tikkanen R, Osborn R, Mossialos E, Djordjevic A, Wharton GA, editors. Canada. International health care system profiles. The Commonwealth Fund; 2020. [Internet]. [Accessed 15 September 2020]. Available from: https://www.commonwealthfund.org/international-health-policy-center/countries/canada.

[26] Anon. What is the Canada health transfer (CHT)? Canada health transfer. Government of Canada; 2011. [Internet]. (Accessed 15 September 2020). Available from: https://www.canada.ca/en/department-finance/programs/federal-transfers/canada-health-transfer.html.

[27] Abedi M. Equalization payments—How they work, and why some provinces are upset. Politics. Global News; 2018. [Online news]. [Accessed 15 September 2020]. Available from: https://globalnews.ca/news/4290676/equalization-payments-canada-provinces/.

[28] Shaw T. Federal financial support to provinces and territories: A long-term scenario analysis. Ottawa: Office of the Parliamentary Budget Officer; 2018.

[29] Anon. Get help with high prescription drug costs. Ontario; 2016. [Internet]. [Accessed 15 September 2020]. Available from: https://www.ontario.ca/page/get-help-high-prescription-drug-costs.

[30] Fair PharmaCare Calculator. Health. British Columbia [Internet]. [Accessed 15 September 2020]. Available from: https://www.health.gov.bc.ca/pharmacare/plani/calculator/calculator.html.

[31] Emanuel EJ. Which country has the world's best health care? New York: PublicAffairs; 2020.

[32] A Guide to Supplementary Health Insurance. Canadian Life and Health Insurance Association.

[33] Tuohy CH. Remaking policy: Scale, pace, and political strategy in health care reform. Studies in comparative political economy and public policy, University of Toronto Press; 2018.

[34] Anon. Mandate and jurisdiction. Patented Medicine Prices Review Board (PMPRB). Government of Canada; 2018. [Internet]. [Accessed 15 September 2020]. Available from: http://pmprb-cepmb.gc.ca/about-us/mandate-and-jurisdiction.

[35] The pan-Canadian Pharmaceutical Alliance. Canada's Premiers [Internet]. [Accessed 15 September 2020]. Available from: https://www.canadaspremiers.ca/pan-canadian-pharmaceutical-alliance-archives/.

[36] OECD. Health at a glance 2019. Paris: OECD Publishing; 2019.

[37] Himmelstein DU, Jun M, Busse R, Chevreul K, Geissler A, Jeurissen P, et al. A comparison of hospital administrative costs in eight nations: US costs exceed all others by far. Health Aff (Millwood) 2014;33(9):1586–94.

[38] Anon. Ontario, Canada. Summary table 2—Operating (2019-20). Ontario; 2019. [Internet]. [Accessed 15 September 2020]. Available from: https://www.ontario.ca/page/summary-table-2-operating-2019-20.

[39] Anon. The system works pretty well and only minor changes are necessary to make it work better, 2016. International health care system profiles. The Commonwealth Fund; 2016. [Internet]. [Accessed 15 September 2020]. Available from: https://www.commonwealthfund.org/international-health-policy-center/system-stats/works-well.

[40] Marchildon GP, Titeu A. Universal prescription drug benefits recommended by citizen's panel on Pharmacare. In: Marchildon GP, Grignon M, Allin S, Tsang J, McKay R, editors. Canada: The health systems and policy monitor. The European Observatory on Health Systems and Policies; 2017. [Online countrypage]. [Accessed 15 September 2020]. Available from: https://www.hspm.org/countries/canada22042013/countrypage.aspx.

[41] Farr MC, Allin S, Grignon M. Canadian pharmacare council's recommendations for efficient and equitable universal prescription drug coverage. In: Marchildon GP, Grignon M, Allin S, Tsang J, McKay R, editors. Canada: The health systems and policy monitor. The European Observatory on Health Systems and Policies; 2019. [Online countrypage]. [Accessed 15 September 2020]. Available from: https://www.hspm.org/countries/canada22042013/countrypage.aspx.

[42] Grignon M, Longo CJ, Marchildon GP, Officer S. The 2018 decision to establish an Advisory Council on adding pharmaceuticals to universal health coverage in Canada. Health Policy 2020;124(1):7–11.

[43] Morgan SG, Boothe K. Universal prescription drug coverage in Canada: long-promised yet undelivered. Healthc Manage Forum 2016;29(6):247–54.

[44] Tuohy CH. Separated at birth: the politics of pharmacare for all in Canada and medicare for all in the United States comment on "universal pharmacare in Canada". Int J Health Policy Manag 2020.

[45] Anon. Wait times for priority procedures in Canada. Canadian Institute for Health Information; 2020. [Internet]. [Accessed 15 September 2020]. Available from: https://www.cihi.ca/en/wait-times-for-priority-procedures-in-canada.

[46] Milne V, Tepper J, Pendharkar S. Four ways Canada can shorten wait times for specialists. healthydebate; 2017. [Internet]. [Accessed 15 September 2020]. Available from: https://healthydebate.ca/2017/02/topic/wait-times-specialists.

[47] Laupacis A. Wait times to see specialists need our attention. healthydebate; 2017. [Internet]. [Accessed 15 September 2020]. Available from: https://healthydebate.ca/opinions/wait-times-specialists.

[48] Palmer KS. How a B.C. court case could change the Canadian health care system. Canadian Medicare on Trial [PDF]. [Accessed 15 September 2020]. Available from: https://quoimedia.com/wp-content/uploads/2020/03/palmer-cdn-medicare-on-trial.pdf.

Chapter 5

Sweden

The big picture

Sweden is often described as a "**welfare state**," stressing equity in access to social benefits and services, including generous policies on parental leave, childcare, disability and unemployment benefits, and pensions. Health care is no exception, with extensive universal benefits and relatively low out-of-pocket (OOP) costs. By most measures, health outcomes are good, health needs are largely met, and there are fewer socioeconomic disparities in access to care than in most wealthy countries. Health behaviors are, in general, excellent, with very low rates of youth and adult alcohol abuse and smoking compared to other European Union countries, due in part to high user taxes [1].

Richard Saltman and Sven-Eric Bergman posit that there are three main features that, historically, have underlain the country's healthcare system [2]. The first is public responsibility, which they date back to the mid-18th century and the establishment of the first state hospitals along with a requirement that doctors treat poor people free of charge. Private insurance still plays only a very small role in financing healthcare services, although there is growing debate about how recent growth in voluntary health insurance (VHI) may ultimately affect equity of access.[a] Moreover, there is no history of private, for-profit hospitals, in contrast with many other countries. The second is a commitment to health-related financial security—not just through reimbursing medical care, but also by providing generous income assistance for accidents, sickness, disability, and old age. The third is an unusual degree of decentralization, with the bulk of authority in the hands of 21 regions (formerly called county councils), whose members are elected by the public every 4 years, and 290 municipalities.

While many countries give key responsibilities for local authorities in delivering healthcare services, Sweden has gone further than others, with most financing coming from local sources. The national government plays an important role in formulating policies to improve geographic equity and providing key information to regional and local authorities to help them manage their populations. Nevertheless, the regions are largely responsible for ensuring the health of their residents through either direct service provision or overseeing the

---

[a] Anders Anell, personal communication, June 2, 2020.

Health Insurance Systems: An International Comparison. https://doi.org/10.1016/B978-0-12-816072-5.00005-5

care of private providers, contracting, and revenue collection. Indeed, almost all hospitals are owned and managed by the regions. While they are no longer able to stop the establishment of private primary care practices, the regions are responsible deciding on which capital investments (buildings and equipment) to fund in their regions [3, p. 70]. In contrast, primary medical education is overseen and financed at the national level although the training of specialists is carried out by the hospitals [3, p. 80].

The Swedish healthcare system has had a stable structure in recent decades, with one major exception. In 2010, the Primary Health Care Choice Reform was enacted, allowing the establishment of private primary care practices typically on a for-profit basis and owned by national or regional corporations. Moreover, patients became free to choose any primary care center they wished and payment to providers followed the choice of individuals. This was in sharp contrast to the previous system that was more top-down, with regions having control over the location of primary care practices based on the healthcare needs of the population [4].

The reform was enacted by a center-right government and has been controversial, with some arguing that the infusion of market competition was necessary to increase access to primary care, and others seeing the legislation as an attack on the Swedish tradition of **solidarity** and equity. By 2016, more than 40% of primary care practices in the country were privately owned, most of them by for-profit firms [4]. Evidence is mixed on the impact of the reforms. On the positive side, the number of primary care visits increased considerably in the first years following the reforms in a country with historically low utilization rates. On the negative side, there is concern—but mixed findings from research studies on the topic [5, 6]—that the reform has benefited the well-off, as physician groups have an incentive to establish practices in areas not only with greater populations, but also with wealthier and healthier patients, potentially creating concomitant problems for poorer and rural areas.

The main criticism of the Swedish healthcare system over the years has been long waiting lists. Sweden is not unique in this; other national health systems covered in this book, particularly Canada and the United Kingdom, have also faced significant queuing problems. It is not terribly surprising that waiting lists would be problematic in health systems that rely on tax funding because governments need to balance health needs against all other national and regional priorities. In spite of a national effort to guarantee that waits are not unduly long, the problem persists [7].

The details

History

Compared to most other countries discussed in this book, Sweden has had a long and unbroken history of direct government involvement in the healthcare system. Although reliance on competition in health care has ebbed and flowed in recent years depending on the political situation, by almost any measure, public ownership, administration, and funding have been and continue to be substantial.

Since the 1860s, county councils held much of the authority over health care, when they were given the authority to establish new hospitals. These hospitals could collect user charges but were required to provide hospital care free of charge to poor patients. The councils (under their new name) have continued their preeminent role until this day [8], with many expanded responsibilities. In 1970, for example, they were also made responsible for overseeing the provision and financing of hospital outpatient services, and in 1998, prescription drugs. In the 1990s, administrative and financial responsibilities for long-term care, elder care, the disabled population, and those with long-term mental illness devolved from the counties to the 290 municipalities [3].

In the area of health insurance, the first voluntary **Sickness Funds** Law for laborers was enacted in 1891. While health insurance was compulsory in several other countries by the early 1920s, this was not true in Sweden until the 1950s. The 1891 legislation did not require that medical benefits be covered and most coverage only provided cash in case of illness, which of course could be used to pay physicians. An estimated 13% of the population was covered by these voluntary arrangements until 1925. Substantial growth in these numbers occurred into the 1930s with the establishment Sickness Funds Law of 1931, which among other things required that medical benefits be provided in addition to cash when a person was ill. Even then, cash benefits predominated. Fund revenues were based mainly on member and employer fees, but there were also government subsidies for registered funds.

In part because of the demand for these medical benefits, growth in coverage occurred rapidly starting in the late 1930s, with nearly half the population covered by the end of World War II. Healthcare coverage expanded greatly after World War II as part of a national effort to improve the welfare of the Swedish people. By 1950, most of the expenditures were for medical rather than cash benefits. Coverage continued to grow quickly, reaching nearly 80% by the time the first compulsory insurance law was approved in 1947 and implemented in the mid-1950s [9].

As was the case in much of Europe, medical technology advanced quickly after the war and care was increasingly hospital based. In Sweden, about 90% of healthcare spending was attributable to hospitals. More care was beginning to be provided in outpatient departments of public hospitals but financial barriers were often serious impediments to poorer patients. In 1970, the county councils assumed responsibility for such services, charging the equivalent of a little over $1 US (1970) for outpatient visits, much less than the previous 25% **coinsurance** rates (the entire fee of which had to be paid up front, with reimbursement for the government share coming later) [10, p. 16]. A parallel change was that hospital physicians became full-time, salaried employees of the publicly owned hospitals, where previously they were paid on a fee-for-service basis for work they had performed on an outpatient basis [11].

The Health and Medical Services Act of 1982 guaranteed coverage for all legal residents, and further specified an enhanced role of the county councils. The councils were responsible for offering "good health and medical services to persons living within its boundaries" and for promoting "the health of all residents," with particular emphasis on economically vulnerable Swedes, including elders and immigrants [10, p. 9, 96]. Another legislative action was enacted in 2010, when all residents were given a choice of primary care provider, and providers were given the freedom to establish private practices (assuming they were accredited by the county council through meeting certain financial, organizational, staffing, and quality requirements)—in contrast to the previous system where county councils had authority over planning the location of practices [12].

Overview of the health insurance system

Swedes do not have health insurance per se. Rather, they are covered by a universal program with automatic enrollment that provides coverage for nearly all healthcare services. A major difference between Sweden and some other countries with government-based healthcare systems is the strong historic role of decentralization: most government effort and power is concentrated at the regional and local rather than the national levels. This is also characteristic of other Scandinavian countries.

Historically, Sweden has had a largely government-run system with most providers being public entities. As noted, more recently, private primary care providers have been permitted to establish practices that compete against traditional public providers but they are strictly overseen by the regions and are subject to the same rules governing such things as reimbursement [3, p. 39]. More than 40% of primary care practices are privately owned [4].

Governance

The Health and Medical Services Act of 1982 specifies that "Health and medical services are aimed at assuring the entire population of good health and of care on equal terms. Care shall be provided with respect for the equal dignity of all human beings and for the dignity of the individual. Priority for health and medical care shall be given to the person whose need of care is greatest" [3, p. 18].

To carry out this and other laws, all three levels of government—national, regional, and local—are involved. Unlike in the United Kingdom, however, the national government is less influential than regional and local governments. Nevertheless, it does perform critical analytic and oversight activities.

The Ministry of Health and Social Affairs has overall responsibility for the health of the Swedish population through research and dissemination activities, oversight, and development of policies. The Ministry has eight boards, some of the most important of which are noted here. The National Board of Health and Welfare is involved in data collection and analysis that results in the development and dissemination of practice guidelines, which help the counties in their own priority setting. The Swedish Council on Technology Assessment in Health Care, as the name implies, evaluates the cost-effectiveness of medical technologies. Similarly, the Dental and Pharmaceutical Benefits Agency carries out similar tasks regarding pharmaceuticals and dental services to help determine which should be included in the county benefits packages [3, p. 25]. In addition, it also makes decisions on provider reimbursement rates for these services.[a] National activities such as these are particularly important as they help ensure that people in different parts of the country receive comparable services.

The bulk of activities are financed and carried out on the county and municipal levels, supplemented with some minor grant funding from the national government. The counties are responsible for the delivery of most health care, including hospital services and primary care, with the 1982 legislation stipulating the broad mission that "Every county council should offer good health and medical services to persons living within its boundaries" [13]. These responsibilities go beyond service delivery and include determining benefits covered, patient cost-sharing levels, and provider fees. Financing and provision of long-term care is the responsibility of the municipal governments.

Financing

Among the countries in this book, Sweden is among the highest with respect to the percentage of expenditures from government or statutorily required sources, at 84% (see Table 13.2). Only 1% is paid by VHI, and 15%, out-of-pocket (OOP) [14, 15].

Revenue comes largely from proportional income taxes levied at both the county and municipal levels. There are national subsidies to the counties to help defray some of the cost of dental care and prescription drugs. Moreover, the national government oversees a tax equalization system so that counties and municipalities with fewer economic resources and/or greater health needs are not disadvantaged [3, p. 58]. As a national health system in the **Beveridge** tradition, Sweden's system does not have premiums.

In 2020, the average county tax rate was 11%, and the average municipal rate, about 21%. The highest combined rate for any region was 35%, and the lowest, 29% [16]. The reason that municipal tax rates are so much higher is that they have to fund a number of other services including primary and secondary education, social services, and sanitation. In contrast, over 90% of county spending is on health care [3, p. 60].

Taxes are high in Sweden, consistent with its reputation as a prototypical social welfare system. Of the 10 countries considered here, Sweden's tax revenue as a percentage of GDP, at 43%, was second only to France in 2015 [17]. Tax rates are somewhat progressive. In 2019, the typical Swede had a marginal income tax rate of 32%, which rose up to a maximum of 57% for incomes up to about $73,000 (US). Above that, the rate was constant [18]. Other sources of revenue include a value-added tax (VAT) of 25%—somewhat higher than most European countries [19]. VATs are generally viewed as regressive because poorer persons pay a greater share of their incomes than wealthier people.

Coverage

Breadth

The Swedish system has universal coverage with automatic enrollment. This was a result of the 1982 legislation discussed earlier. Undocumented children also are covered, as are undocumented adults for emergency and maternity care [15].

Scope

Nearly all services are covered. Two exceptions are adult dental and adult optometry services, although there are some subsidies for dental care as described next.

Depth

Sweden employs a variety of patient cost-sharing requirements that vary across the different counties (except for drugs and dental care), and hence, some of the figures shown are ranges. [At the time of writing, there were about 8 Swedish Krona (SEK) to 1 US dollar.] In general, only adults aged between 20 and 85 have to pay these cost-sharing requirements. They include [1, 20]:

- Physician visits: 120–300 SEK
- Specialist visits: 200–350 SEK (but lower with a primary care referral), with a 12-month cap of 1100 SEK for all physician and specialist visits
- Hospitalizations: 100 SEK per day
- Prescription drugs:
  - 1100 SEK annual **deductible**
  - 50% coinsurance between 1100 and 2100 SEK spending annually
  - 25% coinsurance between 2100 and 3900 SEK spending annually
  - 10% coinsurance between 3900 and 5400 SEK spending annually
  - Maximum 2200 SEK for prescription drugs over a 12-month period.

Prescription drugs are responsible for about one-third of OOP spending, the largest component of any service type [1].

There are limited subsidies for adult dental care; it is free up to age 23. For adult dental procedures, after a deductible of 3000 SEK, patients pay 50% co-insurance of the reference price of the services between 3000 and 15,000 SEK, and 15% above 15,000 SEK over a 12-month period. Although dentists can charge more than the reference price and the patient is responsible for that entire cost, it has been reported that competition among dentists has had a deterrent effect on this practice. Finally, there are small subsidies (300–600 SEK annually) for dental examinations and preventive services [3, p. 64]. Mammography screening is free for women aged 40–74 [3, p. 43].

Voluntary health insurance

Voluntary health insurance plays a more limited role in Sweden than in nearly all of the countries included in the book, with about 10% of the population aged 16–64 possessing it. It is responsible only about 1% of total health expenditures. VHI is mainly provided through group policies funded by employers. The primary purpose is to reduce waits of services [1, 15, 21]. While the exact mechanisms through which VHI reduces waiting time are currently under investigation, it has been contended that because private insurers may pay private providers more than counties do, this can sometimes crowd out publicly funded patients.[b]

Choice

As is typical countries in with Beveridge-style nationalized health systems, Sweden provides universal coverage for a standard set of benefits. There is no choice of insurance or coverage per se because there are no insurance companies outside of a small private insurance sector providing VHI coverage.

While in the past Sweden has put restrictions on free choice of providers, since 2010 patients nationwide have been free to choose any primary care center within their region. Moreover, since 2015, there has also been free choice of outpatient specialist providers. There is not a formal **gatekeeping** system to receive specialist services, but primary care is expected to be the first point of contact. Swedes do need to register with an accredited public or private provider, but most register with a practice rather than a particular physician [15].

To aid consumers in choosing their healthcare providers, there is a great deal of information available on the Internet on such things as waiting times and patient satisfaction for hospitals, primary care physicians, and specialists. Few people appear to use this information. In one study, only 3% of those who made a choice of primary healthcare provider conducted an Internet search [22]. It is not clear whether many people use this information [3, p. 43]; the use of

---

[b] Alexander Kancans and Anna Glenngard, personal communications, March 3, 2020.

similar consumer information in other countries, like the United States, tends to be low [23].

Provider payment

Hospitals

Over 90% of hospitals in Sweden are publicly owned, with the most advanced care carried out at seven public university hospitals. There are only six private hospitals in the country, and three are nonprofit. Sweden has the fewest number of acute inpatient beds per capita of any of the 10 countries in this book [14].

Hospital payment varies across the regions with a mix of global budgets, diagnosis-related groups (DRGs), and performance-based payment based on quality attainment. Global budgeting still dominates in most counties and tends to be based on historical costs, with DRGs were used in only 3 of the 21 regions in 2020.[c] Some regions tried DRGs but reverted to global budgets because it did not increase efficiency. This may have been because physicians, who are generally salaried, did not have an incentive to change their behavior [24].

Physicians

Primary care physicians in Sweden tend to practice in teams with four to five general practitioners and associated staff [15]. Most of them are county employees [25] and are salaried but their practices are paid differently. As in the case of hospitals, payment methods for physician groups vary across the regions although **capitation** is the main method of paying physician groups in all counties. In Stockholm in 2018, 60% of payments were via capitation, 40% by FFS, and a small amount based on **pay-for-performance** (P4P).[d] In the other counties, however, capitation predominates, accounting for more than 80% of total payments [3, p. 67].

While pay-for-performance (P4P) payments account for only a small share of practice incomes, there has been some interest in the topic since 2015, with studies examining the impact of P4P in particular counties that focused on diabetes control [26], appropriate prescribing of antibiotics [27], and medications taken by senior citizens [28]. It is too early to assess its impact on health outcomes, although there is some evidence that providing financial incentives to carry out certain tasks does show some positive effects on care processes. Nevertheless, most regions have moved away from P4P.[c]

Pharmaceuticals

The Dental and Pharmaceutical Benefits Agency, one of the boards of the Ministry of Health and Social Welfare, determines which drugs are covered

---

[c] Anna Glenngard, personal communication, March 3, 2020.
[d] Alexander Kancans, personal communication, February 14, 2020.

under the Swedish national health system. Value-based pricing for brand-name drugs is employed through the use of cost-effectiveness analyses. Generic substitution has been required since 2002 although physicians can appeal this. Patients who request a more expensive drug are responsible for paying the difference between the charge of that drug and the reference price [3, p. 40]. Generic penetration rates are around the middle of the European countries considered here, with 44% of prescriptions, and 15% of total expenditures for generics in 2013.[e] The use of generic vs brand-name drugs, however, is much higher in Germany and the United Kingdom [29]. Generic prices are relatively low. One way in which Sweden has kept them low is by letting companies that sell generics compete with each other by setting their own prices, but providing incentives to patients, physicians, and pharmacists that encourage the use of the cheapest generic alternatives [29].

Assuring access and equity

Sweden is known for its good financial access to medical care. Reported unmet needs are low and do not vary much between the highest and lowest income quintiles or by other socioeconomic factors [1]. An exception is adult dental care, which is not covered very thoroughly; lower income persons are much more likely to report that costs deter them from seeking services [30, 31].

The access problem that has received by far the most attention, historically, is waiting time for services. As stated by Anders Anell and colleagues in 2012,

The Achilles' heel of Swedish health care has been the long waiting times for diagnosis and treatment in several areas. Since the early 1990s, a number of initiatives at both national and local level have been implemented to reduce waiting times and improve access to providers, including reformed payment systems, privatization, introduction of targets and waiting-time guarantees and extra government grants [3, p. 122].

Self-reported data back this up. Among the countries covered in this book in the 2016 Commonwealth Fund survey (all but Japan), Sweden had the second highest rate (after Canada) of people reporting waiting two or more months for a specialist appointment and was tied with the United Kingdom for second (again, after Canada) of people reporting waiting four or more months for elective or nonemergency surgery [30, Appendix 3]. Clearly, the problem persists.

In 2005, to help deal with long waits, the national government implemented the "0–7–90–90" rule. This meant that: (a) a person could receive contact the health system the day in which they sought it; (b) they would be able to meet with a GP within a week; (c) they would be able to get an appointment with a consulting specialist within 3 months; and (d) they would wait no more than

---

[e] Although the OECD has published 2017 numbers on generic market penetration for most of the countries in this book, the most recent data available for Sweden are for 2013.

3 additional months to be treated after being diagnosed—goals that Anell and colleagues call, "quite modest in international comparisons" [3, p. 125]. (Beginning in 2019, the second goal was reduced from 7 to 3 days, although seeing a GP was no longer required, as other authorized primary care providers would count [32].) Data are available on the Internet to help patients navigate toward providers with lower waiting times [3, p. 43]. Despite this guarantee, the country has not been able to meet these goals, although it is quite transparent about the fact. The Web site https://www.vantetider.se/ shows that in 2019, the goals mentioned earlier [(a) through (d)] were met 87%, 77%, 83%, and 76%, respectively—obviously, far lower than one might expect from a guarantee [7]. Performance varies a great deal by region. For example, goal (d) was met only 61% of the time in the lowest performing county, but 96% of the time in the highest [33].

One reform that was enacted in 2010 in part to deal with long waits allowed physicians to establish private primary care practices. Since that time, the number of such practices has grown substantially. These reforms have the potential to reduce waiting lists but the effect appears to be focused on certain urban areas, particularly Stockholm [5, 34]. Moreover, Sweden is still far from meeting the waiting time guarantees established in 2005.

Controlling expenditures

Sweden spends 10.9% of its GDP on health care, which is 6th highest of the 10 countries considered here. This percentage was nearly constant between 2012 and 2019. Per capita spending ranks 4th (see Table 15.3) [14].

As in other tax-financed systems, cost containment is necessary to control tax rates. Because regions are responsible for nearly all healthcare spending, they have a strong incentive to control spending, especially because, by law, they must keep to their annual budgets [15]. They are aided by the national government, which, as noted earlier, evaluates the cost-effectiveness of medical technologies and pharmaceuticals. Nevertheless, the onus falls on the regions, and their cost-containment strategies include:

- Use of global budgets and salaried staff, both in hospitals and for primary care.
- Use of capitation to pay for physician services.
- Employing "**tendering**," in which specialist services or specialized prescription drugs are put out to bid to competing suppliers [15].
- Controlling pharmaceutical prices through various methods, including encouraging generic drug substitution and establishing value-based pricing for both brand-name and generic drug prices.
- Using cost-effectiveness analyses to establish the services covered and prices paid for expensive medical technologies.

Key policy issues

There are a number of issues facing policymakers in Sweden as they consider future reforms. Three are noted here. The first—and the one that has received perhaps the most attention internally—is the struggle with reducing waiting lists. In 2016, Sweden ranked second worst among the 10 countries on waiting time to receive care from a specialist, bettering only Canada [30]. This was 6 years after allowing physicians to establish private practices, and 11 years after putting the "0–7–90–90" rule in place, which was supposed to guarantee that patients would not experience undue delays in receiving care. To help deal with these long waits as well as geographic inequities in waiting time for cancer care, the national government invested $55 million (US) annually between 2015 and 2018 to help shore up the problem [15].

A second issue is the role of privatization. Sweden has been no exception in following the international trend of relying more on market mechanisms in its healthcare system. Compared to other countries, government still has a heavy hand, but this grip has loosened over time, particularly by allowing physicians themselves, rather than regions, to determine where they choose to practice and whether they wish to be for-profit providers. While having the potential to improve responsiveness to patient preferences and reduce waiting lists, there is concern that these practices are establishing themselves in areas that favor those who are younger, healthier, and wealthier [34, 35]. Another related concern is that taking power away from the regions may further challenge efforts to better coordinate care between hospitals, primary care providers, and specialists.

A third and related issue is trying to further reduce disparities in healthcare access and outcomes across geographic areas. This problem exists in nearly all countries, but is even more challenging in Sweden, with vast areas of low population density and few providers. It does not appear that giving physician practices the freedom to establish themselves anywhere they choose has helped, as the vast majority located in areas that already had good geographic access, particularly in the major cities, with none locating in areas showing low service use. Within Stockholm, new practices were established in already well-served parts of the city [35]. One study of the 2010 reforms found that new private practices shied away from areas with older adults living alone and with single parents [36]. The results, however, were more nuanced in that the study found no patterns with regard to income, education, and percentage of the population who were immigrants.

References

[1] OECD and European Observatory on Health Systems and Policies. Sweden: Country health profile 2019. State of health in the EU. Paris: OECD Publishing; 2019.

[2] Saltman RB, Bergman SE. Renovating the commons: Swedish health care reforms in perspective. J Health Polit Policy Law 2005;30(1–2):253–75.

[3] Anell A, Glenngård AH, Merkur S. Sweden: health system review. In: Mossialos E, Busse R, Figueras J, McKee M, Saltman R, editors. Health systems in Transition. Copenhagen: The European Observatory on Health Systems and Policies; 2012.

[4] Kullberg L, Blomqvist P, Winblad U. Market-orienting reforms in rural health care in Sweden: how can equity in access be preserved? Int J Equity Health 2018;17(1):123.

[5] Burstrom B, Burstrom K, Nilsson G, Tomson G, Whitehead M, Winblad U. Equity aspects of the Primary Health Care Choice Reform in Sweden—a scoping review. Int J Equity Health 2017;16(1):29.

[6] Glenngård AH. Experiences of introducing a quasi-market in Swedish primary care: fulfilment of overall objectives and assessment of provider activities. Scand J Public Adm 2016;20(1):71–86.

[7] Waiting times in care. Sweden's Municipalities and Regions [Internet]. [Accessed 17 September 2020]. Available from: https://www.vantetider.se/.

[8] Saltman RB. Structural patterns in Swedish health policy: a 30-year perspective. Health Econ Policy Law 2015;10(2):195–215.

[9] Ito H. Health insurance policy development in Denmark and Sweden 1860–1950. Soc Sci Med 1979;13C(3):143–60.

[10] Glenngård AH, Hjalte F, Svensson M, Anell A, Bankauskaite V. Sweden: health system review. Health Syst Transit 2012;15(5):1–159.

[11] Anell A. The public-private pendulum—patient choice and equity in Sweden. N Engl J Med 2015;372(1):1–4.

[12] Glenngard AH. Pursuing the objectives of support to providers and external accountability through enabling controls—a study of governance models in Swedish primary care. BMC Health Serv Res 2019;19(1):114.

[13] Doupi P, Renko E, Giest S, Dumortier J. Country brief: Sweden. eHealth strategies study. Bonn: European Commission Information Society and Media; 2010.

[14] Anon. OECD health statistics 2020. OECD; 2020. [Online Database]. [Accessed 26 August 2020]. Available from: http://www.oecd.org/els/health-systems/health-data.htm.

[15] Glenngård AH. In: Tikkanen R, Osborn R, Mossialos E, Djordjevic A, Wharton GA, editors. Sweden. International health care system profiles. The Commonwealth Fund; 2020. [Internet]. [Accessed 17 September 2020]. Available from: https://www.commonwealthfund.org/international-health-policy-center/countries/sweden.

[16] Anon. The municipal taxes. Statistics Sweden, Public Finance and Micro-simulations; 2020. [Internet]. [Accessed 17 September 2020]. Available from: https://www.scb.se/hitta-statistik/statistik-efter-amne/offentlig-ekonomi/finanser-for-den-kommunala-sektorn/kommunalskatterna/.

[17] Anon. How do US taxes compare internationally? Briefing book. Tax Policy Center, Urban Institute & Brookings Institution; 2020. [Internet]. [Accessed 18 September 2020]. Available from: https://www.taxpolicycenter.org/briefing-book/how-do-us-taxes-compare-internationally.

[18] Anon. Individual—Taxes on personal income. Sweden. PwC; 2020. [Internet]. [Accessed 18 September 2020]. Available from: https://taxsummaries.pwc.com/sweden/individual/taxes-on-personal-income.

[19] Asen E. VAT rates in Europe. The Tax Foundation; 2019. [Internet]. [Accessed 18 September 2020]. Available from: https://taxfoundation.org/vat-rates-europe-2019/.

[20] Rice T, Quentin W, Anell A, Barnes AJ, Rosenau P, Unruh LY, et al. Revisiting out-of-pocket requirements: trends in spending, financial access barriers, and policy in ten high-income countries. BMC Health Serv Res 2018;18(1):371.

[21] Sagan A, Thomson S. Voluntary health insurance in Europe. vol. 1. United Kingdom: WHO Regional Office for Europe; 2016.

[22] Glenngard AH, Anell A, Beckman A. Choice of primary care provider: results from a population survey in three Swedish counties. Health Policy 2011;103(1):31–7.

[23] Rice T, Unruh L. The economics of health reconsidered. 4th ed. Health Administration Press; 2015.

[24] Ellegard LM, Glenngard AH. Limited consequences of a transition from activity-based financing to budgeting: four reasons why according to Swedish hospital managers. J Health Care Organ Provis Financ 2019;56:1–10.

[25] Kringos DS, Boerma WGW, Hutchinson A, Saltman RB. Building primary care in a changing Europe. Observatory studies series. Copenhagen: European Observatory on Health Systems and Policies; 2015.

[26] Odesjo H, Anell A, Gudbjornsdottir S, Thorn J, Bjorck S. Short-term effects of a pay-for-performance programme for diabetes in a primary care setting: an observational study. Scand J Prim Health Care 2015;33(4):291–7.

[27] Ellegård LM, Dietrichson J, Anell A. Can pay-for-performance to primary care providers stimulate appropriate use of antibiotics? Health Econ 2017;27(1):e39–54.

[28] Odesjo H, Anell A, Boman A, Fastbom J, Franzen S, Thorn J, et al. Pay for performance associated with increased volume of medication reviews but not with less inappropriate use of medications among the elderly—an observational study. Scand J Prim Health Care 2017;35(3):271–8.

[29] Wouters OJ, Kanavos PG, Mc KM. Comparing generic drug markets in Europe and the United States: prices, volumes, and spending. Milbank Q 2017;95(3):554–601.

[30] Schneider EC, Sarnak DO, Squires D, Shah A, Doty MM. Mirror, mirror 2017: International comparison reflects flaws and opportunities for better U.S. health care. Mirror, Mirror: The Commonwealth Fund; 2017.

[31] Glenngård AH, Borg S. Can people afford to pay for health care? New evidence on financial protection in Sweden. Copenhagen: WHO Regional Office for Europe; 2019.

[32] Anell A, Janlöv N, Ljungvall A, Glenngård AH, Zetterberg D. In: Merkur S, editor. The health systems and policy monitor: Sweden. European Observatory on Health Systems and Policies; 2020. [Internet]. [Accessed 18 September 2020]. Available from: https://www.hspm.org/countries/sweden25022013/countrypage.aspx.

[33] Planned specialized care—Operation/Action. Sweden's Municipalities and Regions [Internet]. [Accessed 18 September 2020]. Available from: https://www.vantetider.se/Kontaktkort/Sveriges/SpecialiseradOperation/.

[34] Svanborg-Sjövall K. Swedish healthcare is the best in the world, but there are still lessons to learn. The Guardian; 2014. [Internet]. [Accessed 18 September 2020]. Available from: https://www.theguardian.com/public-leaders-network/2014/jan/03/sweden-healthcare-coordinate-oecd.

[35] Dahlgren G. Why public health services? Experiences from profit-driven health care reforms in Sweden. Int J Health Serv 2014;44(3):507–24.

[36] Isaksson D, Blomqvist P, Winblad U. Free establishment of primary health care providers: effects on geographical equity. BMC Health Serv Res 2016;16:28.

Chapter 6

Australia

The big picture

By most accounts, Australia has a very successful healthcare system. Life expectancy is long for most of the population,[a] cancer survival excellent, and relatively few people die due to causes that timely health care should prevent. At the same time, healthcare spending is a smaller proportion of national income than in any other country included in this book [1]. The system was ranked second overall, and first or second in healthcare outcomes, care process, and administrative efficiency, by the Commonwealth Fund based in its 2016 population surveys across 11 countries, 10 of which (all but Japan) are featured in this book [2].

The system, which is called Medicare, is perhaps most similar to that of Canada (see Chapter 4) [3, p. 56]. Responsibility in Australia is divided between the states and the federal governments, with the former having most of the authority in overseeing the provision of care. The federal government provides grants and subsidies to help the states carry out their responsibilities; most public costs are paid through taxes; and government takes advantage of its purchasing power to control the amount of money it pays for physician services and pharmaceuticals. There is a considerable difference, however, in the role of private insurance. In Canada, insurance is not permitted for services covered by the provincial health systems, while in Australia, its purchase is encouraged by the government.

Indeed, the characteristic that sets Australia apart from most other high-income countries is the role of private insurance to supplement people's national health coverage. Australia has the strongest incentives aimed at inducing citizens to purchase such coverage in the form of considerable subsidies as well as penalties. Those who can afford private insurance enjoy faster access to care, choice of inpatient physician, greater amenities, and coverage for dental care and other services not included in the universal healthcare system.

This system is divisive in part because even relatively wealthy people receive **premium** subsidies to purchase coverage. Moreover, those who can afford it enjoy much shorter average waits for obtaining elective procedures and

---

[a] One exception is the life expectancy of the Aboriginal population, which, while improving, still lags far behind others.

Health Insurance Systems: An International Comparison. https://doi.org/10.1016/B978-0-12-816072-5.00006-7
89

other services provided by specialists—both in private hospitals and as private patients in public hospitals. This is not surprising since these providers can earn more money when they see privately insured patients. There may be a reckoning coming, however, as evidence is mounting that the system is moving toward a "premium death spiral," where adverse selection of older and sicker people into private insurance drives up the premiums so much that they become unaffordable, even with the generous government premium subsidies [4, 5].

The details

History [6][b]

Among the countries included in this book, Australia's system of universal coverage is among the most recent. In fact, private insurance was the dominant form of coverage until the 1970s, with government subsidies to seniors and poorer persons for hospital care, physician services, and pharmaceuticals. In the late 1960s, the country had 78 private insurance funds for medical care and 109 for hospital care. This patchwork of private coverage through voluntary organizations called Friendly Societies, religious organizations, and government subsidies resulted in an estimated 17% of the population without health insurance coverage in the late 1960s [7].

It was not until 1975 that a program resembling the current Medicare system was established. Called Medibank, it was implemented during a Labor government over the strong opposition of the insurance industry and physicians' associations. Medibank provided universal, free coverage for public hospital care and highly subsidized access to medical services. There was still an advantage to having private insurance because it allowed access to private hospitals and specialists practicing in the private hospitals. With the election of a new government, however, Medibank was slowly whittled away and eventually abolished in 1981. In the ensuing few years, the system reverted to one that was more heavily focused on means testing for providing access to free care.

The current Medicare program began in 1984 with the election of another Labor government. It fully covered care in public hospitals for the entire population and provided highly subsidized physician services to everyone as well. Private insurance (which we refer to as voluntary health insurance or VHI) covered things such as care in private hospitals or as a private patient in a public hospital, choice of inpatient physician/surgeon, amenities like a private hospital room, and subsidies for uncovered services like dental care. The overall intention was, according to John Deeble, one of Medicare's architects, to allow "better-off people and those with a strong preference for private treatment to 'opt up' without 'opting out' of the universal scheme to which they all contributed" [6, p. 17].

---

[b] Much of the material in this section comes from Duckett and Nemet [5].

With another change in government in 1996, public policy toward private insurance changed. Previously, coverage rates had fallen after the enactment of Medicare. To bolster private coverage, and thus take pressure off government expenditures, a variety of incentives were enacted, which are detailed later in the section on Voluntary Health Insurance. These incentives increased coverage rates to nearly 50% of the population [6]. To this day, the role of VHI is controversial. According to journalist Dylan Scott, "Over the past 45 years, it's been a pendulum swinging back and forth: Conservative governments try to strengthen the private sector, pushing for the public system to act more as a safety net, while the [Labor] governments focus on investing in and strengthening the public system" [4].

One novel Australian contribution to world health policy began in 1992 with the requirement that new pharmaceuticals be the subject of cost-effectiveness analysis before being listed on the Pharmaceutical Benefits Scheme (PBS) [8, p. 125]. While decisions about which drugs to ultimately include was the responsibility of a government-appointed agency, the Pharmaceutical Benefits Advisory Committee, its decisions were based on economic analyses carried out by health economists [9]. This paved the way for other countries using economic tools to determine which services to cover and how much to pay for them under national health systems. The most notable example is the National Institute for Health and Care Excellence, or NICE, in the United Kingdom.

Overview of the health insurance system

Australia is made up of six states and two main territories. With the exception of some sparsely populated islands with a combined population of fewer than 3000 people, everyone lives on the mainland or the island of Tasmania. The main territories have similar authority as states in the area of health care, so for convenience the chapter refers to both as "states."

The country is viewed by many as having a **single-payer system**. Citizens and some other residents receive coverage automatically. Hospital services including physician care for public patients are fully covered, with outpatient physician services partly reimbursed by government. VHI plays an important role in covering services that are not part of the benefits package, particularly treatment in private hospitals.

An unusual aspect of the Australian system is the different way that public and private hospitals are treated. The country has both public and private hospitals, but within public hospitals, patients can decide for a particular stay whether they will be treated as public vs private patient. Much of the cost of private hospital care is covered by VHI, which about half of the population possesses. Public patients face no out-of-pocket (OOP) costs, but private patients can choose their hospital (public or private) and hospital physicians and often experience shorter waiting time for elective surgery [10]. VHI plays an important role in providing a safety valve for the wealthier people who wish to have greater amenities, shorter waits, and provider choice [4].

Governance

Governmental responsibilities are divided between the national government, called the Commonwealth, the states, and local governments. The original constitution, which became effective at the time of Australia's independence in 1901, left little room for federal involvement in health care. In 1946, it was amended to allow the Commonwealth to have authority in the areas of the "provision of maternity allowances, widows' pensions, child endowment, unemployment, pharmaceutical, sickness and hospital benefits, medical and dental services (but not so as to authorize any form of civil conscription), benefits to students, and family allowances." The parenthetical phrase about conscription effectively removed the possibility that the government could form a National Health Service as England had done 2 years later [11, 12].[c]

The Commonwealth is responsible for determining: which services and pharmaceuticals are covered by national schemes as well as the benefits paid for these services, regulating quality, overseeing private insurance, and providing various subsidies to the states. The states, in turn, oversee public hospitals and, jointly with the Commonwealth, cover preventive and screening services and oversee mental health care. Local governments focus on public health services as well as community health and home care services. A more complete list of which responsibilities fall under which type of jurisdiction is shown in Table 6.1 [13].

Financing

The portion of expenditures covered by government, about 69%, is lower than most of the other countries in this book. It is comparable to Canada and lower than five of the six European countries considered here—all but Switzerland. VHI covers about 10%, with an additional 3% devoted to government financial incentives that subsidize the purchase of VHI [5]. Out-of-pocket (OOP) spending constitutes the remaining 18%. When considering the subsidies, the VHI figure is only exceeded by Canada, and the OOP figure only by Switzerland.

Funds are raised largely through taxes. Taxes on income, profits, and capital gains make up about 60% of tax revenue, and consumption taxes, about 30%, with the remainder coming from payroll and property taxes [14]. The income tax, which is collected by the Commonwealth and not by states, is progressive, with marginal rates varying from 0% for the lowest earners to 45% for the highest. There is also an income tax surcharge. This stands at 2% of income except for those with low incomes. A final levy of between 1% and 1.5% of income is charged to those above an income threshold who do not purchase VHI. In 2019,

---

[c] The Australian Constitution can be amended only if a majority of voters in a majority of states vote in favor of doing so. Sally Wilde (2005) argues that "The irony is that the voters almost certainly believed [in 1946] they were voting for a national health service, or at least voting to give government the power to provide them with a national health service" (p. 46).

TABLE 6.1 Government responsibilities in Australian health care (partial list).

Commonwealth Responsibilities

- Administering the Medicare Benefits Schedule
- Administering the Pharmaceutical Benefits Schedule
- Supporting and regulating private health insurance
- Supporting and monitoring the quality, effectiveness and efficiency of primary care
- Subsidizing aged care services and regulating the aged care sector
- Collecting and publishing health and welfare information and statistics
- Funding health and medical research
- Funding veterans' health care
- Funding community controlled Aboriginal and Torres Strait Islander primary care organizations
- Maintaining the number of doctors in Australia and ensure their equitable distribution
- Buying vaccines
- Regulating medicines and medical devices
- Subsidizing hearing services
- Coordinating national responses to health emergencies

State, Territory, and Local Government Responsibilities

- Managing and administering public hospitals
- Delivering preventive services
- Funding and managing community health services
- Administering public dental clinics
- Administering ambulance and emergency services
- Overseeing food safety and handling regulation
- Regulating, inspecting, licensing, and monitoring health premises

Shared Responsibilities

- Funding public hospital services
- Funding preventive services
- Registering and accrediting health professionals
- Funding palliative care
- Overseeing national mental health reform
- Responding to national health emergencies

Source: The Australian Health System. https://www.health.gov.au/about-us/the-australian-health-system#government-responsibilities.

the threshold was about $90,000 AU for single people and double that for families [15]. [At the time of writing, the exchange rate was $1 (AU) = $0.79 (US)] In contrast, VHI and OOP financing are highly regressive.

Australia is unusual among federal systems in placing so much of revenue generation in the hands of the national government and at the same time putting such a large share of public spending in the hands of the states. This has been called a "vertical fiscal imbalance" and this gap is larger in Australia than elsewhere. States have the major responsibility in paying not only public hospitals but also big-ticket items such as public education. State governments collect only 15% of total tax revenues, and local governments about 3%, with the remaining amount being collected by the Commonwealth. In health care, however, states are responsible for over half of public hospital spending as well as the majority of expenses going toward public and community health centers [3, p. 63, 74].

To compensate for this, large federal transfer payments are necessary to the states. The amount each state is granted from the Commonwealth is determined by the Commonwealth Grants Commission. These amounts vary across states according to their abilities to raise revenues as well as differences in the costs of providing services [3, p. 74, 128]. The fact that they are block grants is important because it means that the states are responsible for excess spending, putting them as risk if they do not control their health expenditures.

Coverage

Breadth

Coverage is automatic for citizens; immigrants with work visas are also eligible for Medicare. Most temporary residents and refugees are not covered, although, as in all countries discussed in this book, everyone with a medical emergency can receive treatment.

Scope

The Medicare program provides coverage for public patient care in public hospitals, ambulatory medical services, diagnostic services, and pharmaceuticals. The Medicare Benefits Schedule (MBS) provides a list of all covered services as well as the benefits paid for them (in a document over 1300 pages long) [16]. Similarly, there is a list of covered drugs—more than 5200—on the PBS [13].

Medicare does not cover hospital care in private hospitals. It also does not cover dental care, eyeglasses, hearing aids, and some types of (allied health) therapies such as physical therapy. There is limited coverage of optometry and dental care for children [17].

Depth

Public hospital care and certain physician care specified in the next paragraph are provided free of charge. Other covered services are subject to patient cost sharing. This can be considerable but there are a variety of OOP maximums as well as lower requirements for poorer and older Australians.

The first factor that determines patient financial liability for physicians' services is whether the doctor uses *bulk billing*. They may choose to do this for some patients and not for others. When bulk billing, the physician agrees to accept the MBS fee as full for their services. This is potentially advantageous for the patient in two ways. First, they do not have to pay cost-sharing requirements, and second, Medicare pays the physician's bill directly. There are advantages and disadvantages for the physician. They do not have to bill the patient, saving resources, and are not at risk of delayed payment or default. The disadvantage is that they cannot receive additional payments beyond the MBS. Bulk billing is most commonly associated with GP services and services that can be ordered directly by GPs. For example, in 2018–19, 85% of GP services were bulk billed, as were 89% of pathology services [18]. Nevertheless, since patients often see more than one physician, a larger percentage—an estimated one-third—do face extra billing for some services they receive during a year [19]. Bulk billing rates are lower on average for specialists, but vary greatly. In 2018–19 bulk billing was used for 32% of specialist services, 59% of obstetrics services, and 11% of anesthetic services.

For nonbulk-billed services, patient liability is determined by the complex interplay between three factors: the size of the gap between what the physician charges and the MBS benefit, whether the service is provided in physician offices or in a hospital inpatient setting, and whether the patient is covered by VHI.

In the simplest scenario, physician services that are provided in physician offices are legislatively excluded from coverage under VHI. In 2018–19, the average patient contribution for all patient-billed, out-of-hospital services was $66 (AU) with higher patient contributions for specialist services ($84 AU) and diagnostic imaging ($110 AU) [18].

For physician services provided in private hospitals, or for patients using private insurance in public hospitals, the MBS covers 75% of the MBS fee and the patient is responsible for 25% of the MBS fee plus any amount charged by physicians exceeding that amount. Private insurance pays for the 25% **coinsurance**; some policies also reimburse the patient all or part of the physician excess charge [20]. Again, there is considerable variation in the charges experienced by patients. Stephen Duckett reports that while "only about 7 percent of all in-hospital medical services are billed … at more than twice the official MBS fee … these bills account for almost 90% of all out-of-pocket medical costs for private hospital patients" [21].

There are also cost-sharing requirements for pharmaceuticals. For most Australians, it is about $41 (AU) per prescription, but for those with a "concession card" it is only about $6.60 (AU) [22]. Concession cards are available to lower-income Australians and some seniors [23]. As discussed in the next section, many patient liabilities are covered by VHI policies.

Because OOP payments can become considerable for pharmaceuticals, there are limits on annual patient liabilities. If those without a concession card spend more than $1487 (AU) during a year on drug copayments, subsequent copayments are lowered to about $6.60 (AU) per prescription. Among those with a concession card, after they spend $317 (AU) on drugs during the year, subsequent prescriptions are free [24].

Voluntary health insurance

Australia is unique among the 10 countries in this book in that it provides strong incentives for its citizens to purchase VHI. Those who do so get a tax break, and those who do not can be penalized. In return for purchasing coverage, policy-holders enjoy access to private care in hospitals, choice of hospital physician/surgeon, more amenities, and shorter waits for services. Because hospital-based physicians can charge considerably more when they treat privately insured patients, there is a strong financial incentive to do so. As discussed under "Assuring Access and Equity," patients with VHI wait only one-third as long for knee replacements compared to their publicly insured counterparts [2].

VHI also often covers dental and optical care and drugs not covered by the PBS. It is prohibited from covering GP visits, office and other outpatient visits, and outpatient diagnostic imaging and testing [25]. In 2019, 44% of the population had VHI coverage for hospital treatment and 54% had coverage for other services (e.g., dental) [26].

The Commonwealth provides various incentives to purchase coverage. One incentive is a system called Lifetime Health Cover. Those who purchase coverage up until the age of 30 are not subject to any surcharges for the rest of their lives if they keep their coverage. Others who purchase VHI later in life, however, are required to pay an additional 2% of premiums for every year that their age exceeds 30. If one purchased coverage at age 40, then, premiums would be 20% higher. (There is a maximum of 70%, and the penalty is removed after a person has had continuous coverage for 10 years [27].) In addition, there is an income tax penalty for those with higher incomes who do not purchase coverage. Individuals/families with incomes above $90,000 (AU)/$180,000 (AU) pay an additional 1%–1.5% in income taxes, the exact percentage depending on how large their income is.

Finally, there is a premium rebate to help everyone except those with very high incomes to purchase coverage. The rebate is about 25% for individuals/families earning less than $90,000/$180,000 (AU), and smaller rebates for those earning up to $140,000/$280,000 (AU) [28]. Because high-income individuals and families receive rebates and are much more likely to purchase private coverage—providing them with better access to care—the system is controversial.

One would expect that these incentives would encourage younger persons, and those with higher incomes, to purchase private insurance. That turns out to be the case although younger people are beginning to exit the market. Of those with hospital coverage, nearly 90% purchased it by age 30, thus avoiding the penalty [26]. Only 22% of Australians in the bottom quintile of the income distribution have coverage, compared to 57% in the top quintile [17].

Annual premiums paid by individuals for basic hospital coverage average about $1000 (AU) and coverage that includes both basic hospital coverage as well comprehensive coverage for other services such as dental care and physiotherapy costs on average about $1750 (AU). Couples pay roughly twice that, and families pay about 2.5 times as much [28]. But there are additional costs as well because private insurance does not cover everything. In particular, if a doctor charges more than 15% above the MBS, the patient is responsible for paying some or all of those charges OOP. As a result, it has been reported that the OOP costs of having a baby, which is almost nothing in the public system, can add up to $5000 AU if a woman uses the private health insurance system [4].

Most of the 37 private insurers operating in Australia in 2020 did so on a for-profit basis [3 (p. 84), 29]. Just two insurers, however, control more than half of the market and the five top companies cover over 80% [3, p. 84]. One of those insurers, Medibank was previously owned by the government but in 2014 became a private company, listed on the Australian stock exchange [30]. Insurers are required to accept all applicants and cannot base premiums on health status, previous healthcare usage, age, or gender [5, 8, p. 35].

Choice

All Australian citizens and documented nonresidents are automatically covered by the Commonwealth and the states for public hospital and physician care and for pharmaceuticals. Beyond that, the degree of patient choice depends to a large extent on whether those accessing hospital care have a VHI policy. Those with private insurance can choose to receive care from a private hospital or as a private patient in a public hospital. This also allows them to choose their inpatient specialists [12]. In contrast, those without private insurance are assigned hospital specialists [31].

There is free choice of general practitioner (GP). A referral from a GP is required prior to receiving specialist services if a person is to receive a subsidy from the Medicare program [17].

Provider payment

Hospitals

A little over half of the Australian hospitals are public, but because private hospitals tend to be smaller, the public ones account for about two-thirds of the total number of beds [17, 32]. Public hospitals are paid by the states on a diagnosis-related group (DRG) system that Australia developed soon after the system was adopted by the US Medicare program. One difference, however, is that states typically put an annual cap on their hospital expenditures to help control incentives to increase the volume of services provided. This is achieved by paying less or even nothing to hospitals when volume exceeds a particular threshold [3, p. 250]. Private insurers use DRGs to some extent but often pay on the basis of costs incurred for certain expensive services. Unlike the states, private insurers can contract with individual hospitals, making them compete for contracts and driving down costs [3, p. 250].

Physicians

GPs generally work in individual or group practices. Specialists, in contrast, can work on a salaried basis in public hospitals or work on a fee-for-service (FFS) basis in private practices—or do both. Those with private practices are still able to contract with both public and private hospitals [8, p. 34, 63].

Except for salaried hospital-based physicians, payment for GPs and specialists is mainly on a fee-for-service FFS basis. Payment is largely based on the MBS fee schedule for GP services since a large majority are bulk-billed. As discussed earlier, however, payment for specialty services is more complicated, being based on such factors as the size of the gap between what the physician charges and the MBS benefit, whether the service is provided in physician offices or in a hospital inpatient setting, and whether the patient is covered by VHI. Thus, the key choice physicians make is whether or not to bulk bill their services, which was discussed earlier under "Depth." There is little in the way of managed care because patients do not have a financial incentive to ally themselves to a network when care is largely free at point of service.

The main deviation from FFS in Australia is the Practice Incentive Program; about 5% of GP revenues are derived from it [17]. The Program, overseen by the Commonwealth, provides augmentation to FFS payments for physicians who engage in activities that enhance quality of care (e.g., use of eHealth, Indigenous health, after-hours activity, practice in rural areas, and collection and review of data that enhance continuous quality improvement) [33].

Pharmaceuticals

Australia is noteworthy in that it was the first country to require that new pharmaceuticals be evaluated for cost-effectiveness before being reimbursed by the national healthcare system [8, p. 52]. The Pharmaceutical Benefits Advisory Committee, an independent body appointed by the government, is responsible for determining which new medicines are covered under the PBS by assessing the effectiveness and cost of new drugs compared to others already on the market. Existing drugs and technologies, however, typically are not subject to such evaluations even if they become outdated [34].

Drug prices generally are set through negotiations between the government and manufacturer. Cost-effectiveness criteria are used in determining price for medicines that provide more benefits than those currently on the market. According to Ezekiel Emanuel, while "there is no formal maximum cost per

QALY [quality-adjusted life-year] threshold, ... the BBAC tries to get drug prices under $34,000 ($50,000 AU) per QALY – which is approximately the threshold in both the UK and Norway" [35, p. 291]. For others, internal **reference pricing** is used, based on the lowest priced therapeutic alternative [36]. A study using 2015 from 10 high-income countries found that unit drug prices were 25% lower in Australia than the average of these countries for six sets of primary care drugs: hypertension, pain, cholesterol, diabetes, stomach preparations, and antidepressants [37].

In spite of these lower drug prices, pharmaceutical spending is not as low as in many countries. Part of the reason is the relatively low use of generic drugs. In 2017, 19% of drug spending was on generics compared to 24% for OECD countries as a whole. The figures for the percentage of prescriptions that were generic was 37%, much lower than the 49% OECD average. The corresponding figure for the United Kingdom was 85% [38]. Part of the reason Australia lags behind other countries is that there is no requirement that pharmacists substitute generic medications when such a product exists, and in fact, only under special circumstances are they allowed to override a physician's brand-name prescription [36].

Assuring access and equity

Equity of access appears to be a larger problem in Australia than in Canada, Sweden, and the United Kingdom, the other three single-payer countries covered in this book. One example regards waiting lists. The Commonwealth Fund's 2016 survey of 11 countries found a large difference in waiting times for specialist appointments between Australians with above- vs below-average incomes. While 9% of the higher-income people reported waiting two or more months for a specialist appointment, the figure for lower-income persons was 19%—a much wider gap than in the other countries [2].

These figures are based on patient reports, so it is useful to examine administrative data. In 2015–16, patient waiting times for public patients in public hospitals were uniformly higher than for patients using private insurance in the same hospitals—generally two to three times longer. To illustrate, median waiting time for a knee replacement was about 75 days for private patients, but 200 days for public patients. Among all hospital procedures, median waiting time was more than twice as long for public patients: 42 vs 20 days [39–41]. Part of the explanation may lie in the fact that private hospitals focus on planned and elective surgeries and treatments, while public hospitals are generally where patients with particularly complex care are channeled.[d]

Another example concerns financial access. In 2014, less than 3% of those in the highest income decile incurred catastrophic health expenditures (defined as spending 10% of income OOP in a given year). The figures for those in the

---

[d] Fran Collyer, personal communication, August 30, 2020.

bottom half of the income distribution was 31%, and for the second poorest decile, 19% [42]. This same pattern is even stronger for pharmaceutical expenditures [3, p. 313].

A final equity issue regards poorer Aboriginal health outcomes, which Stephen Duckett and Sharon Willcox call "appalling" [3, p. 363]. Although the causes of this—and more generally, the determinants of life expectancy worldwide—are determined mainly by factors outside of the medical care system, these disparities have been a focus of Australian government policy for decades. In 2015–17, the gap in life expectancy between Aboriginals and other Australians was 8.6 years for males and 7.8 years for females. This was nevertheless a marked improvement from 10 years earlier, when the gap was 11.5 years and 9.7 years, respectively [43].

Controlling expenditures

Australia devotes less of its national income to health care than any of the countries examined in this book: 9.3% of GDP in 2019. Being a relatively wealthy country, however, Australia's per capita expenditures are not the lowest, with the United Kingdom and Japan spending less (Table 15.3) [44].

One way in which Australia contains its expenditures is by taking advantage of Commonwealth purchasing power to contain hospital and pharmaceutical fees, which is instrumental in controlling increases in the MBS and PBS. One particular tool has been negotiations with both generalist and certain specialist groups (e.g., pathologists and radiologists) to set and adhere to expenditure targets to provide an incentive to control the volume of services provided [3, p. 79].

Moreover, states have a strong incentive to control healthcare spending because they are not permitted to institute income taxes, relying instead largely on block grants from the Commonwealth. States put caps on annual hospital expenditures and also control the supply of hospital beds as well as the healthcare workforce, including the number of trainees [3 (p. 79), 17]. As noted earlier, Australia was the first country to use health technology assessment to determine what drugs are covered under its Medicare program.

Key policy issues

Australia faces many of the same issues of other high-income countries, including an aging population, high obesity rates, and competing priorities for scarce government resources. More so than in other countries, however, policy concerning VHI is a continuing area of focus because of its implications regarding equity in accessing healthcare services. VHI has a role, to a greater or lesser extent, in nearly all of the countries reviewed in this book. VHI in Australia constitutes about the same portion of total health expenses as in France and Canada. But in France, it is possessed by nearly everyone, and in Canada, it only covers services excluded from provincial health plans. Australia differs in that VHI covers only about half of the population *and* it competes against the system of universal coverage for hospital care. Those who purchase it can choose their specialists/surgeons and enjoy shorter waiting times for receiving elective inpatient procedures.

In nearly all countries, wealthier people can choose to spend their own resources to receive better access and sometimes better quality. Australia, however, provides VHI with government premium subsidies to encourage this, at an estimated cost of $6 billion (AU). Given purchasing patterns by income, this is obviously regressive. Wealthier Australians are almost three times as likely to possess VHI coverage, and this, in turn, results in equity problems, particularly in the inpatient setting. In the Commonwealth Fund's 2016 survey of 11 countries, excluding the United States, the gap between those with above- vs below-average income was greatest in Australia in both areas involving waiting for specialist care [2].[e]

Related to this, Fran Collyer and colleagues conclude that there is "rapidly diminishing universality," and, "With elective surgery increasingly being moved into private hospitals and the higher remuneration of surgeons operating in private hospitals, a two-tier system has developed, whereby the least wealthy – and those most in medical need of services – are denied access to timely surgery" [7, p. 280]. Ezekiel Emanuel states that long waiting lists for elective and nonurgent procedures are common, in part because physicians make more by treating private patients, so "there is little reason for physicians practicing in both public and private settings to cooperate with initiatives to reduce public waiting times" [35, p. 298].

A related issue is whether the current system is sustainable. Duckett and Nemet report an incipient "premium death spiral," where VHI premiums spin out of control over time because of adverse selection. There is already evidence of this, with a 30% increase in inflation-adjusted premiums between 2011 and 2019 compared to only an 8% rise in wages. This is due in large measure to more young people dropping coverage and more people age 70 and older people purchasing it—a natural consequence in a marketplace where premiums are **community rated**. Thus, to keep up coverage rates, the government may need to choose whether to increase its premium subsidies or consider spending the resources on other competing priorities—either in the health sector or elsewhere in the economy [5].

---

[e] The two areas were: (a) waiting 2 months or longer for specialist appointment, and (b) specialist lacked medical history or regular doctor not informed about specialist care in the past 2 years. In both cases, those in the bottom half of the income distribution were twice as likely to report the problem as their wealthier counterparts.

References

[1] Tikkanen R, Abrams MK. U.S. health care from a global perspective, 2019: Higher spending, worse outcomes? The Commonwealth Fund; 2020.

[2] Schneider EC, Sarnak DO, Squires D, Shah A, Doty MM. Mirror, mirror 2017: International comparison reflects flaws and opportunities for better U.S. health care. Mirror, Mirror: The Commonwealth Fund; 2017.

[3] Duckett S, Willcox S. The Australian health care system. 5th ed. South Melbourne: Oxford University Press; 2015.

[4] Scott D. Two sisters. Two different journeys through Australia's health care system. Vox; 2020. [Internet]. [Accessed 17 October 2020]. Available from: https://www.vox. com/2020/1/15/21030568/australia-health-insurance-medicare.

[5] Duckett S, Nemet K. Updated: The history and purposes of private health insurance. 2nd ed. Australia: Grattan Institute; 2019.

[6] Duckett S, Nemet K. The history and purposes of private health insurance. 1st ed. Australia: Grattan Institute; 2019.

[7] Collyer F, Harley K, Short S. Money and markets in Australia's healthcare system. In: Meagher G, Goodwin S, editors. Markets, rights and power in Australian social policy. Sydney: Sydney University Press; 2015.

[8] Healy J, Sharman E, Lokuge B. In: Healy J, editor. Australia: Health system review. 5th ed. Health systems in transition, vol. 8. Copenhagen: The European Observatory on Health Systems and Policies; 2006.

[9] Freund DA. Initial development of the Australian guidelines. Med Care 1996;34(12 Suppl):DS211–215.

[10] Johar M, Savage E. Do private patients have shorter waiting times for elective surgery? Evidence from New South Wales public hospitals. Econ Pap 2010;29(2):128–42.

[11] Wilde S. Serendipity, doctors and the Australian constitution. Health History 2005;7(1):41–8.

[12] Day GE, Kerr Jr BJ. Australia. In: Johnson J, Stoskoph C, Shi L, editors. Comparative health systems. 2nd ed. Burlington, MA: Jones & Bartlett; 2018 [chapter 26].

[13] Anon. The Australian health system. Commonwealth of Australia; 2019. [Internet]. [Accessed 17 October 2020]. Available from: https://www.health.gov.au/about-us/the-australian-health-system.

[14] Anon. Taxation revenue, Australia. Australian Bureau of Statistics; 2020. [Internet]. [Accessed 17 October 2020]. Available from: https://www.abs.gov.au/statistics/economy/government/taxation-revenue-australia/latest-release.

[15] Anon. Medicare levy surcharge. Australian Taxation Office; 2020. [Internet]. [Accessed 17 October 2020]. Available from: https://www.ato.gov.au/individuals/medicare-levy/medicare-levy-surcharge/.

[16] Anon. Medicare benefits schedule book. Australian Government Department of Health; 2019.

[17] Glover L, Woods M. In: Tikkanen R, Osborn R, Mossialos E, Djordjevic A, Wharton GA, editors. Australia. International health care system profiles. The Commonwealth Fund; 2020. [Internet]. [Accessed 17 October 2020]. Available from: https://www.commonwealthfund.org/international-health-policy-center/countries/australia.

[18] Anon. Annual medicare statistics. Australian Government Department of Health; 2020. [Internet]. [Accessed 17 October 2020]. Available from: https://www1.health.gov.au/internet/main/publishing.nsf/Content/Annual-Medicare-Statistics.

[19] Hendrie D. Explainer: Bulk-billing rates are at record highs—or are they? The Royal Australian College of General Practitioners; 2019. [Internet]. [Accessed 17 October 2020]. Available from: https://www1.racgp.org.au/newsgp/professional/explainer-bulk-billing-rates-are-at-record-highs-%E2%80%93.

[20] Doctors' Bills. Commonwealth Ombudsman [Guide]. [Accessed 17 October 2020]. Available from: https://www.ombudsman.gov.au/__data/assets/pdf_file/0016/35611/Doctors-Bill-DL-Fyler-Web.pdf.

[21] Duckett S. Saving private health 1: Reining in hospital costs and specialist bills. Grattan Institute; 2019.

[22] Anon. Pharmaceutical benefits. Pharmaceutical benefits scheme. Australian Government Department of Health; 2020. [Internet]. [Accessed 17 October 2020]. Available from: https://www.pbs.gov.au/info/healthpro/explanatory-notes/front/fee.

[23] Drury B. What concession cards are available for seniors and pensioners? SuperGuide; 2020. [Internet]. [Accessed 17 October 2020]. Available from: https://www.superguide.com.au/in-retirement/concession-cards-eligible-what-entitlements.

[24] Anon. PBS safety net thresholds. Australian Government Services Australia; 2020. [Internet]. [Accessed 17 October 2020]. Available from: https://www.servicesaustralia.gov.au/organisations/health-professionals/services/medicare/pbs-safety-net-pharmacists/about-eligible-customers/pbs-safety-net-thresholds.

[25] Anon. What private health insurance covers. Australian Government Department of Health; 2020. [Internet]. [Accessed 17 October 2020]. Available from: https://www.health.gov.au/health-topics/private-health-insurance/what-private-health-insurance-covers.

[26] Anon. Quarterly private health insurance statistics. Statistics. Sydney: Australian Prudential Regulation Authority (APRA); 2019.

[27] Lifetime Health Cover. Commonwealth Ombudsman [Internet]. [Accessed 17 October 2020]. Available from: https://privatehealth.gov.au/health_insurance/surcharges_incentives/lifetime_health_cover.htm.

[28] Silvester B, Jeyaratnam E, Jackson-Webb F. Private health insurance premium increases explained in 14 charts. The Conversation; 2018. [Internet]. [Accessed 17 October 2020]. Available from: https://theconversation.com/private-health-insurance-premium-increases-explained-in-14-charts-92825.

[29] Anon. Register of private health insurers. Australian Prudential Regulation Authority; 2020. [Internet]. [Accessed 17 October 2020]. Available from: https://www.apra.gov.au/register-of-private-health-insurers.

[30] Medibank Private Share Offer. Privatisation. medibank [Internet]. [Accessed 17 October 2020]. Available from: https://www.medibank.com.au/about/company/overview/privatisation/.

[31] Public and private hospitals. How does Australia's Healthcare System work? Bupa [Internet]. [Accessed 17 October 2020]. Available from: https://www.bupa.com.au/healthcare-guide/what-is-australias-healthcare-system#public-and-private-hospitals.

[32] Anon. Hospital resources 2016–17: Australian hospital statistics. Health services series, Australian Institute of Health and Welfare; 2018.

[33] Anon. Types of payments. Australian Government Services Australia; 2020. [Internet]. [Accessed 17 October 2020]. Available from: https://www.servicesaustralia.gov.au/organisations/health-professionals/steps/what-are-practice-incentives-program-payments/51534/types-payments#a1.

[34] Boxall AM. What are we doing to ensure the sustainability of the health system? Parliament of Australia Department of Parliamentary Services; 2011. 4.

[35] Emanuel EJ. Which country has the world's best health care? New York: PublicAffairs; 2020.

[36] Williams G, Loveday C, McKie S. Pharmaceutical pricing and reimbursement. In: Castle G, editor. Pricing and reimbursement 2020—Australia; 2020. Global Legal Group, London, [chapter 3].

[37] Morgan SG, Leopold C, Wagner AK. Drivers of expenditure on primary care prescription drugs in 10 high-income countries with universal health coverage. CMAJ 2017;189(23):E794–9.

[38] Anon. International health data comparisons, 2018. Australian Institute of Health and Welfare; 2018. [Web report]. [Accessed 17 October 2020]. Available from: https://www.aihw.gov.au/reports/phe/237/international-health-data-comparisons-2018/contents/pharmaceutical-market.

[39] Anon. Private health insurance use in Australian hospitals 2006–07 to 2015–16: Australian hospital statistics. Health services series, Canberra: Australian Institute of Health and Welfare; 2017.

[40] Kliff S. What Australia can teach America about health care. Vox; 2019. [Internet]. [Accessed 17 October 2020]. Available from: https://www.vox.com/policy-and-politics/2019/4/15/18311694/australia-health-care-system.

[41] Han E. Patients waiting four times longer than private patients for some operations at public hospitals. The Sydney Morning Herald; 2017. [Internet]. [Accessed 17 October 2020]. Available from: https://www.smh.com.au/healthcare/patients-waiting-four-times-longer-than-private-patients-for-some-operations-at-public-hospitals-20171205-gzyv8x.html.

[42] Callander EJ, Fox H, Lindsay D. Out-of-pocket healthcare expenditure in Australia: trends, inequalities and the impact on household living standards in a high-income country with a universal health care system. Health Econ Rev 2019;9(1):10.

[43] Anon. Deaths in Australia. Australian Institute of Health and Welfare; 2020. [Web report]. [Accessed 17 October 2020]. Available from: https://www.aihw.gov.au/reports/life-expectancy-death/deaths/contents/life-expectancy.

[44] Anon. OECD health statistics 2020. OECD; 2020. [Online Database]. [Accessed 26 August 2020]. Available from: http://www.oecd.org/els/health-systems/health-data.htm.

Universal coverage systems with multiple insurers but no choice

Chapter 7

France

The big picture

A broad review of the literature finds a great deal of enthusiasm for the French healthcare system. Among the 10 countries included in this book, France ranks among the countries with the lowest rate of deaths due to causes that should be avoidable by the healthcare system [1, 2]. Patient out-of-pocket (OOP) spending is low as are levels of unmet need. But there are also a number of problems. Total system spending is viewed as being high and many people with lower incomes claim that they have had a problem paying a medical bill or skipped dental care services because of costs [3]. There are also greater income disparities in unmet need than most of the other European countries considered in this book [2].[a] Physician satisfaction is also low.

While France did not fully achieve universal coverage until 2000—before then an estimated one to 2% of the population was still uninsured [4][b]—its health insurance system dates back to the 19th century. A hallmark of the system has always been the notion of **solidarity**. As colorfully explained by French physician Valerie Newman:

> It would be stupid to say that everyone is equal. Some are rich and some are poor. Some are beautiful, some aren't. Some are brilliant, some aren't. But when we get sick – then, everybody is equal. Everybody must have equal right to the best medical treatment we can provide [5, p. 64].

This, of course, is not entirely true: in all countries, there are greater barriers for those who are socioeconomically disadvantaged, and France is no exception [2]. Nevertheless, OOP spending in France is quite low compared to elsewhere. Perhaps the main access barrier is one that is unique to French among wealthy countries: most people have to pay for their health care up front, which is viewed by people with few economic resources as a considerable impediment. This requirement does not apply to those suffering from 30 or so chronic conditions, who are not subject to OOP costs for treatments of those conditions.

---

[a] The countries referred to here are Germany, the Netherlands, Sweden, and the United Kingdom. Because these data are from a European Union survey, Switzerland is not included.
[b] Victor Rodwin, personal communication, August 3, 2019.

Health Insurance Systems: An International Comparison. https://doi.org/10.1016/B978-0-12-816072-5.00016-X
107

While the government has been trying to change this for many years and has succeeded in doing so for the very poorest of the population, the persistence of the policy is often attributed to the influence of the French physician organizations. In 2014 and 2015, French physicians went on strike largely because of the government's plan to move toward direct reimbursement by insurance companies [6, 7]. The proposed change, originally planned to go into effect in the latter part of 2017, has since been postponed indefinitely [2, 8].

The overall affordability of health care in France continues to be a key issue. In 2018, France was tied for third among all OECD countries in the percentage of GDP spent on health [9, Figure 7.3]. But the cost-containment measures described at the end of the chapter appear to have been effective, at least so far, as exemplified by the fact that this percentage of GDP devoted to health had not budged since 2010 [10, 11, p. 175]. There are, of course, consequences to cost containment particularly in the context of an aging population and the concomitant chronic diseases of its members. In June 2019, French emergency room physicians and nurses staged strikes in dozens of hospitals across the country, warning of the health effects of recent and proposed budget austerity measures such as staffing freezes that have resulted in burnout [12].

The details

History

France has a long history of providing social protections for workers. Originally this was carried out mainly through nonprofit mutual-aid societies, where workers paid contributions and in return received protections for themselves and their families against the loss of income that could come about through illness, pregnancy, disability, old age, and death. These organizations, which date back to the 19th century, were voluntary until the late 1920s. Monika Steffan describes the mutual-aid societies as "non-profit organizations, independent of the state but strictly regulated, and ... managed by their members. They consequently enjoy a high level of public confidence that commercial insurance companies have difficulty acquiring" [13, p. 361].

In 1930, the Act on Social Security required that employees earning below a particular income threshold obtain coverage; this coverage was jointly funded by the employers and the workers. The coverage included financial protection against the costs of illness, maternity, disability, old age, and death. It is estimated that two-thirds of the French population was covered by them in 1939 [11, p. 22].

One major problem was that those who were not salaried workers or who were outside of the labor market were often not covered, although charitable care was sometimes available. Soon after World War II, the protections provided by these mutual-aid societies were subsumed by the passage of the French Social Security ordinances, which also added on social protections (both cash and services) for those otherwise not covered. Coverage became available for all income levels, not just those below a particular threshold. But because **premium** contributions were required, some people remained uninsured [4, 14].

Legislation requiring universal statutory health insurance (SHI) coverage was passed in France in 1999 with implementation of *Couverture Maladie Universelle* (CMU), which among other things provided free coverage for the poor. Previous to that, an estimated one to 2% of French citizens did not have coverage [4]. Because possessing additional health insurance (called complementary health insurance, or CHI, in France) was and still is necessary due to high nominal **coinsurance** rates, one part of the CMU program was the provision of access to free CHI coverage for the poorest French, called CMU-C. In 2004, those with incomes slightly higher than the CMU-C limit were provided premium subsidies to make CHI more affordable [14]. Finally, in 2016, CHI coverage was made compulsory for all private-sector employees, with researchers predicting that over 96% of the French will be covered [15].

Overview of the health insurance system

France has often been viewed as having a healthcare system that, like Germany's, was based on a **Bismarckian** social insurance ideal rather than being a national health program. As discussed earlier, it certainly began that way, with most of the population having job-based coverage as early as the 1930s. Over time, however, the system has morphed into one that in many ways more closely resembles a single-payer system like the ones that characterize Australia, Canada, the United Kingdom, and Sweden. To illustrate:

- People do not have a choice of statutory insurer (although they can choose their CHI company).
- The insurers that provide statutory coverage are often considered quasi-governmental, albeit private nonprofit entities.
- Government plays a leading role in setting provider fees, in consultation with physician trade unions.

There are just two main statutory health insurance funds' insurers in France. Which of the funds a person belongs is determined by employment and occupation status. The largest, covering about 88% of the population, is the national health insurance fund. This fund includes a dozen or so specific occupational groups as well as students and individuals not in the workforce. The agricultural workers' fund represents 5% of the population, while smaller funds cover the remaining 7%. These include national railway employees, the national electricity firm, and some others.[c] The same benefits are available to everyone irrespective of the source of insurance coverage. Moreover, they pay the same

---

[c] Paul Dourgnon, personal communication, October 19, 2019.

fees to hospitals and physicians so no patient is financially disadvantaged when seeking care.

Governance

A major difference between France and the other continental European countries covered in this book is the unusually strong role of government. Activities that are regulated at the national level include fee setting, quality monitoring, and technology assessment. Many other activities are carried out regionally, albeit under the central government's oversight, including planning and public health and healthcare prevention activities and efforts to coordinate care between the different sectors of the healthcare system to meet the needs of all population groups. The French system is not very decentralized in that the regional authorities are chosen by the health ministry and are often viewed as extensions of it.[d]

The French Parliament votes on government recommendations on the overall healthcare spending target for the following year through a system called ONDAM. Regulatory activities are carried out, in large measure, by various branches of the health ministry. Specific responsibilities include allotting the total budget to different sectors (e.g., hospitals, ambulatory care, and mental health), setting hospital fees, overseeing negotiated physician fees, setting drug prices, determining medical school enrollments, and overseeing quality and safety [11, p. 25].

In other countries with multiple insurers, and Germany in particular, the health insurance sector operates largely independently of the government. This is not the case in France, where central government and the SHI system work hand-in-hand in administering the system, jointly determining the services included in the benefit package as well as price and provider fee setting.

Financing

Overall, about 75% of French healthcare spending is through the SHI systems, 13% through CHI, and 7% OOP, with the remaining 5% through miscellaneous government and private sources [11, p. 68]. The financial role of supplemental insurance coverage is greater in France than in nearly all the other countries reviewed here.[e] OOP spending in France is considerably lower on average than in any of the other nine countries, although there is little information available on its distribution by socioeconomic characteristics.[d]

---

[d] Paul Dourgnon, personal communication, August 9, 2019.
[e] VHI also pays a similar share of healthcare expenses in Canada, but it plays a very different role (see Table 13.4). Its main role in France is to cover coinsurance, while in Canada, it focuses almost entirely on uncovered services, which vary by province but which may include prescription drugs, dental, and optical care.

Traditionally, countries that rely on **social health insurance** have raised the bulk of their revenue by taxing a percentage of payroll earnings, typically shared by the employer and employee. France moved away from this system in 1996 and now raises revenue from its employment sector in a different way: it taxes total income rather than just wage income. This not only is more progressive—people with higher labor incomes tend to have higher nonwage incomes as well—but it provides a more stable funding source for the system. Employers, however, still contribute a portion of total payroll: 13% in 2019 [16].

The tax rates on individuals vary according to the source of income. Employees contribute 7.5% of their wages (except for almost half of the population with lower incomes, who contribute 3.8), 8.2% of earnings on capital (e.g., interest and dividends), 6.6% of pension income, and 6.2% of income on benefits such as unemployment insurance [11, p. 77]. Other sources of revenue include taxes on tobacco and alcohol, various taxes on the pharmaceutical industry and CHI companies and on polluting companies [8, 11, p. 78]. The employee contributions are on top of a number of other payroll taxes for so-called social charges and pensions [17].

Coverage

Breadth

Essentially, all French people are covered under the statutory health insurance system. Moreover, the country is more generous than most with regard to undocumented immigrants; those who are poor can, after 3 months of residence [11, p. 71], receive subsidized medical care, although political issues surrounding immigration could change this. Nearly everyone has CHI, which covers coinsurance and additional services such as dental care.

Scope

France's healthcare system covers almost all services, although some, like dentistry and optical care, are covered more thinly than others. Dental care coverage expanded in 2020 with the SHI and dental associations agreeing to cap some prices. It is expected that more than half of dental spending will be fully covered, free from copayments, either through SHI or CHI [2].

Depth

Nominal patient cost-sharing requirements in SHI are high, mainly through substantial coinsurance requirements. Some are listed here, but the actual schedule is far more complicated, and many exceptions are noted in the next paragraph:

- 20% coinsurance for hospital care plus 18 euros per day for inpatient stays
- 30% coinsurance for physician and dentist care
- 40% coinsurance for tests
- 0%–85% coinsurance for prescription drugs, with 35% being typical [11, p. 76].

In spite of this, average per capita OOP spending in France is lower than in any of the other countries discussed in this book. There are two primary reasons for this: there are many exceptions to the coinsurance requirements, and nearly everyone has CHI. The most prominent exception from coinsurance requirements is for those who suffer from any of about 30 long-term or chronic conditions, including cancer, heart problems, stroke, diabetes, liver disease, lung disease, dementia, long-term psychiatric conditions, and a host of others [18, p. 62]. Other exceptions include maternity and newborn care, occupational injuries, and care for the disabled and military pensioners. Low-income patients are exempted from the coinsurance requirements as well [11, p. 74].

Two other aspects about the depth of coverage should be noted. The first is fairly minor: all physician services are subject to a 1-euro **copayment**; drugs, 0.5 euros; and medical transport, 2 euros, all of which is in keeping with European Union recommendations that care not be completely free when services are received. (These fees do not apply to children up to age 18, the poor, and pregnant women, and there is a separate 50-euro annual cap on copayments for physician visits, prescriptions, and dental care [11 (p. 77), 19].) The idea is to dissuade people from using services frivolously without at the same time creating a substantive financial barrier. CHI is prohibited from covering this cost.

The other aspect of coverage depth is far more significant: **balance billing**. There is a long tradition of balance billing in France that still exists today in physicians' private primary and specialty care practices. In fact, one of the reasons CHI is essential is for its coverage of most balance billing. In the past, physicians have sometimes billed for three times the government fee although more recently physician groups have agreed to keep it down to twice as much. Moreover, balance billing can be much higher for services poorly covered by the statutory insurance system, particularly dental and vision care. The fees paid to providers by insurers may be only a few euros for glasses and hearing aids and 200 euros for dentures. In instances like this, the providers may bill more than 10 times this much [8]. As in most countries, the largest sources of OOP spending are prescription drugs, dental care, and vision services [8]. Physicians are not allowed to balance-bill the poor, nor do these patients have to pay up front when they receive care.

Voluntary health insurance

We have kept the term VHI to make it consistent with other chapters, but in France, this additional coverage is called "complementary health insurance," or CHI. In fact, the term "voluntary" longer applies since nearly everyone has coverage. As noted, having CHI is essential in France due to high coinsurance requirements and balance billing by physicians. It is possessed by at least 96% of the population [15]; informational and financial barriers are often the reason why 4% of the French do not have CHI [20, 21]. There are a number of sources. The most common one is through group contracts negotiated by employers for their employees. Premiums are shared, with an estimated average of 56% paid by the employer, and the remainder, the employee [11, p. 88].

VHI typically covers the (high) nominal patient copayments for hospital and physician services, as well as services like dental and vision care, and sometimes amenities like single rooms in hospitals. It varies with regard to how much of balance billing is covered [22, 23].

Beginning in 2016, all employers have been required to provide CHI to their employees and pay at least half of the premiums [20]. In addition, each year policies must reimburse up to 125% of government fees for dental care and 100 euros per year for vision care [22], but balance billing for dental and vision care is often much higher than this.

There is another aspect of the French CHI system, however, that is highly progressive. The poorest French (an estimated 7% of the population) receive CHI from the government for free, and those with slightly higher incomes receive assistance with premiums, resulting in about 11% of the population being completely or partly subsidized via revenues derived largely from progressive taxes [20, 24].

Unlike statutory health insurance in France, which is essentially a government benefit, CHI is sold by hundreds of companies. In 2012, there were 682 CHI insurers, and even that was less than half the number from 10 years earlier [11, p. 88]. A large majority are nonprofit and do not charge more based on health status, but commercial insurers, which comprise about 13% of the market, can do so [11, p. 88]. To discourage this sort of behavior and protect people from facing large balance bills, in 2004 the government began to provide tax incentives to CHI insurers and policyholders to encourage appropriate service usage. By choosing a **gatekeeping** physician, nearly all OOP spending is covered by CHI, including certain preventive care services. In turn, insurers are not supposed to select enrollees on the basis of health status although they can charge more for different age groups.[f] Nearly all CHI policies now conform to this [11, p. 29, 24].

Choice

Choice is a hallmark of the French healthcare delivery system. While there is no choice of SHI insurer, French people have nearly complete freedom in choosing providers, particularly primary care providers and hospitals. Victor Rodwin has noted that professional autonomy[g] is exemplified by "selection of the physician by the patient, freedom for physicians to practice wherever they choose, clinical freedom for the doctor, and professional confidentiality" [4, p. 33].

---

[f] Monika Steffan, personal communication, September 20, 2020.
[g] Rodwin uses the term "liberalism" rather than "professional autonomy," connoting individual freedom.

One exception to this notion of complete freedom of choice is that the French system provides a financial incentive to patients to choose a "treating doctor," who in turn acts as gatekeeper, providing specialist referrals. Patients who seek specialty care without such a referral are reimbursed only 30% of the specialist's, compared to 70% if they are referred; CHI insurers typically do not cover the difference [11, p. 126]. It is noteworthy, though, that when patients are referred to specialty care, they can seek care from any such specialist. Although nearly everyone signs up for a preferred doctor, who in turn is nearly always the patient's regular GP, it is not clear that this has had an impact in reducing unnecessary specialist care [25].

Provider payment

Hospitals

Hospitals in France are a mix of public (35%), private nonprofit (26%), and for-profit (39%). Two-thirds of the beds, however, are in public hospitals [11, p. 100]. Hospital payment is set by the national health ministry, and this responsibility includes setting the fees that are paid to the hospitals. These payments to hospitals are based on a French diagnosis-related group (DRG) system called T2A. The French system is like the American one except that there are far more disease categories: 2200, compared to about 750 in the US Medicare program. Like most DRG-type systems, hospitals receive a fixed payment per patient stay under the T2A system. These are augmented by block grants to encourage hospitals to provide specialized services (e.g., organ transplants), services deemed to be in the interests of the public's health, medical education, and some new medical technologies that have yet to be placed on the national list of covered services [11, p. 94].

One peculiarity of the system is that the fees paid to public and private hospitals differ, and these fees also cover different things. T2A covers all costs for a stay in public hospitals, but in private hospitals, it does not cover physician fees or the costs of certain tests and imaging procedures. This is further complicated by the fact that total inpatient spending is subject to national expenditure targets that are voted on by Parliament and that there are separate targets for the public and private sectors. If volume is higher than predicted, T2A payments will decline the next year. The process has been criticized as being opaque, making it difficult for hospitals to effectively plan since they do not know their revenue streams in future years [26].

Physicians

As is typical internationally, fee-for-service (FFS) payment is the norm in France. In 2011, an estimated 94% of payments to primary care physicians were FFS-based, with the remaining 6% from salary or based on financial incentives, although since that time the latter number has doubled or more.[d] Physicians are increasingly rewarded financially on a per-patient basis for care coordination for their chronically ill patients, complying with quality guidelines, and using electronic means of filing claims. The payment methods for specialists, in contrast, are more varied, with a little over one-third paid on a FFS basis with many of the remainder being paid a salary by hospitals or having a mix of income sources [8].

The fees are set by the health ministry based on negotiations between SHI and physician trade unions [11, p. 20]. As noted, balance billing is common in France, but whether a physician is allowed to do so is based in part on their "sector." Sector 1 doctors cannot balance bill, while those in Sector 2 (an estimated 42% of specialists and 11% of GPs) are permitted to so long as they demonstrate "tact and moderation," [27] which is obviously subjective. Because of the financial and equity problems that can result from balance billing, the SHI controls who and how many physicians can join this sector, limiting new entrants to those with full-time public hospital appointments [11, p. 96, 164].

Interestingly, French primary care physicians are far more likely than those in the other countries covered here to express unhappiness about their incomes. In 2015, 44% of French primary care doctors expressed dissatisfaction. This was higher than any of our countries (Japan, which was not included) [28]. The results are intriguing because the estimated incomes of generalist physicians in France were slightly higher than in the Netherlands and Australia, and almost 30% higher than Swedes [29] (only 18% of whom expressed dissatisfaction) [28].

Pharmaceuticals [30, 31]

Pharmaceutical fees in France are determined through a government economic committee, called CEPS, with input from pharmaceutical manufacturers. The process considers such factors as the medical benefits derived from the drug and the price of substitute drugs already on the market. In addition, the process considers both the prices of comparable drugs as well as the prices paid in other countries, in particular, the United Kingdom, Germany, Italy, and Spain. New drugs are evaluated on a five-point scale with regard to their medical benefit compared to existing products or therapies on the market. The five categories are: major innovation, important improvement, moderate improvement, minor improvement, and no improvement.

Annual price increases after the drug's launch are limited and typically are lowered after 5 years. There is also a national annual limit of growth in drug spending, which, when exceeded, requires drug companies to provide government rebates of 50%–70% [23]. Moreover, patients are given significant incentives to use drugs deemed to be medically effective. Reimbursement for such drugs is 65%, compared to just 15%–30% for others [11, p. 49]. Drugs viewed as irreplaceable, such as HIV drugs, are fully reimbursed, however, as are those used for patients with other chronic diseases.

France has been slower than many other countries to embrace generics but various government policies are being attempted to reverse this. In 2017, only 30% of prescriptions were generic compared to rates exceeding 80% for Germany, the United Kingdom, and the United States (Table 15.6). Among the countries included in this book, only Switzerland had a lower rate than France (23%).

Incentives to increase France's use of generic prescriptions are aimed at patients, physicians, and pharmacists. At the patient level, those who demand brand-name drugs whose benefits are deemed to be insufficient are only reimbursed for 15% of the fee. French physicians have "freedom of prescription" that allows them to choose what drugs to prescribe [32]; however, generics are encouraged through financial incentives [33]. Finally, pharmacists are permitted to substitute generic drugs unless expressly prohibited by the physician on the prescription. They can also earn a higher fee when doing so and, in addition, can earn an annual bonus of up to 3000 euros by meeting certain thresholds for filling generics [11, p. 98].

Assuring access and equity

The French healthcare system is based on the notion of solidarity. In Chapter 2, Martine Bellinger and Philipe Mosse described this as "sharing of resources, equality of all in the face of illness" [34, p. S119]. As further elaborated on by T.R. Reid, "Whenever the French talk about health care, they invoke the concept of 'solidarite', the notion that all French citizens must stick solidly together to help one another in time of need" [5, p. 64]. There is no organized political opposition to this historical tenet.[b]

French health policy exemplifies this mind-set. It is true that there are substantial coinsurance requirements, necessitating possession of CHI, but exceptions are made for those with serious illnesses, the poor, and several other situations.

There are, nevertheless, a number of aspects of the system that have the potential to diminish access and equity. First, approximately 4% of the population has not obtained CHI, although everyone is eligible for it. Second, balance billing is common in France, and CHI does not necessarily cover all of it, and sometimes, covers none of it. Third, statutory health insurance coverage for certain services, notably dentistry, optical care, and hearing aids, is meager—again necessitating CHI. Fourth, the system is complex, particularly for disadvantaged populations. Poorer French need to sign up for their free CHI and the near poor must apply for vouchers that provide subsidies. Cost-sharing requirements are complicated, and electronic medical records lag behind other countries.

There is a fifth barrier unique to France among the countries discussed here. For most care provided by private primary care and specialist physicians, the French have to pay for care up front and wait for their insurance reimbursement. This appears to have indeed impaired access by lower-income persons.

The French government has been concerned about this but has, as yet, been unable to succeed in making wholesale changes to this, in large measure due to opposition of physician groups, who argue that direct payment from the patient is a key component of professional autonomy.[h] This does not mean that the less-advantaged French do not also face other barriers to obtaining care (e.g., income, education, or geographic); income disparities have more of an impact on access to care in France than in several neighboring countries [35].

While wholesale changes have not been made regarding this issue, very recently there have been some helpful developments. In particular, beginning in January 2020, all French people are beginning to have access to certain services free of charge or at very reduced fees (e.g., eyeglasses, dental crowns, and implants, with hearing aids coming in 2021) [36].[i] As will be seen in Chapter 14, findings from the Commonwealth Fund 2016 population survey, which includes all of our countries except Japan, showed substantial cost-related barriers among French with lower than average incomes in 2016, 41% who say that they had a serious problem paying or were unable to pay medical bill—a figure more than double that of all the other countries except the United States [3, Appendix 5]. The 2020 survey, however, found that this disparity had fallen to just 13 percentage points.[j]

Controlling expenditures

France ranked fourth among the counties in this book, spending 11.2% of its national income on health in 2019. In terms of per capita spending, it is 7th, reflecting its somewhat lower average incomes than the other countries (see Table 15.3) [37].

The French healthcare system is one of the most expensive in the world. Some of the tools that France has used in recent year to meet its spending targets include [8, 11 (p. 160), 14]:

- Continuing to set relatively low fees for physicians' services.
- Focusing on prescription drugs in several ways: removing an estimated 600 drugs from the list of approved medications; providing incentives to patients, physicians, and pharmacists to substitute generic for brand-name drugs; and reducing drug prices.
- Moving more surgical services to the outpatient setting and reducing the number of hospital beds and expenditures.
- Providing strong financial incentives to patients to choose a "preferred doctor," who acts as a gatekeeper for specialty referrals, although it is not clear that this has made much of an impact of the use of specialist care.

---

[h] Paul Dourgnon, personal communication, May 25, 2018.
[i] Monika Steffan, personal communication, September 11, 2020.
[j] Roosa Tikkanen, personal communication, September 2, 2020.

- Negotiating with physician organizations to reduce the frequency and the amount of balance billing.
- Employing health technology assessment for all new medical procedures, devices, and prescription drugs before allowing them to be covered by SHI, as well as to determine their reimbursement rates.
- Encouraging better care coordination by (among other things) providing primary care physicians with financial incentives to coordinate the care of their chronically ill patients.

In spite of these, the French system is designed in a way that makes cost-containment challenging. First, OOP costs are low, stimulating strong consumer demand for services. Second, physicians are largely paid on a FFS basis, encouraging higher volumes. Third, French physicians have always demanded a great deal of autonomy, and there is, according to Karine Chevreul and colleagues, of a "strong culture in French medical practice of offering prescriptions for every symptom" [11, p. 162]. Finally, many observers have complained for decades about lack of care coordination, between both inpatient and outpatient sectors, as well as between health care and social care, both of which can have quality, cost, and equity implications [8, 11, p. xxvi]. Ezekiel Emanuel talks of a patient who, "whenever he goes to his physician he makes sure to bring his own X-rays and other test results; otherwise the consulting physician will not be able to access them" [23, p. 143].

One macrolevel method historically used by France is putting an annual expenditure target on health expenditures: ONDAM. Since the mid-1990s, the French Parliament has set such an expenditure target on the following year's total health spending and, at the same time, set premium contribution rates and taxes to fund those expected expenditures [11, p. 24]. The health ministry, in turn, disaggregates the target into such categories as hospital, private ambulatory care, and health and social care; allocates the budget to different sectors of the system; sets hospital fees and drug prices; and oversees the negotiation of physician fees [11, p. 81]. A related success has been what Emanual has concluded to be "remarkable control over drug pricing," with a retail price index far lower than in neighboring Germany and Switzerland [23, p. 163].

Previously, it had been difficult for the French system to stay below this ceiling since there is little in the way of utilization controls; the ceiling would most accurately be viewed as "soft" because it was exceeded almost every year until 2010. Expenditure growth each year between 2010 and 2014, however, was below the ceiling as a result of other cost-containment efforts [11, p. 59].

Key policy issues

There are, of course, concerns that arise when there is such a great focus on cost containment. These include geographic and socioeconomic health disparities as well financial disparities in accessing services. There have been continuing efforts, as yet largely unsuccessful, in having insurers pay providers directly so patients do not have to pay the entire bill first as well as reducing the incidence and amount of balance billing.

In December 2015, France passed a major health reform law designed to address some existing efficiency and equity concerns [11 (p. 173), 38, 39]. Much of the emphasis was on improving health promotion and disease prevention, better coordination of chronic care for the elderly, and extending patient rights. Regarding equity, efforts were to be made to improve geographic equity across the country. More controversially, the extension of direct billing was included, with the original goal of having it in place for all residents by 2017. However, this has continued to draw the ire of the physician community and its implementation is being delayed.

In September 2018, the government put forward a major initiative calling for restructuring the healthcare system, with an additional 400 million euros being invested through an increase in the ONDAM expenditure target. There are three parts of the initiative. The first relates to making medical school training more practical and patient-focused, along with augmenting the pool of physician assistants. The second is to improve coordination of care within geographic regions and in particular, to organize a system of triage where "less serious emergencies" can be treated so as to take the pressure of hospital emergency departments, and well as by distinguishing the roles of community vs specialized hospitals. The third is to improve both the quality and efficiency of hospital care through payment reform, creating financial incentives to encourage quality, and augment the role of nurses as key caregivers in hospitals, in response to concerns that "nursing staff are experiencing a sense of loss of meaning and are left with the impression that there is no time for what really matters nor any opportunities for career development" [40].

References

[1] Gay JG, Parisi V, Devauxi M, De Looper M. Mortality amenable to health care in 31 OECD countries: Estimates and methodological issues. OECD Health Working Papers, Paris: OECD Publishing; 2011.

[2] OECD and European Observatory on Health Systems and Policies. France: Country health profile 2019. State of health in the EU. Paris: OECD Publishing; 2019.

[3] Schneider EC, Sarnak DO, Squires D, Shah A, Doty MM. Mirror, mirror 2017: International comparison reflects flaws and opportunities for better U.S. health care. Mirror, Mirror: The Commonwealth Fund; 2017.

[4] Rodwin VG. The health care system under French national health insurance: lessons for health reform in the United States. Am J Public Health 2003;93(1):31–7.

[5] Reid TR. The healing of America: A global quest for better, cheaper, and fairer Health care. New York: Penguin Press; 2009.

[6] Samuel H. French doctors strike in protest at 'NHS-style' reforms. The Telegraph; 2014. [Online news]. [Accessed 31 October 2020]. Available from: https://www.telegraph.co.uk/news/world-news/europe/france/11310892/French-doctors-strike-in-protest-at-NHS-style-reforms.html.

[7] McPartland B. French doctors strike against health reforms. The Local; 2015. [Online news]. [Accessed 31 October 2020]. Available from: https://www.thelocal.fr/20150313/french-doctors-strike-in-protest-over-health-reforms.

[8] Durand-Zaleski I. In: Tikkanen R, Osborn R, Mossialos E, Djordjevic A, Wharton GA, editors. France. International health care system profiles. The Commonwealth Fund; 2020. [Internet]. [Accessed 31 October 2020]. Available from: https://www.commonwealthfund.org/international-health-policy-center/countries/france.

[9] OECD. Health at a glance 2019. Paris: OECD Publishing; 2019.

[10] OECD.Stat. Health Status. OECD [Web browser]. [Accessed 31 October 2020]. Available from: https://stats.oecd.org/index.aspx?DataSetCode=HEALTH_STAT#.

[11] Chevreul K, Brigham KB, Durand-Zaleski I, Hernández-Quevedo C. France: health system review. Health Syst Transit 2015;17(3):1–218.

[12] Chrisafis A. French medics warn health service is on brink of collapse. The Guardian; 2019. [Online]. [Accessed 31 October 2020]. Available from: https://www.theguardian.com/world/2019/jun/11/french-medics-health-service-collapse-doctors-nurses-protest-outside-french-health-ministry-strikes.

[13] Steffen M. The French health care system: liberal universalism. J Health Polit Policy Law 2010;35(3):353–87.

[14] Kobouloff S, Baiyasi S. France. In: Johnson J, Stoskoft C, Shi L, editors. Comparative health systems: A global perspective. 2nd ed. Burlington, MA: Jones & Bartlett Learning; 2018.

[15] Pierre A, Jusot F. The likely effects of employer-mandated complementary health insurance on health coverage in France. Health Policy 2017;121(3):321–8.

[16] Employer/Employee Social Security Contributions in France. French-Property.com [Internet]. [Accessed 31 October 2020]. Available from: https://www.french-property.com/guides/france/finance-taxation/taxation/social-security/employers-employees.

[17] Social Charges. French-Property.com [Internet]. [Accessed 31 October 2020]. Available from: https://www.french-property.com/guides/france/finance-taxation/taxation/social-security/social-welfare-levy.

[18] Chevreul K, Durand-Zaleski I, Bahrami S, Hernández-Quevedo C, Mladovsky P. In: Hernández-Quevedo C, Mladovsky P, Mossialos E, editors. France: Health system review. 6th ed. Health systems in transition, vol. 12. Copenhagen: The European Observatory on Health Systems and Policies; 2010.

[19] Rice T, Quentin W, Anell A, Barnes AJ, Rosenau P, Unruh LY, et al. Revisiting out-of-pocket requirements: trends in spending, financial access barriers, and policy in ten high-income countries. BMC Health Serv Res 2018;18(1):371. Table 3 Key Out-of-Pocket Payment Requirements in the most Recent Year, by Country.

[20] Steffen M. Universalism, responsiveness, sustainability—regulating the French health care system. N Engl J Med 2016;374(5):401–5.

[21] Gandré C, Or Z. In: Chevreul K, Durand-Zaleski I, Gandré C, Or Z, editors. A specific plan to decrease forgone healthcare. France: The health systems and policy monitor. The European Observatory on Health Systems and Policies; 2019. [Online countrypage]. [Accessed 31 October 2020]. Available from: https://www.hspm.org/countries/france25062012/countrypage.aspx.

[22] Sagan A, Thomson S. Voluntary health insurance in Europe. vol. 1. United Kingdom: WHO Regional Office for Europe; 2016.

[23] Emanuel EJ. Which country has the world's best health care? New York: PublicAffairs; 2020.

[24] Franc C, Pierre A. Compulsory private complementary health insurance offered by employers in France: implications and current debate. Health Policy 2015;119(2):111–6.

[25] Dourgnon P, Naiditch M. The preferred doctor scheme: a political reading of a French experiment of gate-keeping. Health Policy 2010;94(2):129–34.

[26] Or Z. Implementation of DRG Payment in France: issues and recent developments. Health Policy 2014;117(2):146–50.

[27] Choné P, Coudin É, Pla A. Are physician fees responsive to competition? Health, Econometrics and Data Group; 2014.

[28] Anon. 2015 International survey of primary care doctors. The Commonwealth Fund; 2015. [Data]. [Accessed 31 October 2020]. Available from: https://www.commonwealthfund.org/sites/default/files/documents/___media_files_surveys_2015_2015_ihp_survey_topline_11_20_15.pdf.

[29] Papanicolas I, Mossialos E, Gundersen A, Woskie L, Jha AK. Performance of UK National Health Service compared with other high income countries: observational study. BMJ 2019;367:l6326.

[30] Chicoye A, Chhabra A. France—Pharmaceuticals: Global health technology assessment road map. ISPOR; 2009.

[31] Rodwin MA. What can the United States learn from pharmaceutical spending controls in France? The Commonwealth Fund; 2019.

[32] Anon. French code of medical ethics. French National Medical Council; 2013.

[33] Pomey M-P, Denis J-L, Vergnaud S, Préval J, Saint-Lary O. Innovation in physician remuneration in France: what lessons for Canada? Health Reform Obs—Observatoire des Réformes de Santé 2019;7(2).

[34] Bellanger MM, Mosse PR. The search for the Holy Grail: combining decentralised planning and contracting mechanisms in the French health care system. Health Econ 2005;14(Suppl. 1):S119–32.

[35] OECD and European Observatory on Health Systems and Policies. France: Country health profile 2017. State of health in the EU. Paris: OECD Publishing; 2017.

[36] Anon. 100% health reform for eyes, ears and teeth in France. P-O Life; 2020. [Online]. [Accessed 31 October 2020]. Available from: https://anglophone-direct.com/100-health-reform-for-eyes-ears-and-teeth-in-france/.

[37] Anon. OECD health statistics 2020. OECD; 2020. [Online Database]. [Accessed 26 August 2020]. Available from: http://www.oecd.org/els/health-systems/health-data.htm.

[38] Brigham KB, Durand-Zaleski I. In: Chevreul K, Durand-Zaleski I, Gandré C, Or Z, editors. Final passage of health reform law. France: The health systems and policy monitor. The European Observatory on Health Systems and Policies; 2015. [Online countrypage]. [Accessed 31 October 2020]. Available from: https://www.hspm.org/countries/france25062012/countrypage.aspx.

[39] Brigham KB, Durand-Zaleski I. In: Chevreul K, Durand-Zaleski I, Gandré C, Or Z, editors. Assembly vote on final version of health reform legislation. France: The health systems and policy monitor. The European Observatory on Health Systems and Policies; 2015. [Online countrypage]. [Accessed 31 October 2020]. Available from: https://www.hspm.org/countries/france25062012/countrypage.aspx.

[40] Health system transformation strategy. Gouvernement [Online]. [Accessed 31 October 2020]. Available from: https://www.gouvernement.fr/en/health-system-transformation-strategy.

Chapter 8

Japan

The big picture

Japan has the highest life expectancy in the world, with women living to an average age of 87 and men to 81 [1]. There are many reasons for this; Japan's healthcare system, which provides nearly universal and equitable access to high-quality care, is surely one of them. Lifestyle and health habits are likely far more important, however. While the Japanese are becoming increasingly overweight, few reach the level of obesity[a]: 3.7% of Japanese are classified as obese, just one-tenth of the American rate of 38.2% [2]. This is partly the result of the Japanese diet, which relies more on fish, soybean products, and vegetables and less on fat than that of many other countries [3]. Moreover, observers have noted a strong attention to hygiene in daily life and an unusual degree of health consciousness [4]. Similar reasons likely explain the fact that Japan also has the world's lowest infant mortality rates.

The fact that there are multiple reasons why the Japanese live longer should not take away from the accomplishments of the healthcare system, and, in another measure of population health more directly related to health system performance, **mortality amenable to health care** (see Chapter 15), Japan also ranks among the best in the world [5]. What is it, then, about the healthcare system that helps make the Japanese population?

Japan achieved universal coverage earlier than most other countries, in 1961, and did so in a way that helped ensure that nearly everyone was covered for the same benefits and paid the same amounts when seeking care. Equity has always been a hallmark of the system [6 (p. 6), 7].

Universal coverage is carried out by a bewildering array of thousands of insurers to which people are assigned based on their employment, geographic location, or age. But with the major exception of **premium** payments, one's specific insurer does not affect access to care: everyone is covered for the same rich array of services, faces the same cost-sharing requirements (dependent only one age), and importantly, is worth the same amount to hospitals and doctors, thus helping to ensure that one patient does not receive favorable status over another. Few Japanese claim that the costs of care are keeping them from seeking

---

[a] Obesity is defined as a body mass index (BMI) of 30 or more, while overweight is defined as a BMI of 25 or higher.

Health Insurance Systems: An International Comparison. https://doi.org/10.1016/B978-0-12-816072-5.00015-8

it—fewer, in fact, than in the majority of the other countries examined in this book [6, p. 176]. Moreover, Japan has among the highest number of hospital beds, physician visit rates, and high-tech equipment of any country.

Indeed, there is then every reason to expect that the Japanese would have to spend quite a lot for this type of system. But spending is surprisingly low compared to the other countries, with 11.1% of GDP devoted to health in 2019, the 6th highest among the 10 countries covered in this book. This is striking because Japan has by far the oldest population of any country in the world, with 27% of people aged 65 and older. Italy, the country with the second highest figure, is at 23% and none of the other countries reviewed in this book exceeds 21% [8].

Japan's level of spending will almost certainly continue to rise as the population continues to age with little replenishment from births. The country's total fertility rate (births per woman during her lifetime) is 1.48, far lower than population replacement levels of 2.1. In the year 2000, Japan devoted only 7.6% of its economy to health care. The proportionate increase of 46%, to 11.1%, is higher than any of the other nine countries considered here [9].[b] These issues are further magnified by other burgeoning governmental costs associated with aging, and in particular, cash pensions.

These financial challenges are further aggravated by another way in which Japan is exceptional. The central government carries the largest debt in the world, with a level of 2.3 times that of GDP.[c] This is far higher than Greece, at second place with 1.8 times GDP. It is more than double that of the United States (1.1 times GDP), and which ranks second after Japan among the 10 countries considered here [10]. This means that more of Japan's current production needs to be spent on debt repayment—and estimated 25% of the national budget [11]—and therefore less on everything else.

These dual burdens of both health care and pensions will become amplified over time as the age dependency ratio (basically, the number of those too old or young to work divided by the working-age population) continues to rise. Japan had the highest ratio of all OECD countries in 2015, at 0.46; by 2050, it is projected to still be the highest, with a far higher dependency ratio: 0.78 [12]. One recent fiscal consequence has been a large increase in a general consumption tax affecting the entire population, with more increases most likely in the offing.

Japan has a number of tools in its arsenal to control its healthcare expenditures. One factor dwarfs all others: its fee schedule. The Japanese central government sets fees for all medical and surgical procedures and for all prescription drugs. In doing so, medical and surgical fees in particular are extremely low by international standards. This has been effective in controlling how much the

---

[b] One reason that expenditure figures rose was that beginning in 2015, long-term care expenses began to be included in total expenditure data.

[c] All the numbers cited here are before the COVID-19 pandemic, which increased debt considerably in most countries.

country spends on health, although as examined below, may result in a higher quantity and inefficient mix of services provided and consumed. In the case of prescription drugs, Japanese prices appear to be roughly comparable to other countries examined here except for the United States [13, 14].

If Japan had a more unified insurance system, it would likely be easier to deal with the growing financial burden in a coherent fashion. As noted, there are thousands of insurers divided into several groupings, most with different risk pools and therefore varying premiums. The risk pool for those not in the labor force has become increasingly expensive due to its composition, which includes retirees up to the age of 75. Furthermore, the risk pool that includes those aged 75 and older is heavily subsidized by those with employer-based insurance coverage. Nearly half of the money these employers and employees contribute to health care goes not to their own health benefits but to these others. While perhaps speaking well to the egalitarianism of the Japanese healthcare system, the extent to which this trend can continue is a political question. Reo Takaku and colleagues note that "both management and labor have bitterly complained about the transfer payments they have been forced to make..." [15]. In short, Japan faces a ticking time bomb—one that many other countries face, but which is on schedule to detonate earlier than most.

The details

History

Japan began its journey toward universal coverage early, in the 1920s, initially for manual laborers, and for similar reasons as Germany experienced three decades earlier: according to John Campbell and colleagues, as an effort by government and business "to keep workers healthy and ward off the appeal of socialism" [16, p. 18]. But because not everyone is in the workforce, a parallel program for those not engaged in the labor force was developed in the 1930s, administered by the municipalities, and based on geographic location. Coverage, however, was not universal because enrollment in these municipal programs was voluntary. Thus, a large portion of the population remained uninsured.

After World War II, and spurred by the Allied Powers that occupied Japan after the war, there was a push to improve public health and welfare to prevent disease from breaking out, in part to quell the potentially resulting unrest [17]. This was followed soon thereafter by a period of lightning-fast economic growth,[d] with universal coverage being achieved in 1961. As was the case both in Japan and in several European countries from an earlier period, this was partly politically motivated. According to Michael Reich and Kenji Shibuya, one intent was "to weaken the agendas of the Socialist and Communist parties

---

[d] Real (i.e., inflation adjusted) annual economic growth was 9.6% between 1955 and 1970. In contrast, between 1990 and 2011, it was just 1.0%.

by redistributing social resources to industrial workers" [18, p. 1793]. Universal coverage was accomplished mainly on a community-by-community basis, requiring those who were not covered by employer-based systems to obtain coverage through the municipality in which they lived. Various changes have been made over the past five decades, particularly with regard to the older population, but the basis of the original system remains.

Looking back, Japan was an early adopter of health insurance as well as universal coverage. However, some view the segue from voluntary to universal coverage as a missed opportunity to consolidate the healthcare system into a more coherent entity [19]. As stated by John Campbell and colleagues,

> *A negative lesson is that the Japanese government never tried hard to consolidate its health insurance programs, even when there might have been a window of opportunity in 1959. It continually took the path of least political resistance by layering on new and different programs for each group covered—small-firm employees, self- and nonemployees, poor people, and older people. The resulting anomalies and imbalances have continued to plague health policy making and have added to the system's complexity, making it hard to understand—let alone reform [16, p. 25].*

Even if political forces did not allow the merger of employer group plans with those offered by the municipalities, it still might be desirable that some consolidation occur among the over 1700 municipal government plans [19]. A step in that direction was made in 2018, when municipal plans were aggregated at the regional (prefecture) level, although it is too early to know the results of this change.

Overview of the health insurance system

The complexity of the Japanese healthcare system begins with the fact that there are several different sources of coverage depending on employment, geographic location, or age. These are listed here with shares of the population as of 2018[e]:

(a) Employees and dependents of large companies (23% of population)
(b) Public servants and dependents (7% of population)
(c) Employees and dependents of small and medium-sized companies (30% of population)
(d) Community-based coverage for the self-employed, part-time employed, unemployed, or aged 65–74 (26% of population)
(e) Aged 75 or older (13% of population) [6 (p. 56), 20]

The first three categories comprise the Employees' Health Insurance system. More information is provided in Table 8.1.

---

[e] There is one more category, Seaman's Insurance, but this is held by just 0.1% of the population.

TABLE 8.1 Major insurance schemes in Japan, 2019.

Name of insurance scheme	Insurer	Target population	Number of insurers
National Health Insurance	Municipal governments, NHI societies	Self-employed, unemployed, elderly	47 regions and 164 NHI societies
Employees' Health Insurance			
1. JHIA	JHIA	Small and medium-sized companies	1
2. SMHI	Corporate-based health insurance society	Large-sized companies	1388
3. MAS	Mutual-aid societies	Public servants	85
Late-stage medical care system for the elderly	Central, regions, and municipalities	People aged 75 and older	47 administered by coalitions of municipalities at the prefecture level

Notes: *JHIA*, Japan Health Insurance Association; *MAS*, Mutual Aid Societies; *NHI*, National Health Insurance; *SMHI*, Society-Managed Health Insurance.
Sources: Sakamoto H, Rahman M, Nomura S, Okamoto E, Koike S, Yasunaga H et al. Japan Health System Review. vol. 8, no. 1. New Delhi: World Health Organization, Regional Office for SouthEast Asia; 2018. Tables 3.10 and 3.11. Federation of Health Insurance Unions. Health insurance association budget early tabulation results about the outlook for the '2022 crisis.' [in Japanese]. https://www.kenporen.com/include/press/2019/201904222.pdf.

Further complicating the landscape is that there are as few as one, or as many over 1000 sources of health insurance within each of these five categories. While there is a single insurer for employees of small and medium-sized companies, and several dozen for people aged 75 and older run by coalitions of municipalities at the prefecture level,[f] there are large numbers of employer and municipal systems. Why so many health insurance programs? Most large employers have always administered their own programs. Moreover, each of the 47 regions in Japan is required to have a program for the self-employed and others not in the labor force. It bears remembering, however, no matter what program a patient is enrolled in, the services covered and cost-sharing requirements are the same (within an age and income group). As will be seen, the same cannot be said about premium payments.

---

[f] Naoki Ikegami, personal communication, August 5, 2019.

Governance

In Japan, the central government plays a very strong role in overseeing and regulating the healthcare delivery system. The primary governmental body is the Ministry of Health, Labour, and Welfare, but much of the service delivery is overseen by the 47 regions (prefectures) that administer the community-based health insurance plans. As in other wealthy countries, professional organizations are very influential in providing input on policy—particularly the Japanese Medical Association, which represents doctors. One of the most important roles of the central government is administering the national fee schedule, described later. Many activities devolve to the regions and municipalities, which among other things carry out preventive and screening services such as children's checkups, vaccinations, and preventive activities and screening for adults aged 40 and older [6, p. 29].

Financing

Japan is a heavily public-financed system, with 84% of expenditures paid for through compulsory health insurance sources. OOP spending is around the median of the countries in this book—13%—with only a tiny portion of expenses paid through voluntary health insurance (VHI), which, as discussed later, does not focus on healthcare reimbursement but rather on replacing lost income during illness.

The system's complexity is epitomized in its financing structure, and in particular, various ways in which those with different health insurance are cross-subsidized by different levels of government as well as by those with other types of insurance. Nearly half of premiums raised in the large employer sector, for example, are used to help pay the costs of others [15, p. 50].

As in other countries' **social health insurance** systems, historically the bulk of revenue has come from contributions from employers and employees but gradually the system is becoming more reliant on taxes. In 1985, premiums constituted 54% of health revenues, and taxes, 33%. By 2014, taxes had risen to 39%, and premiums had fallen to 49% [6, p. 52]. Part of the shortfall has been made up for by greater reliance on consumption (e.g., sales) taxes. Before 2009, the national consumption tax was 5% tax. It was raised to 8% in 2014 and rose to 10% in 2019. It is noteworthy that this is still far lower than in European Union countries, which are required to have value-added tax rates of at least 15%—a rate exceeded by most. Indeed, the OECD claims that Japan's consumption tax rate is not nearly high enough, recommending a rate of 20%–26% to bring national debt down to an acceptable level. This is certainly unlikely, though, given the many years it has taken to go even from 5 to 10% [21].

For large employers, premiums are shared (often but not always equally) between the employer and employee, the latter's contribution being withheld from wages. Each of the 1400 or so large employers and 85 public employee groups has its own premium rates based on the healthcare expenditures of its workers and their dependents. This creates what economists call a horizontal inequity: two people who otherwise share similar characteristics, but in this casework for different employers, may pay different premium rates. The average premium is about 10% of wages (shared between the employer and employee) [6, p. 52].

In contrast, there is a single organization, the Japan Health Insurance Association (JHIA), that consolidates health insurance coverage for everyone working for a small or medium-sized employer. Increasingly, it has been difficult for it to rely solely on these premiums to pay for health care, so it is now subsidized by about 16% by the central government. The most financially troubled insurance program is the National Health Insurance (NHI), because its risk pool includes more and more elders up to the age of 74.

Earlier it was mentioned that the employment-based system lacks **horizontal equity**, and this is also true of the NHI system for the self-employed, unemployed, and younger seniors. Take, for example, enrollees in the NHI program with household incomes of about $37,000 in 2010. The average premium contribution was 9.3% of income, but it ranged from 4.2% to 17.7%, according to the municipality of residence. Those at the 10th percentile paid 7.6% of their income in premiums, compared to 12.5% for those in the 90th percentile [15]. To make horizontal equity matters worse, premium contribution rates in NHI average triple those in the large employer sectors. This is a particular financial challenge when employees retire; by moving from the employment to NHI systems they often experience a financial shock [7].As noted throughout, Japan has grappled and will do so increasingly, with an aging population. Because their medical costs so much, their inclusion in insurers' risk pools made it difficult to keep premiums manageable. Beginning in 2008, those aged 75 and older were put into their own insurance category, the late-stage medical care system for the elderly. The system is heavily cross-subsidized, with 50% being financed by government, 40% by the working-age population, and the remaining 10% paid through premiums on elder enrollees. The premiums are based on a formula that includes both a fixed amount (about $500) plus an income-related amount (that includes pension income) [22], which often results in a large financial burden on these elders.[g]

Finally, we touch on **vertical equity**: whether the system accounts for the differential financial burden of premiums on those with lower incomes. As discussed in Chapter 2, in most countries, income taxes are progressive while consumption taxes, payroll taxes, and OOP payments are regressive. When these are combined, Japan's system historically has tended to show a largely proportional burden: those with low, middle, and upper-middle incomes pay a similar proportion of income on health care, although the rich pay a lower percentage of income toward health care. This had been the case from 1989 to 2004. The

---

[g] Reo Takaku, personal communication, September 23, 2019.

system was found to be regressive in 2009, the most recent year for which these data were available, but this was likely an anomaly during the world economic recession taking place at that time [6, p. 170].

Coverage

Breadth

Japan is usually viewed as providing universal coverage to citizens and other documented residents. There is, however, a small percentage of the population—mainly those working part-time who are not paying premiums even though their income requires them to do so—that falls through the cracks. Official statistics are not available, but it has been estimated on the order of 1%–3% [6, p. 169].

Scope

Japan's statutory health insurance provides an unusually comprehensive scope of benefits, including most dental care (but not orthodontia). Most services are subject to patient cost-sharing requirements but some services are free or have reduced rates. For example, preventive services for infants and children (check-ups, immunizations, etc.) are free, and very costly treatments such as kidney dialysis and receipt of antiretroviral drugs for AIDS have a modest **copayment** of about $100 per month [23].

In general, only curative services are covered by insurance; adult preventive services are not. For example, in the case of some vaccinations for influenza, patients must pay out of pocket. Financial resources to cover some preventive services such as cancer screening programs are provided by local governments. Consistent with this, insurance benefits do not cover normal childbirth deliveries although emergency deliveries and C-sections are covered. To compensate for this, the government provides cash subsidies to pregnant women to cover most of the costs. Providers generally do not charge more than this, so in essence, childbirth is covered [6, p. 69].

Depth

There is one aspect of Japan's complex financing system that is fairly simple: how much patients are assessed when they seek medical care. There are no deductibles, and patients cannot be **balance-billed**—that is, charged more than the national fee schedule. There is a **coinsurance** rate of 30% for most age groups. Those aged 70–74 pay 20%, and those aged 75 and older pay 10%. There is also a program aimed at lower-income children. Normally, preschoolers pay 20% coinsurance and older children, 30% but, depending on municipality, those whose families are eligible for the program usually pay nothing for their children's outpatient services and prescription drugs [24].

A coinsurance rate of 30% could, of course, pose a tremendous financial burden. This burden is lessened considerably, however, by strict maximums on

OOP spending. The formula is not very simple because it depends on age, income, and how many months in a year patients reach a monthly cap. To provide a single example, suppose a working-age individual had an income somewhere between $32,600 and $67,800 in 2015. Her maximum monthly liability would be $707 plus 1% of expenses above $2356. However, if she reached that maximum more than 3 months in the last 12, she would pay no more than $390 during the remaining months of the year [6, p. 69]. It is because of this OOP limit that Japan's share of health expenditures paid OOP (13%) is lower than the median of the other nine countries considered here (15%).

Voluntary health insurance

Unlike most of the other countries considered in this book, Japan does not have much in the way of VHI in the traditional sense. In those countries, VHI normally covers services not included in the statutory healthcare system (including amenities such private hospital rooms), improves access to services, and/ or reduces patient cost-sharing requirements. In Japan, an estimated 90% of Japanese have coverage that provides income replacement when a person becomes ill, thereby compensating for lost income when a person is unable to work [6 (p. 71), 25]. When obtained through an employer, premiums are typically split between the employer and employee.[h]

Choice

As noted, while there is no choice of insurer, Japanese citizens have a nearly complete choice of hospitals and doctors. Moreover, **gatekeeping** is not commonly employed. .

Provider payment

Hospitals

The central and regional governments of Japan strictly regulate the establishment of new hospitals as well as the expansion of existing hospitals. As in many countries, a large majority of hospitals (81%) are privately owned, and all are nonprofits [6, p. 74]. Japan has more hospital beds (13.2/1000 population), and longer lengths-of-stay (LOS) (16.5 days), than any other OECD country [9]. Part but not nearly all of the discrepancy between Japan and other countries is due to the hospitalization of some older patients as well as psychiatric patients who might be more appropriately served in long-term care (LTC) facilities. It has been estimated that 11% of Japanese hospital expenditures are for LTC compared to an average of 4% in all OECD countries [26].

---

[h] Yusuke Tsugawa, personal communication, July 31, 2019.

Japan has developed a unique way of paying for hospital care: the diagnosis-procedure combination (DPC) system. DPCs are similar to diagnosis-related groups in that patients are categorized based on their diagnosis and the procedures used for treatment, and that hospitals have an incentive to keep patients for a shorter amount of time. What is different is that under DPCs, hospitals are paid per diem amounts, but the per diem rates fall as the patient stays longer, reducing hospitals' financial incentive for excessively long stays. The system, however, does not apply to all hospital stays but instead just over half; excluded are very expensive services included surgery, radiation therapy, anesthesia, and complicated medical procedures [27]. It has been credited with reducing LOS but may have given hospitals an incentive to try to increase admissions, thereby possibly nullifying system-wide cost savings [9, 28]. Researchers have recommended a number of steps to make the system more comprehensive and better align the incentives between hospitals and government [28].

Physicians

Patients visit their doctors in Japan far more often than in the other countries discussed in this book: an average of 12.6 times per year, compared to a median of 6.8 among the other counties discussed here (Table 15.14). One explanation is that unit fees for physician visits are extremely low, providing a financial incentive to see more patients. Patients also sometimes see their physician to obtain refills on their medications.

Unlike the case with hospitals, the central government is not very involved in the regulation of physicians' practices; they can work anywhere they like and patients can see any doctor they wish. Instead, emphasis is placed on the way in which they are remunerated. The central government's Ministry of Health, Labour, and Welfare (MHLW) is responsible for administering a fee schedule that governs nearly all outpatient services—including prescription drugs. It updates the fee schedule every other year. This fee schedule is a hallmark of the Japanese system and is used to control expenditures. Prices apply to all regions in Japan, and providers cannot charge patients amounts in excess of the fee schedule.

While hospital-based physicians are salaried, almost all others are paid almost entirely on a fee-for-service (FFS) basis. The fee schedule lists over 4000 medical services and 130,000 pharmaceuticals. To determine biannual updates, the MHLW carries out both global and microprocesses. The global part involves coming up with a target rate of expenditure increase, which is determined by both the fiscal and political environments [29]. The microprocess relies more on negotiations with provider groups regarding how fees should change relative to each other [30]. While fee levels are mainly based on resource costs, government may increase fees for services it wishes to encourage and reduce them for those whose utilization is viewed as too high [29]. The fee schedule applies to the patients of all insurers so there is not a financial incentive to treat one patient instead of another. This is called an **"all-payer" system** (see Chapter 16).

Prices in the Japanese fee schedule are lower—often much lower—than elsewhere. For example, the fee for a follow-up visit to a physician at a clinic is only about $7 [31]. Payment for an MRI is about $150 in Japan [32], far less than the 2017 figures of over $1430 in the United States, $450 in the United Kingdom, $310 in Switzerland —but only slightly less than $190 paid in the Netherlands [33].

A basic criticism that economists often have of administered price systems is that they can distort behavior—in this case, physicians' behavior. A common response is to provide more of a service when the unit price declines, or perhaps order more tests, to help make up for the loss—called supplier-induced demand. Another response is to substitute different services that pay the physician more. The fact that Japan has the highest average number of physician visits per person among wealthy countries supports the notion that these things are occurring. But distortion can go in the other direction as well. In the case of low MRI prices, another possible response would be for physicians' order the test less often: because the price is so low, the service is a money loser, and it would be better to provide more profitable treatments. In 2002, Japan cut the reimbursement rate for MRIs by 31%, and expenditures fell sharply [29].

Pharmaceuticals

Traditionally Japan has spent much of its healthcare resources on pharmaceuticals. In 2016, 18.6% of total spending was on drugs, higher than any of the other countries in this book. (It was not highest in dollars spent, exceeded by the United States and Switzerland [34].) Part of the reason, historically, has been the low usage of generic drugs. In 2017, only 40% of prescriptions were generic, and just 15% of sales. The 40% figure is far lower than in the United States (90%), United Kingdom (85%), and Germany (82%) [35, Table 10.10, 36]. The government is now engaged in an effort to dramatically increase generic use, with the ambitious goal of reaching 80% by 2020 [37].

To some extent, pharmaceutical prices are formulated and updated in the same way as are physicians' services. The initial prices of new drugs are based on the prices of comparable drugs already on the market, or on the basis of costs when no such drugs already exist. The central government, acting on advice from various interest groups, updates fees periodically for particular drugs.

Once every 2 years, the fee schedules for services and procedures are adjusted, and historically they have nearly always risen. To finance this, the MHLW lowers fees for pharmaceuticals. Rather than negotiating directly with pharmaceutical manufacturers and distributors, the government conducts a market survey of sales prices in the marketplace [29]. As stated by Naoki Ikegami, savings are obtained "by gradually decreasing the profit margins that providers can earn from dispensing drugs," whereby the profits "came from the difference between the fee schedule price and the actual price paid to buy the product" [29]. It is essentially a competitive process: purchasers of pharmaceutical (largely hospital and clinics) can earn more by paying less for the drugs.

Over a more than 20-year period from 1990 to 2012, government was able to grant an increase in medical service fees except for a single year. This was made possible by the fact that the global rate of growth of pharmaceutical fees had been kept *negative* every single year, ranging from annual decreases of 4% to 10% [29]. These low fees imply high usage given that so much of the Japanese healthcare dollar is spent on drugs. Pharmaceutical companies accepted this arrangement because newly developed drugs were not subject to these price controls.

Assuring access and equity

Japanese citizens are less likely than those in other wealthy countries to cite costs as impeding their access to care. Among those aged 50–64, only 2% of Japanese reported forgoing care for financial reasons in the previous year; the figure was less than 1% for those aged 65 and older. Among 10 wealthy European nations to which Japan was compared, none could match it for the older cohort, and only Austria could for the younger cohort [6, p. 176]. Figures using a different database for different age groupings show similar results: 2.9% of those aged 20–65 reported not seeking a healthcare visit due to economic concerns during the previous year; the figure for those aged 65 and older was 1.1% [6, p. 168].

We have already outlined several of the reasons why this is the case: (a) health insurance coverage is nearly universal, (b) a rich array of services, including adult dental care, is covered; (c) patient cost-sharing requirements, while not low, are ameliorated through a system of lower coinsurance rates for potentially vulnerable age groups, and through strict maximums on how much money must be paid OOP; (d) providers cannot charge patients amounts above the mandated coinsurance amounts; and (e) VHI does not exist in the conventional manner, so those with higher incomes or employment status are not overly advantaged. Japan may also have another advantage compared to some other countries: it is more ethnically homogeneous, with 98.5% classified as ethnic Japanese, reducing the importance of ethnic disparities [5].

There are, of course, access and equity concerns. Three are noted here. The first concerns regional variations, as spending by region (prefecture) varies two-fold. One study found that people in the lowest-spending regions who had suffered an out-of-hospital heart attack were about 30% less likely to be alive after 1 month [38]. Moreover, geographic disparities are growing. For example, between 1990 and 2015, death rates, while declining throughout the country, fell by far more in high-performing regions compared to lower-performing ones. While it is difficult to pin down the main causes, including changes in socioeconomic status and health behaviors over time across regions, it has also been hypothesized that differential health system performance may be responsible as well [39].

A second concern relates to the lack of equity—both horizontal and vertical—in premium requirements. Beginning with horizontal equity, those in a health insurance plan provided by one company may pay much more than those in a different one. Another example is that a retired person living in one city may pay much more than somewhere living elsewhere. Vertical equity is also a concern because premiums tend to be lower on average for those working for large companies (Society-Managed Health Insurance, or SMHI) than small companies (JHIA); the former tend to have higher-paid employees. Moreover, premiums are higher in the NHI, which includes an even lower-income group: the self-employed, unemployed, and seniors up to age 75.[g] Nevertheless, some of the vertical equity problems are ameliorated through cross-subsidization of insurance plans via tax-funded government expenditures as well as through explicit assessments on employers and workers in the employment-based plans.

One final access problem is that some Japanese, who are required to purchase coverage, do not do so. (This is why we have used the term "nearly" universal to describe coverage.) Although recent data on the extent of this problem are not available, Naoki Ikegami and colleagues estimated that in 2007, 1.3% of Japanese were not paying premiums, which, they contend, "might bring into question Japan's status as a country with universal coverage" [7, p. 1112]. A similarly sized group might be underinsured because they had not paid their premiums in the previous 18 months. In such cases, they are required to pay for care first and be reimbursed later, something which many may not find affordable—although they can avoid this by applying for public assistance.[f]

Controlling expenditures

Given its population age structure, Japan has been moderately successful in controlling expenditures. How successful, however, depends on how expenditure control is measured. As noted, Japan 5th among the 10 counties discussed here in the portion of GDP spent on health care: 10.9%. But when examining actual monetary spending (and converting Japanese yen to US purchasing power), it ranks 9th (Table 15.3) [40]. This disparity in rankings is a result of the denominator: Japan has the lowest per capita income among the 10 countries [41].

Because Japan's rate of economic growth since the 1990s has been lower than most other wealthy countries, and because its national debt is so high, there is tremendous interest in further controlling expenditures. Japan's major vehicle for controlling healthcare expenditures continues to be its fee schedule. The MHLW has tremendous leverage in negotiating low fees, which are considerably lower than those in most of the other countries covered here. While it is likely that these low fees sometimes stimulate the provision of more services so providers can reap more profits (e.g., recommending more follow-up visits and tests), overall the trend in total healthcare spending closely parallels trends in the fee schedule.

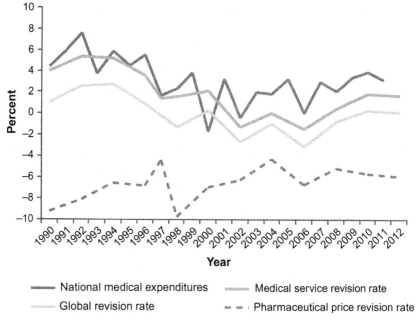

FIG. 8.1   Trends in the fee schedule revision rates and medial expenditures, 1990–2012. *(Source: Ikegami N. Controlling health expenditures by revisions to the fee schedule in Japan. In: Ikegami N, editor. Universal health coverage for inclusive and sustainable development lessons from Japan. Washington, DC: World Bank; 2014.)*

Fig. 8.1 shows the trends between 1990 and 2012 for national medical expenditures, annual changes in medical service and pharmaceutical fees, and an average of changes in those two fees. In every year but one, medical service fees rose. In contrast, pharmaceutical fees fell every single year. Also note the close correlation between changes in overall fees and total medical spending.

There are, of course, other mechanisms for attempting to control healthcare costs, but none plays as large of a role. The government does regulate the number of healthcare facilities, but interestingly, not the equipment used in those facilities. If a hospital or clinic, say, wants to purchase another MRI machine, it is free to do so [40, 42].[i] There is now an incipient movement toward pay-for-performance, where hospitals and physicians are given financial incentives to behave in ways consistent with societal goals, but this (appropriately) is mainly to improve appropriateness and quality.

Key policy issues

Based on the discussion earlier, Japan faces a number of broad policy issues going forward. Some of the most important ones are:

- Enacting methods to control the quantity of services provided, including hospitalization rates and lengths of stay as well as the number of physician visits.
- Enhancing revenue (e.g., through a considerably higher consumption tax) to reduce deficits. Payment of accumulated debt is responsible for a remarkably high one-fourth of the national budget.
- Working to reduce the economic burden on the employed population, who are voicing concerns about the degree to which they are required to cross-subsidize other segments of the population.
- Enhancing horizontal equity so that people working for different companies, and those living in different parts of the country, face roughly equivalent requirements for paying for health insurance.
- Formulating ways to reduce regional disparities in healthcare outcomes.
- More generally, successfully confronting the fact that current revenue sources are insufficient to pay for the medical, social, and residential care of a rapidly aging population.

References

[1] Japan: Life Expectancy. World Health Rankings [Internet]. [Accessed 23 September 2020]. Available from: https://www.worldlifeexpectancy.com/japan-life-expectancy.

[2] Devaux M, Graf S, Goryakin Y, Cecchini M, Huber H, Colombo F. Obesity update 2017. OECD; 2017.

[3] Kurotani K, Akter S, Kashino I, Goto A, Mizoue T, Noda M, et al. Quality of diet and mortality among Japanese men and women: Japan Public Health Center based prospective study. BMJ 2016;352:i1209.

[4] Ikeda N, Saito E, Kondo N, Inoue M, Ikeda S, Satoh T, et al. What has made the population of Japan healthy? Lancet 2011;378(9796):1094–105.

[5] Japan Population 2020 (Live). World Population Review [Internet]. [Accessed 23 September 2020]. Available from: https://worldpopulationreview.com/countries/japan-population.

[6] Sakamoto H, Rahman M, Nomura S, Okamoto E, Koike S, Yasunaga H, et al. Japan: Health system review. vol. 8, no. 1. New Delhi: World Health Organization, Regional Office for Southeast Asia; 2018.

[7] Ikegami N, Yoo BK, Hashimoto H, Matsumoto M, Ogata H, Babazono A, et al. Japanese universal health coverage: evolution, achievements, and challenges. Lancet 2011;378(9796):1106–15.

[8] Anon. Health at a glance 2017. OECD indicators. OECD; 2017. [Chartset]. [Accessed 23 September 2020]. Available from: https://www.oecd.org/els/health-systems/Health-at-a-Glance-2017-Chartset.pdf.

[9] Matsuda S. Health policy in Japan—current situation and future challenges. JMA 2019;2(1):1–10.

[10] Debt to GDP Ratio by Country 2020. World Population Review [Internet]. [Accessed 23 September 2020]. Available from: https://worldpopulationreview.com/countries/countries-by-national-debt.

[11] Kajimoto T. Japan's record financial year 2018 budget puts fiscal discipline in doubt. Reuters; 2017. [Internet]. [Accessed 23 September 2020]. Available from: https://www.reuters.com/article/us-japan-economy-budget/japans-record-financial-year-2018-budget-puts-fiscal-discipline-in-doubt-idUSKBN1EG06I.

[12] OECD. Old-age dependency ratio. Pensions at a glance 2017: OECD and G20 indicators. Paris: OECD Publishing; 2017.

[13] Maruyama M, Tsujimura K, Kasahara M, Yamabe K. Price comparison of new drugs in Japan, EU and US. Value Health 2017;20(9):A655–6.

[14] Miller E. U.S. drug prices vs the world. Drugwatch; 2018. [Internet]. [Accessed 23 September 2020]. Available from: https://www.drugwatch.com/featured/us-drug-prices-higher-vs-world/.

[15] Takaku R, Bessho S, Nishimura S, Ikegami N. Fiscal disparities among social health insurance programs in Japan. In: Ikegami N, editor. Universal health coverage for inclusive and sustainable development lessons from Japan. Washington, DC: World Bank; 2014 [chapter 3].

[16] Campbell JC, Ikegami N, Tsugawa Y. The political-historical context of Japanese health care. In: Ikegami N, editor. Universal Health coverage for inclusive and sustainable development lessons from Japan. Washington, DC: World Bank; 2014 [chapter 1].

[17] MacArthur D. The command structure: AFPAC, FEC and SCAP. In: Reports of General MacArthur, MacArthur in Japan: The occupation: Military phase, vol. 1. Washington, DC: Library of Congress; 2006 [chapter 3].

[18] Reich MR, Shibuya K. The future of Japan's health system—sustaining good health with equity at low cost. N Engl J Med 2015;373(19):1793–7.

[19] Jeong H, Niki R. Divergence in the development of public health insurance in Japan and the Republic of Korea: a multiple-payer versus a single-payer system. Int Soc Secur Rev 2012;62(2):51–73.

[20] Anon. Annual health, labour and welfare report 2018. Japan: Ministry of Health, Labour and Welfare; 2018.

[21] Morita T. OECD: Japan should hike consumption tax to 20–26 percent. The Asahi Shimbun; 2019. [Online news]. [Accessed 24 September 2020]. Available from: http://www.asahi.com/ajw/articles/AJ201904160032.html.

[22] Anon. Late-stage medical care system for the elderly. Osaka Prefecture: Wide Area Union; 2018.

[23] When you incur high medical care costs. IBM Japan Health Insurance Association [Internet]. [Accessed 24 September 2020]. Available from: https://www.ibmjapankenpo.jp/eng/member/benefit/expensive_a.html.

[24] Takaku R. Effects of reduced cost-sharing on children's health: evidence from Japan. Soc Sci Med 2016;151:46–55.

[25] Matsuda R. In: Tikkanen R, Osborn R, Mossialos E, Djordjevic A, Wharton GA, editors. Japan. International health care system profiles. The Commonwealth Fund; 2020. [Internet]. [Accessed 24 September 2020]. Available from: https://www.commonwealthfund.org/international-health-policy-center/countries/japan.

[26] OECD, editor. Key findings: Japan. Health at a glance 2017: OECD indicators; 2017.

[27] Payment System. Japan Health Policy NOW [Internet]. [Accessed 24 September 2020]. Available from: http://japanhpn.org/en/finan2/.

[28] Anderson G, Ikegami N. How can Japan's DPC inpatient hospital payment system be strengthened? Lessons from the U.S. medicare prospective system. Japan-US health policy project, policy recommendation, vol. 2. Center for Strategic and International Studies; Health and Global Policy Institute; 2011.

[29] Ikegami N. Controlling health expenditures by revisions to the fee schedule in Japan. In: Ikegami N, editor. Universal health coverage for inclusive and sustainable development lessons from Japan. Washington, DC: World Bank; 2014 [chapter 5].

[30] Campbell JC, Takagi Y. The political economy of the fee schedule in Japan. In: Ikegami N, editor. Universal health coverage for inclusive and sustainable development lessons from Japan. Washington, DC: World Bank; 2014 [chapter 6].

[31] Follow-up Examination Fee. ShiroBon Net [Internet]. [Accessed 24 September 2020]. Available from: http://shirobon.net/30/ika_1_1_2/a001.html.

[32] Magentic Resonance Computer Tomography (MRI Photograph). ShiroBon Net [Internet]. [Accessed 24 September 2020]. Available from: http://shirobon.net/30/ika_2_4_3/e202.html.

[33] Anon. 2017 comparative price report: International variation in medical and drug prices. International Federation of Health Plans; 2019.

[34] Pharmaceutical spending. OECD [Online data]. [Accessed 24 September 2020]. Available from: https://data.oecd.org/healthres/pharmaceutical-spending.htm.

[35] Paris V, Lopert R, Chapman S, Wenzl M, Canaud M, Mueller M. Generics and biosimilars. In: OECD, editor. Health at a glance 2019: OECD indicators. 2019 ed. Paris: OECD Publishing; 2019.

[36] Anon. Generic drugs. US FDA; 2019. [Internet]. [Accessed 24 September 2020]. Available from: https://www.fda.gov/drugs/buying-using-medicine-safely/generic-drugs.

[37] Anon. The promotion of comprehensive regional medical and long-term care. Annual health, labour and welfare report 2018. Japan: Ministry of Health, Labour and Welfare; 2018.

[38] Tsugawa Y, Hasegawa K, Hiraide A, Jha AK. Regional health expenditure and health outcomes after out-of-hospital cardiac arrest in Japan: an observational study. BMJ Open 2015;5(8):e008374.

[39] Nomura S, Sakamoto H, Glenn S, Tsugawa Y, Abe SK, Rahman MM, et al. Population health and regional variations of disease burden in Japan, 1990-2015: a systematic subnational analysis for the Global Burden of Disease Study 2015. Lancet 2017;390(10101):1521–38.

[40] Anon. OECD health statistics 2020. OECD; 2020. [Online Database]. [Accessed 26 August 2020]. Available from: http://www.oecd.org/els/health-systems/health-data.htm.

[41] Anon. Country comparison: GDP—Per capita (PPP). The world factbook 2020. Central Intelligence Agency; 2020. [Web factbook]. [Accessed 3 September 2020]. Available from: https://www.cia.gov/library/publications/the-world-factbook/fields/211rank.html.

[42] Magnetic resonance imaging (MRI) exams. OECD [Online data]. [Accessed 24 September 2020]. Available from: https://data.oecd.org/healthcare/magnetic-resonance-imaging-mri-exams.htm.

Section C

Universal coverage systems with competing insurers

Chapter 9

Germany

The big picture

Germany set the stage for modern-day health insurance when it developed the first such system in the late 19th century, the rudiments of which still exist today. From its early days, it was based on the notion of **solidarity**, which generally is taken to mean that society takes care of those who need assistance irrespective of their ability to pay. While the initial system obviously has changed dramatically over the past 135 years, Reinhard Busse and colleagues point out "its remarkable resilience: it survived, with key principles intact, different forms of government (an empire, republics, and dictatorships), two world wars, hyperinflation, and the division and subsequent reunification of Germany" [1, p. 882].

The German system represents the prototype of the so-called Bismarckian model (see Chapter 2), with people obtaining health insurance through private, albeit nonprofit, organizations. While some other European countries have moved toward more government involvement in the workings of the healthcare system, Germany continues to take a more hands-off approach, entrusting the most important decision-making to corporatist organizations—that is, nongovernment societal organizations, in this case representing the insurers (or "**sickness funds**") on one side, and provider organizations on the other. There is, of course, government oversight as well as pressure applied to meet national goals of quality, value, and cost containment, with government permitted to intervene when it deems it necessary. However, responsibilities for devising ways of achieving these goals generally are given to these nongovernmental organizations representing competing interests in the healthcare system, as they have legal responsibility to carry out the requirements of the system.[a]

The other unusual feature—unique in Europe—is that universal coverage is not obtained through a single health insurance system, but from a bifurcated one. About seven-eighths of Germans have statutory coverage from nonprofit sickness funds, with the remainder of the population receiving it from private health insurers, a majority of which are for-profit. On average, wealthier and healthier people appear to be disproportionately enrolled in the private system, raising issues of both efficiency and equity [2, p. 265].

---

[a] Bernard Gibis, personal communication, November 12, 2019.

Health Insurance Systems: An International Comparison. https://doi.org/10.1016/B978-0-12-816072-5.00001-8
143

Currently, most people are required to purchase statutory health insurance (SHI)[b] (and are fined if they fail to do so [3])—that is, they are not permitted to obtain their mandatory coverage through private health insurance (PHI).[c] These include most employed persons earning less than 62,550 euros per year in 2020, pensioners, students, and the unemployed; dependents are covered for free if they are not in the labor force. Those earning more than this threshold have a choice of whether to use the SHI system or to purchase PHI [1, 2, p. 121]. Civil servants and most self-employed have a very strong financial incentive to purchase PHI.[d]

The German system is generally well regarded internationally, with excellent financial access, little in the way of waiting lists to receive care, and some good outcomes in specific areas such as cancer care. But other measures of performance are wanting. The Commonwealth Fund, a US foundation, conducts country-specific population surveys in the areas of care process, access, equity, administrative efficiency, and healthcare outcome. In the 2016 surveys, Germany ranked below average among 11 wealthy countries, most of which are included in this book, in all areas except access. An example is **mortality amenable to health care**—that is, the success of the system in preventing deaths that should have been avoided through good preventive or curative care—where among the 10 countries covered here, only the United States and United Kingdom showed lower performance [4]. It ranks similarly in the Healthcare Access and Quality Index, a refinement of mortality amenable to health care (see Chapter 15) [5]. Other issues involve problems in successfully coordinating care, too many hospital beds as well as the provision of too many unnecessary services.

Germany has a reputation of constantly tinkering with its healthcare system [6]. It has faced enormous challenges in the past, such as incorporating the former East Germany into the West's system after reunification in the 1990s, and more recently with the influx of more than a million refugees seeking asylum. At the same time, its aging population, caused by longer life spans and low fertility rates, put continuing financial pressure on the system. Whether the country can continue to meet its challenges by keeping most decisions out of the hands of government through its unique dual system of parallel statutory and private is a key political issue going forward.

The details

History[e]

Germany is usually given credit as being the originator of **social health insurance** in the world, with compulsory sickness, accident, and old-age insurance enacted

---

[b] In this chapter, we use the acronym SHI to denote statutory health insurance. In other chapters, SHI refers to the more general concept of social health insurance (see Glossary).

[c] Although the rest of the book refers to private insurance as VHI, we use the German version, PHI, here to distinguish it from the small market for supplementary health insurance discussed later in the chapter.

[d] Miriam Blumel, personal communication, October 11, 2019.

[e] A compact history can be found in Busse et al. [1].

through the Health Insurance Act of 1883 under the leadership of Chancellor Otto von Bismarck. Workers paid two-thirds of **premium** contributions with employers paying the remaining third. Benefits included payments toward medical care and up to 13 weeks of wages when a worker was sick [7]. Recent econometric research indicates that the Act reduced mortality considerably—by one-third among eligible blue-collar workers by the end of the 19th century. This appears to have been mainly the result of better access to physicians, who in turn may have provided patients with crucial knowledge about preventing infectious diseases [8].

Components of the Act were not new, however, as there was precedent as far back as the Middle Ages when guilds and mutual aid societies provided funds to help workers and their families with the financial consequences of illness and death [1, 9]. Although Bismarck's motives are usually attributed more to staving off socialism than to improving social justice [9], his social programs did provide important protections to some of the working class. Paul Starr asserts that Bismarck "introduced social rights to avoid granting wider political rights" [10, p. 73]. Another motivation sometimes attributed to **Bismarck** is that social insurance provided tangible benefits to people in newly consolidated parts of the country [10].

The German system has always been based on the notion of a social code of solidarity (*Sozialgesetzbuch*), the idea that people's health needs should determine what care they are entitled to, but with financial contributions depending on their ability to pay [11]. Three other aspects of the current system, each discussed below, are also recognizable from the 19th century: having employers and employees sharing in contributions to nonprofit sickness funds based on a person's wages to help ensure affordability, mandatory membership for certain occupation and income groups, and self-regulation rather than direct governmental administration [1].

The 1883 Act hardly provided universal coverage, as only 26% of blue-collar workers, and 10% of the population, initially received social health insurance benefits. This grew to half the population in 1925 as Germany became more industrialized, and as more occupations (including some white-collar), as well as dependents and the unemployed, became subject to mandatory coverage. During the National Socialist period prior to and during World War II, much of the former system was centralized under the Nazi Party, and groups that were discriminated against (and eventually subject to genocide, especially the Jews) were excluded from receiving benefits, although they continued to make payroll contributions while they were still working. During World War II, retired persons were added to the mandatory system. The benefits conferred by SHI also shifted over time, as they did in other countries, away from cash replacement in case of illness toward payment toward benefits in kind, that is, healthcare expenses.

During the Cold War, there were, of course, two different systems: those of West Germany and East Germany. The latter was under the indirect control of the Soviet Union although aspects of the sickness fund model stayed largely intact and coverage was made universal. The system was badly underfunded, however, and population health suffered [1].

After German reunification in 1990, the system reverted to the West German model. Coverage rates had risen to 88% of the population having SHI, approximately where it stands today [2 (p. 25), 9]. The remaining population possesses PHI, a system discussed in the next section.

Soon after reunification, the Health Care Structure Act of 1993 sought to restructure the health insurance system by introducing a greater degree of competition with the hopes of better containing expenditures and making the system more responsive to population preferences. Germans could choose their sickness fund rather than being assigned to one based on their occupation. Coverage became universal based on legislation approved in 2007, but uninsurance rates had been well less than 1% for many years up till that point [12].

Overview of the health insurance system

Unique among European countries, Germany has two parallel systems that provide a primary health insurance: statutory health insurance and private health insurance. A person has coverage through competing health insurance plans from one or the other, and together, the country has achieved universal coverage. In 2019, 87% of Germans had SHI, 11% PHI, and the remaining 2%, including military, police, and refugees, had other governmental coverage. There were 109 SHI sickness funds, all not-for-profit, and 41 PHI funds, a small majority being for-profit [13, 14].

The distinction between the two systems goes back over 100 years. Early iterations of mandatory coverage usually applied to particular occupations and to those whose incomes were below a particular threshold. Others, however, who also wanted coverage purchased it through private health insurers rather than the traditional sickness funds.

Another critical feature of the German system is (and has always been) the large role played by self-regulating corporatist organizations composed of sickness fund insurers and providers, which are legal entities in Germany, and the concomitant relatively small role played by government. According to Reinhard Busse and Miriam Blümel, these groups "have assumed the status of quasi-public corporations," having "the duty and right to define benefits, prices and standards" [2, p. 17]. Interestingly, while corporatist entities have ceded power to government in many other European countries in recent years, mainly to contain costs, the opposite seems to be the case in Germany, where the Federal Joint Committee has taken on increased authority in cost containment [2, p. 61].

Governance

Governance of the German SHI system is carried out jointly by corporatist organizations (mainly groups of sickness funds and providers), the federal government, and the Länder (which are similar to states). The Ministry of Health is the major federal organization. It oversees a number of aspects of the SHI system, pharmaceutical and medical device safety, disease prevention and control, and some medical care research. It also oversees and carries out reallocation of premiums between sickness funds through risk adjustment. There are 16 Länder that oversee a number of areas including hospitals, health professions, local public health, and preventive activities such as reducing substance abuse [2, p. 41–43]. Länder also finance hospital capital costs.

Most authority, however, resides in corporatist entities that compose the Federal Joint Committee. Decision-making is carried out through the Plenary Group, which has 13 voting members: 3 neutral, 5 from the sickness funds, and 5 from provider associations (2 for hospitals, 2 for physicians, and 1 for dentists). There are also five nonvoting members representing patient interests [2, p. 63–64]. The Länder are also represented on certain issues. The Committee's powers are broad and include evaluating and ultimately choosing SHI benefits, pharmaceuticals, and medical technologies to be included in the SHI package; and assessing access to and quality of medical and dental care [1, 2, p. 66].

Financing

In 2017, 84% of total health expenditures were paid by government or compulsory sources, which, along with Sweden, is the highest of any of the 10 countries covered in this book.[f] About 13% was paid OOP, and the remaining 3%, by voluntary health insurance (VHI) and miscellaneous sources [15, Figure 7.8].

There are several sources of revenue in the German healthcare system: SHI contributions, government subsidies, PHI premiums, VHI premiums, and OOP spending. We focus on the first three here, with the other two discussed later.

SHI pays for most of the country's medical care. Wage-related contributions fund over 90% of SHI spending, while general taxes pay for less than 10% [2 (p. 116), 13]. These revenues largely come from a payroll tax of 14.6% (on earnings up to 54,450 euros per year in 2019, making them somewhat regressive), split evenly between the employer and the employee. For people with extremely low incomes, only the employer pays, at a rate of 13% of wages [2, p. 124].

In reality, employees had been paying a bit more than employers—and average of about another 1% of wages—because sickness fund insurers need to charge a supplemental premium to cover their total costs. The burden of these supplemental premiums changed in 2019; they are now split between the employer and employee [13, 16]. Differences in these supplemental premiums vary between sickness funds, most likely a result of administrative efficiencies and imperfect risk adjustment, from 0.3% to 1.8% in 2017, and are one basis of competition among insurers to attract enrollees [1].

Because the country relies so heavily on payroll taxes—that is, wages—to fund health care, this will put additional stress on the financing system as the population ages out of the working force, and at the same time, uses more care. Over time, it is likely that nonwage sources of funding will be necessary, for example, more taxes on nonwage income [17, p. 172].

---

[f] The figure includes the 9% paid by PHI, as having either PHI or SHI coverage is required.

Direct government spending collected from taxes plays a much smaller role. This is used to pay sickness funds to help subsidize premiums for artists and farmers as well as pay for such services as maternity benefits and contraceptives [2, p. 118]. Another way federal authorities become directly involved is through implementing a risk-adjustment financial arrangement. To reduce the incentive for sickness funds to market to healthier people, the scheme reallocates revenues to sickness funds based on age, gender, and the morbidity of members. In 2019, there are about 80 different diseases that enter in the formula—the ones that result directly, or indirectly through comorbidities, in individual expenditures that exceed the average person's spending by 50% or more [2, p. 129].[g] Sickness funds that cover more people with these conditions receive more monies from a central allocation pool, and those with a healthier mix of patients, less.

Private insurance premiums are another source of revenue, with 11% of the German population enrolling in PHI rather than SHI. Only about 9% of total healthcare expenditures are from PHI, reflecting the fact that these enrollees are healthier on average than those in SHI. Unlike statutory coverage, premiums for PHI vary based on age and a person's history of illness. Importantly, though, higher premiums for those who have a history of illness only are charged at time of initial purchase: A person's premiums will not rise more than others if his or her health history worsens over time [2, p. 139]. PHI insurers are also subject to government rules that ensure that older persons do not face unduly high premiums [2, p. 139].[a]

Coverage

Breadth

Between SHI and PHI, coverage is essentially universal, with government enforcing the mandate to purchase. An issue that is particularly important in Germany is health care for refugees seeking asylum. Germany opened its doors more than any other European country, with 1.3 million applications for refugee status (1.6% of the population) between 2015 and 2018. Both German and European laws stipulate that they must receive needed acute care, although chronic care generally is not guaranteed [18].

Scope

The scope of services in Germany is unusually broad, in particular because it includes routine dental care. Other services often excluded from other countries' benefit packages, but which are covered in Germany, are optical care and physical therapy. Some PHI policies have richer benefits than the SHI package, but others cover less [2 (p. 139), 19]. One example where SHI offers more

---

[g] Reinhard Busse, personal communication, November 9, 2019. This is scheduled to include all diseases, not just the 80, beginning around 2020.

comprehensive benefits is in the case of psychotherapy, where up to 80 visits are covered [20].[h]

Depth

SHI coverage is deep. There are relatively modest cost sharing requirements, including 10 euros per day in the hospital up to a maximum of 28 days, and 5–10 euros for pharmaceuticals. Patients choosing drugs exceeding the price of comparably effective but cheaper drugs must pay the difference as well. There is a fixed sum reimbursed for dental procedures, but the patient always faces some cost sharing requirements. There is no cost sharing for physician services, however. Children are not subject to cost sharing, and there is an annual ceiling of 2% of income on copayments (1% for patients with specified chronic conditions) [13, 21]. SHI insurers can offer a choice of other features, such as adding a **deductible** or a rebate if no services are used during the year, but fewer than 4% of members opted for these in 2015 [1].

Voluntary health insurance

The same companies that sell PHI also sell voluntary health insurance (VHI) to those in the SHI system. This is a minor part of the German system, with only an estimated 1% of total expenditures being paid by VHI [15, Figure 7.8]. It covers both supplementary and complementary benefits. Supplementary coverage includes private rooms in hospitals and care by the chief physician, while an estimated 80% of VHI policies cover the cost sharing requirements for dental care [14].

Choice

Those in the SHI market are permitted to choose among dozens of sickness funds that are available nationally in their Länder. Those in the PHI market also can choose among any of the approximately 40 available private insurers. In SHI, the basis of competition is mainly the amount of supplemental contributions and customer service. There is a standardized set of benefits, but some offer additional coverage for particular services (e.g., homeopathic medicine).[d] One complaint is that despite the large number of sickness funds in the SHI system—over 100—they do not appear to compete very actively with each other on the basis of quality [22]. A small proportion of Germans (fewer than 5%) choose plans that engage in selective contracting with preferred providers. Unlike in the Netherlands and the United States, where there has been a strong movement toward consolidation and market power, this has not happened to as large an extent in Germany [1]. While it is easy to switch from one SHI plan to another [23], there do not appear to be public data on how often this occurs.

Germans enjoy free choice of physician and hospital. Primary care **gatekeeping** has never been an important component of the country's healthcare system.

---

[h] Reinhard Busse, personal communication, November 9, 2019.

Provider payment

Hospitals

Germany has a mix of public, private nonprofit, and for-profit hospitals. About half of beds are in the public hospitals, one-third in the nonprofits, and one-sixth in the for-profits—although the for-profit share has been growing in recent years, from 4% of beds in 2004 to 18% in 2019 [13].[i] Compared to all other European Union countries, Germany has both more hospital beds per capita and is also near the top in average length of stay [2 (p. 54), 24]. Many experts consider the glut of hospital beds to be a problem, lowering efficiency and reducing quality since many hospitals are not well equipped [22].

Traditionally, the inpatient and outpatient care sectors have operated separately in Germany. Generally, physicians working in hospitals do not treat patients in outpatient settings, and vice versa.

Hospitals are paid on a DRG basis, a modified version of the one used by Australia, with the system administered by a joint committee of the federal associations for sickness funds and hospitals. There are about 1300 DRGs; these payments cover not only hospital resources but also the salaries of hospital-based physicians [13]. The monetary value of each hospitalization within a DRG category is the same for all hospitals in a Land [2, p. 147]. Capital costs are funded separately through the Länder.

Physicians

Hospital-based physicians are salaried. Ambulatory care physicians generally are paid on a fee-for-service basis subject to fee schedules, one applying to SHI patients and the other to PHI patients. The fee schedule for SHI patients is, according to Konrad Obermann and colleagues, "exceedingly complex," [17, p. 206] in part because fees are reduced for physicians who provide a quantity of services that exceeds a threshold. However, all SHI insurers pay the same fees to doctors for specific services so there is not a financial incentive for a physician to seek one patient over another. This is sometimes called an "**all-payer system**" (see Chapter 16). This does not apply to PHI patients, who, as noted below, are financially more attractive to providers.

The sickness funds do not pay the doctors directly. Rather, each makes an aggregate payment to the regional association representing physicians in that geographic area. The regional association, in turn, pays physician on a fee per service basis, based on a "points"—a measure of the quantity of patients in the practice and the number of services each physician reports during a calendar quarter. These points are determined by the Uniform Value Scale, which are determined by another corporatist committee composed of representatives of sickness funds and physicians. The points are similar to the relative value units used by payers in the United States.

---

[i] Miriam Blümel, personal communication, October 8, 2019.

Each physician is allotted in advance an anticipated aggregate maximum number of patients and points per patient during the calendar quarter, which is based on the volume provided during the previous year. Additional quantities of services delivered that cannot be justified result in a decline in fees; this is a common occurrence as the total number of points submitted by physicians in a region collectively often exceeds the regional budget [22]. Some research has found that some of the practices that reach their reimbursement cap, and thus face declining revenues for providing more services, reduce the number of SHI services they provide at the end of March, June, September, and December; this, in turn, results in a substantial increase in the use of emergency care [25]. Similarly, if physicians prescribe more drugs than an individual target volume established for them by the above committee and are unable to adequately justify it, they are required to return the difference—specifically, the difference between how much they actually prescribed and 115% of their target [2 (p. 149–154, 215), 13].

In contrast, physicians treating PHI patients are not subject to volume restrictions as they are when they treat SHI patients. There is a uniform fee schedule set by the Ministry of Health, but physicians typically charge about double that rate [2, p. 156–157]. Usually, the patient pays the physician directly for care and is reimbursed by their insurer [2, p. 139, 156]. Moreover, unlike in SHI, physicians are not subject to volume restrictions, making such patients financially more attractive [19].

Pharmaceuticals

Germany controls its drug prices through an elaborate procedure of comparing the benefits and costs of new pharmaceuticals to existing ones on the market. When a pharmaceutical company first introduces a new drug into the market, it can freely set its price for the first year. This immediately sets off a process of evaluating if and how much of an additional therapeutic benefit is provided by the new medication. This assessment is usually carried out by an independent commission, the Institute for Quality and Efficiency in Health Care. The evaluation concludes by placing the drug in one of six categories in terms of additional benefit compared to existing drugs: major, considerable, minor, not identifiable (or mixed evidence), none, or less benefit than current drugs on the market [26].

When it is found that there is additional benefit, price negotiation takes place between the national association of sickness funds and the pharmaceutical manufacturer. These negotiations consider both the cost of producing the new drug and how much other countries pay for it. If these negotiations do not result in an agreed price, the case goes to arbitration. If a drug is found to have no additional benefit, sickness funds reimburse no more than the price of the already existing drugs, a system called **reference pricing** [26, 27]. Researchers have found that during the 2012–16 period, drugs found to have a positive benefit nearly always stayed on the market, while 25% of the drugs not shown to have medical benefits were taken off the market [28].

The use of generic drugs is higher in Germany than in most other European countries, with generic medications accounting for over 80% of sales and 35% of revenue in 2017, exceeded only by the United Kingdom [29, Figure 10.10]. This is due in part to the use of reference prices, some requirements for generic substitution for brand-name drugs, and not rewarding pharmacists with additional fees for filling prescriptions with brand-name drugs.

Assuring access and equity

Germans enjoy excellent accessibility to health care. In one cross-European study, almost no Germans said they had to forgo care due to cost, travel distance, or waiting times, and there were almost no differences by income. Only the Netherlands could match the average [14]. Data from the Commonwealth Fund survey of nine of our countries (all but Japan) show the lowest rates of cost-related access problems, both overall and among those with lower incomes, after the United Kingdom [4]. Another European survey shows almost no unmet need for dental examinations due to expense even for those in the lowest income quintiles—which was also true in the Netherlands and the United Kingdom [30].

There are several reasons why Germans enjoy this high level of access. First, the benefit package is among the most comprehensive of any country, as it includes dental care, optical care, and physical therapy. Second, patient cost sharing requirements are modest. Third, there are strict limits on SHI copayments that take into account the affordability of care: No copayments are required for children, and there is a limit of 1% of income for those with chronic conditions, and 2% for other adults.

Over 90% of SHI expenses are funded by a proportional payroll tax. The system is mildly regressive for those with relatively high incomes who choose to remain in SHI and do not have to pay contributions on annual earnings above about 55,000 euros [31].

Perhaps the most significant equity issue concerns the uniquely German feature of parallel SHI and PHI systems; 11% of the population has PHI. While predominantly filled with high-income families, it also contains self-employed persons and civil servants, which reduces but does not eliminate the income disparities between members of the two insurance systems. Younger and healthier persons who are eligible for PHI are financially advantaged because premiums are based, among other things, on health status at time of application. Moreover, in removing these people from the SHI pool, it weakens the overall solidarity of the system [2, p. 265]. Although waiting lists and waiting times are short in Germany compared to other countries, evidence indicates that waiting times for getting an appointment are shorter in PHI, as is the time waiting in the physician's office before being treated [2, p. 269].

Short of eliminating the PHI system, which is highly unlikely given its long history and the fact that it is populated by those who are well off, other options would include moving a greater share of financing of the SHI system away from payroll taxes to general taxes (which are paid by the entire population and do not have maximums on contributions) [2, p. 282], or considering not only wages, but also capital income in funding SHI.

Controlling expenditures

Germany's healthcare spending is above average of the 10 countries reviewed here: In 2018, it was tied for third in per capita GDP spent on health care at 11.2% and also third in average per capita healthcare spending (see Table 15.3) [12]. Traditionally, the country's emphasis has not been on expenditures per se, but rather, on keeping payroll contribution rates stable [2, p. 33–34]. That is possible, however, only if expenditures in the SHI program are kept in check. This is particularly challenging given that government is not generally involved in key decisions about fees.

There does not appear to be one overriding way in which cost control is pursued. Some of the many ways include:

- Relying on consumers to make cost-effective decisions in their choice of health insurance plans.
- Using health technology assessment, cost-effectiveness criteria, and reference prices to reduce SHI spending on prescription drugs [13].
- Reducing physician fees when the quantity of services they provide or drugs they prescribe exceeds a quarterly threshold.
- Encouraging sickness funds to adopt disease management programs to improve the coordination of care between the often-fragmented inpatient and outpatient care systems [1].
- Linking hospital payment more explicitly to quality performance and discouraging provision of low-value services by lower payment [13].

Key policy issues

While most international observers view the German health insurance system positively, it faces a number of challenges. One of the key ones is more long term in nature: securing adequate financing in the wake of an aging population and low fertility rates—the lowest of any of the 10 countries considered here except Japan [32]. In the more immediate term, other issues are more likely to dominate policy discussions.

Germany continues to face challenges with its bifurcated system whereby most of the population is covered by SHI, but over 10% uses the PHI system to secure their primary insurance. This division, in which PHI enrollees tend to be wealthier and healthier than those in SHI, tends to favor these groups in various ways, causing issues not only problems in equity but efficiency as well. In that regard, a European Commission staff report, issued in 2019, concluded that:

> *The legal framework for statutory health insurance and private health insurance creates inefficiencies and challenges the solidarity principle in healthcare. Although several reforms have improved the situation, the current legal framework, which allows people on higher incomes, civil servants and the self-employed to opt out of the statutory health insurance scheme, weakens the risk- and income-based solidarity principle in healthcare. Moreover, doctors can charge patients with private health insurance more than those covered by the statutory health insurance scheme. This creates inequalities in waiting times and the accessibility of medical services. It also incentivises over-provision of health services to private health insurance patients [33, p. 32].*

How to reform the system is not clear. Eliminating PHI would face strong opposition from enrollees, the insurance industry, and the physician community. One alternative would be to increase the proportion of SHI expenditures paid through taxes (which are paid by all Germans), while reducing (the somewhat regressive) payroll contributions, which fall only on those with SHI [2, p. 265].

Another issue is that historically, Germany has had more hospital beds, admissions, lengths of stay, and physician visits than in other European countries. Moreover, relatively little care is devoted to hospital-based outpatient care. This issue goes beyond health insurance but could be partly addressed through provider payment reforms, providing less incentive to hospitalize patients overnight in comparison with treating them, where appropriate, in outpatient and office settings.

A final issue to note is pharmaceutical expenditures, which on a per capita basis are eclipsed only by Switzerland among all European countries [34, Figure 10.2]. According to the European Commission staff report noted above, "Expenditure on pharmaceuticals is high and rising, and recent cost-containment reforms have not been able to stop the increase.... The main reason for the increase [has been] newly licensed patent-protected pharmaceuticals, which account for 45% of Statutory Health Insurance pharmaceutical expenditure" [33, p. 32].

This problem of rising brand-name drug prices is hardly unique to Germany. Moreover, as discussed earlier, the country has high generic penetration and uses cost-effectiveness and reference pricing to help control expenditures. Nevertheless, it may be that more government involvement would be effective, as traditionally price decisions are made through negotiations between corporatist organizations that may not fully represent consumers' interests. Quoting Reinhard Busse and colleagues:

> *Germany's pragmatic policy-making style, with its limited state control of the health system, means that the legislator is charging the same actors with solving*

the problems that they created in the first place: that is, with mandating the Federal Joint Committee, the main self-governance institution of payers and providers, to define areas for quality improvement by selective contracting and pay-for-performance. … [T]he practice of setting policy objectives at the federal level and leaving it to self-governing actors to work out the specifics might need to be reassessed. Going forward, if self-governing actors are too slow, too unambitious, or simply too divided, the government might need to define quality and efficiency targets in the law and be more vigilant about implementation and enforcement [1, p. 894–895].

References

[1] Busse R, Blümel M, Knieps F, Barnighausen T. Statutory health insurance in Germany: a health system shaped by 135 years of solidarity, self-governance, and competition. Lancet 2017;390(10097):882–97.

[2] Busse R, Blümel M. Germany: Health system review. 2nd ed. Health Systems in Transition, vol. 16. European Observatory on Health Systems and Policies; 2014. Copenhagen.

[3] Van Ginneken E, Rice T. Enforcing enrollment in health insurance exchanges: evidence from the Netherlands, Switzerland, and Germany. Med Care Res Rev 2015;72(4):496–509.

[4] Schneider EC, Sarnak DO, Squires D, Shah A, Doty MM. Mirror, mirror 2017: International comparison reflects flaws and opportunities for better U.S. health care. Mirror, mirror: The Commonwealth Fund; 2017.

[5] G.B.D. Healthcare Access Quality Collaborators. Measuring performance on the Healthcare Access and Quality Index for 195 countries and territories and selected subnational locations: a systematic analysis from the Global Burden of Disease Study 2016. Lancet 2018;391(10136):2236–71.

[6] Knox R. History of tinkering helps German system endure. NPR; 2008. [Internet]. [Accessed 26 August 2020]. Available from: https://www.npr.org/templates/story/story.php?storyId=92189596.

[7] Anon. Health Insurance Act of 1883. ImagineWiki; 2009. [Internet]. [Accessed 26 August 2020]. Available from: https://imagine.fandom.com/wiki/Health_Insurance_Act_of_1883.

[8] Bauernschuster S, Driva A, Hornung E. Bismarck's health insurance and the mortality decline. CESifo Working Papers. 2(6601); 2018.

[9] Leith KH, Ledlow G. Germany. In: Johnson J, Stoskoft C, Shi L, editors. Comparative health systems: A global perspective. 2nd ed. Burlington, MA: Jones & Bartlett Learning; 2018.

[10] Reid TR. The healing of America: A global quest for better, cheaper, and fairer health care. New York: Penguin Press; 2009.

[11] Pfaff M, Wassener D. Germany. J Health Polit Policy Law 2000;25(5):907–14.

[12] Anon. OECD health statistics 2020. OECD; 2020. [Online Database]. [Accessed 26 August 2020]. Available from: http://www.oecd.org/els/health-systems/health-data.htm.

[13] Tikkanen R, Osborn R, Mossialos E, Djordjevic A, Wharton GA. International health care system profiles: Germany. The Commonwealth Fund; 2020. [Internet]. [Accessed 26 August 2020]. Available from: https://www.commonwealthfund.org/international-health-policy-center/countries/germany.

[14] OECD and European Observatory on Health Systems and Policies. Germany: Country health profile 2019. Paris: OECD Publishing; 2019.

[15] OECD. Health at a glance 2019. Paris: OECD Publishing; 2019.

[16] Busse R, Blümel M, Quentin W, Spranger A. The health systems and policy monitor: Germany. European Observatory on Health Systems and Policies; 2020. [Internet]. [Accessed 26 August 2020]. Available from: https://www.hspm.org/countries/germany28082014/countrypage.aspx.

[17] Obermann K, Müller P, Müller H, Schmidt B, Glazinski B. Understanding the German health care system. Mannheim Institute of Public Health; 2013.

[18] Bauhoff S, Göpffarth D. Asylum-seekers in Germany differ from regularly insured in their morbidity, utilizations and costs of care. PLoS One 2018;13(5):1–11.

[19] Sagan A, Thomson S. Voluntary health insurance in Europe. vol. 1. United Kingdom: WHO Regional Office for Europe; 2016.

[20] Anon. A guide to psychotherapy in Germany: Where can I find help? Germany. Cologne: Institute for Quality and Efficiency in Health Care (IQWiG); 2006.

[21] Rice T, Quentin W, Anell A, Barnes AJ, Rosenau P, Unruh LY, et al. Revisiting out-of-pocket requirements: trends in spending, financial access barriers, and policy in ten high-income countries. BMC Health Serv Res 2018;18(1):371.

[22] Emanuel EJ. Which country has the world's best health care? New York: PublicAffairs; 2020.

[23] Van de Ven WP, Beck K, Buchner F, Schokkaert E, Schut FT, Shmueli A, et al. Preconditions for efficiency and affordability in competitive healthcare markets: are they fulfilled in Belgium, Germany, Israel, the Netherlands and Switzerland? Health Policy 2013;109(3):226–45.

[24] Anon. Healthcare resource statistics—Beds. eurostat; 2019. [Internet]. [Accessed 27 August 2020]. Available from: https://ec.europa.eu/eurostat/statistics-explained/index.php?title=Healthcare_resource_statistics_-_beds.

[25] Knight B. German doctors give private patients special treatment, says study. DW Akademie; 2018.

[26] Wenzl M, Paris V. Pharmaceutical Reimbursement and Pricing in Germany. OECD Publishing; 2018.

[27] Robinson JC, Panteli C, Ex P. Reference pricing in Germany: Implications for U.S. pharmaceutical purchasing. The Commonwealth Fund; 2019.

[28] Stern AD, Pietrulla F, Herr A, Kesselheim AS, Sarpatwari A. The impact of price regulation on the availability of new drugs in Germany. Health Aff 2019;38(7):1182–7.

[29] Paris V, Lopert R, Chapman S, Wenzl M, Canaud M, Mueller M. Generics and biosimilars. In: OECD, editor. Health at a glance 2019: OECD indicators. 2019 ed. Paris: OECD Publishing; 2019.

[30] European Commission. Health. eurostat; 2020. [Online database]. [Accessed 27 August 2020]. Available from: https://ec.europa.eu/eurostat/web/health/data/database.

[31] Matz-Townsend C, editor. Health insurance options in Germany—2020. In: How to Germany. 1st ed, vol. 8. Pellingen: Chuck Emerson Media Services; 2020.

[32] Plecher H. Countries with the lowest fertility rates 2017. statista; 2020. [Online data]. [Accessed 27 August 2020]. Available from: https://www.statista.com/statistics/268083/countries-with-the-lowest-fertility-rates/.

[33] Anon. Country report Germany 2019: Including an in-depth review on the prevention and correction of macroeconomic imbalances. Brussels: European Commission; 2019.

[34] Paris V, Lopert R, Chapman S, Wenzl M, Canaud M, Mueller M. Pharmaceutical expenditure. In: OECD, editor. Health at a glance 2019: OECD indicators. 2019 ed. Paris: OECD Publishing; 2019.

Chapter 10

Switzerland

The big picture

Switzerland is a small country, and with 8.5 million residents, the fewest of any of the 10 countries examined in this book. Nevertheless, in recent years it has received international accolades as having among the best health care systems. Some of these assessments are based on subjective factors [1] and others on a subjective weighting of objective factors [2]. Its reputation is partially based on country-specific population surveys. One such survey question asked random samples of people in 11 wealthy countries if "the system works pretty well and only minor changes are necessary." Switzerland had the second-highest score among the countries examined in this book, just behind Germany [3]. A related survey, taken in the same countries but with a sample population of only high-need elders,[a] found that the Swiss were most satisfied with one critical metric: the quality of care they receive [4]. Not surprisingly, not all assessments are so positive. In the survey noted above of people in 11 countries (9 of which are included in this book), Switzerland was below the median with regard to measures of the care process, access, and administrative efficiency [5].

While user perceptions are very important, other, more objective measures matter too—perhaps even more so. A common yardstick of the performance of health care systems is **mortality amenable to health care**—essentially, deaths that should have been prevented by a well-functioning medical care system (see Chapter 15). Switzerland's rate has been estimated to be the best among OECD countries [6 (p. 241), 7]. A newer measure in the literature, the Healthcare Access and Quality Index, which further refines the concept of amenable mortality, rated Switzerland as tied for the second in the world among countries with more than a million in population, just below Norway and with a score equal to the Netherlands, Australia, and Finland [8].

Carlo De Pietro and colleagues describe the Swiss system as "combining aspects of managed competition and corporatism in a decentralized regulatory framework shaped by the influences of direct democracy" [6, p. 19]. Both the central and regional governments are important, but key decisions such as fee levels are determined by independent organizations containing representatives

---

[a] "High-need" was defined as either having three or more chronic conditions or having a functional limitation preventing a person from performing a basic activity of daily living.

Health Insurance Systems: An International Comparison. https://doi.org/10.1016/B978-0-12-816072-5.00007-9

from payers and providers, although the government can become involved if negotiations fail.[b] Moreover, unlike in nearly all other countries, many of the most important policies—not just in health—are determined through public referenda.

Switzerland achieved universal coverage through an individual mandate that requires the purchase of health insurance. Policies are sold by approved insurers to individuals; employers are not directly involved. Guaranteed universal coverage came about in 1996—more recently than in other countries—although health insurance had already been mandatory in some cantons (the Swiss equivalent of a state or province). Before that, however, a large segment of the population received their coverage through private insurance, mainly from nonprofit **sickness funds** and also for-profit companies [9]. The tradition of private (albeit, nonprofit) insurance still holds, as does the tradition of relatively high patient cost-sharing requirements. The latter exceeds those of all other countries covered in this book and, it will be shown in Chapter 14, appears to have resulted in greater financial access problems than in most other wealthy countries with universal coverage, particularly for poorer segments of the population.

Another notable feature of the Swiss system is its high expenditures, despite the deterrent of very high OOP spending of its residents. The country has been slow to successfully embrace cost containment strategies used elsewhere such as relying on generic rather than brand-name drugs. It should be kept in mind, though, that Switzerland is also an unusually wealthy country, with a per capita income even higher than the United States, and third only to Ireland and Norway in Europe (among countries with at least 1 million residents) [10]. One might argue, then, that the country has at least so far chosen to invest more of its considerable financial resources in its health care system.

The details

History

Health insurance in Switzerland goes back to the late 19th century. Initially, it was set up by employers, workers' unions, and religious groups to provide workers and their families with financial support when they were unable to work or died, but it eventually covered medical expenses. An estimated 7.5% of the population had such coverage in 1880 [6, p. 22].

The Swiss Constitution requires that certain major initiatives be voted upon by the population at large. After the failure of a federal health insurance proposal at the ballot box in 1900, a new proposal, the Federal Law on Sickness and Accident Insurance, was approved in 1912, stipulating that insurance funds could begin to receive federal subsidies if they agreed to provide particular

---

[b] Monika Diebold, personal communication, November 27, 2019.

benefits. These included open enrollment for most age groups (although higher-risk people could be charged more [11, p. 231]), freedom to change insurers after certain life events, and coverage of inpatient and outpatient care and drugs as well as allowing members to periodically move to another insurer [6, p. 22]. Much of the authority in health care in Switzerland resides locally in the 26 cantons. The 1912 law gave cantons the authority to decide whether possession of health insurance would be mandatory. The first to do was Basel-Stadt, in 1914, and over time, approximately half introduced such requirements, although they did not necessarily extend to all residents [6, p. 23].[c]

As in nearly all high-income countries, insurance coverage in Switzerland expanded greatly after World War II for a variety of reasons: medical care became more effective and along with that, more expensive, necessitating the financial protection afforded by insurance; the number and specialization of skilled medical professionals grew; people's incomes increased rapidly, raising demand; more insurers entered this potentially lucrative market; and lack of coverage was seen to be inconsistent with notions of equity and **solidarity**. Insurance coverage rose from 11% in 1915, to 40% in 1930, and 80% in 1959 [6, p. 23].

Insurance, of course, increases the demand for services by lowering OOP spending, so the rise in insurance coverage naturally led to a need to control expenditures. In 1964, concerned about the amount of money it had to pay in subsidies, the Swiss government amended the 1912 law so that subsidized insurance funds would be required to enact cost-sharing requirements such as **deductibles** and **coinsurance** [6, p. 23]. This legacy lives on more than 50 years later as Switzerland has the highest per capita OOP spending of any wealthy nation.

T.R. Reid provides an account of what happened over the subsequent 30 years:

> In health care .. the basic solidarity of Swiss society became badly strained near the end of the twentieth century. The Swiss health insurance business was coming to resemble the American system. Traditionally, Switzerland had had a network of "mutual," or nonprofit, health insurance plans; workers bought insurance through their employers. But Switzerland is home to some of the world's largest insurance firms. In the 1980s, these private insurance giants learned a profitable lesson from American insurers [which had been] buying up nonprofit health insurers … and converting them into profit-making operations. [F]or-profit health insurance produced fabulous bottom-line results, especially when the insurers were picky about the people they covered and diligent about denying claims … By the early 1990s, Switzerland's health care system was the closest in the world to the American model [12, p. 177].

---

[c]Luca Crivelli, personal communication, July 12, 2020.

In 1990, an estimated 4% of Swiss were without coverage [13]. A task force put together by the government in the early 1990s concluded that reforms were necessary so that (a) insurers do not make profits in the mandatory insurance program, (b) Swiss citizens be mandated to purchase individual coverage, and (c) open enrollment coupled with community-rated premiums would be required. According to Reid, "the reform proposal sparked heated debate with the for-profit insurance industry, the drug industry, and most of the rest of the business community fiercely opposed" [12, p. 179].

Following these recommendations, universal coverage was achieved in 1996 with passage by Parliament, and approval through a public referendum (with a bare majority, just 52% of the vote), of a new Federal Health Insurance Law. (Interestingly, in 2014, the Swiss voters held a referendum moving to a **single-payer system**, but it was soundly rejected [14].) It required that everyone purchase individual health insurance from nonprofit companies[d] that all cover the same set of basic medical benefits through a system of open enrollment with community-rated premiums. About one-fourth of the population receives subsidized coverage due to low incomes [15]. Over time, even opponents became reconciled with the law, and reportedly, insurers' profits rose overall as nonprofit mandatory medical coverage served as a gateway to market other insurance products: both voluntary health insurance (VHI) and nonhealth-related insurance [12].

By European standards, this transition into universal coverage is fairly recent and thus, the notion of nearly free hospital and physician care at the point of service is not necessarily expected or even desired by most of the Swiss population. Nicola Biller-Andorno and Thomas Zeltner state that,

> *[U]nlike countries with a long tradition of a national health service or comprehensive social insurance, Switzerland faces no historical based societal expectation that the state or taxpayers will systematically cover all health care expenses [15, p. 2195].*

Overview of the health insurance system

The Swiss health insurance system is based on publicly regulated, competing, nonprofit private insurers; the typical resident has a choice among 52 of them in 2017 [16, p. 29]. Everyone is required to purchase Mandatory Health Insurance (MHI) coverage, and thus, among citizens and legal residents, there is nearly universal coverage. Those that do not do so within 3 months of eligibility (that is, birth or immigration into the country) are assigned an insurer and pay penalties of 30%–50% more in premiums, depending on the canton in which they reside [17]. Unlike many countries, coverage is individual and not purchased

---

[d] These companies are permitted to make profits on other lines of business, including VHI.

through employer-based sickness funds; dependents must purchase their coverage or, in the case of children, have it purchased on their behalf.

Premium subsidies are available for lower-income individuals. They are financed jointly by the federal government (54%) and cantonal governments (46%, but varying by canton). About 30% of the population receives these subsidies, with about one-fourth of these people pay no premiums at all [6, p. 101].

Switzerland employs managed care, but the degree to which it affects the delivery of care varies with the particular insurance product. About 70% of Swiss belong to an insurance plan that has some limitations in provider choice [16, p. 168]. The most common types are insurers that require the use of primary care gatekeepers or call centers to have access to a specialist. Less common are HMO models where there is a defined network of providers and where providers are paid on a **capitation** basis. (Enrollment in the former outnumbers the latter by 4 to 1 [16, p. 120].) By choosing these plans, enrollees pay less in premiums but do not have the freedom to choose any provider they wish and generally have to go through a primary care **gatekeeping** physician to receive specialist referrals. Younger persons are more likely to join restricted care networks. Because they tend to be healthier and use relatively few services, it implies that these managed care systems are not having a large impact on the overall Swiss health care system as the raw numbers would suggest.[e]

Governance

On the government side, the administration and planning for the Swiss health care system is shared jointly by the federal government, the cantons, and over 2200 municipalities, the last of which are mainly responsible for long-term care, a topic not covered in this book. Historically, the cantons have had the most authority, as the federal government has jurisdiction only over areas explicitly authorized by the constitution. In recent decades, however, the federal government has taken on more authority [6, p. 29]. The Federal Office of Public Health (FOPH), which is under the supervision of the Federal Department of Home Affairs, is responsible for determining which services will be covered by MHI, financing, and monitoring the quality and safety of drugs and devices. The cantons, in turn, oversee the availability and provision of services in their areas, own many of the hospitals and pay for much of hospital care, and assist the federal government in providing poorer persons with subsidies to pay the mandatory health insurance premiums.

As is the case in several other European countries, governments do not control all aspects of health care governance. So-called "corporatist" organizations—consortia of insurers, providers, and sometimes cantons—also have a good deal of authority. MHI insurers are represented by two main associations of member companies. Nearly all physicians belong to a provider association; hospitals

---

[e] Alberto Holly, personal communication, September 17, 2019.

have their own. These payer and provider organizations have the legal authority to negotiate with each other to determine hospital and physician fees. The one that sets hospital (DRG) fees is called SwissDRG SA; it has representatives not only from the insurer and hospital groups but also from the cantons, as cantons own many of the hospitals in the country [6, p. 35]. The organization that sets ambulatory fees, called TARMED Suisse, has equal numbers of the insurer and physician representatives. Between 2004, when TARMED began, and 2014, it was able to reach a consensus on physician fee updates every year. In 2014, however, when such a consensus was not reached, the federal government intervened to settle the disagreement with its legal authority [6, p. 116].

Financing

Switzerland is an outlier among the 10 countries covered in this book, with an unusually large share of total health expenditures financed through OOP spending. In 2017, OECD data shows that 29% of total health care spending was through OOP payments [18].[f] Australia is distant second at 20%, with all other countries relying on OOP for 15% or less of total spending. It is therefore not surprising that share consumed by statutorily mandated health insurance, and government to a lesser degree, at 64%, is the second-lowest after the United States (Table 13.2).

MHI companies determine premiums at the regional level; there are 42 subregions for these purposes among the 26 cantons. Within a subregion, insurers must adhere to what is called "stratified community rating." This means that the company must charge all persons within a particular age range the same premium as everyone else of that age, in that subregion. The age ranges are very broad: 0–18, 19–25, and 26 and older [6, p. 79]; thus, among adults, there is de facto pure **community rating** within subregions.

Premiums are regulated. MHI companies submit proposed premiums to FOPH for approval. Denials or refunds may be required if premiums are judged to be too high, or even if they are deemed to be too low so as to increase the risk of insurer insolvency. The premiums charged are mainly determined through competitive forces, varying in part with the expected costs that insurers expect to incur.

There are thus many variations in premiums both within and between subregions. Other factors that also affect premiums are restrictions on provider choice (e.g., those in managed care networks that have their physician panels tend to

---

[f] Because different countries treat long-term care differently in terms of what percentage of expenditures are paid OOP, these cross-national comparisons should be interpreted cautiously. One example is that while somewhere between 20% and one-third of Swiss OOP are for long-term care, families also receive some cash benefits to help pay these costs. The latter is not included in calculating the OOP percentage.

pay less) and the size of the deductible, both of which are discussed below. It has been estimated that with all of the MHI companies, subregions, age groups, and other allowed criteria, at any one time there are more than 287,000 different premiums in the marketplace [19].

Some insurers, particularly those with a disproportionate share of younger, healthier enrollees, can charge less. To compensate for this, risk equalization activities are carried out at the federal level to reduce incentives of companies to select low-cost enrollees. Until 2011, the formula was quite rudimentary, considering only age and gender. While there was some redistribution of funds between insurers to account for these selection effects, they were generally thought to be inadequate, resulting in companies having an incentive to cherry-pick healthier individuals. To compensate for this, other factors such as prior hospital and nursing home stays, and large pharmaceutical costs, have been added to the formula [6, p. 102, 213],[e] Luca Crivelli reports that the improved formula "had the expected positive effect" [9]. Nevertheless, the abundance of companies and premium arrangements can make consumer-search activities challenging and raise administrative costs [6, p. 100].

Some revenue sources are progressive, but Switzerland relies on more of the regressive sources than most other countries [6, p. 232]. Sources that are generally progressive are income and corporate taxes. Those that are generally regressive include VATs and possibly property taxes (because much of property taxes are paid by renters). Three other types of revenues are generally highly regressive because they are fixed regardless of income: MHI premiums, VHI premiums, and OOP spending [20].

Coverage

Breadth

Practically, all Swiss citizens have MHI coverage. While a few default on their premiums, the government strongly enforces its mandate to purchase coverage [17]. Undocumented residents are eligible for coverage and even premium subsidies, but most do not have coverage because either they are unaware of their entitlement to it or they worry about deportation [6, p. 201].

Scope

All MHI companies are required to offer the same set of benefits. One way that Switzerland goes beyond most other countries is that, as a result of a national referendum, complementary and alternative medicine performed by medical doctors is covered under MHI [21]. The main omission from coverage is dental care, which is also generally not covered by VHI; an estimated 90% of dental costs are paid OOP [6, p. 89]. As in most countries, eyeglasses and contact lenses are not covered except for children [22].

Depth

Comparing Switzerland to the other countries discussed in this book, what stands out is the lack of coverage depth: OOP spending is far higher than in any of the other nine countries. To illustrate, in 2018, per capita OOP spending was over 70% higher than in the United States, the country with the second-highest amount in the world [18]. This appears to be a significant deterrent to seeking care for many people with low incomes.

There are several contributors to OOP spending. The main ones are deductibles and coinsurance; dental care; noncovered outpatient services such as psychologists, physical therapies, home health providers, and ambulance services; and long-term care [6, p. 108].

Everyone who has the age of 19 or older is subject to a deductible of 300 Swiss Francs [at time of writing, 1 Swiss franc (Sw.fr.) equaled $1.10 (US)]. In addition, there is a 10% coinsurance charge for expenses above the deductible, but it is limited to no more than Sw.fr. 700 per year so the annual OOP limit is Sw.fr. 1000 for covered services. Children are exempted from the deductible and are responsible for no more than Sw.fr. 350 per year in coinsurance. For maternity care, there is neither a deductible nor coinsurance. The coinsurance rate is 20% rather than 10% on brand-name drugs when a substitute generic is available. There is also a daily hospital **copayment** of Sw.fr. 15 for adults [6 (p. 107), 23].

The other important facet of cost-sharing in Switzerland is the voluntary deductible. As noted, adults are required to pay an annual deductible of Sw.fr. 300, but people are allowed to choose a higher one to reduce their premiums— as high as Sw.fr. 2500. (Children, who are not ordinarily subject to a deductible, can purchase an insurance policy with a voluntary deductible as high as Sw.fr. 600.) While health insurance companies choose the amount of the discount for those choosing a higher deductible, they are limited to lowering premiums by no more than 50% [6, p. 97]. Estimates vary on the percentage of the population that has chosen a deductible that is higher than the minimum amount, either through their managed care insurance plans or through a conventional plan, but it appears to be a large share, in the range of 40% to slightly over 50% [6, p. 98]. De Pietro and colleagues report that "anecdotal evidence exists that the relatively high annual deductibles … lead to individuals postponing medical care to the next year with potentially adverse consequences for health" [6, p. 231]; there is further empirical support for this conclusion [24, 25].

Voluntary health insurance

VHI, possessed by an estimated 60% of the Swiss population, plays a moderately important role in the country, paying for about 7% of total health care spending [26]. Unlike in many other countries, it is not subsidized by employers although employers do sometimes purchase it as a perk to managers and senior workers.

VHI helps protect these employers by encouraging prompt use of medical care when one of their employees becomes sick because employers are responsible for paying up to 6 months of their employees' sick leave [26]. Importantly, VHI cannot cover patient cost-sharing requirements on MHI-covered services.

There are two kinds of VHI benefits and, oftentimes, a person has to purchase more than one to obtain both benefit types. One type provides private rooms in hospitals and choice of hospital specialist. The other type covers services not included in the MHI benefits, particularly dental care but also such things as the services of psychologists, complementary and alternative medicine, and eyeglasses and contact lenses.

VHI is sold both by companies that sell MHI as well as by for-profit companies. They are permitted to deny enrollment to applicants, not cover preexisting conditions, and charge more to those who are at higher risk. It is estimated that the administrative costs incurred in the VHI market are far higher than in MHI: 18% vs 5% [6, p. 111].

Choice

As discussed earlier, different versions of managed care play a significant role in the Swiss health care system. While the system allows a great deal of choice, choosing to join a managed care plan may reduce provider choice later on—although not the choice of a hospital, as selective contracting between hospitals and insurers is prohibited. The first choice a person makes is the MHI insurer; there were over 50 to choose from in 2017 and, typically, there are several plan choices available from each. Individuals may switch plans as many as two times during a year. An estimated 5%–10% do so at least annually [6, p. 99].

Those not choosing a managed care plan can choose any primary care provider they wish, but premiums tend to be higher. They also have their choice of a hospital as well as specialists who practice outside of the hospital; referrals are not required. People choosing an alternative plan—70% of the population in 2017—generally must stay within their plan's network and need referrals to see a specialist [6, p. 73].

Managed care has grown considerably, from less than 10% of MHI enrollment in 2003 to almost 70% in 2017 [16, p. 168]. Such plans mainly affect care not through managing it so much as requiring that enrollees use a particular panel of physicians. This growth happened largely in the absence of changes in the law. While the parliament approved a bill in 2011 that would have increased the financial penalties for those remaining in traditional insurance, this was strongly opposed by both the physician community and socialist party on different grounds. When it was brought before the voters in a referendum, it failed to pass, garnering only 24% of the votes. This failure has not seemed to have impeded the growth of managed care plans very much. Insured patients find their lower premiums attractive.

Provider payment

Hospitals

Switzerland has a mix of public (21%), nonprofit (25%), and for-profit hospitals (55%). Because public and nonprofit hospitals are larger, they contain nearly two-thirds of total beds [6, p. 124]. Cantons are responsible for paying for just over half of hospital expenses, with MHI companies and patient OOP-spending accounting for the remainder [6, p. 35, 118, 125].

Inpatient hospital care is paid on a DRG basis. Switzerland moved to DRGs in 2012, which is later than most countries. Before that, payment mechanisms varied by cantons, with some hospitals being paid on a per diem basis, a system that encourages longer hospital stays. The company that develops and revises the system, SwissDRG SA, is a corporatist organization jointly owned by the consortium of payers, the consortium of hospitals, and the cantons.

Physicians

The large majority of primary physician payments are paid on a fee-for-service (FFS) basis through a national fee schedule. As in the case of hospitals, fees are negotiated through a corporatist organization with representatives from physicians and insurers, called TARMED. Until 2018, it had revised fees for individual services but had not carried out any systematic revision to try to achieve more equity between generalist and specialist physicians. Beginning in 2018, however, the federal government intervened to make broader changes that are designed to reduce these differences [27]. This included a 10% reduction in payment rates for such common procedures as cataract operations, colonoscopies, and radiation therapy [11, p. 244]. In contrast, hospital-based physicians typically are paid on a salary basis [22].

While FFS dominates, there is some use of capitation and salary in managed care plans. An estimated 10% of payments were made in this way from payers to managed care plans in 2012 [6, p. 117], although most likely not all physicians in these managed care plans were paid via capitation or salary.

Pharmaceuticals

The pharmaceutical industry is an important part of the Swiss economy, with such companies as Roche and Novartis headquartered there. The FOPH sets pharmaceutical prices based on costs of development and production, therapeutic value, and external **reference prices** (i.e., the prices paid in other countries). The inclusion/exclusion of drugs on the list of reimbursed products, and their prices, are assessed by FOPH, with the intent of reassessing the prices of one-third of drugs each year [22]. Those prices deemed to be cost-ineffective are subject to price reductions [6, p. 68]. This occurs commonly; of about 1000 drugs evaluated in 2017, the prices of over one-third were reduced, by an average of 17% [28].

Generic drugs are used far less commonly in Switzerland than in most other high-income countries. In 2017, only 23% of prescriptions were for generics, comprising just 18% of total drug spending. In contrast, Germany's figures were 82% and 35%, respectively (Table 15.6) [29, Figure 10.10]. This is somewhat puzzling in that patients face a higher coinsurance rate for many brand-name drugs (20% rather than 10%), and pharmacists have a financial incentive to dispense them as well. The country is making further efforts to increase the use of generic drugs. One such measure is a requirement that generic medication prices be 20%–50% less than the brand-name price, which in turn reduces the amount that patients pay in coinsurance [22]. Little has been done so far, however, to modify physicians' incentives [6, p. 69]. A related problem is the relatively high prices of generics, which are about double than those in France, the Netherlands, and the United Kingdom [30].

Assuring access and equity

Because OOP spending is so high in Switzerland, there is an obvious concern about how this affects access to care. These concerns are justified, as data from the Commonwealth Fund's 2016 population surveys in 11 countries show that Switzerland has the second-highest rates (after the United States among the 10 countries examined in this book) of residents claiming a cost-related access problem in the past year [5].[8] In addition, twice as many Swiss in the lower half of the income distribution (30%) claim that they had such a problem compared to their wealthier counterparts (15%) [5]. Moreover, the Swiss are more likely to experience catastrophic health care spending, both for those with low and high incomes [31].

Despite per capita OOP spending that exceeds US amounts by 70%, the Swiss have fewer financial access problems than Americans. One reason is that the Swiss have universal health insurance coverage and have had it for 25 years. A second is that there are no cost-sharing requirements for maternity care, and children do not have a deductible (unless their parents choose to have one to reduce premiums) and have an annual OOP maximum of just Sw.fr. 350. Even for adults, there is an Sw.fr. 1000 maximum on OOP spending for services covered by MHI, which is far lower than that of nonpoor Americans face [23]—unless people choose a higher deductible. In the United States, those with employer-sponsored coverage had a maximum averaging about $3900, and individual insurance sold on the ACA exchanges had a maximum of over $6000 [32].

---

[8] Throughout this book, we use Commonwealth Fund data to present financial access across the countries, but it should be noted that other surveys come up with very different results. The Eurostat measure of "self-reported unmet need for medical examination" shows Swiss rates less than 1%, which is less than half the average of 27 OECD countries and lower than France's figure. See Eurostat, Self-reported unmet need for medical examination and care by sex. https://ec.europa.eu/eurostat/databrowser/view/sdg_03_60/default/table?lang=en.

It should be stressed that this cap applies only to MHI-covered services. Coverage for services not included in the public benefit package such as routine dental care, physical therapy, the care of independent psychotherapists, and inpatient long-term care must be paid directly and is not subject to the cap, and indeed, these comprise the majority of patient OOP spending [6].

Historically, among wealthy countries, Switzerland had been found to have among the greatest vertical inequities—that is, poorer people paying a larger share of their incomes toward health care compared to those who are better off [20]. This is still the case because of the high portion of total health spending that is paid OOP as well as the fact that individual premiums are highly regressive [33]. While the poorest 10% of households pay more than 15% of their income on health, this share is around 8% for the richest 10% [6, p. 232].

A related issue is a **horizontal equity**. One study, by Luca Crivelli and Paola Salari, found that there is as much variation in equity between the cantons as there is between Sweden (among the most equitable nations) and the United States. The authors attributed this to the federalist system, whereby cantons have much discretion over such things as the extent to which they subsidize premiums, tax rates, and the mix of revenues raised from MHI premiums vs taxes [34, p. 4].

Crivelli and Salari also posit that the Swiss reliance on consumer choice of health insurance may be aggravating the problem. People choose which MHI plan to join, the deductible level, and whether to be in a managed care plan with a restricted provider network; some people may be better able to make cost-effective choices than others. The authors write that "we cannot exclude the existence of a social gradient in the ability to manage information" [34, p. 9] whereby those, for example, with lower incomes and education levels are making poorer choices.

Controlling expenditures

Switzerland's health care expenditures are among the highest in the world—it usually ranks second after the United States. In 2019, per capita health expenditures were more than 16% higher than in Germany and 44% higher than France. As a share of GDP, Switzerland led Europe, at 12.1%. With this measure, it is less of an outlier, however: Germany and France, which ranked next, spent 11.7% and 11.2% of GDP on health in 2017, respectively (see Table 15.3) [18].[h]

One might expect, then, that cost containment would be a major concern in Switzerland. The country has shied away from a national budget, however, as this is not consistent with its reliance on competition between MHI plans. Moreover,

---

[h] The fact that France is so much lower than Switzerland in the first measure, but is comparable in the second, is simply due to a large difference in the relative wealth of the two countries. In 2017 average per capita income in Switzerland was 40% higher than in France.

its corporatist tradition means that fees are determined by nongovernmental organizations. Instead, it has implemented a handful of policies to control costs in certain segments of the health care sector, although De Pietro and colleagues deemed those aimed at the inpatient sector as "weak" [6, p. 106]. Four of these include:

- High patient cost-sharing requirements.
- Health technology assessment to determine which new medical technologies and pharmaceuticals will be covered.
- Using research on both therapeutic value and payment rates in other countries to keep down the price of prescription medicine.
- Allowing health insurers to market policies containing two features (both of which are voluntary on part of enrollees) that have the potential to control costs: (a) allowing the choice of higher deductibles, and (b) permitting the choice of a managed care plan with primary care gatekeeping and/or a limited provider network.

More recently, in 2018 Switzerland's Federal Council, which is made up of the directors of government departments and which is elected by the natural legislature, approved a new set of cost containment measures to be implemented over the following few years. These include the use of internal reference pricing for paying for pharmaceuticals (e.g., reimbursing only the generic price when a brand-name drug is used), close monitoring of the volume and price of services provided, and "out of the box" pilot projects in such areas as a movement away from fee-for-service in the outpatient sector [35].

Key policy issues

In 2013, the federal government released a strategic plan, *Health2020*, focusing on the challenges that the country faces in health care and possible ways of going forward. The document covers a lot of ground; a great deal of emphasis, for example, is on expanding health promotion and disease prevention activities. In the area of health insurance, some of the recommendations include [19]:

- Simplifying the health insurance system; as noted, there are estimated 287,000 different premiums across the country.
- Improving risk-adjustment mechanisms and providing insurers with reinsurance for their most costly enrollees, so there will be less incentive to cherrypick healthier people.
- More use of health technology assessment in determining covered services and reimbursement rates.
- Improving the system of paying for prescription drugs in ways that will encourage the provision of generic drugs, establish efficient fees, and encourage the use of effective medications.
- Modifying physician payment methods by moving away from pure FFS.

- Reducing the financial burden on the poor by relating cost-sharing requirements to incomes, and eliminating premiums for children in poor- and middle-income families.
- Working with and learn from other countries' accomplishments in health system reform.

References

[1] Carroll AE, Frakt A. The best health care system in the world: which one would you pick? TheUpshot. The New York Times; 2017. [Internet]. [Accessed 2 September 2020]. Available from: https://www.nytimes.com/interactive/2017/09/18/upshot/best-health-care-system-country-bracket.html.

[2] Björnberg A, Phang AY. Euro health consumer index 2018. Health Consumer Powerhouse Ltd; 2019.

[3] Anon. 2016 Commonwealth fund international health policy survey. The system works pretty well and only minor changes are necessary to make it work better, 2016. International health care system profiles. The Commonwealth Fund; 2016. [Internet]. [Accessed 2 September 2020]. Available from: https://www.commonwealthfund.org/international-health-policy-center/system-stats/works-well.

[4] Osborn R, Doty MM, Moulds DB, Sarnak D, Shah A. Commonwealth fund international health policy survey of older adults. The Commonwealth Fund [Survey]; 2017.

[5] Schneider EC, Sarnak DO, Squires D, Shah A, Doty MM. Mirror, mirror 2017: International comparison reflects flaws and opportunities for better U.S. health care. Mirror, Mirror: The Commonwealth Fund; 2017.

[6] De Pietro C, Camenzind P, Sturny I, Crivelli L, Edwards-Garavoglia S, Spranger A, et al. Switzerland: health system review. Health Syst Transit 2015;17(4):1–288.

[7] Tikkanen R, Abrams MK, U.S. health care from a global perspective. higher spending, worse outcomes? The Commonwealth Fund, 2020. [Internet]. [Accessed 27 February 2021]. Available from: https://www.commonwealthfund.org/publications/issue-briefs/2020/jan/us-health-care-global-perspective-2019; 2019.

[8] G.B.D. Healthcare Access Quality Collaborators. Measuring performance on the Healthcare Access and Quality Index for 195 countries and territories and selected subnational locations: a systematic analysis from the Global Burden of Disease Study 2016. Lancet 2018;391(10136):2236–71.

[9] Crivelli L. Consumer-driven health insurance in Switzerland, where politics is governed by federalism and direct democracy. In: Thomson S, Sagan A, Mossialos E, editors. Private health insurance: History, politics and performance. Cambridge: Cambridge University Press; 2020.

[10] Anon. Country comparison: GDP—Per capita (PPP). The world factbook 2020. Central Intelligence Agency; 2020. [Web factbook]. [Accessed 2 September 2020]. Available from: https://www.cia.gov/library/publications/the-world-factbook/fields/211rank.html.

[11] Emanuel EJ. Which country has the world's best health care? New York: PublicAffairs; 2020.

[12] Reid TR. The healing of America: A global quest for better, cheaper, and fairer health care. New York: Penguin Press; 2009.

[13] Anon. History of social security in Switzerland. Federal Social Insurance Office; 2013. [JPG]. [Accessed 3 September 2020]. Available from: https://www.geschichtedersozialensicherheit.ch/fileadmin/redaktion/Zahlen/G14.jpg.

[14] Chaufan C. What can US single-payer supporters learn from the Swiss rejection of single payer? Int J Health Serv 2016;46(2):331–45.

[15] Biller-Andorno N, Zeltner T. Individual responsibility and community solidarity—the Swiss health care system. N Engl J Med 2015;373(23):2193–7.

[16] Anon. Statistique de l'assurance- maladie obligatoire (Compulsory health insurance statistics) 2017. Bern: Office fédéral de la santé publique OFSP (Federal Office of Public Health); 2019. 202 pp.

[17] Van Ginneken E, Rice T. Enforcing enrollment in health insurance exchanges: evidence from the Netherlands, Switzerland, and Germany. Med Care Res Rev 2015;72(4):496–509.

[18] OECD.Stat. OECD. [Web browser]. [Accessed 3 September 2020]. Available from: https:// stats.oecd.org/Index.aspx?ThemeTreeId=9.

[19] Anon. The Federal Council's health-policy priorities. Bern: Federal Department of Home Affairs FDHA; 2013.

[20] Wagstaff A, Van Doorslaer E. Equity in health care finance and delivery. In: Culyer AJ, Newhouse JP, editors. Handbook of health economics. 1st ed, vol. 1B. Amsterdam, North Holland: Elsevier; 2000. p. 893–1910.

[21] Komplementärmedizin D. Complementary medicine in Switzerland now a mandatory health insurance service. Your Health Your Choice; 2017. [Media release]. [Accessed 3 September 2020]. Available from: https://www.yourhealthyourchoice.com.au/news-features/complementary-medicine-in-switzerland-now-a-mandatory-health-insurance-service/.

[22] Sturny I. In: Tikkanen R, Osborn R, Mossialos E, Djordjevic A, Wharton GA, editors. Switzerland. International health care system profiles. The Commonwealth Fund; 2020. [Internet]. [Accessed 3 September 2020]. Available from: https://www.commonwealthfund.org/international-health-policy-center/countries/switzerland.

[23] Rice T, Quentin W, Anell A, Barnes AJ, Rosenau P, Unruh LY, et al. Revisiting out-of-pocket requirements: trends in spending, financial access barriers, and policy in ten high-income countries. BMC Health Serv Res 2018;18(1):371.

[24] Van Winssen KP, van Kleef RC, van de Ven WP. Potential determinants of deductible uptake in health insurance: how to increase uptake in the Netherlands? Eur J Health Econ 2016;17(9):1059–72.

[25] Guessous I, Gaspoz JM, Theler JM, Wolff H. High prevalence of forgoing healthcare for economic reasons in Switzerland: a population-based study in a region with universal health insurance coverage. Prev Med 2012;55(5):521–7.

[26] Sagan A, Thomson S. Voluntary health insurance in Europe. vol. 1. United Kingdom: WHO Regional Office for Europe; 2016.

[27] Kaufmann C, Boes S, Mantwill S. In: Boes S, Mantwill S, Wicki TK, editors. New measures for cost containment and improved efficiency proposed by international expert group. The health systems and policy monitor: Switzerland. European Observatory on Health Systems and Policies; 2017. [Internet]. [Accessed 3 September 2020]. Available from: https://www.hspm.org/countries/switzerland25062016/countrypage.aspx.

[28] Kaufmann C, Boes S, Mantwill S. In: Boes S, Mantwill S, Wicki TK, editors. New evaluation criteria and pricing decisions for pharmaceuticals. The health systems and policy monitor: Switzerland. European Observatory on Health Systems and Policies; 2018. [Internet]. [Accessed 3 September 2020]. Available from: https://www.hspm.org/countries/switzerland25062016/countrypage.aspx.

[29] Paris V, Lopert R, Chapman S, Wenzl M, Canaud M, Mueller M. Generics and biosimilars. In: OECD, editor. Health at a glance 2019: OECD indicators. 2019 ed. Paris: OECD Publishing; 2019.

[30] OECD/WHO. OECD reviews of health systems: Switzerland 2011. OECD reviews of health systems. Paris: OECD Publishing; 2011.

[31] Wagstaff A, Eozenou P, Neelsen S, Smitz M. The 2019 update of the health equity and financial protection indicators database: An overview. World Bank; 2019 [8879].

[32] Claxton G, Rae M, Long M, Damico A. Employer health benefits. San Francisco, CA: Henry J. Kaiser Family Foundation; 2018.

[33] Bilger M. Progressivity, horizontal inequality and reranking caused by health system financing: a decomposition analysis for Switzerland. J Health Econ 2008;27(6):1582–93.

[34] Crivelli L, Salari P. The inequity of the Swiss Health Care system financing from a federal state perspective. Int J Equity Health 2014;13:13–7.

[35] Anon. Contenimento dei costi nel settore sanitario (Cost containment in the healthcare sector). Federal Office of Public Health FOPH; 2018. [Internet news]. [Accessed 3 September 2020]. Available from: https://www.bag.admin.ch/bag/it/home/das-bag/aktuell/news/news-14-09-2018.html.

Chapter 11

Netherlands

The big picture

As colorfully put by Gert Westert and colleagues, "The Dutch live below sea level behind dykes, and history has taught them that solidarity pays off" [1]. More than any other country, the Netherlands has formulated a healthcare system that attempts to marry the typically disparate notions of **solidarity** with reliance on markets. It provides universal coverage with low-to-moderate out-of-pocket (OOP) spending and accessible care for nearly everyone through a system of regulated (or managed) competition.

The driving force of regulated competition is strong reliance on consumer choice of competing health insurance plans. While other countries covered in this book, particularly Germany, Switzerland, and the United States, also use regulated competition, the Dutch system contains more key features [2]. Indeed, it provided a model for the design of healthcare marketplaces included in the US Affordable Care Act (ACA) [3], the difference being that those marketplaces cover less than 10% of the US population. In contrast, in the Netherlands, everyone obtains their coverage through a single national exchange of competing health plans.

This system, which was a radical change from what it replaced, began in 2006. The previous one, composed of private insurance for wealthier citizens and public insurance sold through nonprofit **sickness funds** for others, had been found wanting. The Netherlands was also unusual among wealthy European countries in the early 2000s in that nearly one-third of the population relied on private insurance as their main source of coverage [4]. This exacerbated health inequalities, provided incentives for private insurers to avoid the sick, was prone to waiting lists, gave little incentive to providers to perform better, and had few mechanisms to control spending [5].

The 2006 Health Insurance Act—probably the most fundamental system change among the 10 countries covered in this book since the establishment of the United Kingdom's National Health Service in 1948—hardly happened overnight. In fact, the main principles were laid out nearly 20 years earlier in a document put together by a government-appointed group commonly known as the Dekker Commission. During the ensuing period until 2006, a number of health insurance changes recommended by the Dekker Commission were implemented. Examples included letting sickness funds cover the entire country

Health Insurance Systems: An International Comparison. https://doi.org/10.1016/B978-0-12-816072-5.00011-0
173

and setting the premiums they would charge, and allowing much of the population to choose among these insurance funds during an open enrollment period. To help ensure that competition was on the basis of value rather than selecting the healthiest enrollees, premiums were required to be community rated, and a sophisticated risk adjustment system was implemented to further reduce any advantages to insurers of having healthier enrollees. Efforts were also made to integrate the sickness funds and private insurance, for example, by allowing those turning age 65 with earnings below a certain income threshold to move into a sickness fund. Government also introduced limited cost sharing requirements [6, p. 114]. Arguably, this made the 2006 legislation less of a leap since care would not be free to the patient.

The 2006 Health Insurance Act, however, brought forth a more comprehensive and cohesive set of reforms. More than a dozen years after implementation, debate continues to swirl around the success of the reforms. Most would agree, however, that the Dutch healthcare system is one of the more successful ones among high-income countries, for several reasons: OOP spending is low enough so that financial access barriers are among the lowest in Europe; differences in self-reported unmet need are nearly identical between those with high and low incomes; and many measures of healthcare processes and outcomes are impressive, in part due to an unusually well-developed system of primary care [7]. Whether or not these positive indicators are the result of the 2006 reforms is a matter of contention that is unlikely to be resolved.

Much of the concern around whether regulated competition has been successful as it relates to the health purchasing market—whether insurers are successful in negotiating with providers on behalf of their policyholders to get the highest quality care for the lowest price. There continues to be a great deal of debate as this; answers are difficult to come by in part as a result of a lack of adequate data on quality and outcomes [3, 8, 9].

One problem with systems of regulated competition is market consolidation. Both hospitals and insurers each have an incentive to merge so that they will have more clout during negotiations with each other. This has been how healthcare markets have evolved in the United States and is characteristic of the Netherlands as well. While there is some disagreement over which group has the upper hand, it is unlikely that consumers will be the beneficiaries.

The details

History

The precursors of health insurance in the Netherlands go back to the guild system of the 18th century where workers paid fees to their particular guild, which in turn provided some financial protection for themselves and their families in the case of illness, disability, or death. In the 19th century, both commercial insurers and physician and pharmacist groups began to sell coverage. Soon thereafter, unions offered health insurance coverage themselves so they would not have to rely on commercial insurers. At the very beginning of the 20th century, some employers began to purchase coverage for their employees. At the beginning of World War II, about two-thirds of the population had some coverage [10].

Health insurance became mandatory for all workers below a particular income threshold in 1941 during the German occupation of the country. According to Robert Vonk and Frederik Schut, "The Germany occupation during WWII was of fundamental importance. It reshaped health insurance and introduced the welfare state logic" [4, p. 333]. Those with incomes below a particular level were required to join a nonprofit sickness fund. This system provided uniform benefits and covered dependents as well, with half of premiums coming each from employers and employees. Those not in the labor force could join by paying in voluntarily, while people earning more than the income cut-off could purchase private health insurance [11, p. 19]. But national efforts to provide universal coverage, which had begun as early as 1904, were not fully achieved until more than a century later. It is noteworthy, however, that an estimated 98.5% did have coverage of some sort in 2005, the year before the Health Insurance Act came into effect [12].

This two-tier system of public insurance (for those with lower incomes) and private insurance (for others) was not only inequitable but was inefficient as well. There was little motivation to contain costs, few incentives for providers to increase quality, and there were waiting lists to receive care as well as relatively high administrative costs associated with having two disparate systems operating at arm's length from each other. Other countries, notably England, had achieved universal coverage several decades earlier.

In 1986, the government appointed the Dekker Commission to come up with a way to revamp the Dutch system. While it took nearly 20 years for its main elements to become law, as noted there were a number of incremental legislative changes along the way that eased the transition. The key elements of the Commission's recommendations are listed in the next section. The most fundamental one was merging together the public and private insurance systems into one where all people get the same benefits and are treated equally. Certainly in the case of the Netherlands, one message is that fundamental reform of a healthcare system does not come quickly.

Overview of the health insurance system

The Dutch can choose among 2 dozen or so insurance plans sold by 10 different companies, but 90% of the population are members of the plans sold by just 4 companies [11, p. 33]. Insurance is purchased individually rather than provided through the employment system, although as noted below employers do become involved by forming "collectives." There are several rules that form the key tenets of Dutch regulated competition. These include:

- Mandatory coverage through SHI. Everyone is required to purchase health insurance coverage.

- Open enrollment. Anyone is free to choose any insurer and the insurer cannot turn them down. Moreover, people can choose to switch insurers annually.
- Community rated premiums. Everyone choosing a particular health plan (i.e., health insurance product) is charged the same amount. Different insurers can and do charge different premiums for different health products; indeed, price competition between insurers is one of the key bases of competition.
- Standardized benefits. All insurers must provide the same benefits to aid comparison shopping. One exception is that different insurers may contract with particular providers, although this is not nearly as common as in Switzerland.
- Consumer information is made available to allow comparison of insurers. This includes not only prices but consumer satisfaction and quality [11, p. 46].
- Subsidies. All households with incomes below a certain threshold are entitled to **premium** subsidies. In the Netherlands, those under age 18 receive insurance without having to pay premiums.
- Risk adjustment. Insurers that enroll sicker or more expensive persons receive additional subsidies and those with healthier enrollees forfeit some of the premiums they collect. The Netherlands is known to have among the most sophisticated risk-adjustment systems in the world, although it is still not fully adequate to remove incentives for insurers to seek healthier enrollees. Risk adjustment factors include age, gender, socioeconomic status, source of income, region, pharmaceutical consumption for patients with particular chronic diseases, having chronic conditions typically treated in the hospital, and previous utilization for those without chronic illnesses [11, p. 81].

Unlike in the other European countries covered in the book, insurers providing SHI coverage can be for-profit entities. In reality, though, for-profit insurers never were enthusiastic about participating in such a system because they were pessimistic that they could thrive under the highly regulated environment [4]. Currently, only three SHI insurers are for-profit entities, with a joint market share of about 3%.[a]

Mandatory SHI enrollment is strictly enforced. Those that the government has found not to have purchased coverage within 3 months of being notified are fined, and eventually a bailiff is sent. Those who persist in being uninsured have premiums deducted from their incomes, and generally, these premiums are higher than if the person had chosen his or her own plan. Another set of procedures and fines are applied to those who select an insurer but default on their premiums [13]. To ameliorate this problem, the government provides subsidies to make premiums affordable. All children are fully subsidized, as well as about one-quarter of adults on a sliding scale based on their incomes [14].

---

a. Erik Schut, personal communication, December 23, 2019.

Governance

The Ministry of Health, Welfare, and Sport is the primary government organization responsible for planning and promoting the health of the population. Oversight activities are carried out by an independent organization, the Dutch Health Care Authority, whose mission is to ensure that the system of regulated competition is carried out fairly. The Ministry of Finance has the responsibility to collect revenues and provide premium subsidies for lower-income families to purchase coverage. While the government sets the basic benefits package for SHI, the actual workings of the three markets—health insurance, care provision, and healthcare purchasing—are largely carried out by the insurers, providers, and consumers themselves.

The textbook model of regulated competition has a specific role of government: to set the rules to ensure that competition occurs on the basis of value rather than on having insurers select the healthiest people. Beyond setting such rules and overseeing their implementation, government's role under the textbook model is mainly redistributional: helping to finance premiums for those who cannot afford to pay them [15]. While the Dutch model more closely adheres to this than any other country, its governmental role is greater than in the textbook model, particularly with regard to setting certain healthcare prices and an overall expenditure target.

Indeed, the Dutch model constitutes a hybrid model between regulated competition and direct governmental influence on the marketplace. As noted by Hans Maarse and colleagues, "market principles are combined with an extensive set of public regulations to preserve the public interests in health care and accommodate a smooth transition from the old to the new situation" [8, p. 162]—a transition that continues, at time of writing, 14 years later. These government interventions include establishing a "soft" healthcare budget, which Madelon Kroneman and colleagues state, "indicates the maximum allowed healthcare expenditure. If providers and insurers spend more, the Minister may decide to charge providers to repay the excess…" [11, p. 78]. Negotiations therefore still take place between insurers and providers but government can intercede if it deems spending too high. Government also sets prices for services where promoting competition is likely to be ineffective or unwise, such as for hospital services that are rare or particularly reliant on new technologies, and very expensive drugs provided in inpatient settings such as for cancer treatment.[b]

Financing

About 80% of total health expenditures are paid through the SHI system, with the remaining 20% split between VHI (8%) and OOP (12%). There are two sources of funding for adult SHI coverage, each of which covers half of

---

b. Madelon Kroneman, personal communication, December 23, 2019.

spending: flat premiums (which are community rated, that is, the same for everyone choosing a particular health plan), and income-related premiums. Children under the age of 18 do not pay premiums but instead are funded by tax revenue [11, p. 57]. The premiums average about 1400 euros per year [16, p. 200].

The way in which the two main revenue sources are collected differ. Individuals pay the flat premiums (which are set by the insurer as part of the system of regulated competition) directly to their insurer, while the income-related premiums are sent by the employer to the government tax authority. All revenue is pooled and re-allocated to insurers based on the risk profile of their enrollees, helping to ensure that there is not an undue incentive for insurers to selectively market to healthier persons. In 2020, the payroll tax rate was 6.70%, applied up to an earnings ceiling of about 57,200 euros per year [17]. The self-employed paid a slightly lower rate.

Two of government's major tax-funded expenditures are covering the premiums of those under the age of 18, and subsidizing the health insurance premiums for those with low incomes. These are funded by two sources in fairly equal amounts: an income tax, which is progressive, and a VAT (or sales) tax. VATs are regressive because they take a bigger bite out of the incomes of poorer persons, but the Dutch tax, which is 21% for most goods and services, is adjusted down to 9% for food and some other necessities [11, p. 78].

Coverage

Breadth

Nearly all Dutch are covered by SHI. Those few who do not sign up (an estimated 0.2% of the population in 2014) or who default on premiums are actively pursued by government, using such tools as warnings, fines, and the garnishment of wages. If those are not successful, government purchases coverage on their behalf and charges them [13]. The treatment of undocumented immigrants depends on their immigration status and ability to pay, but in general, there is a system for them separate from SHI [14]. Moreover, providers who treat undocumented individuals who are unable to pay can receive a refund of about 80% of their costs.[b]

Scope

Health insurers are required to offer the same set of government-mandated services. Most healthcare services are included in the benefits package, the main exceptions applying just to adults: dental care (except for major procedures like dental surgery), eyeglasses and contact lenses, and physical therapy. Children up to age 18 are covered for these services. Over 80% of the Dutch have VHI policies, and three-quarters of these cover dental care, meaning that in total, about 63% of the adult population has coverage for some of the costs of dental care.[c]

Depth

SHI coverage in the Netherlands is deep. Except for a **deductible**, most care is provided free of cost sharing requirements. The main cost faced by most people seeking care is a mandatory annual deductible of 385 euros. This does not apply to those under age 18, maternity care, GP care, and to some people with particular chronic conditions who are part of integrated care programs. The deductible was instituted in 2008 at a level of 150 euros but more than doubled to current levels by 2016, which is set for the foreseeable future [18]. There are a few other OOP cost responsibilities such as prescription drugs costing more than the reference price. Providers are not allowed to charge above-established fees, that is, balance bill their patients.

As in Switzerland, the Dutch can voluntarily choose a higher deductible, ranging from an additional 100 to 500 euros, in 100-euro increments. On average, choosing the highest amount results in a reduction in premium rates of 240 euros annually [19]. In 2019, just 13% of the Dutch opted for an optional deductible, far lower than the 40%–50% estimated in Switzerland [20, 21, p. 98]. Those who have been found to be most likely to benefit from choosing a higher deductible are young adults, those likely to have few healthcare expenses, and males [19].

Voluntary health insurance

VHI plays a moderately important role in the Dutch healthcare system. An estimated 84% of the population owns a policy, with VHI paying for 8% of total healthcare expenses [11 (p. 92), 14]. Its main function is to cover services not included in the SHI benefits package, particularly adult dental care, physical therapy, eyeglasses, contraceptives, and prescription drugs costs above the amount reimbursable through SHI coverage [14]. Benefits vary between plans, and therefore, premiums as well. Unlike in Switzerland, it can also cover all or part of the 385-euro mandatory deductible [22].

The market is not regulated. Most people purchase VHI from the company that sells them their SHI coverage, and vice versa. Insurers can turn applicants down (although there is not strong evidence that they have done so) and can charge more to those whom they expect to be high users of medical care [8, 11, p. 92]. Thus, insurers have the ability to use VHI as a way of obtaining healthier

---

c. Ewout van Ginneken, personal communication, October 14, 2019.

patients in their SHI programs. By charging high premiums to those who are unhealthy, it will make VHI unattractive to such persons, who are likely to then shy away from the insurer's SHI plan [23].

Choice

Patients are free to choose any of the approximately two dozen insurers and can switch plans annually. While they can purchase insurance individually, about 70% elect to be part of a collective, which is usually organized through an employer but can also be a patient-oriented or other organization. The attraction of being in a collective is that insurers can give a discount of up to 5% on premiums (it was 10% until 2019 [24]). According to Kroneman and colleagues, collectives are designed "to give the insured more influence ('voice') with health insurers. The threat of the loss of a large number of insured persons may persuade insurers to satisfy the members … and compete on price and quality of care" [11, p. 77]. Collectives have been criticized, however, as constituting a threat to solidarity because evidence indicates that they are a zero-sum game: savings given to collective members result in higher premiums for others [8]. Currently their future is in doubt.^{c}

Although people can switch plans annually, only a small minority do so—between 5% and 10% per year—and even that overestimates the amount of switching because most of those do so under a collective. Only about 2% of people switch per year acting as an individual rather than as part of a collective [25]. Those who do switch tend to be younger, better educated, and healthier, possibly implying that regulated competition may not be serving disadvantaged populations well in this regard [26].

Traditionally, GPs have acted as **gatekeepers** into the rest of the health-care system, with an estimated 93% of patient contacts handled entirely by the primary care provider [11, p. 140]. The Dutch register with a gatekeeper who refers them to specialist and hospital care. In theory, armed with a referral, a patient can choose to go to any hospital. In reality, it is difficult for patients to exert this authority. Kroneman and colleagues state that:

> The free choice of healthcare provider is seen as an important means to improve quality, but in practice citizens hardly make use of this right. People tend to go to the nearest hospital and to the provider that is recommended by their GP. People use the internet to search for information on health and diseases, but they hardly use the available information to choose a healthcare provider. Almost half of the Dutch population (48%) do not have sufficient knowledge, motivation or self-confidence to take an active role in managing their condition [11, p. 172].

There is little in the way of formal managed care arrangements in the Netherlands. Some selective contracting does exist, particularly in pharmaceuticals, hospital care, home services, and mental health care. Patients with insurers who have selective contracts may pay extra for drugs that are not the lowest priced, or hospitals that are out of network. While still in its early stage, selective contracting is likely to grow as insurers are able to collect and verify information on provider quality and costs [8].

Provider payment

Hospitals

All hospitals are nonprofit private institutions. Consistent with regulated competition, insurers negotiate budgets or expenditure caps individually with hospitals based on various aspects of performance, volume, and quality, although Ezekiel Emanual reports that the negotiations "are far from cut-throat" [16, p. 200]. These budgets are then used to derive the prices to be paid for each hospital stay.[d] These payments comprise about 70% of hospital revenues and are based on a Dutch version of **diagnosis-related groups** (DRGs). As is the case in France, the Dutch use far more DRGs than the American Medicare program: 4400 vs 750 [14]. This is partly because the system uses combinations of diagnoses and treatments rather than just diagnostic categories [11, p. 94]. The remaining 30% of reimbursements are set by government for procedures that cannot be planned for in advance (e.g., emergency hospitalizations) or where there are not enough providers to successfully rely on competition (e.g., organ transplantations) [11, p. 168].

Physicians

As of 2015, GPs have been paid in a way to provide incentives for integrated and coordinated care. There are three components to payment [11, p. 100]. The first, which is responsible for about three-quarters of GP income, is a **capitation** fee for each patient under their care, which is a flat fee varying only by age (patients age 65 and older come with a higher fee, as do those whose location is deemed as "deprivation status."). On top of this, GPs can bill for each consultation provided. These fees are set by the Ministry of Health, Welfare, and Sport. The second component of fees is a bundled payment that applies to particular diseases: those with Type II diabetes, chronic obstructive pulmonary disease, asthma, and those with a high risk of cardiovascular disease. Generally these payments, negotiated with insurers, are made to groups of physicians who agree to coordinate care for patients with these diseases. There is a third payment component based on **pay for performance** (P4P), also negotiated with insurers, but it is not as well developed as in other countries and in 2015 was responsible for only 5% of GP income [9].

The fees paid to hospitals under the Dutch DRG system include the monies to be paid to the specialists. The breakdown of how much money the hospital keeps and how much goes to the specialists are negotiated between each

---

d. Erik Schut, personal communication, December 9, 2019.

hospital and the specialists in that hospital.[d] All told, about half of the specialists are paid on a salary basis and half on FFS [11 (p. 100), 14].

Pharmaceuticals

The Dutch healthcare system has used several methods to successfully control pharmaceutical expenditures. Many drugs need to pass cost-effectiveness criteria to be included in the list of covered medicines. A key policy regards "preferred medicines," whereby health insurers decide which pharmaceuticals within a therapeutic category (generally a low-cost generic) will be covered; patients choosing a more expensive one pay the difference under this reference pricing system [11, p. 76].

The Netherlands has embraced generic drugs more than many other countries. In 2017, the share of prescriptions that were generic was 76%, which was not quite as high as the United Kingdom and Germany, but more than double that in France and Switzerland [27]. Patented drug prices generally are set so that they do not exceed those of neighboring countries. Expensive inpatient drugs are usually negotiated between insurers and individual hospitals [14]. As a result of these policies, the growth in pharmaceutical expenditures in the country has been far lower than growth in acute care: only 6% vs more than 50% over the period 2005–14 [11, p. 172]. The government compares actual spending to targeted amounts. In 2012, GP care spending was 11% over their target, while pharmaceutical care, 13% *below* their target [11, p. 172]. This trend (albeit at a lower rate) continued at least through 2014 [14].

Assuring access and equity

Accessibility to care is generally considered to be high in the Netherlands: there is: universal coverage with premium subsidies for an estimated 36% of the population [11, p. 189]; cost sharing requirements that are low to moderate; an SHI benefit package that is comprehensive except for adult dental care (but with a large share of the population having VHI to cover that); and excellent geographic access, with 99% of the population within 10 minutes of a GP or pharmacy by car and nearly as easy access to the nearest hospital [28]. Significantly, few people report unmet medical-care needs and there is almost no difference in that regard between those in the lowest- vs highest-income quintiles [7].

As in all countries, there are major differences in health and life expectancy by socioeconomic status (SES). The Netherlands also shows substantial differences in healthcare usage by SES. The more highly educated Dutch use specialist and dental care about 30% more than those with low education, while those with low education use hospital care about 35% more often than their better educated compatriots [29]. It is not clear which factor is more responsible for this: affordability or sophistication in using the healthcare system.

Because health insurance is sold and subsidized on a national basis, there is little problem with geographic financial equity. This contrasts with Japan, where those in certain parts of the country face substantially higher financial requirements. **Vertical equity** is more of an issue due to the way in which the system in financed. While some tax revenue is raised through a progressive income tax, other is raised through VATs, which are regressive. Most revenue is derived from a proportional payroll tax that is capped for those who earn above a specific threshold, making it somewhat regressive [11, p. 77]. Individual premiums are also regressive since they are invariant with income.

Controlling expenditures

As a wealthy country, surpassed in per capita income only by Switzerland and the United States among the 10 countries covered in this book, one would expect the Netherlands' healthcare spending to be high. As compared to the other nine countries, this is not the case. Among the 10 countries included in this book, per capita expenditures are the 9th lowest in terms of percentage of GDP spent on health care—10.0% in 2019—after Australia (see Table 15.3). (Per capita spending in euros ranks 5th due to the country's comparatively high per capita GDP [27].) This figure grew considerably in the 2000s, rising from 7.5% in 2000 to 10.2% in 2010, but has fallen slightly by 2019 [27]. Nevertheless, as in other countries, the specter of a rapidly aging population and its concomitant chronic illnesses, a low fertility rate, and the proliferation of medical technologies continue to make cost containment a high priority [7].

Spending increases have been limited in recent years through a variety of mechanisms, some competition-oriented and others more regulatory in nature. The system of insurers competing for consumers and being fully at risk for losses, a hallmark of regulated competition, is likely to be some part of the answer, but as discussed below, several researchers doubt that this has been a major driver of cost containment. Another competitive strategy has been raising cost sharing. Between 2008 and 2016, the annual SHI deductible rose more than 2.5-fold, from 150 to 385 euros. There is some evidence that this reduced demand as there was a fourfold increase between 2010 and 2013 in the percentage of adults reporting access problems due to costs. But by 2016, the percentage had almost returned to 2010 levels, perhaps because people had become accustomed to paying more [18].

The implementation of regulated competition in the Netherlands has been criticized by some with regard to one particular component: difficulties insurers have in effectively negotiating with providers. Some researchers have concluded that even though insurers have consolidated, hospitals and GPs have the upper hand in negotiations, at least for certain specialties and in certain regions. This is in part due to a large number of mergers among hospitals (almost none of which have been turned down by government authorities) and both a well-organized group of GPs of whom the public has high regard, alongside low regard for insurers [3, 9, 30]. This led Kieke Okma and Luca Crivelli to conclude that "bilateral monopolies of insurers and providers emerged that all but defeated government competition policy in health care" [30, p. 108]. Others disagree, concluding that the power balance is more tilted toward the insurers due to their considerable market consolidation [31].

Other strategies used in the Netherlands to control spending have been more regulatory in nature. Some of them include:

- A "soft" annual healthcare budget for total healthcare expenditures, whereby providers can be held responsible for exceeding this amount (e.g., cutting provider fees or requirement repayment) [11, p. 78]. As reported by Joost Wammes and colleagues:

  In 2013, an agreement signed by the minister of health, all health care providers, and insurers set a voluntary ceiling for the annual growth of spending on hospital and mental care. When overall costs exceed that limit, the government has the ability to control spending via generic budget cuts. The agreement included an extra 1 percent spending growth allowance for primary care practices in 2014 and 1.5 percent in 2015–2017, provided they demonstrate that their services are a substitute for hospital care [14].

- Government setting maximum hospital prices for certain procedures such as transplants and emergency hospitalizations.
- The use of health technology assessment to determine the services to be included in the SHI benefit package.
- Control of pharmaceutical prices through such means as keeping reimbursement no higher than in other European countries and using reference pricing to encourage the use of cheaper drugs [11, p. 207].

Key policy issues

Even after a decade of experience with regulated competition, Maarse and colleagues argue that "the ongoing reform must be viewed as reform in progress" [8, p. 163]. Kroneman and colleagues state that "future health policy will be mainly directed towards fine-tuning and optimizing the reforms: the focus will remain on improving quality and containing costs" [11, p. 184]. Regarding quality, the government initiated a campaign called "Quality pays off," with elements which include:

- Encouraging insurers to reduce the mandatory deductible when patients use contracted providers.
- Improving risk adjustment to further encourage insurers to accept those with chronic illnesses. One study found that Dutch insurers are paid far less than their costs for enrollees in poor health, having chronic conditions, or who were treated by a specialist in the last year. In contrast, they are overcompensated for those in good health, without chronic conditions, and who have not used services in the past year [32].

● Providing further incentives to providers to make P4P arrangements based on quality outcomes.

● Being more vigilant about further mergers and counteracting the deleterious effects of previous ones [11, p. 184].

Regarding the last of these, Frederik Schut and Marco Varkevisser state that "To prevent further consolidation and anticompetitive coordination, strict enforcement of competition policy is crucially important for safeguarding the potential for effective insurer-provider negotiations about quality and price" [9, p. 126]. The other tenet of effective regulated competition is the availability and use by consumers of good information about quality and prices. In 2015, the Ministry and a consortium of insurers agreed to have all insurers provide comparable information, including breaking down components of the premiums (including profits). There is also a government-sponsored website that is designed to make it easier to compare the providers contracted with different health plans [11, p. 184]. How effective these will be is uncertain as first it is necessary to develop easy-to-understand and robust measures of both processes and outcomes that consumers will use—a hurdle that has not been overcome by any country that employs regulated competition.

Thus, a significant challenge going forward for the Netherlands is getting to a point where health system competition is truly based on value—that is, quality in relation to price. But as in all such systems, there is a tension between improving competition and, at the same time, encouraging cooperation to improve the coordination of care. Providers need to cooperate with each other in an effective integrated care delivery system. This is difficult to achieve if laws encouraging competition keep providers from cooperating with each other as part of large integrated systems.[d]

References

[1] Westert GP, Burgers JS, Verkleij H. The Netherlands: regulated competition behind the dykes? BMJ 2009;339:b3397.

[2] Van de Ven WP, Beck K, Buchner F, Schokkaert E, Schut FT, Shmueli A, et al. Preconditions for efficiency and affordability in competitive healthcare markets: are they fulfilled in Belgium, Germany, Israel, the Netherlands and Switzerland? Health Policy 2013;109(3):226–45.

[3] Van Ginneken E, Swartz K, Van der Wees P. Health insurance exchanges in Switzerland and the Netherlands offer five key lessons for the operations of US exchanges. Health Aff (Millwood) 2013;32(4):744–52.

[4] Vonk RAA, Schut FT. Can universal access be achieved in a voluntary private health insurance market? Dutch private insurers caught between competing logics. Health Econ Policy Law 2019;14(3):315–36.

[5] Daley C, Gubb J. In: Clarke E, Bidgood E, editors. Healthcare systems: the Netherlands. London: Civitas; 2013.

[6] Exter A, Hermans H, Dosljak M, Busse R. Health care systems in transition: Netherlands. 6th ed. vol. 6. Copenhagen: WHO Regional Office for Europe on behalf of the European Observatory on Health Systems and Policies; 2004.

[7] OECD and European Observatory on Health Systems and Policies. Netherlands: Country health profile 2019. State of health in the EU, vol. 2. Paris: OECD Publishing; 2019.

[8] Maarse H, Jeurissen P, Ruwaard D. Results of the market-oriented reform in the Netherlands: a review. Health Econ Policy Law 2016;11(2):161–78.

[9] Schut FT, Varkevisser M. Competition policy for health care provision in the Netherlands. Health Policy 2017;121(2):126–33.

[10] Anon. Origin of health insurance. Zorgverzekering Informatie Centrum; 2019.

[11] Kroneman M, Boerma W, Van den Berg M, Groenewegen P, De Jong J, Van Ginneken E. Netherland: health system review. Health Syst Transit 2016;18(2):1–239.

[12] Van de Ven WP, Schut FT. Universal mandatory health insurance in the Netherlands: a model for the United States? Health Aff (Millwood) 2008;27(3):771–81.

[13] Van Ginneken E, Rice T. Enforcing enrollment in health insurance exchanges: evidence from the Netherlands, Switzerland, and Germany. Med Care Res Rev 2015;72(4):496–509.

[14] Wammes J, Stadhouders N, Westert G. In: Tikkanen R, Osborn R, Mossialos E, Djordjevic A, Wharton GA, editors. Netherlands. International health care system profiles. The Commonwealth Fund [Internet]; 2020. [Accessed 13 September 2020]. Available from: https://www.commonwealthfund.org/international-health-policy-center/countries/netherlands.

[15] Enthoven AC. The history and principles of managed competition. Health Aff (Millwood) 1993;12(Suppl):24–48.

[16] Emanuel EJ. Which country has the world's best health care? New York: PublicAffairs; 2020.

[17] Anon. Dutch Health Insurance Act. Netherlands: Other taxes. PwC; 2020. [Internet]. [Accessed 13 September 2020]. Available from: https://taxsummaries.pwc.com/netherlands/individual/other-taxes#:~:text=Dutch%20Health%20Insurance%20Act&text=an%20income%2Drelated%20contribution%20(6.7,tax%20authorities%20by%20the%20employer.

[18] Rice T, Quentin W, Anell A, Barnes AJ, Rosenau P, Unruh LY, et al. Revisiting out-of-pocket requirements: trends in spending, financial access barriers, and policy in ten high-income countries. BMC Health Serv Res 2018;18(1):371.

[19] Van Winssen KPM, Van Kleef RC, Van de Ven WPMM. How profitable is a voluntary deductible in health insurance for the consumer? Health Policy 2015;119(5):688–95.

[20] Anon. Inzicht in het overstapseizoen. Verzekerden in beeld. Netherland: Vektis Intelligence; 2019.

[21] De Pietro C, Camenzind P, Sturny I, Crivelli L, Edwards-Garavoglia S, Spranger A, et al. In: Busse R, editor. Switzerland: Health system review, vol. 17. Copenhagen: Health Systems in Transition; 2015.

[22] Sagan A, Thomson S. Voluntary health insurance in Europe. vol. 1. United Kingdom: WHO Regional Office for Europe; 2016.

[23] Van Kleef RC, Van Vliet RC, Van de Ven WP. Risk equalization in the Netherlands: an empirical evaluation. Expert Rev Pharmacoecon Outcomes Res 2013;13(6):829–39.

[24] Anon. Health insurance via work? The discounts are being cut next year. DutchNews.nl; 2019. [Internet]. [Accessed 13 September 2020]. Available from: https://www.dutchnews.nl/news/2019/09/health-insurance-via-work-the-discounts-are-being-cut-next-year/.

[25] Van Ginneken E, Waitzberg R, Barnes A, Quentin W, Smatana M, Rice T. Choosing payers: can insurance competition strengthen person-centred care? In: Nolte E, Merkur S, Anell A, editors. Achieving person-centred health systems: Evidence, strategies and challenges. United Kingdom: Cambridge University Press and European Observatory on Health Systems and Policies; 2020 [chapter 9].

[26] Boonen LH, Laske-Aldershof T, Schut FT. Switching health insurers: the role of price, quality and consumer information search. Eur J Health Econ 2016;17(3):339–53.

[27] OECD.Stat. OECD [Web browser]. [Accessed 3 September 2020]. Available from: https:// stats.oecd.org/Index.aspx?ThemeTreeId=9.

[28] Van den Berg MJ, Kringos DS, Marks LK, Klazinga NS. The Dutch Health Care Performance Report: seven years of health care performance assessment in the Netherlands. Health Res Policy Syst 2014;12:1.

[29] OECD and European Observatory on Health Systems and Policies. Netherlands: Country health profile 2017. State of health in the EU, vol. 1. Paris: OECD Publishing; 2017.

[30] Okma KG, Crivelli L. Swiss and Dutch "consumer-driven health care": ideal model or reality? Health Policy 2013;109(2):105–12.

[31] Schut E, Sorbe S, Høj J. Health care reform and long-term care in the Netherlands. 1010 ed. OECD Economics Department Working Papers, Paris: OECD Publishing; 2013.

[32] Van de Ven WP, Van Kleef RC, Van Vliet RC. Risk selection threatens quality of care for certain patients: lessons from Europe's health insurance exchanges. Health Aff (Millwood) 2015;34(10):1713–20.

Section D

Systems without universal coverage

Chapter 12

United States

The big picture

The scope of the US health care system is difficult to comprehend, much less to summarize. In 2017, the World Health Organization (WHO) estimated global spending on health to be $7.8 trillion [1]. That year, US spending was $3.5 trillion. If the WHO estimate is accurate, it means that 45% of world health care spending is accounted for by a country with only 4% of the world's population. It is not just this magnitude that makes it challenging to encapsulate the key features of the system, however. In fact, there is not a single system. Rather, health insurance in the United States is a combination of numerous government programs and private organizations. Different types of insurance arrangements exist for population groups, and within a particular group, government and the private insurance sector may operate independently or in close cooperation.

Government involvement in health insurance was minimal until the mid-1960s, when the two main federal programs, Medicare for seniors (and later some of the disabled population) and Medicaid for some but not all of the poor, were enacted. From the beginning, government involvement faced political obstacles, some raised by the medical community, which did not want government to interfere either with the physician-patient relationship or with the remuneration systems providers had established with private insurers. These historical remnants are seen throughout the system today. One example is that when Medicare enacted a prescription drug benefit in the early 2000s, coverage could be obtained only through private insurers. A second, even more vivid example is represented by the title and first sentence of the law that established Medicare. That section of the law is entitled, "Prohibition Against Any Federal Interferences," and reads:

> *Nothing in this [law] shall be construed to authorize any Federal officer or employee to exercise any supervision or control over the practice of medicine or the manner in which medical services are provided, or over the selection, tenure, or compensation of any officer or employee of any institution, agency, or person providing health services; or to exercise any supervision or control over the administration or operation of any such institution, agency, or person. [2]*

Reading this, it's hard to imagine that this is a federally funded and operated program.

Health Insurance Systems: An International Comparison. https://doi.org/10.1016/B978-0-12-816072-5.00019-5
191

Whether and how Americans obtain insurance depend on their circumstances, such as the type of job they have, their age, and their income. People who work for large- and medium-sized employers usually obtain job-based coverage offered through private insurance companies. Seniors aged 65 and older and some of the disabled population receive it through the federal Medicare program, but even then, about one-third are enrolled through Medicare-approved and subsidized private insurance companies. Some of the poor and near-poor who do not have access to other coverage receive Medicaid, but this varies greatly by state. Those who do not have any of the above sources can purchase individual insurance coverage, which may be subsidized depending on their income—or they may remain uninsured. No other country in this book ties coverage so strongly with an individual's life circumstances.

When considering the US health insurance as a whole, a few characteristics stand out. First, the system is extraordinarily expensive by almost any measure. Compared with the nine other countries described in this book, the United States devotes almost 60% more of GDP to health, and health care spending per capita is double [3, Figures 7.1 and 7.2]. This is not because Americans use more services; rather, it results from higher prices [4]. Second, financial access is poor: Nearly one-tenth of the population lacks coverage and even more are underinsured, resulting in one-third of Americans saying that they experienced cost-related barriers to obtaining medical care in the past year—twice as high as any of the other nine countries [5]. Third, many health care outcomes are poor. For example, **mortality amenable to health care**, a measure of deaths that should be prevented by timely medical care (discussed in Chapter 15), is higher in the United States than in the other countries and is more than double that of Switzerland [6, Figure 3.9]. These facts imply that Americans are getting low value for their health care spending, although some observers disagree [7].

One thing that many experts agree upon is that the United States has shown a great deal of innovation in devising insurance products that push the boundaries of organizational innovation. HMOs have been a major part of the system for decades, and newer models of care, most notably Accountable Care Organizations, provide mechanisms for rewarding the provision of high-value care. The United States (along with the United Kingdom) leads the world in devising **pay-for-performance** (P4P) schemes to pay hospitals and physicians. These payment methods often blend the more effective features of fee-for-service, **capitation**, and salary to counter some of their individual shortcomings when used alone [8]. Nevertheless, results are still mixed on the impact of these organizational and payment innovations on health outcomes [9].

The most salient development in recent US health policy was passage of the Patient Protection and Affordable Care Act (ACA) in 2010, with its major provisions implemented 4 years later. The law has been highly controversial, with Democrats generally supportive and favoring expansion, and Republicans calling for its repeal. In fact, in 2017 major provisions of the law survived repeal by a single vote in the 100-member US Senate. Later that year, though, one major component of the legislation—the mandate that everyone obtains coverage or pays a penalty—was effectively repealed by setting the penalty at $0, effective in 2019. At time of writing, the Supreme Court is considering a lawsuit brought about by 20 states to declare the entire law unconstitutional.

Despite the fraught political environment, the ACA has had a major impact on the US health insurance market. Most notably, the uninsurance rate has fallen from about 16% to 9% [10]. Moreover, health insurance products must cover 10 essential health benefits and provide a minimum array of covered services. People can no longer be turned down for individual coverage or charged more based on their health status or past use of services. In all but 12 of the 50 states, all poor and near-poor residents are eligible for Medicaid; previously, they often had to meet strict income, asset, and situational characteristics (e.g., being a parent of a dependent child). Future developments, and in particular whether efforts toward universal coverage will advance or retreat, will depend heavily on which political party is in power.

The details

History

Health insurance in the United States is a relatively recent development, and government programs providing coverage are even more so. Through the early 20th century, medical care was provided almost entirely through the private sector without the aid of health insurance. The first instance of insurance occurred in 1929, when a hospital in Texas sold prepaid hospital insurance to a group of school teachers. The idea caught on in part because such an arrangement provided guaranteed revenues to hospitals during the Great Depression.

During the 1930s, nonprofit hospitals in different parts of the country banded together to provide hospital insurance under the name Blue Cross. Under these arrangements, patients could choose any hospital they wished. This coverage obviously was limited because it did not include physicians' bills. In the late 1930s, an analogous nonprofit organization, Blue Shield, was formed to provide insurance coverage for physicians' services—again, allowing the patient free choice of physician. Coverage was mainly sold to employers.

The early Blue Cross and Blue Shield plans used **community-rated** premiums, where all groups were charged the same amount irrespective of the risk profile of their members. This left an opening for commercial insurers, which emerged in the marketplace after World War II. By using **experience rating**, these companies were able to get a foothold in the market by appealing to employers with younger and healthier workers. Under experience rating, premiums were based on the health status and expected cost of the particular group being insured. Eventually, Blue Cross and Blue Shield had to follow suit, after which there was relatively little distinction between the pricing behavior of nonprofit and for-profit insurance. More recently, many Blue Cross and Blue Shield plans moved from nonprofit to for-profit status.

During this period, possession of health insurance rose dramatically, from 6 million people in 1939 to 75 million (half the US population) by 1950, driven by such factors as greater emphasis on hospital care and its associated costs, higher living standards, and demand for tax-favored coverage by labor [11, p. 32]. Regarding the latter, during World War II, there was a domestic labor shortage. Fearing that inflation would surge as businesses raised wages to compete in the labor market, the US government froze wages. In response, business offered additional nonwage benefits, including health insurance. These were soon ruled to be exempt from taxation, making it desirable for unions and workers to seek broader benefits. When wage controls were removed, it was still beneficial for workers to have a greater share of total compensation coming from these fringe benefits because wages were subject to taxes [12].

By 1965, when Medicare and Medicaid were enacted, 156 million Americans—80% of the population—were insured [13, p. 34]. This growth was mainly driven by coverage through employment, which benefited from the major tax break just noted. This made it far cheaper for people to obtain coverage through the workplace. Coverage through employment became the norm and still is to this day.

Publicly funded coverage began in 1965 with the establishment of the Medicare and Medicaid programs. Medicare covered Americans aged 65 and older (and later disabled individuals), and Medicaid covered some poor Americans. Passage of the legislation was exceedingly difficult as it was strongly opposed by the medical lobby. Compromise was necessary on several issues, the most important being that hospitals would be paid on the basis of their costs and physicians on the basis of their charges. These were obviously inflationary; it wasn't until 1983 that hospital payment moved to a **diagnosis-related group** (DRG) basis, where government paid a fix fee for patients with a particular hospital diagnosis, and 1992 until physician payment became based on costs rather than charges.[a] Prescription drug coverage for the Medicare population began in 2006. The drug benefit is administered through private prescription drug insurers, with premiums subsidized by Medicare and the exact benefits depending on the particular plan purchased.

Medicare is administered by the federal government and Medicaid by the states with contributions from the federal government. One problem with the original Medicaid program was that only about one-half of poor Americans were eligible for coverage. People not only had to meet income requirements but also certain categorical eligibility rules. These rules varied by state. In some states, coverage was limited to those aged 18 and younger, parents of dependent children, and some disabled persons. Most also restricted eligibility to those who possessed no more than minimal assets. As a result, over 15% of the US population were uninsured.

---

[a] In an effort to control outpatient (Part B) spending, the Medicare Economic Index was implemented in 1975. It restricted the increase in physician fees to a combination of growth in the costs of practice and general earnings [14].

The ACA became law in 2010. It halved the uninsurance rate in the United States by increasing both public and private health insurance coverage. Private coverage rose through health insurance marketplaces, allowing for the purchase of subsidized individual coverage. Public coverage increased through an expansion of the Medicaid program. Both are discussed in more detail below.

Overview of the health insurance system

Unlike other high-income countries, the United States does not have a single, national health insurance system. Rather, there are several separate systems in play. A slight majority of the US population has private health insurance coverage, with a large majority of them possessing group coverage through an employer. Sizable percentages of the population have Medicare and Medicaid; others purchase individual coverage (often subsidized), and still others have coverage from government programs such as the Veterans Health Administration and the Indian Health Services. In 2017, about 46% of Americans had employer-based coverage, 7% individual coverage, 18% Medicare, and 27% Medicaid [11, pp. 117–118].[b]

Unlike the other nine countries examined here and nearly every other high-income country, there is a sizeable portion of the population that is uninsured. The uninsurance rate was an estimated 9.2% of the population, or about 29.6 million people, in 2019 [10]. Several factors are responsible for this: Coverage is not required and is unaffordable to some, others choose to forgo coverage even if they can afford it, many poor and near-poor persons in 12 states are not eligible for Medicaid coverage, and undocumented individuals find it extremely difficult to obtain coverage.

If a person is not eligible for Medicare or Medicaid, employment-based coverage is desirable because premiums are almost always subsidized by an employer and are tax-favored. It is not always available, however, because many small employers choose not to provide it; only employers with 50 or more employees are required to offer coverage; some employees, particularly those who work part-time, usually are not eligible; and even if it is offered, employees may find premiums unaffordable.

Individual private insurance can be purchased through the ACA's marketplaces or directly. Even if purchased directly from an insurer, the ACA requires that insurance policies conform to the rules governing the ACA marketplaces. The advantage of using the marketplace is that the federal government provides **premium** subsidies for those with incomes up to four times the poverty level on a sliding scale, which means that subsidies are available to the middle class. In 2020, the poverty level was $12,760 for an individual and $26,200 for a family of four, meaning that individuals with incomes up to about $51,000 and families with incomes up to about $105,000 received at least some subsidization.

---

[b] Because some people have coverage from multiple sources, these numbers are not strictly additive.

Insurers that participate in the marketplaces must accept all applicants and cannot charge more to those who have preexisting medical conditions. They are, however, allowed to charge older persons up to three times as much as younger persons.

Medicare covers health insurance expenses for almost all seniors aged 65 and older as well as disabled individuals. It is divided into four parts. Part A covers hospital and other facility expenses (excluding physician charges). Part B covers physicians' services, outpatient care, medical equipment, tests and imaging, and some home health care. Part D covers prescription drugs. Parts A, B, and D are sometimes called "traditional Medicare" to distinguish it from Part C, Medicare Advantage.

Over one-third of beneficiaries choose to enroll in Medicare Advantage. Typically, they pick a managed care plan through which they receive care, which in turn receives a risk-adjusted capitation payment from Medicare. Enrollees are willing to limit their choice of provider to those in the network because Medicare Advantage plans often cover benefits that are not included under traditional Medicare's Parts A and B, including vision, hearing, and dental care [11, p. 124]. It should be noted that Medicare provides only a limited coverage for nursing home care, the bulk of which is paid for either by Medicaid or out-of-pocket.

Medicaid is a state-run program that is subsidized by the federal government. Until the Medicaid expansion that began in 2014, it covered only about half of poor Americans [15].[c] This was in large part because many states employed strict categorical requirements (e.g., coverage of adults was limited to parents of dependent children and the disabled) and very low income and asset maximums. This still holds in the dozen states that have not expanded Medicaid. In Texas during 2020, for example, among nondisabled adults, only parents of dependent children were eligible for Medicaid—and only if their income did not exceed 17% of the federal poverty level—that is, if did not exceed an *annual* income of $3700 [16].

The ACA changed that by expanding Medicaid to cover all Americans with incomes below 138% of the poverty level. Even though the federal government was paying at least 90% of the costs of Medicaid expansion, some states objected, and in 2012, the Supreme Court found this provision of the law to be unconstitutional. As a result, Medicaid expansion became optional for states. As of January 2020, 12 of the 50 states had not expanded coverage.

Parallel to Medicaid, there is a Children's Health Insurance Program (CHIP) that provides insurance coverage to children who are in families with incomes

---

[c] The exact percentage of poor Americans covered by Medicaid before the implementation of the ACA's expansion is not possible to calculate. In the US Census Bureau's estimates of health insurance coverage by source and income, all government programs are lumped together. In 2013, all government health insurance programs combined covered 59% of those with incomes below the poverty level.

above the Medicaid eligibility threshold. This federally funded program, administered by the states, is aimed at lower-income families who do not have access to employer-based coverage and who would find private insurance coverage difficult to afford.

Governance

The principle government agency that administers public health insurance is the Centers for Medicare & Medicaid Services (CMS), part of the Department of Health and Human Services (DHHS). CMS runs both the Medicare program and the federal portion of Medicaid. Other DHHS agencies include the Indian Health Services, the Centers for Disease Control and Prevention, the Food and Drug Administration, and the National Institutes of Health. The Veterans Health Administration is a separate, cabinet-level agency.

State governments are responsible for administering the Medicaid and CHIP programs and also are responsible for regulating private health insurance through state insurance commissions.[d] Other roles carried out by states and/or localities include operating public acute care and psychiatric hospitals; providing preventive services through health departments, clinics, and community health centers; and public health activities such as regulating restaurant safety [11, p. 92]. States also regulate the licensure of physicians.

Financing

Because the country does not have a single health insurance program, the financing of US health care is complex. Overall, in 2018 public insurance spending (41%) exceeded private insurance spending (34%), with 15% spent by other programs[e] and 10% spent out-of-pocket (OOP) [17]. The reason that public insurance spending exceeds that of private is that even though more people have private than public coverage, those covered by the public sector—particularly seniors, disabled persons, and those in nursing homes—use more services on average. Financing is best understood by examining the main sources of coverage: private health insurance, Medicare, and Medicaid. After that, we discuss the overall equity of the financing system.

Private health insurance

Just over half of the country's 330 million people are covered by private health insurance. There are two main types of private coverage in the United States: employment-based and individual. Since 2014, employers with more than 50

---

[d] States do not have the authority to regulate self-insured employer plans. Instead, this is regulated by the federal government through the Employee Retirement Income Security Act.

[e] "Other" spending includes a mix of public and private sources, including worksite health care, the Indian Health Service, and other state and local programs.

employees have been required to offer coverage to their employees or pay a tax. In 2019, 57% of firms in the country offered health insurance benefits, but this varied greatly by firm size: The figure is about 100% for firms with 1000 or more workers, compared with 47% for firms with 3–9 workers. If one examines coverage in terms of workers rather than firms, a different picture emerges, with 90% of employees working for companies that offer health benefits to at least a portion of their workforce. But working for a firm that offers coverage is not enough as only 80% of employees are *eligible* for coverage; those who are not eligible primarily work part-time or are temporary. Finally, not everyone who is eligible *enrolls*; some have other sources of coverage, such as through a spouse, but others find their share of the premium to be unaffordable. As a result of all of these factors, 39% of those employed in firms that offer coverage are not enrolled—typically, those who are younger and have lower incomes [18].

By international standards, premiums are expensive, hardly surprising given the high cost of the American health care system. In 2020, the average annual cost of single coverage was $7470, and family coverage, $21,342—particularly striking in that these insurance policies are subject to substantial **deductibles** and **coinsurance** requirements. Most of the premiums were paid by the employer; the employee share averaged 17% for single coverage, and 27% for family coverage. Nevertheless, the employee share is significant: $1243 for single coverage and $5588 for family coverage [19].

As noted earlier, employer contributions are not counted as part of employee income, and therefore, employees do not have to pay taxes on the value of these contributions. This tax break is quite sizable—$260 billion in 2019, compared with actual government spending of $1.2 trillion [20]. That is, almost 20% of resources devoted by government to health care is forgone revenue due to this tax exclusion. The tax break is generally viewed as regressive because those with higher incomes receive greater savings [21], because they are more likely to have employer-sponsored health insurance, have more comprehensive and therefore expensive policies, and face higher marginal tax rates. One provision of the ACA would have penalized companies that provided extremely generous health plans (dubbed "Cadillac" plans) by charging the employer a 40% surtax on premiums exceeding a threshold. This provision, however, was repealed even before it was implemented as it faced political opposition from both the left and right.

Medicare

About 60 million Americans are eligible for Medicare. Medicare employs a variety of financing schemes. Part A of Medicare, covering hospital insurance, is financed through a payroll tax, equal to 2.9% of wages, split evenly between the employer and the employee. Because people with very high incomes (over $200,000 for individuals and $250,000 for couples) pay an extra 0.9% tax on income above those thresholds—another provision of the ACA—overall, the funding is progressive.

Part B, covering physician and some other outpatient services, is technically voluntary, although nearly all Medicare beneficiaries choose to enroll it in because 75% of premium costs are subsidized by the federal government. It is financed through a combination of general government revenues and beneficiary-paid premiums. In 2020, premiums were about $1700 per year, but they were higher for individuals earning $85,000 or more and couples earning more than $170,000. The highest-earning group, those with incomes of $500,000 of more, were responsible for paying nearly $6000 yearly in premium costs. Nevertheless, the financing of Part B is still largely regressive because for the vast majority of beneficiaries, monthly premiums are the same irrespective of income.

Like Part B, Part D, which covers prescription drugs, is financed through a combination of government revenues and beneficiary-paid premiums. Also like Part B, government pays about 75% of total costs and beneficiaries pay the remaining 25% in premiums out-of-pocket. These premiums vary according to which private insurance plan is chosen by the beneficiary, and averaged about $500 annually in 2018. But (again like Part B) those with higher incomes are required to pay a premium surcharge that can reach almost $1000 annually for those with the highest incomes [22].

Part C, Medicare Advantage, is financed in the same manner as the other parts of Medicare. Beneficiaries who choose to be in Medicare Advantage plans pay the Part B premiums, and those with high incomes pay a surcharge. Just under half of beneficiaries pay an additional premium to cover the extra benefits, depending on the plan they choose [23]. Participating insurers and managed care plans, in turn, receive a monthly capitation payment from Medicare that is risk-adjusted based on a number of factors, including the beneficiary's health conditions.

Because Medicare coverage has a number of gaps, nearly 90% of beneficiaries obtain some form of supplemental coverage. Those with low incomes are dually covered with Medicaid. Beneficiaries with a former employer offering retiree coverage for their employees (about 30% of seniors) often receive subsidized coverage that fills in some of Medicare's gaps. Medicare Advantage plan owners receive benefits not covered by other beneficiaries. Still others purchase "Medigap" policies: unsubsidized private insurance policies that cover some of the coverage and cost-sharing gaps in Medicare. Unlike most health insurance in the United States, where regulation of insurance is mostly left to the states, Medigap is regulated at the federal level. This dates back to the 1980s and Congressional hearings that documented abuses in the marketing and sale of such coverage [24]. What is novel about Medigap benefits is that they are standardized: All insurers must sell identical benefit packages, making comparison shopping easier. The average Medigap plan costs about $1800 annually in 2018 [25].

Medicaid

About 74 million Americans are eligible for Medicaid. Medicaid is jointly funded by the federal and state governments through general tax funds, with about 60% of funding coming from the federal government. The percentage varies by state, varying from 50% to 77%, using a formula based on per-capita income in the state relative to the national average. As noted, the federal government pays 90% of costs for those eligible for coverage through the ACA's Medicaid expansion. While the federal government pays the majority of Medicaid costs, the states pay a significant portion, so much so that the only state budget item that is larger is primary and secondary education [11, p. 135].

Equity of financing

Paul Jacobs and Thomas Selden conducted a detailed analysis of changes in equity in the country's financing system between 2005 and 2016. They found that overall, US health care financing was regressive at the beginning of this period but was largely proportional by the end. That is, each income grouping spent about the same percentage on health care. Table 12.1 summarizes their results. In 2005, Americans in the bottom 20% of the income distribution spent about 27% of their income on health care, while those in the top 10% spent 16% of income or less. By 2016, the percentages were almost equal: 23% for the low-income group, vs 21%–22% for the high-income group. The authors attribute this major movement toward equity in financing to a number of factors, both macroeconomic (e.g., the impact of the Great Recession; changes in tax policy) and health policy. Among the health policy reasons were the expansion of enrollment in public programs, particularly Medicaid; implementation of the Medicare prescription drug benefit; and the Affordable Care Act [26].

Coverage

Breadth

Health insurance coverage in the United States is far narrower than in any of the other countries examined here—and indeed, among the 36 countries that were members of the OECD in 2018, only Mexico had a lower coverage rate. About 9% of the US population lacked health insurance coverage in 2018 [27]. While this is far below the 16% of Americans who were uninsured before the major provisions of the ACA were enacted in 2014, most analysts still consider it a major shortcoming of the US health care system.

Costs or lack of a job with health benefits or limited Medicaid coverage in a state are by far the major reasons for uninsurance. The uninsured are much more likely to lack a regular source of care and face access barriers to obtaining medical care and prescription drugs [27]. Hispanic or Latinos are particularly affected, with uninsurance rates in 2018 of 19% among those aged below 65, more than double those of Whites (8%), and considerably higher than Blacks (11%) [28]. Income is also a major determinant. In 2017, among those younger than 65, 18% of Americans with incomes below 200% of the poverty level were uninsured, compared with just 4% for those with incomes four or more times greater than poverty [29, Table 47].

TABLE 12.1 Percent of household income spent on health care, by income category, 2005 and 2016.

	2005	2016
Bottom 20%	27%	23%
21%–40%	24%	25%
41%–60%	20%	23%
61%–80%	18%	22%
81%–90%	17%	20%
91%–95%	16%	21%
96%–99%	15%	21%
Top 1%	14%	22%

Source: Jacobs PD, Selden TM. Changes in the equity of us health care financing in the period 2005-16. Health Aff (Millwood) 2019;38(11):1791–1800.

Scope

There are few national data available on the scope of coverage because there is not a single insurance program in the United States. As was the case in discussing financing, it is necessary to examine the major insurance programs separately.

Employed-Based Coverage: While comprehensive data are lacking, in general, it can be said that nearly all hospital and doctor visits as well as prescription drugs are covered in job-based health insurance plans. In addition, large companies in particular are likely to make available and contribute to the premiums associated with dental care (63%) and vision care (33%) [18].

Individual Coverage: Those with individual health insurance coverage enjoy a broad array of services as required by the ACA, which stipulates that all individual insurance policies, irrespective of whether they are purchased through the ACA marketplaces or directly through insurance companies, cover 10 categories of "essential health benefits." These include hospital, physician and other ambulatory services; emergency care; pregnancy and newborn care; prescription drugs; lab services; mental health care; rehabilitative services; and preventive and wellness care [30]. The primary services not required are dental and vision care.

Medicare Coverage: Medicare covers inpatient, outpatient, and prescription drug services. The main uncovered services are most dental care, vision care, and hearing care. In addition, coverage for nursing home care is extremely limited. It does not include custodial care—that is, care for those needing help with their daily activities—which is the type of care received by most nursing home residents. Skilled nursing care is covered on a limited basis: Only the first 100 days is reimbursed, with very high daily copayments ($176, in 2020) starting on the 21st day of the stay; the stay must begin with 30 days of a hospital discharge that lasts a minimum of 3 days and must be for the same condition as the hospitalization, and treatment must be ordered by a physician [31]. As a result, Medicare pays only about 15% of nursing home care.[f] Most of the rest is split fairly evenly between Medicaid and OOP payments [29, Table 44].

Medicaid Coverage: The program's coverage is relatively broad but varies by state. The federal government requires that states cover such services as inpatient and outpatient hospital care, physician and nurse practitioner services, laboratory and radiology services, nursing home and home health care for those aged 21 and older, health screening for those under age 21, and family planning. At their option, states may choose to cover (and therefore receive the federally matched funding for) prescription drugs, dental care, durable medical equipment, eyeglasses, care provided by professionals other than doctors and nurse practitioners, rehabilitation services, various types of institutional care, and home and community-based services [11, p. 134]. There may be limits to these benefits, however, such as capping the number of visits covered. While optional, all states do cover prescription drugs. Finally, while millions of Americans are covered by Medicaid for nursing home stays, before becoming eligible they are required to essentially impoverish themselves by "spending down" nearly all of their financial assets.

Depth

Like scope of coverage, depth also varies by type of insurance.

Employer-Based Coverage: This typically has large deductibles and significant coinsurance or **copayment** requirements. One desirable feature is that unlike Medicare, there is nearly always an annual maximum of OOP payments, although the limit may be very high. The following are average cost-sharing requirements for single (as opposed to family) coverage in 2019 [18]:

- Deductibles: $1655
- Cost sharing for primary care office visits: $25
- Cost sharing for specialty office visit: $40
- **Out-of-pocket maximum**: $4065

These figures vary by type of plan, e.g., HMO, PPO, high-deductible, which are discussed under "Choice," below.

Individual Coverage: Depth of cost sharing in individual plans depends on the "metal tier" of the plan. Under the ACA, all individual insurance policies are classified as Platinum, Gold, Silver, or Bronze. The distinction is that they need

---

[f] It is not possible to calculate the exact percentage of nursing home costs paid by Medicare because the national health accounts dataset combines nursing home facilities with continuing care retirement communities.

to cover at least 90%, 80%, 70%, or 60% of expected claims costs, respectively. In general, the higher metal tiers have higher premiums but lower cost-sharing requirements, although it is difficult to generalize much beyond that since insurance companies can choose their own amounts. One state where it is possible to generalize is California because it has standardized benefits within each metal tier. In 2020, the cost-sharing requirements for Bronze, Silver, and Gold plans (the more common ones) in California were [32]:

- Bronze:
  - Deductible: $6300 individual, $12,600 family
  - Doctor visit copayment (primary care/specialist): $65–$95
  - OOP maximum: $7800 individual, $15,600 family
- Silver:
  - Deductible: $4000 individual, $8000 family
  - Doctor visit copayment (primary care/specialist): $40–$85
  - OOP maximum: $7800 individual, $15,600 family
- Gold:
  - Deductible: $0
  - Doctor visit copayment (primary care/specialist): $30–$65
  - OOP maximum: $7800 individual, $15,600 family

Enrollees whose income is below 250% of the poverty level are eligible for lower cost sharing but only if they select a Silver plan.

Medicare Coverage: This coverage is not very deep. In 2015, Medicare paid only 54% of total medical and long-term care expenses for its beneficiaries.[g] As noted earlier, because of this nearly 90% of enrollees obtain supplemental coverage. The following are some of the cost-sharing requirements under traditional Medicare in 2020—many of which are covered by supplementary insurance:

- $1408 deductible per hospital stay
- Daily copayments of $352 for stays between 61 and 90 days, and twice that for longer stays
- $176 daily copayment for covered skilled nursing home stays starting on the 21st day, and lasting until coverage ends on the 100th day
- $198 annual deductible for Part B expenses
- 20% coinsurance on remaining Part B covered expenses

There is no annual out-of-pocket maximum.

Patient expenses for Part D, the prescription drug benefit, vary according to which private insurance plan is chosen by the beneficiary. The benefit is unusually complex and has changed over time, and also depends on whether a

---

[g] This computation was made by the Kaiser Family Foundation for the author based on the 2015 Medicare Current Beneficiary Survey data.

patient's particular drugs are classified as preferred generic, generic, preferred brand, nonpreferred brand, or specialty [33].

Like Part D plans, Part C plans are purchased through private insurers, which can offer the specific benefits they wish. Plans may choose to have annual deductibles as well coinsurance or copayments. Moreover, companies often offer more than one plan [34]. Typically, they provide more benefits than traditional Medicare.

Medicaid Coverage: The depth of coverage for Medicaid varies considerably across the states. On the surface, coverage appears to be deep in that cost-sharing requirements for covered services typically are zero or negligible. But coverage can be shallower for three reasons: (a) Some states have obtained waivers from the federal government to charge premiums and cost-sharing requirements, and in a few instances require evidence that the beneficiary is working, looking for work, or caring for a dependent; (b) in many states, it is extremely difficult to find a nearby physician who will accept Medicaid patients, due largely to the program's low payment rates; and (c) there usually are restrictions on the number of services that will be paid for [11, p. 134]. Regarding the latter, prescription drugs offer an example. While all states provide some coverage, most require a copayment, often $3 per prescription. There may also be limits on quantities and requirements that the program provide prior authorization [35]. Even though the copayment levels may seem small, the Medicaid population is poor and often finds them unaffordable. There is a substantial literature showing that poorer persons are deterred from filling prescriptions through these requirements [36].

Voluntary health insurance

Voluntary health insurance (VHI) does not apply to the US health care system in the way it does in other countries. In all of the other countries covered in this book except for Japan, VHI helps pay for services, amenities, or patient cost-sharing requirements that are not part of the national health system. The United States has no such system. There is one type of insurance that is a close correlate: Medigap policies purchased individually by some Medicare beneficiaries, described earlier. Altogether, premiums for these policies make up less than 1% of US health care spending.

Choice

A hallmark of the American health care system in choice, although typically the upstream choice of a health plan results, downstream, in limiting the numbers of providers available in a person's network.

Plan choice

Beginning with choice of health plan, like most other aspects of the system, the availability and extent of choice depends on the type of insurance a person has. Among those with job-based coverage, in general those working for large firms have a choice of plans, while others do not. The actual plans from which workers choose are usually determined by employee benefit managers working at these companies, often with the advice of consulting firms.

Interestingly, people with individual coverage through the ACA marketplaces had more choices than those obtaining it from employers. In 2020, there were an average of 4.5 insurers participating in each state, and these insurers each typically offered multiple plans—not just choices between the four metal tiers, but different plans within metal tiers. Using Chicago, Illinois, as an example, there were 9 Bronze, 17 Silver, and 7 Gold plans available. One company alone offered 11 different Silver choices, varying on such factors as deductible ($0–$7050), copayments for physician visits ($30–$45 for primary care), copayments for generic drugs ($10–$36), cost sharing for emergency room care, coverage of dental care, and premiums, which ranged from $329 to $386 per month for someone receiving no subsidies [37]. Research has shown that consumers have great difficulty navigating their choices both in this market and in the Medicare Part D prescription drug market [38–40]. California only allows standardized plans, with a few other states including New York and Massachusetts having both standardized and nonstandardized ACA plans. Standardization of benefits within metal tiers eases the challenges of "too much choice" [41].[h]

Plan choice under Medicare depends on whether a person chooses to stay in traditional Medicare or enroll in Medicare Advantage (Part C). Traditional Medicare is an anachronism in the US health care system in that beneficiaries can go to any hospital or doctor that they wish. (This is true in many of the other countries' systems covered in this book.) Moreover, referrals from a primary care physician are not required. In contrast, those in Medicare Advantage must stay within their plan's provider network. Going outside of the network either is not allowed or will result in substantially higher patient OOP spending. Medicaid is more difficult to generalize about. Most but not all states contract with managed care plans, but the ability of consumers to choose among competing plans varies widely.

Provider choice

Choice of provider in the American health care system depends on the type of health plan that one is enrolled in. The only major health insurance that offers free choice of provider—both hospital and physician—is traditional Medicare. In nearly all others, there is a limited network of contracted providers.

There are five major types of health plans offered in the United States: conventional plans, health maintenance organizations (HMOs), preferred provider

---

[h] The disadvantage of standardization is that it does not allow people to tailor plan benefits to their particular needs.

organizations (PPOs), point-of-service plans (POSs), and high-deductible health plans (HDHPs). At the risk of overgeneralizing, they are defined as follows [42]:

Convention plans do not have provider networks. Enrollees can seek care from any hospital or physician without a penalty. The only significant example of conventional coverage in the United States are Parts A and B of the Medicare program. HMOs are managed care organizations that provide health care on a prepaid basis through a defined network of providers. Except in the case of an emergency that occurs while traveling, they usually provide no coverage for treatment by out-of-network providers. Moreover, referral to specialists by a primary care **gatekeeping** physician typically is required. There are two main types of HMOs. Group or staff models are single organizations like Kaiser Permanente, where members go to receive all of their care. They have a staff of providers who work full-time for the organization. The other, more popular type of HMO is the network-type model, where the HMO is not a place per se. These are sometimes called "HMOs without walls," in which the HMO contracts with multiple hospitals and physician groups. These hospitals and groups may also contract with many other HMOs. Thus, unlike in the group/staff model, network-type HMOs have overlapping provider panels.

POS plans are very similar to network-type HMOs. The main difference is that enrollees can seek care from providers outside of the network at an additional fee. As in the case of HMOs, referral to specialists by a primary care gatekeeping physician typically is required.

PPOs share a key trait with HMO and POS plans: There is a network of providers. Like POS plans, those in PPOs can go outside of the network for an additional fee. PPOs usually do not require that patients be referred by a primary care doctor before seeing a specialist, and this distinguishes them from POS plans. Physician reimbursement may also vary, with PPO doctors more likely to be paid on a fee-for-service basis than in other types of managed care plans.

According to US regulations, high-deductible plans must have a deductible of at least $1400 annually for single coverage and $2800 for family coverage in 2020. It bears pointing out that these deductible minimums are typical in the United States for all health plans, not just HDHPs. In addition, HDHPs must include some sort of savings account that is used to pay deductibles, coinsurance, and copayments. In one version, the health savings account (HSA), employers and enrollees pay a plan premium, and the employer may contribute to an employer-administered savings account. The employee also can contribute to this account and use funds in the account to pay for medical services on a pretax basis. Moreover, funds that are not spent can be set aside for spending in a future year. Money in the HSA is portable if a person changes jobs. At age 65, accrued cash in the HSA can be spent on nonmedical expenses without a penalty.

In the job-based market, PPO plans are most popular, with 47% of enrollment, followed by 31% for HDHPs, 13% for HMOs, and 8% for POS plans. There is almost no (1%) conventional coverage [19]. One-third of Medicare enrollees are in Medicare Advantage, mainly HMOs and PPOs. The remaining two-thirds have traditional Medicare. About 70% of Medicaid enrollees are in managed care plans [43], mainly HMOs.

Provider payment

Hospitals

The United States has a mix of private nonprofit, for-profit, and public hospitals. More than half (57%) are nonprofit, one quarter (25%) for-profit, and the remainder (19%) public [44]. Because the nonprofits tend to be larger, they contain over 70% of the total beds [45]. The total number of beds, 2.8 per 1000 population, is relatively low from an international standpoint, and occupancy rates are the lowest among the countries examined here (along with the Netherlands), at 64% in 2017 [46, Figures 9.6 and 9.8].

Physicians treat patients in both inpatient and outpatient settings, unlike in Germany, where a given physician will provide services in either one or the other setting. Nevertheless, about 40% of US physicians are employed by hospitals because of a recent upsurge in hospitals acquiring medical practices [47].

The overriding method for paying hospital inpatient care is through diagnosis-related groups (DRGs). DRGs were first used in the United States for the Medicare program in 1983 and quickly diffused to both state Medicaid programs and private insurers—and later throughout the world. Actual payment rates vary by insurer. An analysis by the Kaiser Family Foundation concluded that, "private insurance payments are consistently greater, averaging 199% of Medicare rates for hospital services overall, 189% of Medicare rates for inpatient hospital services, 264% of Medicare rates for outpatient hospital services…" [48]. Non-DRG payment methods are also employed. State Medicaid programs, for example, vary in how they pay for hospital inpatient care, with some employing such methods as capitation payment rates, per diems, and/ or cost-based reimbursement [11, p. 167]. DRG payments are often adjusted through P4P reimbursement schemes, which consider quality indicators and/or costs. The next section provides an example of P4P in the context of physician payment based on Medicare's Accountable Care Organization (ACO) payment system.

Physicians

Physician payment methods in the United States are quite varied; to adequately describe them would require a chapter of its own. One obvious reason for such complexity is that there are so many different insurance programs, each using its own payment schemes. But another reason is that payments from health plans often do not go directly to the physicians. Consider a health plan that contracts with a multispecialty physician group practice. The plan might pay the group a fee for each service provided or it might provide a capitation payment for every enrolled patient who seeks care from the practice. Even if it does the latter, that does not mean that physicians in the practice are capitated. Irrespective of how the practice is paid, it may choose to pay its doctors on a FFS basis, with payments sometimes adjusted to reward parsimonious use of services. One estimate is that in 2013, almost 95% of physician office visits in the United States were paid on a FFS basis, with capitation accounting for only 5%—a sharp decline from 15% in the late 1990s [49]. A more recent estimate is that in 2017, while about one-third of all physician payments were not purely based on FFS payment, only about one-eighth of total physician payments put the provider at financial risk if quality or cost goals were not met [50, p. 35].

The predominant way of paying physicians under FFS is through fee schedules. The one used by Medicare is the basis of many of those used by private insurers and Medicaid. The Medicare Fee Schedule is based on "resource-based relative values." That is, fees are supposed to be proportional to the amount of time and effort expended by the physician; shorter, less intensive visits are paid less than those requiring more time and effort. A common complaint is that specialty care and testing are overpaid compared with primary care.[i]

In 2018, the Medicare payment rate was about $45 for an uncomplicated visit lasting 10 minutes compared with $74 for one lasting 15 minutes [52]. But average payments vary greatly by insurer. In 2017, Medicare paid on average only 75% as much as PPOs operating in the private insurance sector. This varied by type of service as well (and also by geography): It was 80% for typical office visits, but 59% for coronary bypass graft surgery [53, p. 117]. Medicaid, in turn, pays considerably less than Medicare: an average of only 72% of the Medicare rates, meaning it pays on average only about half of what private insurance does [54]. It is hardly surprising, then, that many Medicaid beneficiaries have a hard time finding doctors who will treat them in their private offices. In 2014, 71% of physicians said they would accept a new Medicaid patient into their practice compared with 85% for Medicare and 90% for private insurance. The Medicaid figure for psychiatrists was only 36% [55].

In recent years, Medicare and other insurers have increasingly used incentive reimbursement techniques to adjust payment to both hospitals and doctors. These P4P programs are often called "value-based" payment systems. An example is provided by Accountable Care Organizations (ACOs). ACOs are voluntary organizations of providers (hospitals, doctors, and other health professionals) that agree to coordinate patient care with each other to improve quality and efficiency and control costs. They are provided financial incentives to do so [11, p. 129]. To illustrate, in 2019 Medicare used 23 quality measures

---

[i] This was not supposed to be the case. The main reason that Medicare moved to the resource-based system in the early 1990s was to raise payments for primary care, which were generally recognized to be undercompensated compared with specialty care. Over time, however, the relative values have reverted toward favoring the care provided by specialists. A major reason appears to be the specialist groups that have outsized power in an advisory committee that recommends fee changes to the Medicare program [51].

spanning patient and caregiver experience, care coordination and patient safety, preventive health, and care for at-risk populations (those needing mental health, diabetes, and blood pressure care) [56]. ACOs started with Medicare but they are now part of the payment schemes of some state Medicaid programs and commercial insurers as well.

ACOs are quite common in Medicare, covering 11 million participants in 2020—about one out of every five program beneficiaries [57].[j] A review of 42 scientific articles published between 2010 and 2016 concluded that findings on ACOs' impact on health outcomes were mixed. There was no indication, however, that quality of care was diminished, which was a significant conclusion because ACOs did appear to reduce inpatient and emergency department usage [9].

Pharmaceuticals

The US pharmaceutical market is enormous. In 2018, it was estimated to be $485 billion, constituting 40% of the total estimated global spending of $1.2 trillion [58]. It is profitable too, with average profits generally ranging from 15% to 20%, more than double those of large companies in other industries [59]. Controlling drug prices has therefore become a leading policy issue in the United States.

Polices concerning the inclusion of particular pharmaceuticals as covered insurance benefits and the amount that insurers pay for these drugs are completely different in the United States than in the other nine countries examined in this book. Most of the other countries carry out assessments of the benefits and costs of new drugs, either to decide whether they will be covered by insurance or to determine how much insurers will pay for them, or both. In addition, nearly all of the countries either set pharmaceutical price levels or engage in explicit negotiations with manufacturers. A common tool is to use external **reference prices**—that is, what other countries are paying for the same drugs. None of these activities are carried out by the US federal government. Similarly, private insurers generally do not make coverage decisions on the basis of benefit-to-cost assessments, although they may consider assessments of the value of new pharmaceuticals in negotiations with manufacturers.

Key players in the market are pharmaceutical benefit managers (PBMs). PBMs are companies that administer drug plans in both commercial and public health insurance plans, covering more than 270 million Americans [60]. Among other things, they establish drug formularies (lists of covered drugs) and negotiate drug prices and rebates with pharmaceutical manufacturers [50, p. 35, 44]. Rebates are discounts that these pharmaceutical companies give to PBMs

---

[j] One curiosity is that Medicare beneficiaries do not explicitly enroll in ACOs, and in fact, most likely have no idea that they are a members of one. Rather, groups of providers enroll in the program. For purposes of reimbursement, patients are "assigned" to the provider who treats them most often.

to encourage them to include their drugs in formularies. Rebates are controversial—with Congressional proposals to ban them in the Medicare program—in part because consumers may not directly benefit from them. Rebates may not be fully passed on from the PBM to the insurer, and the OOP costs paid by the patient typically are based on the drug's list price prior to subtracting the rebate [61]. An even larger criticism is that because PBMs are paid in part on the percentage discount they negotiate off a drug's list price, they have an incentive to include more expensive and even less cost-effective drugs on formularies [62]. More generally, some observers have complained that they constitute another expensive middle-man in the health care system [63].

The US Congress prohibits Medicare from negotiating prices with drug manufacturers. The 2003 legislation that established the Medicare Part D program includes a "noninterference" clause, which says that the program "may not interfere with the negotiations between drug manufacturers and pharmacies and [insurer] sponsors" nor can it "require a particular formula or institute a price structure for the reimbursement of coverage part D drugs" [64]. Thus, any control over the prices that insurers pay would be achieved through the competitive marketplace. The idea is that drug insurance plans compete with each other on the basis of premiums. To keep their premiums competitive, they would attempt to be effective negotiators (through their PBMs). This same sort of negotiation is the basis of efforts to control prices in the employer-based insurance market.

Many question the effectiveness of current US policy that prohibits government negotiations and relies instead on competition. As noted earlier and shown in Table 15.5, brand-name drug prices are far higher in the United States than in other countries—often more than double. There are several proposals before the US Congress that would either allow the federal government to negotiate prices or use other methods of lowering drug prices [65]. Polls show that the US public strongly supports the federal government using its power to lower drug prices through negotiations [66] so the issue is likely to remain on the political agenda.

One area where the United States has led most countries is in the use of generic drugs, where it is estimated that generic medications comprise 89% of all prescriptions, although this accounts for only 26% of total drug spending [50 (p. 35, 43), 67]. The 89% figure is similar to the United Kingdom but higher than the other countries covered here. The 26% figure is also higher than most of our countries and similar to Canada, but lower than the United Kingdom (36%) and Germany (35%) [68, Figure 10.10]. This mainly reflects the high cost of brand-name drugs in the United States.

Assuring access and equity

United States has constructed far more financial barriers to accessing care than the other countries. It starts with nearly 10% of the population lacking any coverage but does not end there. Because cost-sharing requirements are often very high, an even larger portion of the population is sometimes considered to be underinsured. The Commonwealth Fund, a US foundation, defines this as insured people who (a) incurred out-of-pocket costs (excluding premiums) exceeding 10% of income, or (b) incurred OOP costs exceeding 5% of income for those with incomes below 200% of the poverty level, or (c) faced a deductible of 5% or more of income. Defined this way, 28% of adults aged 19–64 were defined as underinsured in 2018. Adding the 12% uninsurance rate among that age group [69, Table 2], a full 40% of American adults below the age of 65 would be defined as uninsured or underinsured. The main reason the underinsurance figure is so high is that 29% of those with employer-provided coverage faced very large deductibles [70].

Some of these people do not spend up to their deductibles, implying that even though they may lack adequate financial protection in a given year, it does not necessarily result in catastrophic spending. Other data, however, show that many Americans *do* experience catastrophic levels of OOP spending. Data from the World Bank shows that in 2010 (the latest year available), 13.5% of Americans in the lowest-income quintile spent more than 10% of their income on OOP costs. The figure did not exceed 3.5% in France, Germany, Sweden, and the United Kingdom; for the other countries, the data are shown in Fig. 14.9 [71].

Uninsurance and underinsurance are not randomly distributed in the population. In 2018, 29% of Americans who did not complete high school were uninsured, as were 15% of people whose education did not go beyond high school graduation. This is compared with approximately 5% for people with a college degree or higher [69, Table 3]. (Patterns by income and by race and ethnicity were discussed earlier, under breadth of coverage.) The same is true for the underinsured. The Commonwealth Fund estimates that more than half of the US population with incomes below 200% of the poverty level—57%—are underinsured compared with only 22% of those with higher incomes. Moreover, like those who lack any coverage, the underinsured are about twice as likely to skip recommended tests, treatments, or follow-ups; not visit a doctor or clinic when experiencing a medical problem; and not get needed specialist care [72]. Finally, uninsurance varies sixfold by state of residence. Nearly 18% of Texas residents are uninsured compared with 3% in Massachusetts [73]. Among low-income adults below the age of 65, 14% of people in Medicaid expansion states were uninsured in 2018, compared with 34% in nonexpansion states [74].

Americans who are uninsured or otherwise cannot afford coverage, including many of the undocumented population, can usually access some types of care. One common source is community health centers that are usually available in low-income neighborhoods, as well as emergency care. The Emergency Medical Treatment and Labor Act (EMTALA), which has been law since 1986, requires hospitals that participate in the Medicare program to stabilize patients seeking treatment before releasing them, or transferring them to a facility that has that capability regardless of their ability to pay [75]. Nevertheless, over the years, many hospitals have been convicted of "dumping" uninsured patients back into the community before they are stabilized [76]. In addition, community health centers provide free outpatient care, also regardless of ability to pay. They are supported by federal, state, and local governments as well as philanthropic organizations.

It is sometimes asserted that while there are financial access barriers in the United States, people do not have to wait to obtain services. The evidence, however, appears to be more nuanced. Insured Americans generally do not have to wait very long to obtain testing and imaging services, see specialists, or receive elective procedures. Access to primary care, however, can involve waiting. Unfortunately, the OECD health database does not report US waiting time for medical procedures because the data are not routinely collected. Self-reported waits (and one measure of doctor-reported waits) are available from the Commonwealth Fund's international surveys (Table 15.13). (Japan is not included.) Among the nine countries with data, the United States ranked 7th in providing the ability to access a doctor or nurse the same or next day. In contrast, it ranked 3rd in providing for short waits for specialist appointments and elective surgery, and was around the median regarding waiting time in the emergency room, difficulty getting after-hours care, and doctor reports on how long it takes to get imaging examinations like CTs and MRIs [5].

Controlling expenditures

The United States is a major outlier internationally in health spending. According to US health accounting data, which gives estimates about 5% higher than the OECD data used here for international comparisons, in 2018 per-capita health expenditures totaled $11,172, equaling 17.7% of GDP [77]. Both are approximately 40% higher than Switzerland, the world's second ranked country [3, Figures 7.1 and 7.3].

Not surprisingly, the many health insurance systems in the United States are continually engaged in efforts to control spending. These efforts are too numerous to explore. Suffice to say that most cost control in the private sector comes from individual employers or insurers, often in the form of insurers competing for discounts from providers, which reduces premiums they and their employees must pay. Most cost control for public payers is in the form of administratively set prices. Patient cost sharing is a second method of cost control in private plans.

To provide a broader context on US expenditure control, it is helpful to consider cost containment methods that are commonly used in other countries, but not very much in the United States. There are two primary examples: price controls and health technology assessment.

Unit prices for health care services are far higher in the United States than in other countries (Tables 15.4 and 15.5). This is true across the board—hospital, physician services, brand-name drugs—with the one exception being generic drugs [78]. Although there is disagreement about why this is the case, most likely it is at least partly a result of government's lack of involvement in price negotiation. In the employer-based market and the ACA marketplaces, prices are set through negotiations between providers and private insurers. This may not be very effective, however, because the provider market is monopolized in many areas. To provide a single example, in California, hospitals in certain parts of the states are "vertically integrating" by buying up physician practices at a fast pace, leading them to take advantage of their monopoly power to raise hospital prices and ultimately causing large increases in premiums [79]. In a study examining the United States as a whole, it was found that in 72% of more than 100 urban areas studied, the hospital market was highly concentrated [80]. In 2018, over half of physicians were part of health systems, along with more than 70% of hospitals [81].

Thus, there are limits to relying on the marketplace to control spending. An alternative used elsewhere is for government to use its market power as a huge buyer of goods and services to keep prices down. While Congress has prohibited the Medicare program from negotiating drug prices with pharmaceutical manufacturers, it has not restricted the Veterans Health Administration (VHA) from engaging in such negotiations. As a result, the VHA pays about 40% less than Medicare for its drugs [82]. Similarly, other countries employ external reference pricing for drugs. Most countries base their pharmaceutical prices on the prices paid by a reference groups of other countries to help ensure that they do not overpay for drugs. This tool is not used in the United States.

Lack of government involvement transcends the prescription drug market. Indeed, unlike any of the other countries discussed in this book, the United States is unique in eschewing the use of health technology assessment to determine what services are covered by government insurance programs as well as in setting their prices. Hospitals and clinics can purchase as much equipment (e.g., MRI machines) as they wish, and insurers generally pay for the tests so long as they are ordered by a physician.

More generally, there are two overall methods of controlling health care spending: supply-side rationing and demand-side rationing [83]. Supply-side rationing involves either providing fewer resources to the health care system or changing providers' incentives toward providing care more parsimoniously. In contrast, demand-side strategies are aimed at quelling patient demand. Both methods are used by all countries, but on balance, the United States relies more on demand-side interventions, mainly through deductibles, coinsurance, and copayments. It is difficult to determine how effective these methods have been. As noted, cost sharing in employment-based insurance is very high, but it is difficult to know how much higher premiums would be in their absence. One curiosity is that the two countries covered in this book that have the highest patient cost-sharing requirements, Switzerland and the United States, also have the highest per-capita spending. Unfortunately, it is not possible to determine the direction of causality. One possibility is that patient cost sharing has been ineffective. But another is that because these countries spend so much, they have felt compelled to control spending by charging patients more. In either case, there are serious repercussions regarding financial access, particularly among those with low incomes.

Many on the left point to the large administrative expenses associated with a system of competing insurers [84]. One needs to look no further than to hospitals that hire reimbursement specialists to maximize their DRG payments, and to physicians' offices where a cadre of administrative clerks wrestle with the multitude of health plans from a multitude of insurers. Moreover, the prominence of corporate involvement and the for-profit insurance status of insurers participating in the primary health insurance systems are unusual internationally. Most agree that there is a great deal of waste in the US system, with estimates on the order of 25% of total health care spending [85], but there are no easy ways to reduce it [86].

As noted, both public and private insurers are actively engaged in efforts to improve value in the US health care visits. Examples include ACOs, expanding medical homes, bundling services rather than paying providers on a purely FFS basis, other forms of incentive payment, and focusing more on disease prevention so as to reduce the need for treatment. All of these efforts are ongoing, and it is too soon to conclude which will constitute "best practices" in the future.

In sum, cost containment in the US system is a major challenge. This relates not only to the multiplicity of insurers but also to politics of health care policy. There is an adage in academic circles that cost containment is so hard because every dollar of contained costs is taking away a dollar of income from someone [87]. Earlier, we identified high prices as the main culprit in the United States spending being so much more than other countries. While it is tempting to conclude that the United States needs to reduce prices to those paid in other countries, the politics of this are hardly straightforward. As noted by Tal Gross and Miriam Laugesen,

> *[I]t is this type of discussion that makes health policy enduringly frustrating. One can imagine policies that would be powerful enough to bring American health care prices in line with prices in other countries. We could induce dramatic cuts to Medicare reimbursement rates and all-payer rate setting. It is unlikely that blunt cuts will be tolerated politically; even the smallest payment reforms have tended to be diluted such that they lack the penalties and claw-backs that are necessary. ... Therefore, the policies that are politically viable are sufficiently toothless and watered-down that they have little chance of moving the needle [88, p. 786].*

Key policy issues

The US health care system is beset with enormous problems. Spending is far higher than in all other countries even after adjusting for national wealth (Figures 15.1 and 15.2), but most indicators of access to care and many related to health care outcomes are poor. The system is also rife with disparities in access and outcomes. The Latino population is three times as likely to be uninsured as are Whites [89] and face numerous impediments to obtaining coverage [90].[k] Historically, Blacks have experienced both higher mortality and morbidity, the consequence of a history of racism and discrimination that dates back hundreds of years. Its consequences are still found today. As of August 2020, on a per-capita basis, compared with Whites, Blacks had Covid-19 hospitalization rates that were almost five times as great, and death rates that were more than double [91].

While the causes of these access and outcome disparities are numerous and complex, the health insurance system is at least partly at fault. Calls for its reform are the norm although there is much disagreement about how fundamental the reform should be. These calls are aimed at correcting numerous problems, including:

- Financial barriers in accessing services, brought about by uninsurance and underinsurance.
- Poor outcomes in areas in which the health system is at least partly to blame, including **mortality amenable to health care**, infant and maternal mortality, and hospitalization and re-hospitalization for preventable conditions. (It should be noted, however, that one bright side in comparative performance is cancer care—screening rates are higher and mortality lower than in most other high-income countries for several common cancers [92].)
- Disparities in both access and outcomes by race and ethnicity, education, and income.
- Extremely high spending in general, and spending on administration in particular.

Some observers believe that part of the problem is an overemphasis on medical spending with insufficient attention paid to social spending and to the socioeconomic determinants of health [93]. An example is provided by "deaths of despair," defined as mortality from suicide, narcotic drugs, and alcohol-related causes. These doubled between 2000 and 2017 [94], and one result was an unprecedented reduction nationally in life expectancy among Whites aged 25–54 during this period, the demographic found to be most susceptible [95]. The emphasis on socioeconomic determinants, however, is especially relevant to racial and ethnic minorities and those with lower income and education, as well as recent immigrants. More emphasis on these factors would lead to greater spending on such things as affordable housing, education, neighborhoods, employment, and social support [96].

Returning to the health insurance system, two types of reform are often suggested: incremental vs fundamental. The ACA provided an example of

---

[k] These challenges include laws that prevent Latino undocumented individuals and families from obtaining coverage, the disproportionate growth of the Latino population in states that have not expanded Medicaid coverage (e.g., Texas), and the lack of Latino physicians.

incremental reform, albeit a large dose of it. It kept the current structure of public and private insurance, strengthening both by increasing financial access to insurance. Reform of the ACA would likely involve increasing insurance coverage rates by raising the income threshold for receiving premium subsidies and expanding Medicaid to cover more people. Fundamental reforms could include moving to a Canadian-style, **single-payer system** or to an **all-payer system** like those in France, Germany, and Japan. Such reforms, however, will face tremendous opposition from insurers, the provider community, and conservatives. Up till now proposals for fundamental reform have not made any serious legislative inroads.

Even incremental reform is challenging. Ten years after its passage, the ACA is still highly controversial, with more than one-third of the American public viewing it unfavorably [97]. As in other countries, then, the direction and success of future reforms will depend on which party is in political power. Even with a change in power, implementing reforms like those discussed here are not a given.

References

[1] Global Spending on Health. A world in transition. Global report. Geneva: World Health Organization; 2019.

[2] Prohibition Against Any Federal Interference. Compilation of the Social Security Laws. Social Security Administration [Internet]. [Accessed 21 September 2020]. Available from: https://www.ssa.gov/OP_Home/ssact/title18/1801.htm.

[3] OECD. Health expenditure: health expenditure per capita. In: Health at a glance 2019. Paris: OECD Publishing; 2019 [chapter 7].

[4] Anderson GF, Hussey P, Petrosyan V. It's still the prices, stupid: why the US spends so much on health care, and a tribute to Uwe Reinhardt. Health Aff (Millwood) 2019;38(1):87–95.

[5] Schneider EC, Sarnak DO, Squires D, Shah A, Doty MM. Appendices. In: Mirror, mirror 2017: International comparison reflects flaws and opportunities for better US health care. Mirror, Mirror. The Commonwealth Fund; 2017.

[6] OECD. Health status: avoidable mortality (preventable and treatable). In: Health at a glance 2019. Paris: OECD Publishing; 2019 [chapter 3].

[7] Atlas SW. In excellent health: Setting the record straight on America's health care. Hoover Institution Press; 2012.

[8] Robinson JC, Shortell SM, Li R, Casalino LP, Rundall T. The alignment and blending of payment incentives within physician organizations. Health Serv Res 2004;39(5):1589–606.

[9] Kaufman BG, Spivack BS, Stearns SC, Song PH, O'Brien EC. Impact of accountable care organizations on utilization, care, and outcomes: a systematic review. Med Care Res Rev 2019;76(3):255–90.

[10] Keisler-Starkey K, Bunch LN. Health insurance coverage in the United States: 2019. Washington, DC: United States Census Bureau; 2020.

[11] Rice T, Rosenau P, Unruh LY, Barnes AJ, van Ginneken E. United States of America: health system review. Health Syst Transit 2020;1–441.

[12] Caroll AE. The real reason the U.S. has employer-sponsored health insurance. The Upshot. The New York Times; 2017. [Online news]. [Accessed 21 September 2020]. Available from:

https://www.nytimes.com/2017/09/05/upshot/the-real-reason-the-us-has-employer-sponsored-health-insurance.html.

[13] Rice T, Rosenau P, Unruh LY, Barnes AJ. United States of America: health system review. Health Syst Transit 2013;15(3):1–431.

[14] Dutton Jr BL, McMenamin P. The Medicare Economic Index: its background and beginnings. Health Care Financ Rev 1981;3(1):137–40.

[15] Smith JC, Medalia C. Health insurance in the United States: 2013. Current population reports. Washington, DC: United States Census Bureau; 2014.

[16] Anon. Medicaid income eligibility limits for adults as a percent of the federal poverty level. State health facts. Kaiser Family Foundation; 2020. [Internet]. [Accessed 21 September 2020]. Available from: https://www.kff.org/health-reform/state-indicator/medicaid-income-eligibility-limits-for-adults-as-a-percent-of-the-federal-poverty-level/?currentTimeframe=0 &sortModel=%7B%22colId%22:%22Location%22,%22sort%22:%22asc%22%7D.

[17] Kamal R, McDermott C, Cox C. Chart: Total national health expenditures, 1970 and 2018. Health insurance is a growing share of total health expenditures and out-of-pocket spending is a smaller portion than in 1970. Peterson-KFF [Diagram]. [Accessed 21 September 2020]. Available from: https://www.healthsystemtracker.org/chart-collection/u-s-spending-healthcare-changed-time/#item-nhe-trends_total-national-health-expenditures-1970-and-2018; 2020.

[18] Claxton G, Rae M, Damico A, Young G, McDermott D, Whitmore H. Employer health benefits. San Francisco, CA: Henry J. Kaiser Family Foundation; 2019.

[19] Claxton G, Damico A, Rae M, Young G, McDermott D, Whitmore H. Health benefits in 2020: premiums in employer-sponsored plans grow 4 percent; employers consider responses to pandemic. Health Aff (Millwood) 2020;2018–28.

[20] Anon. Tax breaks for employer-sponsored health insurance. National Bureau of Economic Research; 2020. [Internet]. [Accessed 21 September 2020]. Available from: https://www.nber.org/aginghealth/2010no1/w15766.html.

[21] Iselin J, Stallworth P. Who benefits from health-care related tax expenditures? Tax line. Tax Policy Center, Urban Institute and Brookings Institution; 2016. [Internet]. [Accessed 21 September 2020]. Available from: https://www.taxpolicycenter.org/taxvox/who-benefits-health-care-related-tax-expenditures.

[22] Anon. An overview of medicare. Medicare. Kaiser Family Foundation; 2019. [Internet]. [Accessed 21 September 2020]. Available from: https://www.kff.org/medicare/issue-brief/an-overview-of-medicare/.

[23] Jacobson G, Freed M, Damico A, Neuman TA. Dozen facts about medicare advantage in 2019. Medicare. Kaiser Family Foundation; 2019. [Internet]. [Accessed 21 September 2020]. Available from: https://www.kff.org/medicare/issue-brief/a-dozen-facts-about-medicare-advantage-in-2019/#:~:text=1.,doubled%20over%20the%20past%20decade&text=In%20 2019%2C%20one%2Dthird%20(,rate%20in%202017%20and%202018.

[24] McCormack LA, Fox PD, Rice T, Graham ML. Medigap reform legislation of 1990: have the objectives been met? Health Care Financ Rev 1996;18(1):157–74.

[25] Anon. What is the average cost of medicare supplement insurance? MedicareAdvantage.com; 2020. [Internet]. [Accessed 22 September 2020]. Available from: https://www.medicareadvantage.com/costs/average-cost-of-medicare-supplement#:~:text=The%20average%20Medigap%20premium%20cost,actually%20paid%20by%20Medigap%20beneficiaries.

[26] Jacobs PD, Selden TM. Changes in the equity of US health care financing in the period 2005-16. Health Aff (Millwood) 2019;38(11):1791–800.

[27] Tolbert J, Orgera K, Singer N, Damico A. Key facts about the uninsured population. Uninsured. Kaiser Family Foundation; 2019. [Internet]. [Accessed 22 September 2020]. Available from: https://www.kff.org/uninsured/issue-brief/key-facts-about-the-uninsured-population/.

[28] Anon. Uninsured rates for the nonelderly by race/ethnicity. State health facts. Kaiser Family Foundation; 2018. [Internet]. [Accessed 22 September 2020]. Available from: https://www.kff.org/uninsured/state-indicator/rate-by-raceethnicity/?currentTimeframe=0&sortModel= %7B%22colId%22:%22Location%22,%22sort%22:%22asc%22%7D.

[29] Anon. Health, United States, 2018—Data finder. Trend tables. CDC; 2018. [Internet]. [Accessed 22 September 2020]. Available from: https://www.cdc.gov/nchs/hus/contents2018. htm#Table.

[30] HealthCare.gov. What Marketplace health insurance plans cover. Health benefits & coverage. U.S. Centers for Medicare & Medicaid Services; 2020. [Internet]. [Accessed 22 September 2020]. Available from: https://www.healthcare.gov/coverage/what-marketplace-plans-cover/.

[31] Anon. Medicare's limited nursing home coverage. ElderLawNet, Inc; 2020. [Internet]. [Accessed 22 September 2020]. Available from: https://www.elderlawanswers.com/medicares-limited-nursing-home-coverage-6705#:~:text=Many%20people%20believe%20that%20 Medicare,home%20stay%20will%20be%20covered.

[32] Coverage levels/Metal tiers. Covered California [Internet]. [Accessed 22 September 2020]. Available from: https://www.coveredca.com/individuals-and-families/getting-covered/coverage-basics/coverage-levels/#.

[33] Medicare.gov. What medicare part D drug plans cover. U.S. Centers for Medicare & Medicaid Services; 2020. [Internet]. [Accessed 22 September 2020]. Available from: https://www. medicare.gov/drug-coverage-part-d/what-medicare-part-d-drug-plans-cover.

[34] Anon. Medicare advantage. Medicare. Kaiser Family Foundation; 2019. [Internet]. [Accessed 22 September 2020]. Available from: https://www.kff.org/medicare/fact-sheet/medicare-advantage/.

[35] Anon. Medicaid benefits: Prescription drugs. State health facts. Kaiser Family Foundation; 2018. [Internet]. [Accessed 22 September 2020]. Available from: https://www.kff.org/medicaid/state-indicator/prescription-drugs/?currentTimeframe=0&sortModel=%7B%22colId% 22:%22Location%22,%22sort%22:%22asc%22%7D.

[36] Ghosh A, Simon K, Sommers BD. The effect of health insurance on prescription drug use among low-income adults: evidence from recent Medicaid expansions. J Health Econ 2019;63:64–80.

[37] HealthCare.gov. View health & dental plans. U.S. Centers for Medicare & Medicaid Services; 2020. [Internet]. [Accessed 23 September 2020]. Available from: https://www.healthcare. gov/see-plans/#/plan/results.

[38] Sinaiko AD, Kingsdale J, Galbraith AA. Consumer health insurance shopping behavior and challenges: lessons from two state-based marketplaces. Med Care Res Rev 2019;76(4):403–24.

[39] Abaluck J, Gruber J. Choice inconsistencies among the elderly: evidence from plan choice in the medicare part D program. Am Econ Rev 2011;101(4):1180–210.

[40] Zhou C, Zhang Y. The vast majority of Medicare Part D beneficiaries still don't choose the cheapest plans that meet their medication needs. Health Aff (Millwood) 2012;31(10):2259–65.

[41] Corlette S, Ahn S, Lucia K, Ellison H. Missed opportunities: State based marketplaces fail to meet stated policy goals of standardized benefit designs. ACA implementation—Monitoring and tracking. Urban Institute; 2016.

[42] Anon. Health insurance plan types and definitions. National Conference of State Legislatures; 2011. [Internet]. [Accessed 22 September 2020]. Available from: https://www.ncsl. org/research/health/health-insurance-plan-types-and-definitions.aspx.

[43] Medicaid Managed Care Market Tracker. State health facts. Kaiser Family Foundation [Online data collection]. [Accessed 22 September 2020]. Available from: https://www.kff.org/data-collection/medicaid-managed-care-market-tracker/.

[44] Anon. Hospitals by ownership type. State health facts. Kaiser Family Foundation; 2018. [Internet]. [Accessed 22 September 2020]. Available from: https://www.kff.org/other/state-indicator/hospitals-by-ownership/?currentTimeframe=0&sortModel=%7B%22colId%22:%22Location%22,%22sort%22:%22asc%22%7D.

[45] Anon. Hospital beds per 1,000 population by ownership type. State health facts. Kaiser Family Foundation; 2018. [Internet]. [Accessed 22 September 2020]. Available from: https://www.kff.org/other/state-indicator/beds-by-ownership/?currentTimeframe=0&sortModel=%7B%22colId%22:%22Location%22,%22sort%22:%22asc%22%7D.

[46] OECD. Health at a glance 2019. Paris: OECD Publishing; 2019.

[47] Masterson L. Hospitals now employ more than 40% of physicians, analysis finds. Healthcare Dive; 2019. [Internet]. [Accessed 22 September 2020]. Available from: https://www.healthcaredive.com/news/hospitals-now-employ-more-than-40-of-physicians-analysis-finds/548871/.

[48] Lopez E, Neuman T, Jacobson G, Levitt L. How much more than medicare do private insurers pay? A review of the literature. Medicare. Kaiser Family Foundation; 2020. [Internet]. [Accessed 22 September 2020]. Available from: https://www.kff.org/medicare/issue-brief/how-much-more-than-medicare-do-private-insurers-pay-a-review-of-the-literature/#:~:text=Based%20on%20the%20reviewed%20studies,inpatient%20hospital%20services%2C%20264%25%20of.

[49] Zuvekas SH, Cohen JW. Fee-for-service, while much maligned, remains the dominant payment method for physician visits. Health Aff (Millwood) 2016;35(3):411–4.

[50] Emanuel EJ. Which country has the world's best health care? New York: Public Affairs; 2020.

[51] Laugesen MJ, Wada R, Chen EM. In setting doctors' medicare fees, CMS almost always accepts the relative value update panel's advice on work values. Health Aff 2012;31(5).

[52] Anon. Physician fee schedule 2019 proposed rule faculty practice solutions center [presentation]. [Accessed 22 September 2020]. Available from: https://www.aamc.org/system/files/c/2/490826-physicianfeeschedule2019proposedrule.pdf; 2018.

[53] Anon. Medicare payment policy. Report to the Congress. Washington, DC: The Medicare Payment Advisory Commission (MedPAC); 2019.

[54] Anon. Medicaid-to-medicare fee index. State health facts. Kaiser Family Foundation; 2016. [Internet]. [Accessed 22 September 2020]. Available from: https://www.kff.org/medicaid/state-indicator/medicaid-to-medicare-fee-index/?currentTimeframe=0&sortModel=%7B%2colId%22:%22Location%22,%22sort%22:%22asc%22%7D.

[55] Holgash K, Heberlein M. Physician acceptance of new medicaid patients: what matters and what doesn't. Health Affairs; 2019. [Online blog]. [Accessed 22 September 2020]. Available from: https://www.healthaffairs.org/do/10.1377/hblog20190401.678690/full/.

[56] Anon. Quality measurement methodology and resources. Medicare shared savings program. Centers for Medicare & Medicaid Services (CMS); 2019.

[57] Anon. Shared savings program fast facts. Centers for Medicare & Medicaid Services (CMS); 2020. [Online data]. [Accessed 22 September 2020]. Available from: https://www.cms.gov/files/document/2020-shared-savings-program-fast-facts.pdf.

[58] Pharmaceutical Commerce. Global pharma spending will hit $1.5 trillion in 2023, says IQVIA. MultiMedia Pharma Sciences, LLC; 2019. [Internet]. [Accessed 22 September 2020]. Available from: https://pharmaceuticalcommerce.com/business-and-finance/global-pharma-spending-will-hit-1-5-trillion-in-2023-says-iqvia/.

[59] Anon. Drug industry: Profits, research and development spending, and merger and acquisition deals. Report to congressional requesters. United States government accountability Office; 2017.

[60] Our industry. Pharmaceutical Care Management Association [Internet]. [Accessed 22 September 2020]. Available from: https://www.pcmanet.org/our-industry/.

[61] Anon. Prescription drug rebates, explained. Kaiser Family Foundation; 2019. [Video]. [Accessed 24 September 2020]. Available from: https://www.kff.org/medicare/video/prescription-drug-rebates-explained/.

[62] Seeley E, Kesselheim AS. Pharmacy benefit managers: Practices, controversies, and what lies ahead. The Commonwealth Fund; 2019.

[63] Kane A. The problem with PBMs. The Progressive Policy Institute; 2018.

[64] Subpart 2—Prescription Drug Plans; PDP Sponsors; Financing. Compilation of the social security laws. Social Security Administration [Internet]. [Accessed 24 September 2020]. Available from: https://www.ssa.gov/OP_Home/ssact/title18/1860D-11.htm.

[65] Cubanski J, Neuman T, True S, Freed M. What's the latest on medicare drug price negotiations? Kaiser Family Foundation; 2019.

[66] Witters D. In U.S., 66% report increase in cost of prescription drugs. Gallup; 2020. [Online news]. [Accessed 24 September 2020]. Available from: https://news.gallup.com/poll/308036/report-increase-cost-prescription-drugs.aspx.

[67] Anon. Generic drug access & savings in the U.S. Association for Accessible Medicines; 2017.

[68] Paris V, Lopert R, Chapman S, Wenzl M, Canaud M, Mueller M. Generics and biosimilars. In: OECD, editor. Health at a glance 2019: OECD indicators. 2019 ed. Paris: OECD Publishing; 2019.

[69] Berchick ER, Barnett JC, Upton RD. Health insurance coverage in the United States: 2018. Current population reports. Washington, DC: United States Census Bureau; 2019.

[70] Anon. More adults are underinsured, with the greatest growth occurring among those with employer coverage. The Commonwealth Fund; 2019.

[71] Wagstaff A, Eozenou P, Neelsen S, Smitz M. The 2019 update of the health equity and financial protection indicators database: An overview. World Bank; 2019 [8879].

[72] Collins SR. Testimony: The growing cost burden of employer health insurance for U.S. families and implications for their health and economic security. The Commonwealth Fund; 2019.

[73] Conway D. Percentage of people with public health insurance up in 11 states, down in two. State-by-state health insurance coverage in 2018. United States Census Bureau; 2019. [Internet]. [Accessed 25 September 2020]. Available from: https://www.census.gov/library/stories/2019/11/state-by-state-health-insurance-coverage-2018.html.

[74] Haley J, Zuckerman S, Karpman M, Long S, Bart L, Aarons J. Adults' uninsurance rates increased by 2018, especially in states that did not expand medicaid—Leaving gaps in coverage, access, and affordability. Health Affairs; 2018. [Blog]. [Accessed 25 September 2020]. Available from: https://www.healthaffairs.org/do/10.1377/hblog20180924.928969/full/#:~:text=Furthermore%2C%20consistent%20with%20other%20data,this%20period%20in%20nonexpansion%20states.

[75] Anon. Emergency Medical Treatment & Labor Act (EMTALA). U.S. Centers for Medicare & Medicaid Services; 2012. [Internet]. [Accessed 25 September 2020]. Available from: https://www.cms.gov/Regulations-and-Guidance/Legislation/EMTALA.

[76] Terp S, Wang B, Burner E, Connor D, Seabury SA, Menchine M. CME information: civil monetary penalties resulting from violations of the Emergency Medical Treatment and Labor Act (EMTALA) involving psychiatric emergencies, 2002 to 2018. Acad Emerg Med 2019;26(5):470–8.

[77] Hartman M, Martin AB, Benson J, Catlin A, National Health Expenditure Accounts Team. National health care spending in 2018: growth driven by accelerations in medicare and private insurance spending. Health Aff (Millwood) 2020;39(1):8–17.

[78] Wouters OJ, Kanavos PG, Mc KM. Comparing generic drug markets in Europe and the United States: prices, volumes, and spending. Milbank Q 2017;95(3):554–601.

[79] Scheffler RM, Arnold DR, Whaley CM. Consolidation trends in California's health care system: impacts on ACA premiums and outpatient visit prices. Health Aff (Millwood) 2018;37(9):1409–16.

[80] Johnson B, Kennedy K, Rodriguez S, Hargraves J. Healthy marketplace index. [Interactive site]. [Accessed 25 September 2020]. Available from: https://healthcostinstitute.org/research/hmi-interactive; 2020.

[81] Furukawa MF, Kimmey L, Jones DJ, Machta RM, Guo J, Rich EC. Consolidation of providers into health systems increased substantially, 2016–18. Health Aff 2020;39(8):1321–5.

[82] Frakt A. What if medicare's drug benefit was more like the VA's? The Incidental Economist; 2011. [Online blog]. [Accessed 25 September 2020]. Available from: https://theincidentaleconomist.com/wordpress/what-if-medicares-drug-benefit-was-more-like-the-vas/#:~:text=The%20VA%20pays%2040%25%20less,the%20most%20popular%20200%20drugs.

[83] Ellis RP, McGuire TG. Supply-side and demand-side cost sharing in health care. J Econ Perspect 1993;7(4):135–51.

[84] Himmelstein DU, Campbell T, Woolhandler S. Health care administrative costs in the United States and Canada, 2017. Ann Intern Med 2020;172(2):134–42.

[85] Shrank WH, Rogstad TL, Parekh N. Waste in the US health care system: estimated costs and potential for savings. JAMA 2019;322(15):1501–9.

[86] Glied S, Sacarny A. Is the US health care system wasteful and inefficient? A review of the evidence. J Health Polit Policy Law 2018;43(5):739–65.

[87] Anderson G. Uwe Reinhardt's 'Priced Out' offers lessons in health care costs for all. STAT; 2019. [Opinion]. [Accessed 25 September 2020]. Available from: https://www.statnews.com/2019/05/14/uwe-reinhardt-priced-out-lessons-health-care-costs/.

[88] Gross T, Laugesen MJ. The price of health care: why is the United States an outlier? J Health Polit Policy Law 2018;43(5):771–91.

[89] Profile: Hispanic/Latino Americans. Office of Minority Health Resource Center [Online data]. [Accessed 25 September 2020]. Available from: https://minorityhealth.hhs.gov/omh/browse.aspx?lvl=3&lvlid=64.

[90] Ortega AN, Rodriguez HP, Vargas Bustamante A. Policy dilemmas in Latino health care and implementation of the Affordable Care Act. Annu Rev Public Health 2015;36:525–44.

[91] Anon. COVID-19 hospitalization and death by race/ethnicity. CDC; 2020. [Online data]. [Accessed 25 September 2020]. Available from: https://www.cdc.gov/coronavirus/2019-ncov/covid-data/investigations-discovery/hospitalization-death-by-race-ethnicity.html.

[92] OECD. Quality and outcomes of care: survival for other major cancers. In: Health at a glance 2019. Paris: OECD Publishing; 2019 [chapter 6].

[93] Braveman P, Gottlieb L. The social determinants of health: it's time to consider the causes of the causes. Public Health Rep 2014;129(Suppl. 2):19–31.

[94] Anon. Long-term trends in deaths of despair. United States Congress, Joint Economic Committee; 2019. [Internet]. [Accessed 25 September 2020]. Available from: https://www.jec.senate.gov/public/index.cfm/republicans/2019/9/long-term-trends-in-deaths-of-despair.

[95] Kochanek KD, Arias E, Bastian BA. The effect of changes in selected age-specific causes of death on non-Hispanic white life expectancy between 2000 and 2014. National Center for Health Statistics; 2016. p. 250.

[96] Artiga S, Hinton E. Beyond health care: The role of social determinants in promoting health and health equity. Kaiser Family Foundation; 2018.

[97] Anon. KFF health tracking poll: The public's views on the ACA. Health Reform; 2020. [Internet]. [Accessed 25 September 2020]. Available from: https://www.kff.org/interactive/ kff-health-tracking-poll-the-publics-views-on-the-aca/#?response=Favorable- -Unfavorable &aRange=twoYear.

Part III

Cross-country comparisons

Chapter 13

System characteristics

In this chapter, we examine some of the characteristics of the 10 health care systems. Data come from several sources. The main source is the Organization for Economic Co-operation and Development (OECD), which provides hundreds of comparisons of health care system metrics across its 37 member countries—including all 10 of the countries examined in this book. The OECD data are particularly well suited because the organization has worked for decades to develop valid and standardized measures of health systems and their performance. Through a collaborative effort between the OECD, the World Health Organization, and European Commission, countries are provided with a detailed guidance on how to measure and report their data to help ensure the accuracy of cross-national comparisons [1].

The majority of the OECD data that were used in constructing the tables both in this chapter and in Chapter 15 can be found in the annual publication, *Health at a Glance*. The most recent version at the time of writing was 2019, which contained information as recent as 2017 and 2018. An even more current source of data is from the OECD's interactive website, OECD Health Statistics [2], because it is updated more often. This website provides details on the variables that are collected from member nations as well as links to methodologies [3]. In addition, the OECD collects data on health system characteristics of member countries [4].

There are also a number of miscellaneous data sources that we draw upon, including information for the Commonwealth Fund's international surveys of patients and physicians. Some other cross-national data sets are available but are used on sparingly here, primarily because they do not include enough of our 10 countries. One example is Eurostat [5], which, by presenting data only on European countries, covers at most only six of the countries.

This chapter features 11 tables covering various aspects of the countries and their residents as well as health care systems characteristics. More tables are included in Chapter 15, which covers the topic of efficiency. The tables contained in this chapter are grouped into three subsections: context, health system features, and health.

Context

Table 13.1 provides information on various aspects of each country's populations. Five of the countries, namely, the United States, Japan, Germany, France,

Health Insurance Systems: An International Comparison. https://doi.org/10.1016/B978-0-12-816072-5.00012-2

TABLE 13.1 Population characteristics.

Country	Population (millions), 2018 (1)	Percent population age 65+, 2018 (2)	Fertility rate (children/woman), 2018 (3)	Per-capita GDP, 2019 (4)	Poverty rate, 2017 (5)	Gini coefficient before taxes and transfers, 2017[a] (6)	Gini coefficient after taxes and transfers, 2017[a] (6)
Australia	25.0	15.7%	1.7	$ 48,534	12.4%	0.45	0.33
Canada	37.1	17.2%	1.5	$ 45,851	12.1%	0.44	0.31
France	66.9	19.8%	1.8	$ 43,074	8.1%	0.52	0.29
Germany	82.9	21.5%	1.6	$ 50,140	10.4%	0.50	0.29
Japan	126.4	28.1%	1.4	$ 42,226	15.7%	0.50	0.34
Netherlands	17.2	19.0%	1.6	$ 52,772	8.3%	0.45	0.29
Sweden	10.2	19.9%	1.8	$ 50,574	–	0.43	0.28
Switzerland	8.5	18.4%	1.5	$ 66,290	9.2%	0.39	0.30
United Kingdom	66.4	18.3%	1.7	$ 44,234	11.7%	0.51	0.36
United States	327.2	16.0%	1.7	$ 60,705	17.8%	0.51	0.39

[a]Australia data are for 2018, Japan for 2015.
Sources: (1) Population. OECD. https://data.oecd.org/pop/population.htm. (2) Elderly population. OECD. https://data.oecd.org/pop/elderly-population.htm#indicator-chart.
(3) Fertility rates. OECD. https://data.oecd.org/pop/fertility-rates.htm#indicator-chart. (4) OECD.Stat. Level of GDP per capita and productivity. OECD. 2020. https://stats.oecd.org/
Index.aspx?DataSetCode=PDB_IV. GDP in US dollars. (5) Poverty rate. OECD. https://data.oecd.org/inequality/poverty-rate.htm. Data for Japan are for 2015; Netherlands for 2016;
Australia and United Kingdom for 2018. (6) OECD.Stat. Income Distribution Database. OECD. https://stats.oecd.org/viewhtml.aspx?datasetcode=IDD&lang=en.

and the United Kingdom, are relatively heavily populated compared with the others. There is sharp break after that, with Canada, the 6th most populated, having just over half the population of France and the United Kingdom. Switzerland's population is one-fortieth that of the United States.

What's most notable about the age distribution is Japan's very high proportion of seniors, with 28.1% of the population aged 65 or over, far greater than the next highest country, Germany, at 21.5%. All of the countries have fertility rates below the replacement level of 2.1 children per woman. Japan's low level of 1.4 is particularly challenging in the long run in light of the high burden presented by its large older population.

While all of the countries are among the wealthiest in the world, just how wealthy they are varies considerably. The richest, Switzerland, has a per-capita GDP that is 57% higher than Japan's. The United States joins Switzerland in being considerably wealthier than the other eight in terms of per-capita GDP. This is particularly noteworthy in light of the fact that the US poverty rate, 17.8%, is higher than any of the other countries. Japan also has a relatively high poverty rate of 15.7%.

The poverty figures imply that certain countries have income distributions that are more equal than others. This is shown in the last two columns, where the Gini coefficients are presented. The **Gini coefficient** is a measure of income inequality. It ranges from 0 to 1, with higher figures indicating a more unequal distribution. Figures are shown both before and after taxes and transfer payments. After taxes and transfers, the USA has the most unequal distribution of income among the 10 countries. The countries with the least skewed posttax/transfer income distribution are France, Germany, the Netherlands, Sweden, and Switzerland.

Another measure of income inequality is the S80/S20 (not shown in table), which provides the ratio of average incomes earned by the top 20% of the population divided by the average income earned by the bottom 20% of the distribution. Five of the 10 countries with the lowest ratio in 2017 are tightly bunched between 4.1 and 4.6: Sweden, the Netherlands, France, Germany, and Switzerland. The United States has by far the highest ratio: 8.4. The remaining countries have ratios between 5.1 and 6.5 [6].

Health system features

Table 13.2 shows how the 10 countries raise the revenues to fund their health care systems: through government or compulsory schemes, private voluntary health insurance (VHI), and out-of-pocket (OOP) spending. Six of the countries are tightly bunched with regard to government/compulsory insurance, where it accounts for between 79 and 84% of total revenue, but the other four, Australia, Canada, Switzerland, and the United States show considerably smaller proportions. In Australia and Canada, VHI plays a relatively larger role than in the other countries. Switzerland relies on OOP spending much more than any other

TABLE 13.2 Sources of health care revenue, 2017.

Country	Government/ compulsory	Voluntary (private) insurance	Out-of-pocket
Australia	69%	10%	18%
Canada	70%	13%	15%
France	83%	7%	9%
Germany	84%	1%	13%
Japan	84%	2%	13%
Netherlands	82%	6%	11%
Sweden	84%	1%	15%
Switzerland	64%	7%	29%
United Kingdom	79%	3%	16%
United States	45%	35%	12%

Notes: Figures may not add up to 100% because "Other" category is not shown. In Germany, substitutive voluntary health insurance is classified as government/compulsory.
Sources: Data for all countries except the United States are from: OECD. Health at a Glance 2019, Figure 7.8. https://www.oecd-ilibrary.org/social-issues-migration-health/health-at-a-glance-2019_4dd50c09-en. Data for the United States are from: Health, U.S., 2018, Table 44. https://www.cdc.gov/nchs/data/hus/2018/044.pdf.

country, accounting for 29% of total revenue, with the next highest country, Australia, far lower at 18%. The figures in Table 13.2 for the United States are very different than the other nine countries because it has a much higher voluntary sector through employer-based private insurance; there is no requirement that people have health insurance. There was an individual mandate with relatively small financial penalties between 2014 and 2018 but it is no longer in effect. Only 45% of revenue is accounted for by government/compulsory sources, far below the next lowest figure (64% in Switzerland).

The 12% percentage for OOP in the United States may seem surprisingly low given the high cost-sharing requirements discussed in Chapter 12. In spite of this, the United States ranks 2nd after Switzerland in per-capita OOP spending among the 10 countries. This US OOP burden may not look high as a percentage compared with other revenue sources, but given the very large total spending, even 12% results in a very large amount of OOP spending per person.

Some information about governance and public funding appears in Table 13.3. There is a great deal of variation in all three columns: locus of governance, sources of public funding, and the number of insurers in the public or compulsory system. Regarding the latter, the four countries with only one public insurer, namely, Australia, Canada, Sweden, and the United Kingdom are

TABLE 13.3 Governance and public financing.

Country	Major locus of governance	Major source of public financing	Number of insurers in public or compulsory system
Australia	Shared between national, state, and local	Taxes	1
Canada	Provincial	Taxes	1
France	Shared between national and regional	Taxes and social insurance contributions	2[a]
Germany	Corporatist organizations[b]	Social insurance contributions	Approximately 110
Japan	Shared between national, regional, and local	Taxes and premiums	Over 1500
Netherlands	National government and corporatist organizations[b]	Premiums	Approximately 25
Sweden	Counties and localities	Taxes	1
Switzerland	Shared between national, cantons, and local	Premiums	Approximately 50
United Kingdom	National (separately for each of the four countries)	Taxes	1
United States	Shared between national, state, and employers	Taxes and premiums	Over 1000 (see Note)

Note: A plurality of Americans receive their insurance through thousands of employers although typically they have only a small handful of choices and many have only a single option available. Those purchasing individual insurance in the health care marketplaces often have 30 or so choices, depending on state. Medicare beneficiaries who choose to enroll in Medicare Advantage plans often can choose between several dozen options. Medicaid beneficiaries sometimes have a choice among managed care plans; this varies by state.
[a]While there are two main statutory health insurance funds in France, there are several smaller funds covering a several specific groups such as railway employees and miners.
[b]These are consortia of insurers and provider groups that negotiate with each other fees and other matters of mutual interest. Government generally takes a hands-off approach but can intervene if negotiations fail.
Source: The country-specific chapters in this book.

sometimes called "single-payer systems." In contrast, in Japan and the United States there are more than 1000 insurers if one recognizes that most large companies in the United States are self-insured.[a]

Table 13.4 describes the role of VHI in eight of the countries; the concept does not apply very well in the United States and VHI is almost nonexistent in Japan. Recall that VHI is secondary insurance, supplementing countries' mandatory or compulsory primary health insurance systems. The table shows that:

- VHI usually provides complementary and/or supplementary benefits. Complementary means paying for the patient cost-sharing requirements for services covered under the public program, while supplementary means paying for services or amenities not covered by the public plan (e.g., dental or optical care, a private room in a hospital). Which roles VHI takes on varies a great deal between countries (see Chapter 2 for more details.)
- Ownership varies considerably as well. VHI is nearly universal in France but plays only a small role in the United Kingdom, with the other countries falling in between. In terms of how much of total health spending is covered by VHI, its biggest roles are in France, Canada, and Australia.
- VHI is often provided through employers, which tends to favor those who are better off financially. In some countries, companies can screen and even deny coverage to those with preexisting conditions. Its ownership is actively encouraged by the Australian government through both premium rebates and financial penalties.
- There are two types of VHI in Germany. For the 11% of the population not covered by the public system (many of those with high income, the self-employed, and civil servants), it provides coverage that substitutes for the public system. For others, it plays only a very minor role largely because the German benefits package is extremely generous.

Table 13.5 provides several measures of the supply of resources available in each country. Beginning with the number of practicing physicians per 1000 population, there is a large amount (almost twofold) of variation. Japan, the United States, Canada, and the United Kingdom have relatively low physician densities, with Germany, Sweden, and Switzerland on the higher end of the spectrum.

The second column shows the percent of physicians who are classified as providing primary care. These numbers should be viewed with caution because different countries choose to classify physicians in different ways. With the

---

[a] When a company self-insures, it takes on (some of) the risk of the health care costs of its employees. Typically, self-insured employers contract with health insurance companies to carry out administrative tasks like claims processing, for a fee. There are various tax and regulatory advantages to self-insurance but it does put the company at risk if it experiences high and unexpected health insurance claims. As a result, many also purchase stop-loss coverage from an insurance company, where, for an additional fee, they are protected against such large and unexpected costs.

TABLE 13.4 Role of voluntary health insurance.

Country	Type	(a) % Pop (b) % THE[a]	Benefits	Comment
Australia	Complementary and Supplementary	(a) 47% (b) 10%[a]	Complementary covers costs of stays in private hospitals, dental, and other care. Supplementary provides faster access and more choice of providers in hospitals.	Government encourages purchase of VHI through tax breaks and penalties. There is open enrollment and community-rated premiums within age groups. 22% of lowest-income quintile are covered, vs 57% of highest-income quintile.
Canada	Mostly Complementary	(a) 67% (b) 13%	For services not covered by provincial plans, particularly drugs, dental care, and private rooms in hospitals.	94% of premiums paid through employers, unions, or other groups.
France	Complementary and Supplementary	(a) 95% (b) 14%	Covers copayments and **balance billing** on hospital and physician services, dental and other care, as well as private rooms in hospitals.	Mainly obtained through employment. Premium vouchers are provided to those with lowest incomes, but overall poorer people pay a greater percentage of income for VHI. Generally, VHI is not used to avoid waiting lists.
Germany	Substitutive	(a) 11% (b) <8%	Provides coverage in lieu of statutory health insurance coverage.	Available to those with higher incomes, public employees, and the self-employed. Provides individual rather than group coverage. Premiums are risk-rated initially but not upon renewal; the typical buyer healthier and wealthier.
Germany	Complementary and Supplementary	(a) 11% (b) 1%	Copayments for dental and other care, treatment by chief physician in hospitals, and private hospital rooms.	A very minor component of the Germany system

Continued

TABLE 13.4 Role of voluntary health insurance.—cont'd

Country	Type	(a) % Pop (b) % THE[a]	Benefits	Comment
Netherlands	Complementary	(a) 84% (b) 6%	Covers dental and other care, and costs for drugs above the amount covered by the statutory system. Does not provide faster access.	Insurers can screen applicants and rates are not regulated. It is usually purchased from providers of statutory insurance. VHI is not used to avoid waiting lists or increase choice of provider.
Sweden	Supplementary	(a) 5%–10% (b) 1%	Quicker access to specialists and elective treatments	Paid for by employers.
Switzerland	Complementary and Supplementary	(a) 72% (b) 7%	Covers costs not included in statutory insurance plans, especially dental care, and free choice of hospital physician and private rooms in hospitals. Also provides coverage for certain drugs and faster access to specialists.	Insurers can screen applicants and refuse coverage.
United Kingdom	Complementary and Supplementary	(a) 11% (b) 3%	Provides faster access for elective services in hospitals and choice of private provider and private rooms. Some plans cover costs of dental care.	Insurers can screen applicants and not cover preexisting conditions. Premiums are risk-rated. Mostly paid for by employers.

[a]Notes: % THE is the percent of total health expenditures accounted for by VHI. % Pop is the percentage of the population with voluntary health insurance. The percentage THE in Australia is closer to 13% rather than 10% if one includes the cost to the government of premium rebates.
Sources: Sagan A, Thomson S. Voluntary health insurance in Europe. vol. 1. United Kingdom: WHO Regional Office for Europe; 2016. Country Profiles. International Health Care System Profiles. The Commonwealth Fund. https://www.commonwealthfund.org/international-health-policy-center/countries. Country Health Profiles 2019. OECD. http://www.oecd.org/health/country-health-profiles-EU.htm. Other sources included the European Observatory on Health Systems and Policies' country-specific books in its Health Systems in Transition (HiT) series. https://www.euro.who.int/en/about-us/partners/observatory/publications/health-system-reviews-hits.

TABLE 13.5 Provider supply and selected equipment, 2017 or 2018.

Country	Practicing physicians per 1000 population, 2018 (1)	Percent primary care (2)	Practicing nurses per 1000 population, 2018 (3)	Hospital beds per 1000 population, 2018 (4)	MRI units per million population, 2017 (5)	CT scanners per million population, 2017 (6)
Australia	3.8	45%	11.9	3.8	14.2	64.8
Canada	2.7	48%	10.0	2.5	10.0	15.3
France	3.2	54%	10.5	5.9	14.2	17.4
Germany	4.3	45%	13.2	8.0	34.7	35.1
Japan	2.5	43%	11.8	13.0	55.2	112.3
Netherlands	3.7	47%	11.1	3.2	13.0	13.5
Sweden	4.3	33%	10.9	2.1	14.0	18.5
Switzerland	4.3	48%	17.6	4.6	23.1	39.3
United Kingdom	2.8	45%	7.8	2.5	7.2	9.5
United States	2.6	43%	11.7	2.9	37.6	42.6

Sources: (1, 3, 4) Data are from: OECD.Stat. https://stats.oecd.org/Index.aspx?ThemeTreeId=9. (3) United States and France data are from OECD. Health at a Glance, 2019, Figure 8.10, and are for 2017. https://www.oecd-ilibrary.org/social-issues-migration-health/health-at-a-glance-2019_4dd50c09-en. (4) Australia data are for 2016; Germany and the United States are from 2017. (5, 6) Data at from OECD. Health at a Glance, 2019, Figure 9.3. UK data are for 2014. https://www.oecd-ilibrary.org/social-issues-migration-health/health-at-a-glance-2019_4dd50c09-en. (2) Data are from: Papanicolas I, Woskie LR, Jha AK. Health care spending in the United States and other high-income countries. JAMA. 2018;319(10):1024–39. Fig. 5, row 2. Years vary.*

exception of Sweden's low figure, which may not be meaningful [7],[b] the countries are fairly similar with respect to the proportion of physicians who are in the field of primary care, with eight of the 10 countries falling between 43% and 48%.

The US figure of 43% may seem surprising high to some and inconsistent with much of the literature [8]. It is consistent, however, with research by Miriam Laugesen, who contends that the issue is mainly definitional [9]. She writes, "The OECD restricts its definition of generalists to a limited group of physicians, which includes family practitioners, general practitioners, and 'other generalists'." In the United States, however, primary care physicians often are trained as general internists, pediatricians, and sometimes obstetricians/gynecologists. The US figure of 43% is consistent with the fact that over half of all physicians visits in the country are defined as being for primary care [9].

Most countries have similar densities of nurses, but there are two exceptions, with Switzerland employing a very large number and the United Kingdom, a small number, so much so that some are citing it as a "crisis." This will likely be aggravated by **Brexit** in part because a relatively large share of nurses—15%—there are foreign-born [10 (p. 859), 11].

Japan and Germany both have very high numbers of hospital beds. Sweden, Canada, the United Kingdom, and the United States have relatively few compared with the other countries. While this probably reflects an oversupply in Japan and Germany, it may also reflect population preferences, which in turn may further signify what people are used to having. Many experts consider the large number of hospital beds to be a problem, lowering efficiency and reducing quality since many hospitals are not well equipped [12]. Part of the discrepancy between Japan and other countries is due to hospitalization of some older patients and psychiatric patients who might be more appropriately served in long-term care facilities. It has been estimated that 11% of Japanese hospital expenditures are for LTC compared with an average of 4% in all OECD countries [13].

The last two columns of Table 13.5 show the availability of two imaging technologies: MRI units and CT scanners. Japan and the United States show the highest availability, with the United Kingdom showing the lowest for both. Japan has almost eight times as many MRI units per million population as the United Kingdom, and about 12 times as many CT scanners. Interestingly, this does not necessarily translate into greater use of these imaging technologies. Japan is second in CT scan use per 1000 population (after the United States) and third in MRI examinations (see Table 15.15).

Table 13.6 provides an overview of hospital and physician payment methods and related information. The countries vary greatly in terms of whether referrals

---

[b.] It has been noted by Toralf Hasvold that "there is not a sharp distinction between primary care and specialized hospital care, as owners and governing bodies (county) are the same..." [7]. As a result, the low Swedish figure may not be especially meaningful.

TABLE 13.6 Providers and payment methods.

Country	Referral needed for specialty care	Hospital payment methods	Physician payment methods	Role of managed care
Australia	Yes	DRGs	FFS	Small
Canada	In most provinces	Global budgets	FFS in most provinces; mix of capitation, salary, and P4P in Ontario	Small
France	Usually	DRGs	FFS	Small
Germany	No	DRGs	Ambulatory: FFS Inpatient: salary	Small
Japan	Rarely	Per diems	FFS	Small
Netherlands	Yes	Mainly DRGs	Capitation, FFS, and P4P	Small
Sweden	No, but primary care is usually the first point of contact	Global budgets, DRGs, and P4P	Capitation, FFS, and P4P	Small
Switzerland	Yes	DRGs	FFS, a small amount of capitation, with salary for hospital-based specialists	Depends on definition[a]
United Kingdom	Yes	Global budgets, DRGs, and P4P	Capitation, Salary, P4P	Small
United States	Usually no, but varies by insurance type	Mainly DRGs	Mainly FFS and P4P, with salary for some hospital-based specialties	Large

[a]About 70% of the Swiss have insurance plans that employ selective contracting of providers. A much smaller percent, however, are in plans that actively manage the care provided to patients.
Sources: The country-specific chapters in this book.

are needed before seeking specialty care. Diagnosis-related groups (DRGs) are the predominant method of paying for hospital inpatient stays but by no means the only way, with Canada employing hospital global (annual) budgets and Japan paying on a per diem basis. Sweden and the United Kingdom use a variety of methods. There is perhaps even more variation in physician payment methods, which is not surprising since primary care and specialty physicians are often paid in different manners. The data therefore are not easily summarized, with fee-for-service, **capitation**, salary, and mixes of those three payments methods all in use. Finally, managed care currently plays a large role mainly in the United States; in Switzerland, it depends on how the concept is defined (see table footnote).

Table 13.7 provides some data on the wages of generalist physicians, specialist physicians, and hospital nurses. These data should be viewed with a great deal of caution because there is little uniformity in the way compensation

TABLE 13.7 Provider incomes, 2017.

Country	Ratio, generalist MD income to average wages (1)	Ratio, specialist MD income to average wages (2)	Hospital nurses, 2018 (3)
Australia	1.9	3.8	$77,871
Canada	3.1	4.9	$56,147
France	2.9	4.9	$38,229
Germany	4.4	5.4	$54,704
Japan	–	–	$42,100
Netherlands	2.4	3.6	$65,887
Sweden	–	2.3	–
Switzerland	–	–	$76,053
United Kingdom	1.7	3.3	$47,736
United States	3.8	5.5	$77,670

Notes: For (1, 2), the data are for self-employed physicians in Australia, Canada, France, Germany, and the Netherlands, and for salaried physicians in Sweden and the United Kingdom. All figures in US dollars.
Sources: (1, 2) OECD. Ch. 8: Health Workforce: Remuneration of doctors (general practitioners and specialists). OECD. Health at a Glance 2019, Figure 8.8. https://www.oecd-ilibrary.org/social-issues-migration-health/health-at-a-glance-2019_4dd50c09-en. (3) OECD.Stat. Health Care Resources: Remuneration of health professionals. OECD. 2020 https://stats.oecd.org/index.aspx?queryid=30025#. Data for Australia are for 2017; France for 2016; Germany for 2014; United Kingdom for 2015. US data are for 2019 and from: Tank A. Physician salary report 2020: Salaries rising prior to COVID-19 impacts. Weatherby Healthcare. 2020 https://weatherbyhealthcare.com/blog/annual-physician-salary-report. Guzman G. Household Income: 2018. United States Census Bureau. 2019. https://www.census.gov/content/dam/Census/library/publications/2019/acs/acsbr18-01.pdf.

data are collected across countries. Moreover, some countries are not included in the OECD data. (The omission of Switzerland is unfortunate because there are some reports that Swiss physician income is very high, with a government agency reporting average annual incomes in 2018 of over $600,000 for neurosurgeons and gastroenterologists, and over $500,000 for oncologists, anesthetists, and radiologists [14].) The first two columns of the table show the ratio of wages for generalists and specialists to average wages in the respective countries. Of the countries shown, income ratios are highest in the United States, Germany, Canada, and France. The ratio of 2.3 for Swedish specialists compared with average wages in the country is perhaps emblematic of more economic equality in the Scandinavian countries. Pay for hospital-based nurses also varies considerably, with annual wages of Australia and US nurses double that of the French.

The final data in this section are shown in Table 13.8, on patient cost-sharing requirements. This is from a 2018 study, providing a great deal of information on deductibles, **coinsurance**, **copayment**, and extra billing requirements, along with protection mechanisms the countries put in place. All figures are in the country's currency. The data are not easily summarized and instead provided as a reference source. Note that some of these costs are covered by VHI.

Health

Major indicators of lifespan are shown in Table 13.9. Life expectancy at birth is fairly uniform, with Japan and Switzerland a bit higher than the other countries and the United States considerably lower—2.5 years below the second-lowest country, Germany. The United States and Germany also perform the lowest with regard to additional life expectancy at age 65. Japan, France, and Switzerland perform the best. Infant mortality rates (deaths per 1000 live births) vary more, with the US rate about three times as high as the rates in Japan and Sweden. Canada also performs poorly. Many factors affect infant mortality, some of which are largely unrelated to the health care system.

There is even more variation in maternal mortality, but it should be kept in mind that the figures are deaths per 100,000 live births rather than per 1000, as was the case for infant mortality. The US rate of 17.4 is more than five times as great as in the Netherlands and Germany. Excluding the United States, Canada and France did not perform as well as the other countries.

Table 13.10 shows health risks: smoking, alcohol consumption, and overweight/obesity among adults and children. Smoking rates are particularly low (12% or less) in Sweden, the United States, Canada and Australia, but double that (25%) in France. Alcohol consumption is highest in France and Germany, but fairly uniform among the other countries, with Sweden and Japan having

TABLE 13.8 Patient cost-sharing requirements, 2018.

Country	Deductibles	Coinsurance and copayments	Extra billing and reference prices	Protection mechanisms
Australia	None	*Specialist ambulatory care:* Coinsurance (15%) *Prescriptions:* Copayment: AUD38.30 *Hospital care:* Coinsurance (25%) at private hospitals	Physicians may bill above fee schedule Private hospitals may bill above fee schedule	*Prescriptions:* Reduced copayment for low income families and children *Ambulatory care:* Coinsurance cap; cap on OOP for extra billing for low income and children
Canada	For prescriptions (depending on province)	*Prescriptions:* Copayment or coinsurance (depending on province)	None	*Prescriptions:* Provincial regulations determine OOP caps and exemptions *Low income:* Various provincial programs cover OOP costs Tax credits for individuals whose medical expenses exceed 3% of annual income
England	None	*Prescriptions:* Copayment: GBP8.40 *Dental care:* GBP19.70, 53.90, or 233.70, depending on type of service	None	*Exemptions:* Children, low income, certain diseases, + for prescriptions and eye tests also aged 60+ Annual cap on prescription copayments

France	None	*Physician visits:* Coinsurance (30%) + €1 copayment per visit and lab test/X-ray *Prescriptions:* Coinsurance (15%–100%) + €0.5 copayment *Inpatient care:* Coinsurance (20%) + copayment €18/day *Dental care:* Coinsurance (30%) + copayment €1 Additional copayment for expensive care (>€120): €18 (once per visit or stay)	20% of physician bills above fee schedule Reference prices exist for dental care, glasses, dentures, hearing aids (covering as little as 10% of costs)	Children exempted from copayments Patients with one of 32 severe chronic diseases exempted from coinsurance Low income (10% of population) receive free VHI, free vision care, free dental care Complementary VHI covers coinsurance Hospital copayment limited to 31 days €50 caps on copayments each for physician visits, prescriptions, and dental care
Germany	None	*Prescriptions and medical aids:* 10% coinsurance (min €5, max €10) per prescription *Hospital copayment:* €10 per day *Home nursing, physiotherapy, etc.:* Coinsurance (10%) + €10 per prescription	Reference prices exist for crowns and dentures (covering about 50% of normal treatment), prescriptions, and medical aids.	*Exemption:* Children under age 18 Maximum cost sharing (does not apply to OOP above reference prices): 2% of annual income (1% for patients with chronic conditions)
Japan	None	30% coinsurance (lower for ages 70 and older)	None	**Out-of-pocket maximum**, varying by income (see Chapter 8)

Continued

TABLE 13.8 Patient cost-sharing requirements, 2018.—cont'd

Country	Deductibles	Coinsurance and copayments	Extra billing and reference prices	Protection mechanisms
Netherlands	€385 for all services except primary care	Coinsurance (20%–25%) for noncontracted care (only for certain insurance policies)	*Prescriptions:* OOP above reference price *Medical devices and aids:* OOP above reference prices	***Deductible** exemptions:* Children <18, maternal care, integrated care programs
Sweden	*Prescriptions:* 1100 SEK (for adults >18) *Dental care:* 3000 SEK (for adults >22)	*Copayments* (varying across the 21 county councils): *Primary care:* 120–200 SEK per physician visit *Specialist care:* 200–350 SEK per physician visit (reduced if referred from primary care) *Hospitalization:* 100 SEK/day for adults >19 *Medical devices/aids:* copayment for different types of devices/aids Coinsurance (determined at national level): *Prescriptions:* 50% between 1100 and 2100 SEK, 25% between 2100 and 3900 SEK, 10% between 3900 and 5400 SEK (max 2200 in copayments for each 12-month period) *Dental care:* 50% between reference prices of 3000 and 15,000 SEK, 15% for reference prices above 15,000 SEK (applies for each 12-month period)	*Dental care:* OOP above reference prices *Medical devices/aids:* OOP above reference prices; extra billing for medical devices/aids not covered in some county councils (e.g., multifocal lenses in cataract surgery, advanced hearing aids)	*General exemptions:* Children and young adults <22 for dental care, <18 for prescription drugs, <20 for health services Two separate copayment caps for each 12-month period: – Visits to primary and outpatient specialist care combined: 1100 SEK – Prescription drugs: 2200 SEK

Switzerland	All services: min. CHF300, max CHF2500	*Coinsurance:* 10% of all costs above deductible *Hospital copayment:* CHF 15/day	*Medical aids:* Patients pay OOP above reference price	Children (<19 y): no deductible (or voluntary between CHF 100 and CHF 600); Maximum for coinsurance: CHF700/ year (children: CHF350/year) Exemptions for preventive and maternal care
United States	*Employer plans* Average: $1505 *Medicare:* Hospital care: $1340 Physician services: $183 Drugs: Varies by plan	*Employer plans:* Average coinsurance: 19% primary, specialist, and hospital *Average copayment:* US$25 (primary), US$38 (specialist), US$336 (hospital) *Prescriptions:* Coinsurance 17%–38%, Copayment: US$11–110 *Medicare:* Hospital care: No copayment for first 60 days, US$335/day until day 90 *Physician services:* 20% coinsurance *Prescriptions:* Varies by plan	Usually not allowed	*Employer plans:* Average cap on user charges: US$3822 *Medicare:* No cap

Notes: Most figures are for 2016.
AUD, Australian dollars; CHF, Swiss Franc; GBP, British Pounds; SEK = Swedish Krona.
Sources: (1) Rice T, Quentin W, Anell A, Barnes AJ, Rosenau P, Unruh LY, et al. Revisiting out-of-pocket requirements: trends in spending, financial access barriers, and policy in ten high-income countries. BMC Health Serv Res 2018;18(1):371. (2) Chapter 8 of this book.

TABLE 13.9 Major measures of mortality.

Country	Life expectancy at birth, 2017 (1)	Additional life expectancy at age 65, 2017 (2)	Infant mortality, 2018 (3)	Maternal mortality, 2018 (4)
Australia	82.6	21.0	3.1	4.8
Canada	82.0	20.7	4.7	8.6
France	82.6	21.6	3.8	8.7
Germany	81.1	19.7	3.2	3.2
Japan	84.2	22.0	1.9	3.6
Netherlands	81.8	20.0	3.5	3.0
Sweden	82.5	20.4	2.0	4.3
Switzerland	83.6	21.4	3.3	4.6
United Kingdom	81.3	20.0	3.9	6.5
United States	78.6	19.4	5.8	17.4

Sources: (1, 2) are from: OECD. Health at a Glance 2019. https://www.oecd-ilibrary.org/social-issues-migration-health/health-at-a-glance-2019_4dd50c09-en. (1) Figure 3.1. (2) Figure 11.3. (3) OECD.Stat. Health Status: Maternal and infant mortality. OECD. 2020. https://stats.oecd.org/index.aspx?queryid=30116#. Deaths per 1000 live births. Data for United States are for 2017. (4) OECD.Stat. Health Status: Maternal and infant mortality. OECD. 2020. https://stats.oecd.org/index.aspx?queryid=30116#. Deaths per 100,000 live births. Data for France are for 2012; Switzerland and the United Kingdom, for 2017.

the lowest rates. Japan has by far the lowest obesity/overweight statistics. The United States has the highest overweight/obesity rates for both age groups followed by Australia, the United Kingdom, and Canada.

In spite of Americans showing poorer results in several health and health risk measures, they rate themselves as healthier than the residents of all of the other countries except Canada (Table 13.11). Eighty-eight percent of Americans said they were in good or very good health in 2016. Curiously, only about 35% of Japanese people felt that their wealth was good or very good, but only 14% said that their health was "bad or very bad"; thus, they preferred not to express either of the extreme choices. Among the other countries, Germany and France show lower self-assessed health status. These cross-national results need to be viewed with caution, however, because cultural and language differences between countries affect the way survey respondents answer questions about their health [15].

TABLE 13.10 Health risks, 2017.

Country	Smoking rate (1)	Alcohol consumption in liters (2)	Obesity (adults) (3)	Overweight and obesity (children), 2016 (4)
Australia	12.4%	9.4	30.4%	36.0%
Canada	12.0%	8.1	26.3%	33.9%
France	25.4%	11.7	17.0%	32.4%
Germany	18.8%	10.9	23.6%	28.7%
Japan	17.7%	7.2	4.4%	17.5%
Netherlands	16.8%	8.3	13.4%[a]	26.9%
Sweden	10.4%	7.1	13.1%[a]	25.2%
Switzerland	19.1%	9.2	11.3%[a]	23.0%
United Kingdom	17.2%	9.7	28.7%	32.5%
United States	10.5%	8.9	40.0%	43.0%

[a]*Self-reported. Self-reported measures are usually 5%–10% points lower than measured values.
Sources: From OECD. Health at a glance 2019: OECD indicators. Paris: OECD Publishing; 2019,
https://doi.org/10.1787/4dd50c09-en. (1) Figure 4.2. Percent of population aged 15+ smoking
daily. Data for Australia are for 2016; France for 2018. (2) Figure 4.4. Liters per capita among
population aged 15+. Data for Australia, Germany, and the United States are for 2016. (4)
Figure 4.14. Percent of population aged 5–9 overweight (including obesity). Data for all countries are
measured values. (3) OECD Health Statistics 2020—Frequently Requested Data. OECD [xls]. 2020,
http://www.oecd.org/health/OECD-Health-Statistics-2020-Frequently-Requested-Data.xls. Data for
France are for 2015; Germany for 2012; the United States is for 2016. Data for Netherlands, Sweden,
and Switzerland are self-reported; data for other countries are measured values.*

TABLE 13.11 Adults rating health as good or very good, 2016.

Country	
Australia	85.2%
Canada	88.5%
France	67.4%
Germany	65.4%
Japan	35.5%
Netherlands	76.1%
Sweden	76.5%
Switzerland	80.2%
United Kingdom	74.8%
United States	87.9%

Sources: OECD. Health at a Glance 2019, Figure 3.24. https://www.oecd-ilibrary.org/social-issues-migration-health/health-at-a-glance-2019_4dd50c09-en. Data for France are for 2014; Australia, Canada, and Sweden for 2015; Japan for 2017.

References

[1] OECD/Eurostat/WHO. A system of health accounts 2011: Revised edition. Paris: OECD Publishing; 2017.

[2] Anon. OECD health statistics 2020. OECD; 2020. [Online Database]. [Accessed 26 August 2020]. Available from: http://www.oecd.org/els/health-systems/health-data.htm.

[3] Anon. Guidelines for completing the questionnaire. OECD health data questionnaire. 2020. OECD Publishing; 2019.

[4] Health Systems Characteristics. OECD Health System Characteristics Survey. OECD [Internet]. [Accessed 4 November 2020]. Available from: https://www.oecd.org/els/health-systems/characteristics.htm.

[5] Data. Health. Eurostat [Online data]. [Accessed 4 November 2020]. Available from: https://ec.europa.eu/eurostat/web/health/data.

[6] Income inequality. OECD [Online data]. [Accessed 4 November 2020]. Available from: https://data.oecd.org/inequality/income-inequality.htm.

[7] Hasvold T. Sweden. In: Kringos DS, Boerma WGW, Hutchinson A, Saltman RB, editors. Building primary care in a changing Europe: Case studies, vol. 40. Copenhagen: European Observatory on Health Systems and Policies; 2015.

[8] The Number of Practicing Primary Care Physicians in the United States. Agency for Healthcare Research and Quality. 2011(12-P001-2-EF).

[9] Laugesen MJ. Do other countries have a better mix of generalists and specialists? J Health Polit Policy Law 2018;43(5):853–72.

[10] Gilroy R. NHS workforce being 'hollowed out' by registered nurse shortages. Nursing Times; 2019. [Internet]. [Accessed 4 November 2020]. Available from: https://www.nursingtimes.net/news/workforce/nhs-workforce-being-hollowed-out-by-registered-nurse-shortages-28-11-2019/.

[11] OECD.Stat. OECD [Web browser]. [Accessed 3 September 2020]. Available from: https://stats.oecd.org/Index.aspx?ThemeTreeId=9.

[12] Emanuel EJ. Which country has the world's best health care? New York: PublicAffairs; 2020.

[13] Key Findings: Japan. Health at a glance 2017: OECD indicators. OECD; 2017.

[14] Xuequan M. Doctors' salaries in Switzerland exceed expectations: Gov't report. Xinhua; 2018. [Internet]. [Accessed 4 November 2020]. Available from: http://www.xinhuanet.com/english/2018-10/30/c_137567506.htm#:~:text=General%20practitioners%2C%20who%20provide%20primary,an%20underestimate%2C%20the%20authors%20said.

[15] Spitzer S, Weber D. Reporting biases in self-assessed physical and cognitive health status of older Europeans. PLoS One 2019;14(10):e0223526.

Chapter 14

Equity

Equity and efficiency are the two key broad measures of a successful health care system. This chapter focuses on equity, while Chapter 15 examines efficiency—that is, which countries are getting the most value for their investments in health care.

Equity is defined here as it is used in common speech, being synonymous with the concept of fairness, and operationalized through the idea that people in different income or other socioeconomic groups be treated equally through the health care system in their countries. This is, admittedly, a limited definition; other critical dimensions include gender equity and equity across racial and ethnic groups. The lack of cross-national data on such dimensions, however, limits our inquiry. Box 14.1 discusses equity in more detail.

While equity and efficiency are examined in separate chapters, they are intertwined. The desire to contain health care expenditures, particularly public money, in quest of greater efficiency, has forced countries to enact policies that can sacrifice equity. Two prominent examples discussed throughout this book are greater reliance on private supplemental voluntary health insurance plans that are more typically available to those of higher means, as well as employing higher patient cost-sharing requirements. The twin issues of equity and efficiency are brought together in Chapter 16.

Measuring equity

We use data that meet two criteria. First, the data must include measures that mainly reflect the influence of the health insurance system rather than other factors. This removes from consideration many measures of health outcomes. Life expectancy and infant mortality, for example, are determined by factors that arguably are influenced more by socioeconomic (SES) factors, social policies and protections, individual behaviors, and environmental factors than by medical care [1, 2]. Cross-national data on those two measures are provided in Table 13.9.

Second, data are used if they allow the comparison of people who are in higher SES groups with those who are in lower SES groups *within* a country. This is necessary for two reasons. First, some countries have greater resources than others, so they are better able to lower barriers to obtaining care. Simple cross-country comparisons may reflect differences in wealth rather than differences

Health Insurance Systems: An International Comparison. https://doi.org/10.1016/B978-0-12-816072-5.00018-3

BOX 14.1   Definitions of equity.

In economic definitions of the term, there are two types of equity: horizontal and vertical. **Horizontal equity** implies that similar people are treated the same with respect to some characteristic; this is akin to the concept of equality. The term is commonly used in the tax literature and connotes that people with similar incomes and/or assets should incur the same tax liabilities. Horizontal equity is used somewhat differently in the health economics literature, however, where it usually means equal treatment for those with equal health needs. In contrast, **vertical equity**, according to Gavin Mooney (1996, p. 99), is "the unequal but equitable treatment of unequals." An example in health care is waiving patient cost-sharing requirements for people below a certain income threshold.

Sources: Mooney G. And now for vertical equity? Some concerns arising from aboriginal health in Australia. Health Econ 1996;5(2):99–103 (p. 99). Wagstaff A, Van Doorslaer E. Equity in health care finance and delivery. In: Culyer AJ, Newhouse JP, editors. Handbook of health economics, vol. 1B. 1st ed. Amsterdam, North Holland: Elsevier; 2000. p. 893–1910.

---

attributable to their health insurance systems. By comparing groups of people in different SES categories within a country, we partly control for this confounder. The second reason is that each country has its own history and institutional background. To illustrate, in Chapter 2 we discussed two methods of controlling the use of health care resources: supply-side vs demand-side rationing. The United Kingdom focuses mainly on the former, and the United States, the latter. We would therefore expect that people would face a different set of barriers in the United Kingdom (waiting to obtain services) than in the United States (being able to afford care). These different contexts make it prudent to focus on differences within each country by comparing different population groups, rather than across disparate countries and their health care systems.

Almost all of the measures of equity used here compare those with higher vs lower incomes; a single one compares low- and high-education groups. Four sources of data are used, although not every data set includes all 10 countries, with Japan nearly always being absent. These sources are[a]:

- The Commonwealth Fund's 2016 survey of adults in nine of our countries (all but Japan) [3]. It should be noted that just before this book was published, the Commonwealth Fund released data from its 2020 survey. Because the survey was carried out during the beginning of the Covid-19 pandemic, this may have affected people's responses in ways that do not reflect longer-term patterns. As a result, we use the 2016 findings in the body of chapter but include a discussion of the 2020 findings in the chapter's Appendix.

---

[a] The World Health Organization released a report in 2019, titled "Can People Afford to Pay for Health Care," that provides cross-national data on catastrophic spending. It is not used here because only four of the 10 countries were included: France, Germany, Sweden, and the United Kingdom.

- OECD data published in its book, *Health at a Glance, 2019*, based on various national surveys [4]. 2014 data are used in most of the data presented here.
- Eurostat, a database from the European Commission with data compiled from a variety of sources, but only for the six European countries in the book [5]. The most recent data are for 2014.
- The World Bank's Health Equity and Financial Protection Indicators study, a compilation of consumer surveys and other data from 183 countries, and which includes several of our 10 [6]. Unfortunately, the most recent cross-national data for catastrophic health care spending—the variables examined here—are for 2010.

Understandably, each organization that collects and compiles data uses its own methodology, including definitions and survey techniques. Individual results therefore need to be viewed with caution, but we can be more confident when disparate data sources reveal similar findings.

Table 14.1 provides definitions, comparison groups, sources, and years for 17 measures of equity meeting the aforementioned criteria. They are divided into four categories to aid in interpreting the results later in the chapter: (a) cost-related barriers; (b) catastrophic spending; (c) health system barriers; and (d) perceptions of quality and coordination.

Findings

Cost-related and other barriers

Fig. 14.1 shows self-reported cost-related access problems for obtaining medical care in the past year (2016), comparing people with below vs above average income. For convenience, we sometimes refer to these groups as the lower and higher halves of the income distribution.[b] Interestingly, the five countries that show the most problems for both income groups also exhibit the greatest *differences* between the two income groups. In these countries—Australia, Canada, France, Switzerland, and the United States—over 20% of those with below average income cited a cost-related access problem.

We focus on differentials between the income groups as well as how the lower-income groups compare across countries. It is not surprising that the largest self-reported barriers are in the United States given that 43% of Americans below age 65 have been classified as being either uninsured or underinsured [7]. The fact that Switzerland had the second greatest barriers for those with lower incomes also is not surprising because almost

---

[b] To determine which survey respondents are in the upper vs. lower part of the income distribution, the Commonwealth Fund first informs the respondent of the average income in their country and then asks them if theirs is: much higher, somewhat higher, around average, somewhat lower, or much lower. The group responding "around average" are not included in the statistics presented. Source: Roosa Tikkanen, personal communication, November 6, 2020.

TABLE 14.1 Measures of equity.

Variable	Comparison	Source	Year	Figure number
Cost-related barriers				
Had a medical problem but did not visit doctor because of cost in the past year	Below vs above average income	Commonwealth Fund	2016	14.1
Needs-adjusted probability of visiting a doctor	Lowest vs highest income quintile	OECD	2014	14.2
Had a serious problem or unable to pay medical bills	Below vs above average income	Commonwealth Fund	2016	14.3
Skipped dental care or checkup due to cost in the past year	Below vs above average income	Commonwealth Fund	2016	14.4
Unmet needs for dental examination due to expense	Lowest vs highest income quintile	Eurostat	2016	14.5
Unmet needs for dental examination due to expense	Lowest vs highest education group	Eurostat	2016	14.6
Share of population who visited a dentist	Lowest vs highest income quintile	OECD	2014	14.7
Share of women aged 20–69 screened for cervical cancer	Lowest vs highest income quintile	OECD	2014	14.8

Catastrophic spending

Spent more than 10% of income out of pocket	Lowest vs highest income quintile	World Bank	2010	14.9
Spent more than 25% of income out of pocket	Lowest vs highest income quintile	World Bank	2010	14.10

Health system barriers

Have regular source of care	Below vs above average income	Commonwealth Fund	2016	14.11
Somewhat or very difficult to get after-hours care	Below vs. above average income	Commonwealth Fund	2016	14.12
Waited 2 months or longer for specialist appt.	Below vs. above average income	Commonwealth Fund	2016	14.13

Perceptions of quality and coordination

Rated medical care from regular provider as fair or poor	Below vs above average income	Commonwealth Fund	2016	14.14
Regular doctor always or often spent enough time and explained things understandably	Below vs above average income	Commonwealth Fund	2016	14.15
Regular doctor always or often knew important information about medical history	Below vs above average income	Commonwealth Fund	2016	14.16
Specialist lacked medical history, or regular doctor not informed about specialist care	Below vs above average income	Commonwealth Fund	2016	14.17

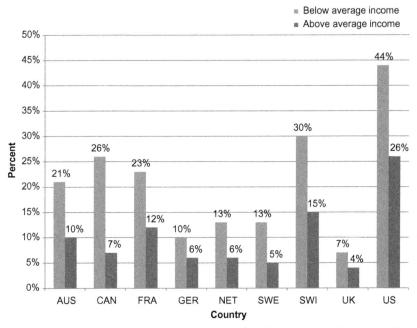

FIG. 14.1   Any cost-related access to medical care problem in the past year, by income, 2016 (below vs above average income). *(Source: Schneider EC, et al. Mirror, mirror 2017: International comparison reflects flaws and opportunities for better U.S. health care. The Commonwealth Fund; July 2017.   https://www.commonwealthfund.org/sites/default/files/documents/___media_files_ publications_fund_report_2017_jul_schneider_mirror_mirror_2017.pdf.)*

30% of health care spending there is out of pocket (Table 13.2). Canada reports the third largest barriers among residents with below average income. This is attributable to lack of government coverage for prescription drugs and dental care, and the fact that possession of voluntary health insurance (VHI) tends to be skewed toward those in the labor market and higher-skilled jobs. It is somewhat surprising that France shows these access barriers given that per capita out-of-pocket (OOP) spending there is low. The reason probably relates to patients often having to pay upfront for medical care before receiving insurance reimbursement, which is discussed further below. Finally, cost-related access problems in Australia may stem from the uneven distribution of VHI (favoring wealthier people), coupled with substantial OOP spending that can occur when physicians do not bulk-bill services (see Chapter 6).

In contrast, four countries show far fewer cost-related access problems for those with lower incomes: Germany, the Netherlands, Sweden, and the United Kingdom. This is likely because these countries (a) tend to provide comprehensive benefits in their public programs, (b) have relatively low patient cost-sharing

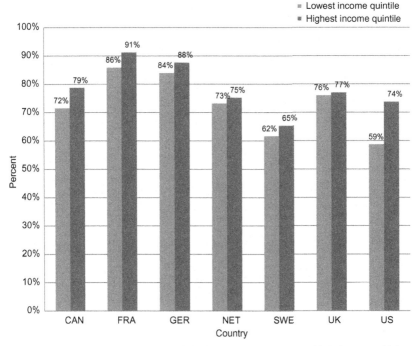

FIG. 14.2 Needs-adjusted probability of visiting a doctor, by income, 2014 (lowest vs highest income quintile). *(Source: OECD. Health at a glance 2019. OECD indicators. Figure 5.5.)*

requirements including the low annual OOP maximums, and (c) VHI represents a small proportion of total national health expenditures.[c]

Fig. 14.2 shows the probability of visiting a doctor, adjusting for the fact that people in lower SES groups have greater health care needs, on average [8]. These data compare those in the lowest vs highest income quintile and are for 2014. Of the seven countries for which we have data, the United States shows by far the greatest disparities, with those in the highest income quintiles having a probability of 15 percentage points higher than those in the lowest income quintile. Differences in Canada (7 percentage points) and France (5 percentage points) exceeded those in other countries, with the United Kingdom showing the most equity: a 1 percentage point difference.

Fig. 14.3 shows whether respondents said they had "a serious problem paying or were unable to pay your medical bills." Almost all countries had considerable differences between those with higher vs lower incomes, with France, the United States, and Switzerland having the largest differences, and the United

---

[c] In the case of Germany, we are referring to low ownership rates for traditional VHI. As discussed in Chapter 9, 11% of the population has private health insurance that substitutes for public coverage.

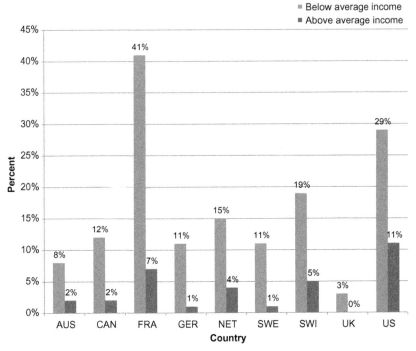

FIG. 14.3   Serious problems paying or unable to pay medical bills, by income, 2016 (below vs above average income). *(Source: Schneider EC, et al. Mirror, mirror 2017: International comparison reflects flaws and opportunities for better U.S. health care. The Commonwealth Fund; July 2017. https://www.commonwealthfund.org/sites/default/files/documents/___media_files_ publications_fund_report_2017_jul_schneider_mirror_mirror_2017.pdf.)*

Kingdom having almost no one reporting this problem. The most noteworthy result is for France, where 41% of those whose income is below average reported these problems in paying medical bills, compared to only 7% for high-income French. This is striking in light Figs. 14.9 and 14.10, below, where it is shown that very few low-income French people incurred catastrophic out-of-pocket spending. Moreover, per capita OOP spending in France is the lowest among the 10 countries [9] and nearly everyone has VHI, including the very poor whose premiums are fully subsidized. The main reason, discussed at some length in Chapter 7, is that historically, in most cases individuals have had to pay medical bills directly and wait for reimbursement, which causes a strain on lower-income persons who have little in the way of savings. There have been repeated policy efforts to change this and it appears that progress is being made. The Commonwealth Fund's 2020 survey showed that the percentage of lower-income persons citing this problem had dropped from 41% to 16% in just 4 years (see Appendix Table). Perhaps as a result, the 2020 survey also showed a large drop in the percentage of lower-income people citing cost-related barriers compared to the numbers as shown in Fig. 14.1 [10].

Figs. 14.4 through 14.7 illustrate financial access barriers to receiving timely dental care. They are from three different data sources that word questions somewhat differently, examine different sets of countries, and compare different subsets of the population. Fig. 14.4, from the Commonwealth Fund, is advantageous because it includes all of our countries except Japan, showing whether respondents skipped dental care or dental checkups because of the cost. The overall pattern is similar to Fig. 14.1, which illustrated medical rather than dental care, and shows that five of the same countries—Australia, Canada, France, Switzerland, and the United States —had the greatest barriers. The one additional country with relatively large barriers is Sweden, which is the case because adult dental care is not part of the country's benefit package, although as described in Chapter 5, there are subsidies available to defray some of the costs. In these five countries, between 27% and 45% of those with lower-than-average incomes said they skipped care because of cost in the past year. In contrast, the figures for Germany, the Netherlands, and the United Kingdom were 18% or less. Germany is particularly impressive because there was almost no difference by income, clearly a result of the country's very generous public dental coverage.

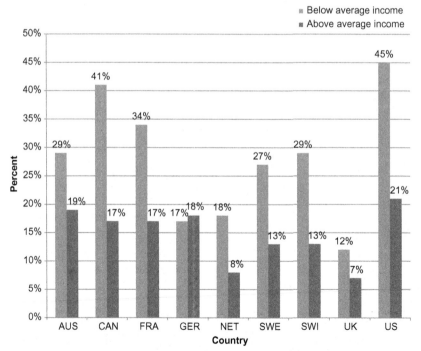

FIG. 14.4   Skipped dental care or checkup because of cost in the past year, by income, 2016 (below vs above average income). *(Source: Schneider EC, et al. Mirror, mirror 2017: International comparison reflects flaws and opportunities for better U.S. health care. The Commonwealth Fund; July 2017. https://www.commonwealthfund.org/sites/default/files/documents/___media_files_ publications_fund_report_2017_jul_schneider_mirror_mirror_2017.pdf.)*

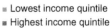

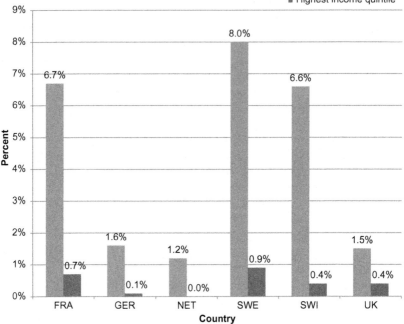

FIG. 14.5 Unmet needs for dental exam, by income, 2016 (lowest vs highest income quintile). *(Source: Eurostat. Unmet health care needs: Statistics. 2020.)*

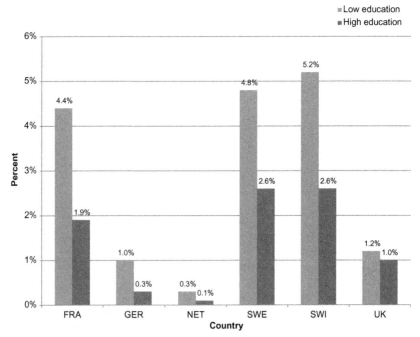

FIG. 14.6 Unmet needs for dental exam, by education, 2016 (lowest vs highest education group). *(Source: Eurostat. Unmet health care needs: Statistics. 2020.)*

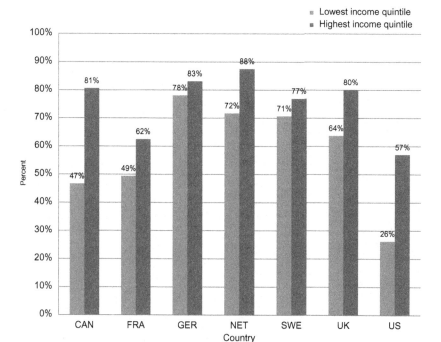

FIG. 14.7 Share of population who visited a dentist, by income, 2014 (lowest vs highest income quintile). *(Source: OECD. Health at a glance 2019. OECD indicators. Figure 5.6.)*

More detail among the six European countries can be gleaned through the Eurostat database, which reports on unmet needs for dental examination by comparing the lowest vs the highest income quintiles (Fig. 14.5) and lowest vs highest among three educational attainment categories (Fig. 14.6) in 2016. Consistent with the previous figures, the highest barriers were in France, Sweden, and Switzerland. Disparities in these three countries were quite large—severalfold between the income quintiles. Differences by education were a little less stark. It should be kept in mind that other factors, such as the availability of dentists particularly in rural areas, could also result in unmet needs.

Fig. 14.7 provides a final measure of access to dental care, from the OECD: the share of the population that visited a dentist in 2014. Seven countries are represented in the data. Where the largest disparities occur are in the United States and Canada. Canada shows a 34 percentage point difference in the probability of visiting a dentist between the lowest and highest income quintiles, and the United States, almost as large, at 31 percentage points. There are few such disparities in Germany, undoubtedly because adult dental care is covered by the public insurance program. Interestingly, Sweden also shows little difference by income even though adult dental care is not a benefit of the public system (although as noted earlier, there are subsidies provided to users).

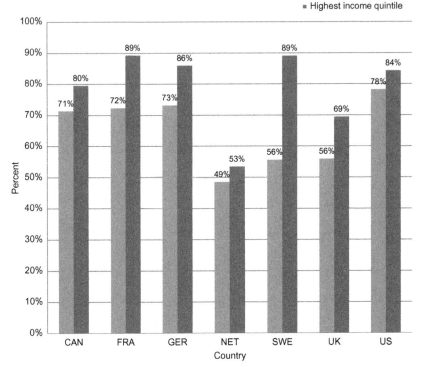

FIG. 14.8   Share of women aged 20–69 screened for cervical cancer, by income, 2014 (lowest vs highest income quintile). *(Source: OECD. Health at a glance 2019. OECD indicators. Figure 5.7.)*

Differences by income in France, the Netherlands, and the United Kingdom are between 13 and 16 percentage points.

The final measure in this category of cost-related barriers is the percentage of women aged between 20 and 69 who received cervical cancer screening in 2016 (Fig. 14.8). It should be recognized that this is an imperfect measure because different countries have varying norms regarding at what ages women should be screened. The United States, Canada, and the Netherlands showed few disparities (between 4 and 9 percentage points when comparing the highest and lowest income quintiles). The other countries had 13–17 percentage point differences except for Sweden, which showed a remarkable 33 percentage point difference. It is not entirely clear what makes Sweden different from neighboring countries in this regard [11].

Catastrophic spending

The next two figures relate to catastrophic spending: spending 10% or more (Fig. 14.9) or 25% or more (Fig. 14.10) of income OOP during the year. The

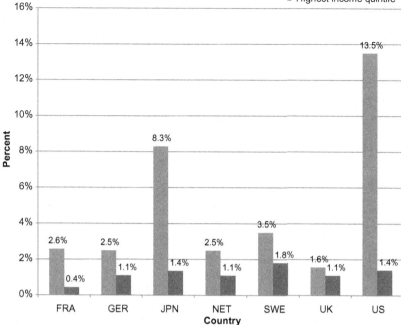

FIG. 14.9 Spent more than 10% of income out of pocket, by income, 2010 (lowest vs highest income quintile). Note: US data are for 2012. *(Source: World Bank. Health equity and financial protection indicators. 2020.)*

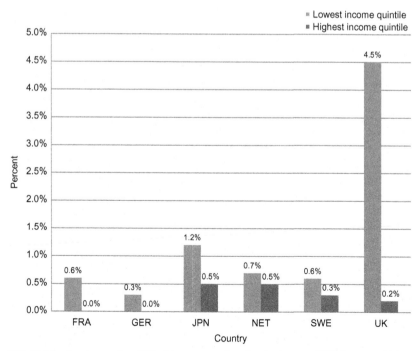

FIG. 14.10 Spent more than 25% of income out of pocket, by income, 2010 (lowest vs highest income quintile). Note: US data are for 2012. *(Source: World Bank. Health equity and financial protection indicators. 2020.)*

data, from the World Bank, were available for only five of the countries[d] and mostly for 2010. The United States is an outlier among those in the lowest income quintile, with 13.5% spending more than 10% of their income out of pocket in 2012 (a figure that had risen to 14.4% in 2018). The percentage did not exceed 3.5% in any of the other countries except for Japan (8.3%). A similar pattern was evident when examining 25% of income spent out of pocket: the figure for the lowest income quintile in the United States was 4.5%, but none of the other countries exceeded 1.2%.

Health system barriers

The next three measures relate to being able to use care. The measures—having a regular doctor or place of care, difficulty in obtaining after-hours care, and waits for two or more months for a specialist appointment—were chosen because those with low SES might encounter greater impediments in these aspects of access. In nearly all countries, having a regular doctor or place of care did not vary much between those in the lower and upper halves of the income distribution (Fig. 14.11). The main exception was the United States, where there was a 9 percentage point difference, with only 84% of those with below-average incomes reporting a regular source. This is not surprising given that almost 10% of the United States population is uninsured and that far more transfer between insurance coverage sources (each of which may have different provider panels) when their income, job, or other circumstances change.

Having difficulty accessing after-hours care was a problem for the majority of people in nearly all of the countries, the main exception being the Netherlands, where only one-fourth of residents reported difficulty (Fig. 14.12). There were few noticeable patterns by income. Those with lower-than-average incomes tended to report difficulty a little more often, except that in the United Kingdom there was very little income disparity.

Finally, regarding waiting 2 months or more before seeing a specialist, absolute levels were highest in Canada, the United Kingdom, Sweden, and Australia, in that order (Fig. 14.13). But patterns by income are somewhat curious. In two countries, Australia and the United States, the poorer parts of the population, were twice as likely to report waiting this long—a substantial disparity although it should be kept in mind that relatively few Americans had to wait this long. In contrast, in France and the United Kingdom, the wealthier people reported

---

[d] Data are available from the OECD's Health at a Glance 2019 book on two more countries, Australia and Japan. These are shown in Table 15.11. The definition of catastrophic spending is different, as are the years, and the figures are for the entire population rather than by income subgroups. But the percentages of people experiencing catastrophic costs are largely similar across the two data sets (when using the 10% of income threshold rather than 25%). Neither data set includes Canada, the Netherlands, or Switzerland, the latter being particularly unfortunate given that OOP spending is so high there.

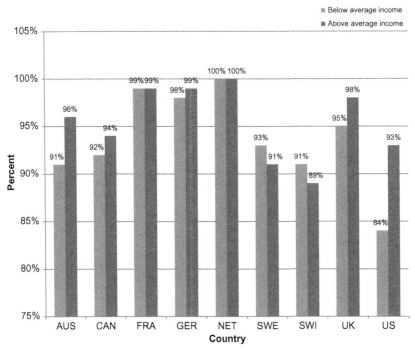

FIG. 14.11 A regular doctor or place of care, by income, 2016 (below vs above average income). *(Source: Schneider EC, et al. Mirror, mirror 2017: International comparison reflects flaws and opportunities for better U.S. health care. The Commonwealth Fund; July 2017. https:// www.commonwealthfund.org/sites/default/files/documents/___media_files_publications_fund_ report_2017_jul_schneider_mirror_mirror_2017.pdf.)*

a *greater* likelihood of waiting. This is one of the few instances in any of the equity data collected for this paper where those with lower SES report that they are *advantaged*. However, this counterintuitive finding did not appear in the 2020 Commonwealth Fund survey data.[e] No data are reported for Germany, but other data sets show that queuing in Germany is rare.

Perceptions of quality and coordination

The final four figures illustrate people's perceptions regarding the process of care. The variables examined are: rating medical care from regular provider as fair or poor (Fig. 14.14), regular doctor always or often knew important information about medical history (Fig. 14.15), regular doctor always or often spent enough time and explained things understandably (Fig. 14.16), and specialist lacked medical history, or regular doctor not informed about specialist care

---

[e] Roosa Tikkanen, personal communication, September 2, 2020.

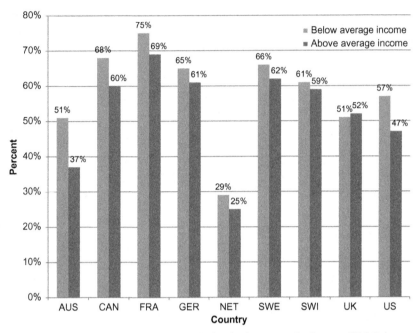

FIG. 14.12   Somewhat or very difficult to obtain after-hours care, by income, 2016 (below vs above average income). *(Source: Schneider EC, et al. Mirror, mirror 2017: International comparison reflects flaws and opportunities for better U.S. health care. The Commonwealth Fund; July 2017. https://www.commonwealthfund.org/sites/default/files/documents/___media_files_ publications_fund_report_2017_jul_schneider_mirror_mirror_2017.pdf.)*

(Fig. 14.17). In each, people in the upper vs lower halves of the income distribution are compared.

The United States was always among the three countries with the largest differential between below vs above average incomes. The French were also noteworthy as showing the highest differential by income for two measures: rating of the quality of care from regular source of provider and regular doctor knowing important information about one's medical history. Germans showed high differentials for two measures: regular doctor always or often spending enough time and explaining things understandably, and regular doctor knowing important information about one's medical history.

There were some other findings of interest. The percentage of higher-income Germans rating the quality of care from the regular provider as fair or poor was zero. Both the French and Swedes showed a great deal of dissatisfaction in this measure, but most noteworthy was the gap by income in France: 19% for lower-income persons vs 5% for higher-income. The British had an unusual pattern, with wealthier people being less satisfied than poorer persons.

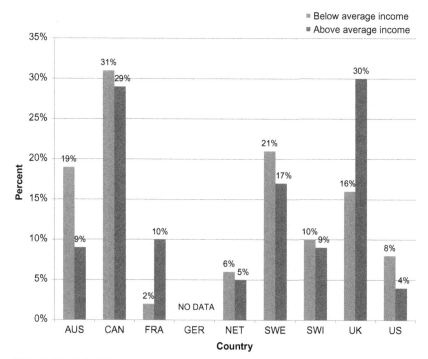

FIG. 14.13 Waited 2 months or longer for specialist appointment, by income, 2016 (below vs above average income). *(Source: Schneider EC, et al. Mirror, mirror 2017: International comparison reflects flaws and opportunities for better U.S. health care. The Commonwealth Fund; July 2017. https://www.commonwealthfund.org/sites/default/files/documents/__media_files_publications_fund_report_2017_jul_schneider_mirror_mirror_2017.pdf.)*

Lack of data on disparities in health outcomes

It is unfortunate that no comparative data could be found that show disparities in the equity of health outcomes that can be attributed mainly to the health care system. In particular, it would be desirable to know of differences in **mortality amenable to health care** by SES group. One study from Canada showed that amenable mortality rates among those in the lowest income quintile more than double those in the highest income quintile [12]. This raises two issues. First, are such ratios higher or lower in other countries? And second, could this mean that the concept of amenable mortality is capturing the direct impact of SES as well as the quality of the medical care system? This issue is addressed in Chapter 15.

Interpretation of the equity findings

The findings can be understood most clearly by dividing them into issues relating to affordability (cost-related barriers and catastrophic spending), as shown

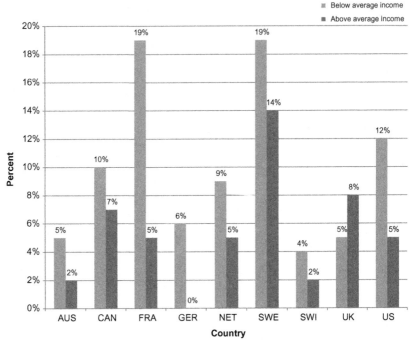

FIG. 14.14 Rated medical care from regular provider as fair or poor, by income, 2017 (below average vs above average income). *(Source: Schneider EC, et al. Mirror, mirror 2017: International comparison reflects flaws and opportunities for better U.S. health care. The Commonwealth Fund; July 2017. https://www.commonwealthfund.org/sites/default/files/documents/___media_files_ publications_fund_report_2017_jul_schneider_mirror_mirror_2017.pdf.)*

in Figs. 14.1 through 14.10, and health system barriers and perceptions of quality and coordination (Figs. 14.11 through 14.17).

Affordability

In considering these findings, it is useful to revisit a figure that appeared in Chapter 2. It is replicated here as Fig. 14.18. There are two cubes. The larger one represents total health care spending in a country, and the smaller one, public spending. Note that the term "public" is used loosely and includes any insurance that is required to be purchased. The difference between the two cubes is expenditures that are the responsibility of the patient. They can be paid either OOP or through VHI.

Explanations of each of the three dimensions are necessary for understanding the graph. Along the horizontal axis, going from right to left, shows *breadth*: the extent to which the whole population is covered. Those without insurance coverage must either pay for all services OOP or obtain substitute health insurance. Paying OOP is common in the U.S. for those without coverage, and obtaining substitute coverage occurs in Germany. The axis going from front to

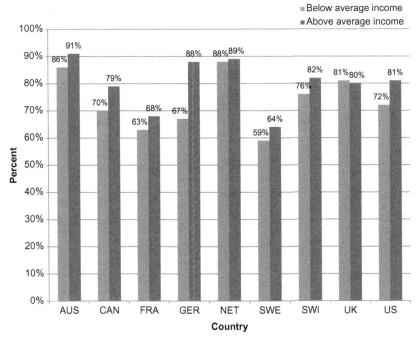

FIG. 14.15 Regular doctor always or often spent enough time and explained things understandably, by income, 2016 (below average vs above average income). *(Source: Schneider EC, et al. Mirror, mirror 2017: International comparison reflects flaws and opportunities for better U.S. health care. The Commonwealth Fund; July 2017. https://www.commonwealthfund.org/sites/default/files/documents/___media_files_publications_fund_report_2017_jul_schneider_mirror_mirror_2017.pdf.)*

back shows *scope*: the extensiveness of the services that are covered. If country covers more services (e.g., dental care), public spending constitutes a larger portion of this axis. Services that are uncovered are either paid OOP or through supplementary VHI. The vertical axis shows *depth*: the portion of costs paid for covered services. In countries with higher cost-sharing requirements, people pay more in OOP spending or through complementary VHI.

The data from our countries strongly imply that equity is enhanced when national health care systems are more comprehensive: they cover everyone and nearly all important services with low patient cost-sharing requirements. In such instances, people will have less of a need for owning a VHI policy to cover the gaps. At the same time, such systems necessarily involve more spending on part of public entities; the money has to come from somewhere.

It is worth mentioning that equity could be enhanced in a very different way: by providing comprehensive benefits to lower-income persons, subsidized by those who are well off.[f] This approach has not been chosen by the

---

[f] Corrina Moucheraud, personal communication, November 12, 2020.

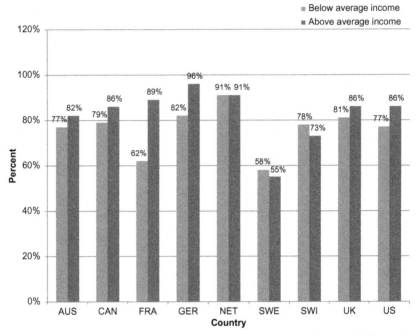

FIG. 14.16 Regular doctor always or often knew important information about medical history, by income, 2016 (below vs above average income). *(Source: Schneider EC, et al. Mirror, mirror 2017: International comparison reflects flaws and opportunities for better U.S. health care. The Commonwealth Fund; July 2017. https://www.commonwealthfund.org/sites/default/files/documents/___media_files_ publications_fund_report_2017_jul_schneider_mirror_mirror_2017.pdf.)*

nine countries with universal coverage. Part of the reason is that it is easier to get political support for tax-supported programs when the taxpayers also benefit directly. The exception is the United States, where Medicaid is provided to most but not all people with lower incomes. However, while benefits generally are comprehensive and financial liability low, those on Medicaid often do not have access to the same providers because program reimbursement rates usually are very low.

We have not discussed how countries finance their health care systems, although it is presented in the country-specific chapters. Box 14.2 considers financing from a cross-national perspective.

Table 14.2 summarizes the nine countries' performance on affordability. The overall assessment (column 2) is subjective, based on material from the country-specific chapters (column 3) and examples from the data presented in this chapter's figures (column 4). Japan is not included because of lack of data.

Overall, the United States fared the worst and Canada, second worst with regard to equity in affordability. In contrast, the United Kingdom performed the best. Germany, the Netherlands, and Sweden are assessed as being above average, and Australia and France as average; and Switzerland as below

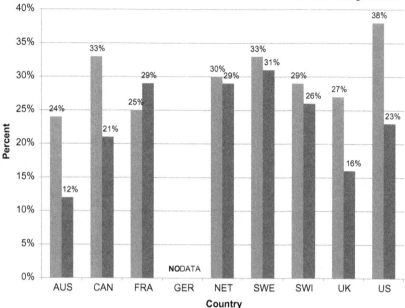

FIG. 14.17   Specialist lacked medical history or regular doctor not informed about specialist care, by income, 2016 (below average vs above average income). *(Source: Schneider EC, et al. Mirror, mirror 2017: International comparison reflects flaws and opportunities for better U.S. health care. The Commonwealth Fund; July 2017. https://www.commonwealthfund.org/sites/default/files/documents/___media_files_publications_fund_report_2017_jul_schneider_mirror_mirror_2017.pdf.)*

average. The table provides reasons for the assessment and some examples from the figures.

We suggest that four factors appear to determine the level of affordability of health care: providing universal coverage (breadth), having a comprehensive benefits package (scope), keeping cost-sharing requirements low (depth), and not overly relying on VHI.

Universal coverage

It is hardly surprising that universal coverage improves affordability of heath care. The fact that the United States has the greatest (overall and dental) cost-related disparities by income is due in part—but only in part—to its lack of breadth in coverage, with almost 10% of the population being uninsured. The uninsurance rates among documented residents in the other eight countries are nearly zero. It is not just uninsurance that is the problem. The Commonwealth Fund has estimated that in 2020, 31% of working-age *insured* persons also suffered from underinsurance, much of it due to facing high **deductibles** [7].

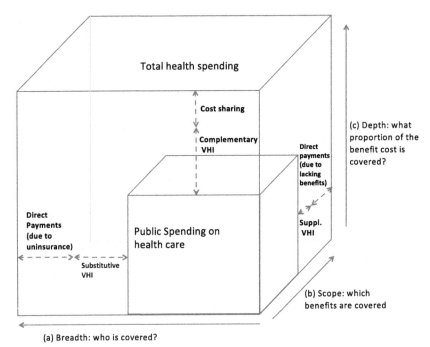

FIG. 14.18   The components of health insurance coverage. *(Sources: Busse R, Schlette S. Health policy developments 7/8 focus on prevention, health and ageing and human resources. Gütersloh: Verlag Bertelsmann Stiftung; 2007; Rice T, Quentin W, Anell A, Barnes AJ, Rosenau P, Unruh LY, et al. Revisiting out-of-pocket requirements: trends in spending, financial access barriers, and policy in ten high-income countries. BMC Health Serv Res 2018;18(1):371.)*

Moreover, these problems are likely accentuated because physicians and dentists are paid relatively little by the Medicaid program (which covers many poor and near-poor Americans) compared to people with private insurance, making it harder to find a provider.

Comprehensiveness of benefits package

When there is a broader scope of services covered by statutory insurance, there is less of a need to rely on VHI, which is often unevenly distributed across the population. The most important public benefit that is covered the least fully across the countries is dental care, with only Germany, Japan, and the United Kingdom covering all adults for clinically appropriate care. This is likely the reason why, for example, over 40% of those in Canada with lower-than-average income reported skipping dental care or checkups in the past year, the second highest to the United States: nearly all dental spending is privately financed in Canada. It was not just Canada and the United States, however, that showed barriers to obtaining dental care. Most of the other countries where adult dental care

BOX 14.2   A note on financing.

The financing of health care has only an indirect impact on access to care. This is because the financing system does not provide a direct barrier to those seeking care at the point of service, unlike, say, cost-sharing requirements. Rather, financing may have an impact through what economists refer to as an income effect; that is, in more regressive systems, poorer persons have less money to purchase all goods and services, including their share of health care.

In the previous chapter, Table 13.2 provides a breakdown of each of the 10 countries' total health expenditures according to the percentage associated with (a) government/compulsory insurance, (b) private/voluntary health insurance, and (c) OOP spending. Six of the countries are tightly bunched, with between 79 and 84% of total expenditures financed by public sources, but four others—Australia, Canada, Switzerland, and the United States —are considerably lower. Thus, they rely more on VHI and OOP.

Both VHI and OOP financing tend to be regressive, and OOP spending, highly so. VHI is usually regressive for two reasons: premiums tend to be fixed irrespective of income and subsidies are often available to those in the labor force, who on average are better off financially. OOP is regressive because cost-sharing requirements rarely differ by income. For example, a $20 **copayment** for a prescription presents a much greater financial barrier to a poorer person than a wealthier one.

Australia and Canada have a considerably larger role in terms of total spending on VHI, and Switzerland relies on OOP spending much more than any other country, funding 29% of health expenses that way, with the next highest country, Australia, far lower at 18%. The figures for the United States are very different from the other nine countries because it has a much higher voluntary sector, mainly because there is no requirement that people have health insurance. There is, however, another element that needs to be considered: how the public spending component is financed (Table 13.3).

It would be ideal if there were a single metric that would indicate whether the financing of a health care system, overall, is progressive or regressive. It turns out that there is such a metric; it is called the **Kakwani index**. Research in the late 1990s by Adam Wagstaff, Eddy van Doorslaer, and colleagues calculated this index in the health care financing systems for several of our countries: France, Germany, the Netherlands, Sweden, Switzerland, the United Kingdom, and the United States. In general, the authors found that funding from income taxes is more progressive than funding from social insurance, and both tend to be more progressive than funding from premiums and consumption taxes. In those respects, the single-payer countries (Australia, Canada, Sweden, and the United Kingdom), which rely more on tax payments to finance health care, exhibit greater progressivity.

Unfortunately, the research, which relies on collecting extensive consumption data from each country, has not been replicated across multiple countries since then (Van Doorslaer, E., personal communication, October 26, 2018). During this 20-year time period, financing systems have changed considerably in most of the countries so their findings about progressivity do not necessarily apply today.

Sources: Wagstaff A, Van Doorslaer E. Equity in health care finance and delivery. In: Culyer AJ, Newhouse JP, editors. Handbook of health economics, vol. 1B. 1st ed. Amsterdam, North Holland: Elsevier; 2000. p. 893–1910. Kakwani NC. Measurement of tax progressivity: an international comparison. Econ J 1977;87(345):71–80.

TABLE 14.2 Summary of findings: Equity of affordability.

Country	Overall assessment	Reasons for assessment (− or +)[a]	Examples[b]
Australia	Average	− Relatively high cost-sharing requirements when services are not bulk billed − Substantial reliance on VHI, with higher-income persons more likely to own it − Few subsidies and no free care for children (except dental) + Free public hospital care	• Average in most indicators
Canada	Second least equitable	− Does not cover adult prescription drugs − Narrow scope of coverage outside of hospital and doctor's office − Substantial reliance on VHI − Few subsidies for children for prescription drug costs + Free care in hospital and doctor offices	• Among highest disparities in cost-related barriers to medical care • Highest dental access disparities
France	Average	− Liquidity problems for poorer persons caused by often having to pay bills upfront prior to reimbursement + VHI provided free to the poor + Cost-sharing exemptions for children	• Major dental access disparities • Greatest disparities in facing problems paying medical bills
Germany	Above average	− People with higher income more likely to have substitutive, private insurance + Physician visits free at point of service + Most comprehensive dental coverage + Generous cost-sharing reductions for children	• Among fewest disparities in cost-related barriers to medical care • Almost no disparities in dental access

Country	Rating	Coverage features	Access/disparity notes
Netherlands	Above average	− Limited adult dental coverage + Few cost barriers after initial deductible + Generous cost-sharing exemptions for children, including dental care	• Above average in most indicators
Sweden	Above average	− Limited adult dental coverage − Low-income women do not get some cancer screening + Modest cost-sharing requirements + Generous cost-sharing exemptions for children, including dental care	• Major dental access disparities
Switzerland	Below average	− Very high OOP requirements − Relatively few subsidies for low-income persons + Some cost-sharing exemptions and reductions for children	• High disparities in cost-related barriers to medical care • Major dental access disparities
United Kingdom	Most equitable	+ Broad benefit package + Almost all care free at point of service + Generous cost-sharing exemptions for children, including dental care	• Among countries with fewest disparities in cost-related barriers to medical care
United States	Least equitable	− Only country with uninsurance − High cost-sharing requirements − Uneven scope of services − Large reliance on private insurance + Some cost-sharing exemptions for poor and near-poor children	• Among highest disparities in cost-related barriers to medical care • Highest dental access disparities • Largest incidence of incurring catastrophic spending

[a] Source: Chapters 3 through 12.
[b] Source: Figs. 14.1 through 14.10.

is not part of the public benefit package—France, Sweden, and Switzerland—also showed considerable cost-related access problems.

Cost-sharing requirements

As just noted, the uninsurance rate alone cannot explain why nearly half of Americans, and many in the low-SES populations in several other countries, report cost-related problems in accessing doctors, and why so many poor Americans experience catastrophic levels of health care spending. The three countries with the highest per capita out-of-pocket costs are Switzerland, the United States, and Australia. Each of these countries shows a significant lack of depth in coverage: either relatively high deductibles or **coinsurance** for hospital and/or physician services and relatively high limits on OOP spending.

The problem is aggravated in the United States by high unit prices and the risk of facing even greater liabilities when people use out-of-network physicians. An issue that has received a great deal of attention in the United States is the so-called surprise medical billing. This occurs when, unbeknownst to the insured patients, they are treated by a nonnetwork provider who may charge (sometimes exorbitant) additional fees that are not covered by insurance policies. Emergency services are especially susceptible, where nearly 20% result in this a surprise bill—with figures almost as high for inpatient hospital stays [13].

One way in which most of the countries in this book enhance the equity of their health insurance systems is by exempting children from most cost-sharing requirements. By waiving these requirements, they reduce barriers that may impede families from seeking care when their children need it. The countries that provide the most generous exemptions—usually including dental care—are France, Germany, Sweden, and the United Kingdom. The least generous countries in this regard are Australia, Canada, and the United States.[g]

The role of VHI

When national health system benefit packages cover a narrow scope of services or exhibit a lack of depth in coverage, many in the population will feel compelled to obtain VHI to cover the gaps. In terms of the percentage of total health expenditures covered, VHI plays the most important role in the Australian and Canadian health care systems, where it constitutes 10% and 13% of total health expenditures, respectively (Table 13.4). (The Australian figure is closer to 13% when one includes government financial incentives that subsidize the purchase of VHI [14].) In fact, two of the three countries besides the United States and Switzerland with the largest income-related disparities in cost-related access are Australia and Canada. It is plausible that those with lower incomes in these two countries are disadvantaged through their lack of access to VHI. France also relies a good deal on VHI but is unique in that all employers are required to

---

provide access to VHI for their workers, with the government paying the premiums for others with low incomes.

Health system barriers and access and quality issues

Unlike the case of affordability, where there are clear linkages between health insurance system characteristics and access disparities, such relationships are less clear in relating system characteristics to health system barriers and quality. Occasionally, there is a clear link, particularly with regard to health system barriers. It is hardly surprising, for example, that there is a gap by income group regarding having a regular source of medical care in the United States (Fig. 14.11). The 9% of the population without health insurance is part of the reason; another reason is that many people with Medicaid coverage find it difficult to find a local doctor who will accept the program's low reimbursement rates [15].

The country that showed the largest gap in waiting time to see a specialist was Australia, with 19% of those with lower-than-average income distribution reporting waits of two or more months, compared to only 9% of those with higher-than-average income. These self-reported data are confirmed by administrative data. In 2015–16, patient waiting times for public patients in public hospitals were uniformly higher than for patients using private insurance in the same hospitals—generally two to three times longer. In the case of knee replacement surgery, private patients waited an average of about 75 days while public patients waited 200 days. Among all hospital procedures, median waiting time was more than twice as long for public patients: 42 vs 20 days [16–18]. These differences almost certainly stem from the fact that wealthier people are more likely to own VHI policies.

Linkages between the health insurance system and perceptions of quality and coordination are even less clear, with the United States being the only country that consistently stood out in showing large disparities. The explanation is likely the same as just mentioned: those without coverage or with Medicaid may find that their care is not as satisfactory as those with employer-based coverage or Medicare.

Spending does not buy equity

In considering the data in Chapters 13 through 15, a final conclusion is clear from the data. Countries that spend more do not appear to be buying equity. The two with the highest spending, as measured both by percentage of GDP devoted to health and per-capita expenditures, are the United States and Switzerland, and both show among the most inequities. In contrast, the lowest spending country, the United Kingdom, has among the fewest equity issues in the measures we have examined. The data do not support reverse pattern, however, as Australia shows a number of equity issues and its spending is also among the lowest.

There is a somewhat more distinct pattern when examining the percentage of total spending through government or compulsory health insurance programs (Table 13.2). There are four countries with percentages that are far lower than the others: Australia (69%), Canada (70%), Switzerland (64%), and United States (45%). These were the four countries with the greatest equity problems.

Beyond this, it is not possible to draw further conclusions from the data presented here. More detailed cross-country analyses are necessary to aid policy makers in instituting best international practices in augmenting health care equity.

Appendix: 2020 Commonwealth Fund equity results

During the months of March through May of 2020, the Commonwealth Fund fielded its survey of adults in 11 countries, nine of which are the main focus of this book. Data were not collected from Japan. As this time period coincided with the beginning of the Covid-19 pandemic, it is possible that people's responses to the survey would be colored by their experiences with the medical care system during the pandemic and would not be reflective of longer-term needs. Because of this, the body of the chapter used data from the 2016 Commonwealth Fund survey. The Appendix Table provides responses to the same nine variables for which there were data in both 2016 and 2020. The one question not asked in 2020 was the quality of care provided by their regular provider; it was only asked in Switzerland in 2020.

Some of the main differences between the two survey years are noted here. It is not possible to know whether changes were because of the performance of the health care system, Covid-19, or other factors:

- Perhaps the most notable change in any country was the decline in disparities in France, for two measures: having a serious problem or being unable to pay medical bills, and regular doctor always or often knowing important information about medical history. In 2016, 41% of French respondents in the lower half of the income distribution cited having a serious problem. This plummeted to 16% in 2020; the concomitant reduction in disparities by income level fell from 34 to 13 percentage points. As discussed in Chapter 7, historically most French people have had to pay their medical bills directly and then file for reimbursement, which can be very difficult financially on those with lower incomes. Very recently, however, this appears to be changing, first, because more lower-income people do not have to pay anything for most services through government subsidization of universal VHI, and second, starting in January 2020, all French are beginning to have access to certain services free of charge or at very reduced fees (e.g., eyeglasses, dental crowns, and implants, with hearing aids coming in 2021) [19].[h] The one

---

[h] Monika Steffan, personal communication, September 11, 2020.

other significant reduction in disparities in France between the two survey years is harder to explain: why the disadvantage that poorer persons showed (in relation to wealthier persons) in their regular doctor knowing important information about their medical history fell from 27 to 5 percentage points.

- In all nine measures, disparities declined or stayed the same in Australia between 2016 and 2020. The disparity in cost-related access problems fell from 11 to 5 percentage points, and those encountering difficulties in obtaining after-hours care declined from 14 to 6 percentage points. It is not clear why this is the case, although it is notable that several of the changes were the result of access decreasing for those in the higher half of the income distribution—rather than improved access for those in the lower half of the distribution.[g]

- Disparities also fell in Switzerland. Most notably, there was a reduction in differences by income group in citing cost-related access problems, from 16 percentage points in 2016 to 5 points in 2020. The Netherlands, on the contrary, showed an increase in disparities on several measures. The reasons explaining the changes in both countries are not obvious.

- In the 2016 survey, there was an anomalous finding that wealthier people in France and the United Kingdom said they had to wait longer for specialist appointments than lower-income persons. That was no longer the case in 2020. The change was quite dramatic in the United Kingdom. In 2016, the wealthier half of the income distribution were 14 percentage points *more* likely to say that they had to wait two or more months for a specialist appointment. In 2020, they were 13 percentage points *less* likely to say so. Whether this is related to Covid-19, other reasons related to the health care system, or sampling or related statistical issues is not clear.

Appendix Table: Results from the Commonwealth Fund 2020 international health policy survey.

	AUS		CAN		FRA		GER		NET		SWE		SWI		UK		US	
	L	H	L	H	L	H	L	H	L	H	L	H	L	H	L	H	L	H
Had cost-related access problem in the past year	24	19	21	7	14	6	15	9	20	9	19	6	26	21	12	7	50	27
Had serious problem or unable to pay medical bills	10	5	13	2	16	3	9	2	12	3	16	2	14	3	7	3	36	9
Skipped dental care or checkup due to cost in the past year	35	30	40	16	26	11	23	17	19	8	29	17	34	18	27	18	51	21
Have regular source of care	94	94	89	94	96	95	96	94	98	99	87	86	95	92	97	99	85	92
Somewhat or very difficult to get after-hours care	48	42	64	55	57	50	55	51	35	24	54	53	49	48	62	59	58	44
Waited 2 months or longer for specialist appointment	30	19	42	44	34	26	22	14	14	10	37	37	8	11	42	29	10	9
Regular doctor always or often spent enough time and explained things understandably	86	87	76	81	74	85	84	84	83	91	62	64	82	85	66	73	74	85
Regular doctor always or often knew important information about medical history	85	90	82	86	81	86	89	90	86	93	59	48	82	82	69	76	81	90
Specialist lacked medical history, or regular doctor informed about specialist care	36	27	28	31	17	19	27	21	15	9	20	18	21	15	25	17	50	49

L = residents in the (approximate) lower half of the country's income distribution. See "footnote b" for precise definition.
H = residents in the (approximate) upper half of the country's income distribution. See "footnote b" for precise definition.

Source T Tikkanen, personal communication, September 2, 2020.

References

[1]   National Research Council, Institute of Medicine. In: Woolf SH, Aron L, editors. Shorter lives, poorer health. US health in international perspective. Washington, DC: National Academies Press; 2013.

[2]   Woolf SH. Necessary but not sufficient: why health care alone cannot improve population health and reduce health inequities. Ann Fam Med 2019;17(3):196–9.

[3]   Schneider EC, Sarnak DO, Squires D, Shah A, Doty MM. Mirror, mirror 2017: International comparison reflects flaws and opportunities for better U.S. health care. Mirror, Mirror: The Commonwealth Fund; 2017.

[4]   OECD. Health at a glance 2019. Paris: OECD Publishing; 2019.

[5]   European Commission. Health. eurostat; 2020. [Online database]. [Accessed 27 August 2020]. Available from: https://ec.europa.eu/eurostat/web/health/data/database.

[6]   Health Equity and Financial Protection Indicators (HEFPI). The World Bank [Internet]. [Accessed 9 November 2020]. Available from: http://datatopics.worldbank.org/health-equity-and-financial-protection/.

[7]   Collins SR, Gunja MZ, Aboulafia GN. U.S. health insurance coverage in 2020: A looming crisis in affordability. The Commonwealth Fund; 2020.

[8]   Devaux M. Income-related inequalities and inequities in health care services utilisation in 18 selected OECD countries. Eur J Health Econ 2013;16(1):21–33.

[9]   OECD.Stat. OECD [Web browser]. [Accessed 3 September 2020]. Available from: https://stats.oecd.org/Index.aspx?ThemeTreeId=9.

[10] Doty MM, Tikkanen RS, FitzGerald ME, Fields K, Williams RD. Income-related inequalities in affordability and access to primary care in eleven high-income countries. Health Aff 2021;40(1):113–20.

[11] Broberg G, Wang J, Ostberg AL, Adolfsson A, Nemes S, Sparen P, et al. Socio-economic and demographic determinants affecting participation in the Swedish cervical screening program: a population-based case-control study. PLoS One 2018;13(1):e0190171.

[12] Khan AM, Urquia M, Kornas K, Henry D, Cheng SY, Bornbaum C, et al. Socioeconomic gradients in all-cause, premature and avoidable mortality among immigrants and long-term residents using linked death records in Ontario, Canada. J Epidemiol Community Health 2017;71:625–32.

[13] Pollitz K, Rae M, Claxton G, Cox C, Levitt L. An examination of surprise medical bills and proposals to protect consumers from them. Peterson-KFF; 2020.

[14] Duckett S, Nemet K. Updated: The history and purposes of private health insurance. 2nd ed. Australia: Grattan Institute; 2019.

[15] Holgash K, Heberlein M. Physician acceptance of new medicaid patients: what matters and what doesn't. Health Affairs; 2019. [Online blog]. [Accessed 22 September 2020]. Available from: https://www.healthaffairs.org/do/10.1377/hblog20190401.678690/full/.

[16] Anon. Private health insurance use in Australian hospitals 2006–07 to 2015–16: Australian hospital statistics. Health services series, Canberra: Australian Institute of Health and Welfare; 2017.

[17] Kliff S. What Australia can teach America about health care. Vox; 2019. [Internet]. [Accessed 17 October 2020]. Available from: https://www.vox.com/policy-and-politics/2019/4/15/18311694/australia-health-care-system.

[18] Han E. Patients waiting four times longer than private patients for some operations at public hospitals. The Sydney Morning Herald; 2017. [Internet]. [Accessed 17 October 2020]. Available from: https://www.smh.com.au/healthcare/patients-waiting-four-times-longer-than-private-patients-for-some-operations-at-public-hospitals-20171205-gzyv8x.html.

[19] Anon. 100% health reform for eyes, ears and teeth in France. P-O Life; 2020. [Online]. [Accessed 31 October 2020]. Available from: https://anglophone-direct.com/100-health-reform-for-eyes-and-ears-and-teeth-in-france/.

Chapter 15

Efficiency

At first glance, efficiency would seem to be a straightforward concept, comparing how much output is attained from the use of a given set of inputs. Measuring these elements in health would appear to be "beguilingly simple," according to Jon Cylus and colleagues, "represented … as a ratio of resource consumed (health system inputs) to some measure of valued health system outputs they create" [1, p. 7]. While this sounds encouraging, implementing it turns out to be anything but straightforward. Cylus and colleagues go on to say:

> Yet putting this simple notion into practice can be complex. Within the health system as a whole, there is a seemingly infinite set of interlinked processes that could independently be evaluated and found to be efficient or inefficient. This has given rise to a plethora of apparently disconnected indicators that give glimpses of certain aspects of efficiency, but rarely offer a comprehensive overview [1, p. 7].

While the emphasis of this book has been health insurance systems, in most cases it is not possible to isolate the impact of health insurance from other parts of overall health systems, particularly the delivery of care. System outcomes examined in this chapter, such as reductions in mortality and morbidity that should be treatable by the health care system, waiting for care, and satisfaction (among others), are the result of not only insurance but also critical inputs such as the quantity and quality of the health care workforce and the organizational and technical processes employed.

As will be seen, no effort is made to come up with an overall ranking of systems: there are too many outcome measures that span health, access, and spending, with some countries performing well in some and poorly in others. (Chapter 16 will present some rankings compiled other researchers and organizations.) Nevertheless, examining particular areas of performance can provide important insights on best practices.

Measuring the efficiency of health care systems

Defining efficiency

In this chapter, we employ the simple definition of efficiency presented earlier: how much output is attained from the use of a given set of inputs. Output is defined as the desirable outcomes that society obtains from its health care system.

Health Insurance Systems: An International Comparison. https://doi.org/10.1016/B978-0-12-816072-5.00014-6

Traditionally, these fall under the categories of access, quality (objective and subjective), and spending. They are operationalized here as falling into several categories:

- Lower mortality and morbidity from causes that should be treatable by the health care system
- Access to care:
  a. Affordability
  b. Waiting for care
  c. Use of care
- Satisfaction with the health care system

Comparative data availability across the 10 countries dictated which specific measures were used.

The main input is total health care spending, measured either as per-capita expenditures or as the percentage of **gross domestic product** (GDP) devoted to health. Secondary measures, such unit prices for services and pharmaceuticals, and the supply of doctors, hospitals, nurses, and technologies, will also be examined to better understand the different ways that countries marshal their spending on health care.

Attributing performance to the health care system: The case of mortality

To evaluate the successes and failures of each country's health care system in achieving maximum efficiency, it is necessary to pick performance measures that can be attributed, at least to a significant extent, to the system rather than other factors. This is easier to do for financial protection and satisfaction but less so for health outcomes. Both mortality and morbidity are certainly affected by the health care system in general, and health insurance in particular, but also by a myriad of other factors.

Consider infant mortality. As shown in Table 13.9, the US rate of 5.8 deaths per 1000 live births is about three times as large as in Japan (1.9) and Sweden (2.0). Canada's rate of 4.7 deaths per 1000 live births is more than double. To what extent are the health care systems responsible? There is little consensus on this issue. One possible explanation for the high rate in the United States is the large number of uninsured and underinsured Americans, making prenatal care unaffordable to many and resulting in more preterm births, but that would not explain Canada's high rate: coverage there is universal and free at point of service. A partial explanation for the Canadian rate is the lack of supply of maternity care providers, that is, obstetricians-gynecologists and midwives [2]. Having said that, while the health care system can have an impact on reducing infant mortality, particularly by making prenatal care more accessible, national differences in rates are almost certainly determined mainly by social and behavioral factors.

One promising measure of health system performance in reducing deaths is **mortality amenable to health care** (sometimes called mortality from treatable causes). It, and a more recent refinement, the Healthcare Access and Quality (HAQ) index, attempt to measure deaths that should have been averted by a well-functioning health care system.[a] Rates for each of the 10 countries covered in this book will be presented in Table 15.7, and the concept is defined and critiqued in Box 15.1. While we will use amenable mortality and related measures in this chapter as indicators of health system performance, it should be kept in mind that nearly all health care outcomes are the result of multiple factors, not just the health care system.

Input and outputs examined

Table 15.1 provides information for the inputs examined in this chapter. It is divided into health care spending, prices, and labor and equipment. Table 15.2 shows the measures of outcomes. This table is divided into mortality, morbidity, access (affordability, waiting for care, use of care), and satisfaction with the health care system. Each table also includes the data sources and the years examined.

Findings

The findings are divided into two sections: inputs and outcomes.

Inputs

Health care spending

Table 15.3 presents four sets of figures relating to health care spending: health expenditures as a share of GDP, health expenditures per capita, the percentage of health spending devoted to governance and finance administration, and public social spending as a share of GDP. Health expenditures per capita are expressed in purchasing power parities (PPPs), a method that adjusts disparate national monetary currencies to equalize purchasing power across countries [3].

The first two measures are prominent in international discussions because they provide an aggregate of the value of all of the inputs devoted to the health care system. As is well known, by either measure the United States is an international outlier. US spending of $11,072 per capita in 2019 was more than double the median of the other countries ($5418). The United States devoted 17% of GDP to health care compared with between 9 and 12% in the other countries—about 40% more than the second-highest country, Switzerland. The United Kingdom had the lowest per-capita spending dollar amount; Australia spent the lowest share of its GDP on health.

---

[a] See Box 15.1 for an explanation of the HAQ index.

Box 15.1 Measures of mortality that should be averted by a well-functioning health care system.

Mortality rates are determined by a myriad of factors. Some relate to the effectiveness of the health care system, but others are primarily the result of other factors: a country's wealth and its distribution, the age and demographic structure of the population, and health behaviors such as smoking and diet, to name just a few.

In studying health care systems, one seeks to find measures that relate most closely to system characteristic rather than these other factors. We briefly discuss three such measures here. The first, and most commonly used metric, is **mortality amenable to health care**. This is sometimes referred to as mortality from treatable causes. Ellen Nolte and Martin McKee list over 30 diseases included in their measure of amenable mortality. These include:

- Infectious diseases: intestinal and several other types of infection, tuberculosis, whooping cough, measles.
- Tumors: colon and rectum, skin, breast, cervix, testis, Hodgkin's disease, leukemia
- Diabetes
- Ischemic heart disease (Note: only 50% of such deaths count as amenable to health care)
- Other circulatory diseases (chronic rheumatic heart disease, hypertension, cerebrovascular)
- Respiratory diseases, including influenza and pneumonia
- Surgical conditions (peptic ulcer, appendicitis, abdominal hernia, cholelithiasis and cholecystitis, nephritis and nephrosis, benign prostatic hyperplasia)
- Misadventures to the patient (i.e., fatal injuries caused by medical errors)
- Maternal, congenital, and perinatal condition (maternal death, congenital cardiovascular anomalies, perinatal deaths excluding stillbirths)
- Other conditions (diseases of the thyroid, epilepsy)

In most cases, any deaths before the age of 75 for these conditions are included, but in some instances, only deaths occurring prior to reaching a particular age are.

One potential criticism is counting exactly half of the heart disease deaths, which is clearly an arbitrary estimate of how often the health care system is mainly responsible. A deeper criticism is that there is good evidence that people in more disadvantaged population groups have higher rates of amenable mortality, further implying that factors in addition to the health care system are partly responsible. Iris Plug and colleagues examined mortality data from 14 European countries by educational attainment, concluding that "a lower educational level is associated with a substantial higher mortality from causes thought to be amenable to medical intervention ... [and that there is no] evidence for a role of health care..." This is a something of an indictment of the concept; if amenable mortality is picking up social factors, how we can attribute differences in rates across countries to their health care systems?

In response to this sort of criticism, Sara Allin and Michel Grignon argue that amenable mortality is a reasonable measure of the effectiveness of a health care system if the goal is to improve "timely access to high-quality care when needed..." The argument is as follows: If, as a result of social factors, a country or region has

Box 15.1 Measures of mortality that should be averted by a well-functioning health care system—cont'd

more amenable mortality, then it is the responsibility of the health care system to devote more resources to compensate. To illustrate, consider pneumonia, a cause of death amenable to timely health care intervention, they write,

Given the state of medical art today, no one younger than 75 should die of pneumonia. Smoking is a known cause of pneumonia and, as a result, a region with a higher proportion of smokers will have to devote more resources towards preventing, detecting and treating pneumonia than a region with fewer smokers; if it fails to do so, it can be considered a less effective health system.

The **Healthcare Access and Quality (HAQ) index** provides a refinement of the concept of mortality amenable to health care. This index was developed and implemented by researchers across the world as part of the Global Burden of Diseases, Injuries, and Risk Factors Study, which ranks health care performance in 195 countries. Countries are scored on a scale ranging from 0 to 100, with the highest-rated countries garnering a 97 score (Iceland and Norway) and the lowest, a score of 19 (Somalia and the Central African Republic). The methodology goes beyond mortality amenable to health care by seeking to standardize causes of death in each of the countries and by adjusting these death rates for environmental and behavioral risks.

Mortality from preventable causes is a broader measure of deaths that can be prevented by the greater health care system because it includes deaths that result from risky health behaviors such as smoking and excess alcohol consumption and narcotic drugs. Also included are deaths that are almost entirely extrinsic to the health care system such as suicide and road accidents. Being a broader measure, preventable mortality rates are about 75% higher than amenable rates.

(Sources: Nolte E, Mckee CM. In amenable mortality—Deaths avoidable through health care—Progress in the US lags that of three European countries. Health Aff 2012;31(9):2114–22. Appendix Exhibit A1. Plug I, Hoffmann R, Artnik B, Bopp M, Borrell C, Costa G, et al. Socioeconomic inequalities in mortality from conditions amenable to medical interventions: do they reflect inequalities in access or quality of health care? BMC Public Health. 2012;12:346. Allin S, Grignon M. Examining the role of amenable mortality as an indicator of health system effectiveness. Health Policy 2014;9(3):12–9. G.B.D. Healthcare Access Quality Collaborators. Measuring performance on the Healthcare Access and Quality Index for 195 countries and territories and selected subnational locations: a systematic analysis from the Global Burden of Disease Study 2016. Lancet 2018;391(10136):2236–71. OECD. Avoidable mortality (preventable and treatable). Health at a glance 2019: OECD Indicators. Paris: OECD Publishing; 2019.)

The reason that these two measures are not so highly correlated is that per-capita expenditures are also affected by how wealthy the country is. To illustrate, France and Germany both devote fairly similar amount of % of GDP to health (11.2% vs 11.7%, respectively), but Germany spends 24% more per person because it is a wealthier country. It is therefore useful to observe how health care spending compares across the countries when one controls for national wealth.

Figs. 15.1 and 15.2 show these comparisons. In Fig. 15.1, we look at the relationship between per-capita health care spending and GDP per capita. To

TABLE 15.1 Measures of inputs.

Construct	Specific measures	Sources	Years	Table number
Health Care Spending				
Total, administrative, social	Spending as share of GDP, per-capita spending, % spent on governance and finance administration, public share of spending	OECD	2018	15.3
Prices				
Selected medical prices	Bypass surgery, knee replacement, normal delivery, MRI scan, colonoscopy	Healthcare Cost Institute	2017	15.4
Selected pharmaceutical prices	Six prescription drugs	Healthcare Cost Institute	2017	15.5
Labor and Equipment				
Provider supply and selected equipment	Doctors, nurses, and beds per person, % doctors in primary care, MRI units, and CT scanners per person	OECD, Papanicolas et al.	2017	15.6

Sources: OECD. Health at a glance 2019. Paris: OECD Publishing; 2019. OECD Health Statistics 2020. OECD. http://www.oecd.org/els/health-systems/health-data.htm. Hargraves J, Bloschichak A. International comparisons of health care prices from the 2017 iFHP survey. Health Care Cost Institute; 2019. https://healthcostinstitute.org/in-the-news/international-comparisons-of-health-care-prices-2017-ifhp-survey. Papanicolas I, Woskie LR, Jha AK. Health care spending in the United States and other high-income countries. JAMA 2018;319(10):1024–39.

TABLE 15.2 Measures outcomes.

Construct	Specific measures	Sources	Years	Table number
Mortality				
Avoidable and hospital mortality	Preventable causes, treatable causes, HAQ index, opioid-related, 30-day hospital for AMI and stroke	OECD, GBD 2016 Healthcare Access and Quality Collaborators	2016, 2017	15.7
Cancer 5-year survival rates	Breast, colon, lung	OECD	2010–14	15.8
Morbidity				
Safe care	Asthma, COPD, diabetes hospitalizations; medical, medication, or lab mistake	OECD, Commonwealth Fund	2016–17	15.9
Access: Affordability				
Health care coverage	% with: public coverage, any coverage, dental coverage	OECD, miscellaneous	2017	15.10
Catastrophic spending	% households	OECD	2011–17	15.11
Cost-related access problems	Miscellaneous	Commonwealth Fund	2016	15.12

(Continued)

TABLE 15.2 Measures outcomes—cont'd

Construct	Specific measures	Sources	Years	Table number
Access: Waiting for Care				
Self-reported waiting times	Same day, after-hours, and emergency care; specialist appointments and elective surgery	Commonwealth Fund	2016	15.13
Access: Use of Care				
Physician and hospital usage	Doctor visits, hospital discharges, length of stay	OECD	2017	15.14
Use of selected procedures	Miscellaneous	Commonwealth Fund	2013 and 2017	15.15
Generic drug market	Share of volume and share of value attributed to generics	OECD	2017	15.16
Immunization rates	DPT (children), influenza (senior)	OECD	2018–19	15.17
Satisfaction with the Health Care System	Works pretty well vs fundamental changes needed vs needs to be completely rebuilt	Commonwealth Fund	2016	15.18

Sources: OECD. Health at a glance 2019. Paris: OECD Publishing; 2019. OECD Health Statistics 2020. http://www.oecd.org/els/health-systems/health-data.htm. G.B.D. Healthcare Access Quality Collaborators. Measuring performance on the Healthcare Access and Quality Index for 195 countries and territories and selected subnational locations: a systematic analysis from the Global Burden of Disease Study 2016. Lancet 2018;391(10136):2236–71. Schneider EC, Sarnak DO, Squires D, Shah A, Doty MM. Mirror, mirror 2017: International comparison reflects flaws and opportunities for better U.S. health care. Mirror, Mirror: The Commonwealth Fund; 2017. https://www.commonwealthfund.org/sites/default/files/documents/___media_files_publications_fund_report_2017_jul_schneider_mirror_mirror_2017.pdf.

TABLE 15.3 Health care spending, 2019.

Country	Health expenditures per capita (1)	Health expenditures as a share of GDP (2)	Percent of health spending on governance and finance administration (3)	Public social spending as a share of GDP (4)
Australia	$5187	9.3%	3.4%	17.8%
Canada	$5418	10.8%	3.1%	17.3%
France	$5376	11.2%	5.6%	31.2%
Germany	$6646	11.7%	4.7%	25.1%
Japan	$4823	11.1%	1.7%	21.9%
Netherlands	$5765	10.0%	3.8%	16.7%
Sweden	$5782	10.9%	1.7%	26.1%
Switzerland	$7732	12.1%	3.9%	16.0%
United Kingdom	$4653	10.3%	1.9%	20.6%
United States	$11,072	17.0%	8.8%	18.7%

Sources: (1) and (2): OECD health statistics 2020. OECD; 2020. http://www.oecd.org/els/health-systems/health-data.htm. (3) OECD health statistics 2020. OECD; 2020. http://www.oecd.org/els/health-systems/health-data.htm. Data for Australia and Japan are for 2017. (4) OECD. Social spending. https://data.oecd.org/socialexp/social-spending.htm.

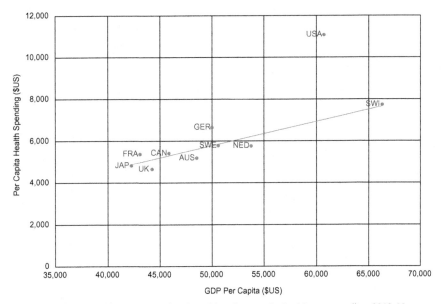

FIG. 15.1 Relationship between national wealth and per-capita health care spending, 2019. Note: The trend line is based on data from all of the countries except for the United States. *(Sources: OECD Health Statistics 2020 and OECD.Stat. 2020 (Level of GDP per capita and productivity, US dollars, constant prices, 2015 PPPs).)*

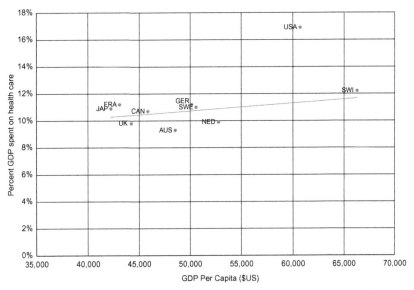

FIG. 15.2 Relationship between national wealth and proportion of GDP spent on health care, 2019. Note: The trend line is based on data from all of the countries except for the United States. *(Sources: OECD Health Statistics 2020 and OECD.Stat. 2020 (Level of GDP per capita and productivity, US dollars, constant prices, 2015 PPPs).)*

make the relationship clearer, we have added a line that best connects the data points for all of the countries except the United States. The results are quite revealing: per-capita health care spending and national wealth show a tight, largely linear relationship. If one knows only one thing—how wealthy one of these nine countries is—one can quite accurately predict per-capita spending on health care. One thing that this graph clarifies is that Switzerland is not an outlier: its per-capita spending of over $7700 is consistent with its wealth.

While there are some deviations along the line, they are relatively small. Germans spend a little more than would be predicted, while the British spend a little less. The enormous outlier is the United States.

Fig. 15.2 uses the same approach, but instead uses percentage of GDP devoted to health as the measure of health care spending. The resulting graph is similar to the previous one, demonstrating that the relationship between health care spending and national wealth is largely consistent for the nine countries, as is the outlier status of the United States.[b]

The third column of Table 15.3 illustrates one aspect of administrative costs: the proportion of health care spending devoted to payers' governance, finance, and administration. It is important to recognize that this reflects only a portion of health care administration. It does not include, for example, the large portion of resources devoted to providers' administration, e.g., in hospitals and physicians' offices. These costs, not reflected here, are particularly high in the United States for a variety of reasons, including the personnel time devoted to such activities as confirming coverage and validating claims with insurance companies, as well as the effort it takes to negotiate payment rates between individual insurers and individual providers rather than having it done collectively [4]. The table still shows the United States as something of an outlier, spending 8.8% on these particular administrative activities, exceeding the next highest country, France, by over three percentage points. In contrast, Japan, Sweden, and the United Kingdom each devoted less than 2% of total health care spending to these activities. It should be noted that US administrative spending is far lower in public insurance programs like Medicare: an estimated 1.3% of total program expenditures [5].

The last column shows public social spending as a share of GDP. One of the main components of such spending is public old-age pensions. Seven of the 10 countries are tightly bunched, devoting between 16% and 22% of GDP to public social spending. Three countries, however, spend more: France (31%), Sweden (26%), and Germany (25%). US social spending is typical of the other countries; its 18.7% share ranks 6th among the 10 countries.

---

[b] There is a small difference between the lines in Figs. 15.1 and 15.2. In Fig. 15.1, Switzerland falls on the same line as the other 8, non-US countries. In Fig. 15.2, however, the line between those 8 countries is relatively flat. If it were drawn based on just those 8 countries, Switzerland would be above the line.

Irene Papanicolas and colleagues examined US social spending in comparison with the other nine countries in this book (plus Denmark) to try to explain the factors responsible for the United States being a health care spending outlier. Their analysis concluded that:

> US social spending appears to be similar to that in other high-income OECD countries. This finding calls into question the belief that higher health care spending is due to a lack of investment in social determinants. In particular, given that the United States did not appear to be an outlier with regard to utilization of [health care] services, it is unlikely that a lack of social spending results in higher health care spending due to a misallocation of resources that results in greater need (and overutilization.) [6, p. 1034].

A much more plausible explanation for high US spending is high unit prices.

Prices

Researchers have recognized for at least two decades that, at least from an accounting standpoint, the primary reason why the United States spends so much more than other countries is its high unit prices, rather than higher utilization [7]. Data on comparative unit prices, however, are sparse. One source for several of our countries is a collaboration between the International Federation of Health Plans and the Health Care Cost Institute, a US-based independent, nonprofit research organization [8]. Periodically, the Federation publishes price comparisons for selected procedures and prescription drugs; 2017 data are provided in Tables 15.4 and 15.5.

Table 15.4 lists the unit prices for five medical procedures: bypass surgery, knee replacement, normal delivery, MRI scan, and colonoscopy. This is a subset of the 14 procedures included in the Federation's international comparison of health care prices, published in 2019 [9]. Data for each procedure are available from either 4 or 5 of the 10 countries. US prices are from claims data for commercially insured Americans with employer-based coverage; they do not reflect payment rates from the Medicare and Medicaid programs. Prices from the other countries come from unpublished local industry sources.

A clear pattern emerges from the table: unit prices in the United States are much higher than in the other countries for all five of the procedures. Using bypass surgery as an example, the US price of about $78,000 is more than double the other four countries listed, and nearly seven times as high as the Dutch price. In almost all cases, prices in the Netherlands are the lowest of the listed countries, and generally average about one-fifth as high as in the United States (varying by procedure).

Another international comparative study involved the prices for cardiac implant devices such as stents and pacemakers, comparing US prices with four European countries, including France, Germany, and the United Kingdom through 2014. Depending on the device, US prices were between two and six times as high in Germany and the United Kingdom compared with the United States [10].

TABLE 15.4 Selected medical prices, 2017.

Country	Bypass surgery	Knee replacement	Normal delivery	MRI scan	Colonoscopy
Australia	$35,800	$18,557	$6089	–	–
Canada	–	–	–	–	–
France	–	–	–	–	–
Germany	–	–	–	–	–
Japan	–	–	–	–	–
Netherlands	$11,673	$7508	$3638	$193	$708
Sweden	–	–	–	–	–
Switzerland	$32,010	$18,333	$5141	$310	$582
United Kingdom	$24,440	$12,659	$9009	$452	$1936
United States	$78,104	$29,583	$11,167	$1432	$2874

Sources: Hargraves J, Bloschichak A. International comparisons of health care prices from the 2017 iFHP survey. Health Care Cost Institute |News|; 2019. https:// healthcostinstitute.org/in-the-news/international-comparisons-of-health-care-prices-2017-ifhp-survey. Prices are in 2017 US dollars.

Table 15.5 shows comparative prices for 6 prescription drugs, selected from the 11 listed in the Federation's report. US drug prices reflect discounts from the wholesale price but not manufacturer rebates, so on average they may be inflated by about 18% or so [11]. Prices from the other countries are from unpublished industry sources, except for the United Kingdom, which are from a British national formulary survey. For all but one of the drugs, the US price is about double that of the next highest-priced country. Using Harvoni as an example—a drug used to treat chronic hepatitis C—the US price of about $32,000 is about double that in Germany, the Netherlands, Switzerland, and the United Kingdom.

Another study, by Kang and colleagues, used price data on 79 single-source brand-name drugs that had been sold in the United States for at least 3 years, comparing prices to those in the United Kingdom, Japan, and Ontario. On average, the "estimated US post-rebate price index was 3.6 times higher than the UK price, 3.2 times higher than the Japanese price, and 4.1 times higher than the Ontario post-rebate price, on average" [11, p. 807]. In contrast, drug prices were very similar in the other three countries, which may have been due to their benchmarking their own prices against those paid by other countries.

A final study of comparative prices involved expenditures on cancer drugs and included eight of our countries (all but Switzerland and the Netherlands). Specifically, it examined the correlation between health gains as measured by reduction in potential life years lost and increases in spending on cancer drugs 2004 and 2014. Although the United States spent more on these drugs, utilization was often lower, implying that prices were higher. Investments in these drugs were at least twice as cost-effective in each of the other countries compared with the United States. In France and Sweden, these investments were about six times as effective mainly because their prices so much lower [12].

Table 15.6 provides information on labor and technology inputs. Because we included this table in Chapter 13, the discussion will be abbreviated here. It provides several measures of the supply of resources available in each country: physician, nurse, and hospital bed supply per population unit; similar information for MRI units and CT scanners; and the percentage of physicians who are considered in their countries to be providing primary care. The data show:

- Countries vary a great deal in how they employ labor inputs. Germany, Sweden, and Switzerland have relatively high physician-population ratios, while the United States, Canada, Japan, and the United Kingdom have fewer physicians to care for their populations. There is not as much variation in nurse-to-population ratios, with the exception that Switzerland employs nurses more than the other countries, and the United Kingdom, less than the others. Part of these differentials may result from nurses having different clinical responsibilities across the countries.
- The ratio of physicians who practice primary care does not vary by a large amount. The low Swedish figure is probably the result of how primary care

TABLE 15.5 Selected pharmaceutical prices, 2017.

Country	Herceptin	Immunoglobulin	Kalydeco	Enbrel	Harvoni	Xarelto
Australia	–	–	–	–	–	–
Canada	–	–	–	–	–	–
France	–	–	–	–	–	$107
Germany	$48	$41	$17,781	$2270	$14,566	$107
Japan	–	–	–	–	–	–
Netherlands	$24	$17	$15,860	$773	$12,778	$59
Sweden	–	–	–	–	–	–
Switzerland	$47	$33	$21,340	$1566	$13,613	$77
United Kingdom	$133	$27	$18,060	$922	$16,761	$65
United States	$211	$97	$23,874	$4635	$31,618	$379

Sources: Hargraves J, Bloschichak A. International comparisons of health care prices from the 2017 iFHP survey. Health Care Cost Institute [News]; 2019. https://healthcostinstitute.org/in-the-news/international-comparisons-of-health-care-prices-2017-ifhp-survey. Prices are in 2017 US dollars.

TABLE 15.6 Provider supply and selected equipment, 2017 or 2018.

Country	Practicing physicians per 1000 population, 2018	Percent primary care	Practicing nurses per 1000 population, 2018	Hospital beds per 1000 population, 2018	MRI units per million population, 2017	CT scanners per million population, 2017
	(1)	(2)	(3)	(4)	(5)	(6)
Australia	3.8	45%	11.9	3.8	14.2	64.8
Canada	2.7	48%	10.0	2.5	10.0	15.3
France	3.2	54%	10.5	5.9	14.2	17.4
Germany	4.3	45%	13.2	8.0	34.7	35.1
Japan	2.5	43%	11.8	13.0	55.2	112.3
Netherlands	3.7	47%	11.1	3.2	13.0	13.5
Sweden	4.3	33%	10.9	2.1	14.0	18.5
Switzerland	4.3	48%	17.6	4.6	23.1	39.3
United Kingdom	2.8	45%	7.8	2.5	7.2	9.5
United States	2.6	43%	11.7	2.9	37.6	42.6

Sources: (1), (3), (4) Data are from: OECD.Stat. https://stats.oecd.org/Index.aspx?ThemeTreeId=9. (3) US and France data are from: OECD. Health at a Glance 2019. Paris: OECD Publishing; 2019, Figure 8.10, and are for 2017. (4) Australia data are for 2016; Germany and the United States are from 2017. (5), (6) Data at from: OECD. Health at a glance 2019. Paris: OECD Publishing; 2019, Figure 9.3. UK data are for 2014. (2) Data are from: Papanicolas I, Woskie LR, Jha AK. Health care spending in the United States and other high-income countries. JAMA 2018;319(10):1024–39, Fig. 5, row 2. Years vary.

is defined in the country. The US figure of 43% of physicians practicing primary care may seem surprising high given its reputation for favoring specialist care, but as described in Chapter 13, is supported by two recent studies [6,13].

- Hospital bed-to-population ratios also vary a great deal, with Japan and Germany having higher ratios, and Sweden, Canada, the United Kingdom, and the United States having the fewest beds. Some (but probably not most) of this variation can be explained by some countries using a portion of inpatient hospital beds for long-term care patients. For example, it has been estimated that 11% of Japanese hospital expenditures are for long-term care [14].
- Japan and the United States have more MRI units and CT scanners per million population than the other countries, and the United Kingdom and Canada, the fewest.

Outcomes

Mortality

Table 15.7 shows several measures of mortality that can arguably be attributed, at least broadly, to the health care system: mortality from preventable causes; mortality from treatable causes (also called "mortality amenable to health care" or "amenable mortality") and a refinement of the measure, the Healthcare Access and Quality (HAQ) index; and 30-day hospital mortality rates for acute myocardial infarction (AMI) and stroke. Box 15.1 explains how preventable mortality, treatable mortality, and the HAQ index are calculated.

Looking at the first three columns of Table 15.7, several countries stand out in terms of high or low performance:

- Switzerland performed the best on all three measures, with Australia, Japan, and Sweden also performing well
- The United States performed worst on all three measures
- The United Kingdom performed second lowest overall, and Germany, third lowest

The results were different for the two hospital mortality rates, with the Netherlands performing best and the United Kingdom worst. The most notable difference was that the United States performed second-best for the 30-day mortality rate from stroke, an indicator of high-quality inpatient care. Because Switzerland was missing one of the two measures, it is difficult to assess how it fared overall. One curiosity is that Japan performed best in stroke mortality, but next to last in AMI mortality. It is impossible to know from the data, however, if this is a real phenomenon or rather if causes of death are coded differently than in other countries.

Table 15.8 focuses on cancer survival rates. It is difficult to provide an overall performance rating because three countries did not record data for breast

TABLE 15.7 Avoidable and hospital mortality.

Country	Mortality from preventable causes per 100,000 population, 2016	Mortality from treatable causes per 100,000 population, 2016	HAQ index, 2016	30-day hospital mortality rate, AMI, 2017	30-day hospital mortality rate, stroke, 2017
	(1)	(2)	(3)	(4)	(5)
Australia	96	49	96	3.8	6.0
Canada	117	59	94	4.8	7.9
France	106	48	92	5.6	7.1
Germany	120	66	92	8.5	6.0
Japan	87	51	94	9.7	3.0
Netherlands	101	52	96	3.5	5.3
Sweden	93	51	95	3.9	5.7
Switzerland	85	40	96	–	5.4
United Kingdom	119	69	90	7.0	8.8
United States	175	88	89	5.0	4.2

Sources: All data except HAQ index (3) are from: OECD. Health at a glance 2019. Paris: OECD Publishing; 2019. (1), (2) Figure 3.9. Data for Canada and France are for 2015. (4) Figure 6.18. Age-sex standardized rates for acute myocardial infarction (AMI) per 100 patients aged 45+. (5) Figure 6.15. Age-sex standardized rates per 100 patients aged 45+. (3) HAQ (Healthcare Access and Quality) Index: G.B.D. Healthcare Access Quality Collaborators. Measuring performance on the Healthcare Access and Quality Index for 195 countries and territories and selected subnational locations: a systematic analysis from the Global Burden of Disease Study 2016. Lancet 2018;391(10136):2236–71. 2016 data, p. 2243, first column.

TABLE 15.8 Cancer 5-year survival rates, 2010–14.

Country	Breast cancer (1)	Colon cancer (2)	Lung cancer (3)
Australia	89.5%	70.7%	19.4%
Canada	88.6%	67.0%	21.3%
France	–	63.7%	17.3%
Germany	86.0%	64.8%	18.3%
Japan	89.4%	67.8%	32.9%
Netherlands	–	63.1%	17.3%
Sweden	–	64.9%	19.5%
Switzerland	86.2%	67.3%	20.4%
United Kingdom	85.6%	60.0%	13.3%
United States	90.2%	64.9%	21.2%

Sources: OECD. Health at a glance 2019. Paris: OECD Publishing; 2019. (1) Figure 6.29. (2) Figure 6.33. (3) Figure 6.35.

cancer deaths. Nevertheless, some generalizations are possible from the data that are available:

- Overall, Japan performed the highest, with lung cancer survival rates that far exceeded all other countries.
- The United States, Australia, and Canada also performed well
- The United Kingdom performed the lowest in all measures
- France, Germany, and the Netherlands also performed poorly

Morbidity

The three measures in Table 15.9, which are labeled as indicators of safe care, provide a very imprecise understanding of how well different health care systems keep people healthy; comparative performance data on morbidity across countries is scarce. The first two columns provide administrative data on hospital admissions that should not occur very often if a health care system provides good timely preventive and primary care, with asthma and chronic obstructive pulmonary disease (COPD) in column 1 and diabetes in column 2. The third column uses data from patient self-reports of having experienced a medical or lab mistake.

Japan reported by far the fewest asthma and COPD hospitalizations. Data were not available for diabetes, but given the very low obesity rate (Table 13.10), this rate is likely to be low as well. Switzerland was the country that was

TABLE 15.9 Indicators of safe care.

Country	Asthma and COPD hospital admissions, adults per 100,000 population, 2017 (1)	Diabetes hospitalizations, adults per 100,000 population, 2017 (2)	Experienced a medical, medication, or lab mistake in past 2 years, 2016 (3)
Australia	403	144	11%
Canada	253	96	15%
France	150	151	8%
Germany	289	209	7%
Japan	58	–	–
Netherlands	236	59	10%
Sweden	169	79	17%
Switzerland	138	73	14%
United Kingdom	281	74	11%
United States	268	170	19%

Note: *COPD*, chronic obstructive pulmonary disease.
Sources: (1) and (2) are from: OECD. Health at a glance 2019. Paris: OECD Publishing; 2019. (1) Figure 6.9. Age-sex standardized rates for asthma and chronic obstructive pulmonary disease (COPD); Data for Japan are for 2011; France and Switzerland for 2015; Australia, Netherlands, and United States for 2016. (2) Figure 6.12. Age-sex standardized rates; Data for France and Switzerland are for 2015; Australia, Netherlands, and United States for 2016. (3) Schneider EC, Sarnak DO, Squires D, Shah A, Doty MM. Mirror, mirror 2017: International comparison reflects flaws and opportunities for better U.S. health care. The Commonwealth Fund. 2017. https:// www.commonwealthfund.org/sites/default/files/documents/___media_files_publications_fund_ report_2017_jul_schneider_mirror_mirror_2017.pdf. Appendix 2B.

consistently the highest-performing country for the first two measures, while Australia, Germany, and the United States performed consistently poorly. With respect to self-reported medical or lab mistakes, in this area Germany performed best—a sharp contrast with most of the other indicators discussed so far. France also performed well. The United States showed the lowest performance, with 19% of survey respondents reporting such an error in the past 2 years. These findings must be viewed with caution, however, because self-reported experiences of medical errors may be affected by such things as cultural factors that affect people's willingness to report these errors as well as issues very specific to each country such as the medical malpractice environment.

Access: Affordability

All countries except the United States provide health insurance coverage for practically all documented residents (Table 15.10, column 1). The United States, in contrast, had an uninsurance rate of about 9%. The second column of the table shows the source of the coverage, in particular, the percentage of the population with public or mandatory coverage. Germany is one of the countries with universal coverage that allows some of its citizenry to purchase private health insurance as a substitute for the public program. As a result, about 89% of the population is listed as having public coverage (see Chapter 9). The low US figure for public or mandatory coverage—just over one-third of the population—mainly reflects enrollment in the Medicare and Medicaid programs, which cover seniors, many of the poor and near-poor, and some of the disabled population.

Table 15.10 also summarizes dental coverage. The countries that cover nearly the entire population are Germany, Japan, and the United Kingdom, although in the United Kingdom, there are substantial patient cost-sharing requirements. Other countries provide coverage for subgroups of the population, most commonly for children and/or poor persons, and sometimes for senior citizens.

Table 15.11 provides the percentage of households that incur catastrophic spending, which is defined by the OECD as spending 40% or more of resources out-of-pocket in a year. Resources are defined as household income minus a standard amount for spending on food, rent, and utilities. Researchers have found that this measure of catastrophic spending is more effective than others in capturing the burdens faced by poor families.[c] Data are available for only seven of the 10 countries. Among the seven, catastrophic spending is far more likely to occur in the United States than in the other countries. The rate exceeds 7%, which is more than double the rate in any other country and five times the rate in the United Kingdom. This reflects the lack of universal coverage as well as underinsurance, particularly the high annual deductibles faced by much of the population.

Catastrophic spending, of course, reflects services that are used. The other side of affordability is having trouble accessing care due to its costs. Table 15.12 shows the results from population survey data regarding experiences with five different aspects of cost-related access: accessing medical care and dental care, problems with insurers paying for care, problems

---

[c] Jonathan Cylus and colleagues compared four definitions of catastrophic spending. The traditional method defined the concept as a percentage of total income spent on health care in a given year—usually 10% or 25%. The study found that this method "overestimates financial hardship among rich households and underestimates hardship among poor households" [23, p. 599]. It was concluded that the alternative method, presented here, is the most effective of the four in capturing the concept.

TABLE 15.10 Health care coverage, 2017.

Country	Percent of population with any coverage (1)	Percent of population with public or mandatory coverage (2)	Dental care coverage (3)
Australia	100.0%	100.0%	Limited coverage for children
Canada	100.0%	100.0%	Generally not covered except for some older adults
France	99.9%	99.9%	Limited coverage for low-income residents
Germany	100.0%	89.4%	Covered
Japan	100.0%	100.0%	Covered except for orthodontia
Netherlands	99.9%	99.9%	Coverage for children
Sweden	100.0%	100.0%	Coverage for children
Switzerland	100.0%	100.0%	Not covered
United Kingdom	100.0%	100.0%	Covered, with significant copayments
United States	90.8%	35.9%	Varies by health insurance program

Sources: (1), (2) OECD. Health at a glance 2019. Paris: OECD Publishing; 2019. Figure 5.1. Data for Japan are for 2016. The figures in column 2 were modified by the author. Health at a Glance provides figures for public coverage, listing the Netherlands and Switzerland at 0%. However, both countries have mandates that require the purchase of insurance, so they fit the definition of public coverage used here, which includes mandatory coverage. (3) The country-specific chapters in this book.

coming up with the money to pay medical bills, and experiencing OOP spending of $1000 in the past year. Data were not available for Japan. Some of the patterns that appear are:

- The United States consistently showed the greatest cost-related access problems, often occurring many times as often as in other countries.
- Switzerland also exhibited these problems, particularly for obtaining medical care and experiencing high OOP expenses. Nearly half of the Swiss (46%) reported OOP spending of $1000 or more in the past year. The only other country above 16% was the United States (36%).

TABLE 15.11 Share of households with catastrophic spending.

Country	Year	Percent
Australia	2016	3.2%
Canada	–	–
France	2011	1.9%
Germany	2013	2.4%
Japan	2014	2.6%
Netherlands	–	–
Sweden	2012	1.8%
Switzerland	–	–
United Kingdom	2014	1.4%
United States	2017	7.4%

Sources: OECD. Health at a glance 2019. Paris: OECD Publishing; 2019. Figure 5.13. Households are defined as in current catastrophic spending if they spend 40% or more of resources on out-of-pocket costs in a year. Resources are defined as household income minus a standard amount for spending on food, rent, and utilities.

- The United Kingdom, in contrast, showed the fewest cost-related access problems for each of the five measures.
- Cost-related access problems were also low in Germany, the Netherlands, and except for dental care, in Sweden.

Access: Waiting for care

Self-reported data on waiting to receive care is provided in Table 15.13. The five measures capture different aspects of health care delivery: primary, after-hours, emergency, specialist, and surgical care. Data from Japan were not available. Beginning with countries that report longer waiting time, the main pattern is that Canada ranked poorest in four of the five measures. Sweden also showed consistently longer waits than the other countries, ranking between 6th and 8th on all of the measures. The United Kingdom had among the lowest waits for primary and after-hours care, but longer waits for specialty and surgical care.

The country that consistently showed low waiting time was the Netherlands, which performed best on two measures and in the top four in the others. France and Germany also performed well: best or second best in three measures. The other countries were inconsistent performers. While the United States performed third best for specialist and surgical care, it was in the middle of the pack for the other measures. Australia and Switzerland had mixed results, depending on the measure.

TABLE 15.12 Cost-related access problems, 2016.

Country	Had any cost-related access problem to medical care in past year	Skipped dental care or checkup because of cost in past year	Insurance payment denied or less than expected	Had a serious problem paying for or unable to pay medical bills	OOP for medical bills greater than $1000 in past year
Australia	14%	21%	9%	5%	16%
Canada	16%	28%	14%	6%	15%
France	17%	23%	24%	23%	7%
Germany	7%	14%	8%	4%	5%
Japan	–	–	–	–	–
Netherlands	8%	11%	8%	7%	7%
Sweden	8%	19%	2%	5%	4%
Switzerland	22%	21%	12%	11%	46%
United Kingdom	7%	11%	1%	1%	4%
United States	33%	32%	27%	20%	36%

Sources: Schneider EC, Sarnak DO, Squires D, Shah A, Doty MM. Mirror, mirror 2017: International comparison reflects flaws and opportunities for better U.S. health care. The Commonwealth Fund; 2017. https://www.commonwealthfund.org/sites/default/files/documents/___media_files_publications_fund_report_2017_jul_ schneider_mirror_mirror_2017.pdf. Appendix 3 under Affordability.

TABLE 15.13 Self-reported waiting times, 2016.

Country	Saw doctor or nurse on same or next day, last time needed medical care	Somewhat or very difficult to obtain after-hours care	Waited 2+ hours for care in emergency room	Waited 2+ months for specialist appointment	Waited 4+ months for elective/ nonemergency surgery
Australia	67%	44%	23%	13%	8%
Canada	43%	63%	50%	30%	18%
France	56%	64%	9%	4%	2%
Germany	53%	64%	18%	3%	0%
Japan	–	–	–	–	–
Netherlands	77%	25%	20%	7%	4%
Sweden	49%	64%	39%	19%	12%
Switzerland	57%	58%	26%	9%	7%
United Kingdom	57%	49%	32%	19%	12%
United States	51%	51%	25%	6%	4%

Sources: Schneider EC, Sarnak DO, Squires D, Shah A, Doty MM. Mirror, mirror 2017: International comparison reflects flaws and opportunities for better U.S. health care. The Commonwealth Fund; 2017. https://www.commonwealthfund.org/sites/default/files/documents/___media_files_publications_fund_report_2017_jul_ schneider_mirror_mirror_2017.pdf. Appendix 3 under Timeliness.

Access: Use of care

Health care utilization rates are a highly imperfect measure of health system efficiency, for the simple reason is that it is often ambiguous whether more or less usage is a good or bad thing. Are populations better off, for example, if they visit their physicians more often? This could be the case if this helps people better manage their chronic conditions and therefore could reduce the need for more expensive hospital admissions. But at some point, efficiency will fall if people get less benefit after repeatedly seeing their doctors. Moreover, a low number of visits could mean that the health system is efficiently substituting more appropriate care—for example, using nurse practitioners or physician assistants for tasks where an MD might not be necessary. The same ambiguity applies to procedures. Are more hip replacements better than fewer? This depends not only on the health of the population, but also on cultural or other norms regarding the best way to treat medical problems.

In an effort to reduce unnecessary utilization, an effort called "Choosing Wisely" was begin in the United States in 2012 and has now been extended to over 20 countries [15]. Clinical specialty societies develop lists of procedures and tests that are clinically ineffective or even harmful to patients with particular medical conditions. As yet, there is not enough international comparison statistics to judge the success of our 10 countries in reducing such usage. It should also be noted that there are some instances when more care is clearly better than less care. Experts agree, for example, that if a greater proportion of the population receives immunizations or cancer screening tests, this is an indicator of greater efficiency.

Table 15.14 shows some key summary measures of service utilization: number of doctor consults (i.e., visits) per year, hospital discharge rates, and average length of hospital stays. The average number of doctor consults varies severalfold across the countries, with the Japanese figure of 12.6 being more than four times as large as the Swedish figure of 2.8 (column 1).[d] One factor that may be partly responsible for Japan's high figure is that unit fees for physician visits are extremely low—about $7 for a follow-up visit to a physician or at a clinic [16]. Low fees could induce patients to return more often, and could also encourage physicians to ask them to do so to increase their incomes. Germany also has a very high visit rate, averaging about 10 visits per year. While such high visit rates may appear to be wasteful, one cannot discount the possibility that people in these countries are accustomed to seeing the doctor more often, and would be dissatisfied if they were not able to.

The hospital discharge rate, an indicator of how often people are hospitalized (column 2), shows somewhat more uniformity. While Germany's rate of 255 per 1000 population is considerably higher than those of the other

---

[d] Japan's visit rate is not the highest. The OECD data show that Koreans see their doctors an average of 17 times per year.

TABLE 15.14 Physician and hospital usage, 2017.

Country	Average number of doctor consultations (1)	Hospital discharge rates per 1000 population (2)	Average hospital length of stay (3)
Australia	7.7	181	5.6
Canada	6.8	84	7.4
France	6.1	182	9.9
Germany	9.9	255	8.9
Japan	12.6	128	16.2
Netherlands	8.3	96	5.0
Sweden	2.8	131	5.7
Switzerland	4.3	171	8.1
United Kingdom	–	131	6.9
United States	4.0	125	6.1

Sources: OECD. Health at a glance 2019. Paris: OECD Publishing; 2019. (1) Figure 9.1. Data for France and Japan are for 2016; the United States for 2011. (2) Figure 9.7. Data for Australia and France are for 2016; the United States for 2010. (3) Figure 9.9. Data for Australia, France, and the United States are for 2016.

countries, seven of the remaining nine are clustered between 125 and 182. Part of the reason for Germany's high rate is its history of providing the vast majority of specialist care in an inpatient hospital setting, with relatively little attention devoted to hospital-based or other outpatient care. A related explanation may be the large number of hospital beds (adjusted for population) compared with other European countries. The two countries with very low discharge rates are Canada and the Netherlands (84 and 96 per 1000 population, respectively).

Except for Japan, hospital length of stay (column 3) shows the tightest pattern of the three columns, with averages falling between 5 and 10 days. France and Germany have longer stays (about 10 and 9 days), and the Netherlands, Australia, and Sweden shorter (between 5 and 6 days). As discussed in Chapter 8, Japan's high figure can only partly be explained by the hospitalization of some older patients and psychiatric patients who might be more appropriately served in long-term care facilities [17].

Table 15.15 shows the utilization rates for seven procedures: MRI examinations, CT scans, coronary bypass (CABG) and angioplasty procedures, hip and knee replacements, and C-sections. The data are too voluminous to summarize

TABLE 15.15 Use of selected procedures, 2017.

Country	MRI examinations per 1000 population	CT scans per 1000 population	CABG procedures per 100,000 population, 2013	Angioplasty procedures per 100,000 population, 2013	Hip replacements per 100,000 population	Knee replacements per 100,000 population	C-sections (percent of births)
	(1)	(2)	(3)	(4)	(5)	(6)	(7)
Australia	45	126	53.8	166	195	213	33.7%
Canada	51	153	56.1	158	159	191	27.7%
France	114	190	30.0	213	248	175	19.7%
Germany	143	149	67.7	368	309	223	30.2%
Japan	112	231	–	–	–	–	–
Netherlands	51	94	54.4	241	238	159	16.2%
Sweden	–	–	32.2	193	240	132	16.6%
Switzerland	74	110	49.4	196	307	251	31.9%
United Kingdom	62	92	28.7	125	181	145	27.4%
United States	111	256	79.0	157	–	–	32.0%

Sources: All data except (3), (4) are from: OECD. Health at a glance 2019. Paris: OECD Publishing; 2019. (1) Figure 9.4. Data for Germany are for 2016; Japan for 2014. (2) Figure 9.5. Data for Germany are for 2016; Japan for 2014. (5) Figure 9.12. Data for Australia are for 2016; Netherlands for 2016. (6) Figure 9.13. Data for Australia are for 2016; Netherlands for 2014. (7) Figure 9.16. Data for the United States are for 2015; Australia for 2016. Coronary artery bypass graft (CABG) and angioplasty data are from: OECD. Cardiac procedures. Health at a glance 2015: OECD Indicators. Paris: OECD Publishing; 2015. (3), (4) OECD. Health at a glance 2015: OECD Indicators. Paris: OECD Publishing; 2015. Figure 6.16. Data for Switzerland are for 2008; the Netherlands and the United States for 2010; Australia and Canada for 2012.

here. Data were available for Japan for only two of the seven services. A few noteworthy patterns are:

- The United States, Japan, and France have high rates for both imaging procedures, although Germany is the highest for MRIs. The Netherlands, the United Kingdom, and Australia have low rates for both.
- There is little consistency of high vs low use among the countries for the two cardiac procedures. This is not surprising because they can be used as substitutes for each other. The one exception is Germany, which shows high utilization of both procedures—particularly angioplasty, with rates 50% higher than the next highest country—and the United Kingdom, which has the lowest for both.
- The placement of Germany (high) and the United Kingdom (low) was also true of joint replacement surgery. Usage rates in Switzerland were also high for both. Unfortunately, the OECD did not have internationally comparable data for the United States.
- C-section rates varied about twofold between countries. There were three countries where C-sections were performed less than 20% of the time: France, the Netherlands, and Sweden. In the other countries, rates fell between 27% and 34%.

Table 15.16 illustrates the use of generic drugs, specifically, the share of pharmaceuticals dispensed and the share of total pharmaceutical value accounted for by generics. The share of prescriptions that are generic shows tremendous variation, from a high of 89% in the United States and 85% in the United Kingdom, to a low of 23% in Switzerland. The shares when examining the dollar value of drugs differ considerably, however, with the United States falling to fourth. The two countries where generics account for the greatest share of total drug spending are the United Kingdom and Germany, at about 35%. The fact that the United States performs well in one measure but not the other points to its efficiency in pharmaceutical utilization but inefficiency in pricing.

Finally, Table 15.17 shows the percentage of children vaccinated for diphtheria, tetanus, and pertussis (DTP) and the percent of seniors aged 65 and older vaccinated for influenza. DTP rates were largely uniform, varying from a low of 91% in Canada to a high of 97% in Sweden. There was somewhat more variation for influenza, with a 35% rate in Germany compared with 72% in the United Kingdom and 69% in the United States. The low rate in Germany has been attributed to some seniors believing that the vaccine causes the flu, as well as mistrust in the vaccine and the perception that contracting flu is not dangerous [18].

Satisfaction with the health care system

In its 2016 international surveys, the Commonwealth Fund asked adult respondents to assign their country's health care system to one of three categories:

TABLE 15.16 Generic drug market, 2017.

Country	Share of generics in pharmaceutical market, by volume	Share of generics in pharmaceutical market, by value
Australia	37.0%	19.0%
Canada	76.0%	27.0%
France	30.2%	15.5%
Germany	82.3%	34.6%
Japan	40.2%	15.0%
Netherlands	75.6%	17.9%
Sweden	44.0%	15.0%
Switzerland	22.8%	17.9%
United Kingdom	85.3%	36.2%
United States	89.0%	26.0%

Sources: Data for all countries except Australia, Sweden, and the United States are from: OECD. Health at a glance 2019. Paris: OECD Publishing; 2019, Figure 10.10. Data for France are for 2013. Data for Australia are from: AIHW. International health data comparisons, 2020. Canberra: Australian Institute of Health and Welfare; 2020. Data for Sweden are for 2013, and are from: Wouters OJ, Kanavos PG, McKee M. Comparing generic drug markets in Europe and the United States: prices, volumes, and spending. Milbank Q 2017;95(3):554–601. Data for the United States for 2016, and are from: Generic drug access & savings in the U.S. Association for Accessible Medicines; 2017.

(a) "works pretty well and only minor changes are necessary" vs (b) "there are some good things but fundamental changes are needed," vs (c) the "system has so much wrong that we need to completely rebuild it." These were mutually exclusive choices so the percentages within a country sum to approximately 100%.

The most noticeable result is how unpopular the US system is (Table 15.18). Only 19% rated it in the first category, and 23% in the third. The latter number far exceeds the other countries, all of which fell below 10%. Germany and Switzerland had health care systems that garnered the most support, with about 60% putting it into the first category, and only 3%, the third. There were some small differences between the other countries, but one should not parse them too much since language and cultural factors could affect responses.

Interpretation of the findings

We divide the findings into those relating to inputs vs outputs. With the exception of the United States, which spends far more than the other countries, total input use, as represented by total health care spending per capita, is roughly similar in the other nine countries after accounting for each country's wealth.

TABLE 15.17 Selected immunization rates.

Country	Percent of children vaccinated for diphtheria, tetanus, and pertussis, 2018 (1)	Percent of population aged 65+ vaccinated for influenza, 2019 (2)
Australia	94.6%	–
Canada	91.0%	59.0%
France	96.3%	51.0%
Germany	93.0%	34.8%
Japan	99.0%	48.0%
Netherlands	93.5%	62.7%
Sweden	97.0%	52.2%
Switzerland	95.9%	–
United Kingdom	94.0%	72.0%
United States	94.0%	68.7%

Sources: (1) OECD. Child vaccination rates. https://data.oecd.org/healthcare/child-vaccination-rates.htm#indicator-chart. (2) OECD. Influenza vaccination rates. https://data.oecd.org/healthcare/influenza-vaccination-rates.htm#indicator-chart.

Because of this, we argue that for those nine countries, one can assess efficiency by focusing on outputs. That does not hold for the United States, however, where one needs to compare both differences in spending and outputs with those in other countries.

Why should we adjust for a country's wealth when assessing efficiency? In support of this way of proceeding, nearly all research has found that health care services are the sort of product where the citizenry demands more when their countries are better off financially.[e] Among high-income countries, higher wealth generally translates into proportional (or more) increases in health care spending [19]. It is hardly surprising that the people in a country would demand more health services as general wealth rises, or that countries would translate

---

[e] In economics, if the demand for a good rises with income, it is called a "normal" good. Sometimes textbooks further subdivide normal goods, with those whose income elasticity of demand exceeds a value of 1 being called "luxury" goods. The income elasticity of demand is defined as the percentage change in demand divided by the percentage change in income. Some previous research has found health care to have an income elasticity exceeding a value of 1, which would qualify it as a luxury good [19]. While demanding more health care when it is easier to afford may not seem like a luxury, it does highlight how desirable most people find it to be.

TABLE 15.18 Satisfaction with health care system, 2016.

Country	System works pretty well, only minor changes necessary	Some good things, but fundamental changes are needed	System has so much wrong that we need to completely rebuild it
	(1)	(2)	(3)
Australia	44%	46%	4%
Canada	35%	55%	9%
France	54%	41%	4%
Germany	60%	37%	3%
Japan	–	–	–
Netherlands	43%	46%	8%
Sweden	31%	58%	8%
Switzerland	58%	37%	3%
United Kingdom	44%	46%	7%
United States	19%	53%	23%

Sources: (1) 2016 Commonwealth fund international health policy survey. The system works pretty well and only minor changes are necessary to make it work better, 2016. International health system profiles. The Commonwealth Fund [Internet]; 2016. https://www.commonwealthfund. org/international-health-policy-center/system-stats/works-well. (2) 2016 Commonwealth fund international health policy survey. There are some good things in our health care system, but fundamental changes are needed to make it work better, 2016. International health system profiles. 2016. https://www.commonwealthfund.org/international-health-policy-center/system-stats/fundamental-changes-needed. (3) 2016 Commonwealth fund international health policy survey. Our health care system has so much wrong with it that we need to completely rebuild it, 2016. International health system profiles. The Commonwealth Fund; 2016. https://www. commonwealthfund.org/international-health-policy-center/system-stats/completely-rebuilt. UK data for the United Kingdom are for England only.

those demands into greater aggregate health care spending. Moreover, wealthier countries also have higher wages and prices in general, translating into higher total spending.

Inputs

Total spending

Figs. 15.1 and 15.2 provided strong evidence that nine of the countries (all but the United States) spend roughly the same amount on health care when accounting for each country's wealth. Indeed, nearly all of the differences that exist in both per-capita expenditures and the share of GDP devoted to health are explained by differences in national wealth. To illustrate, Switzerland spends 54% more per capita on health care than Japan, but per-capita income is 57% higher.

The United States is a clear outlier. If the same relationship between wealth and spending is held as in the other nine countries, in 2018 the United States would have spent $4000 *less* on health care per capita. It would have also devoted only 11.3% of its GDP to health care rather than the actual figure of 16.9%.

Components of spending

We also examined some components of spending: medical and pharmaceutical prices and the supply of providers and selected equipment. Of particular note are the very low unit prices paid in the Dutch system for both medical procedures and pharmaceuticals (Tables 15.4 and 15.5), which are even considerably lower than UK prices—a country noted for its strong regulation of prices based on comparative effectiveness research and cost-effectiveness analyses. Note, however, that comparative pharmaceutical price data were available for only 5 of the 10 countries.

In terms of inefficient use of inputs, one might point to:

• Prices for procedures and drugs in the United States that are several times higher than in some of the other countries.
• The very high inpatient bed ratios in Japan and Germany, and high concentration of CT scanners in Japan.
• The low nurse-to-population ratios in the United Kingdom.

It is difficult to make broad-brush conclusions that go beyond this. Consider the number of practicing physicians per 1000 population. It is difficult to say whether the low figures in Japan, the United States, Canada, and the United Kingdom are signs of efficiency or shortage, or rather whether the high numbers in Germany, Sweden, and Switzerland are instead signs of inefficiency, or instead, an indicator of employing sufficient resources. This indeterminacy is even more salient when one realizes that population expectations differ across countries.

Outputs

The findings on outputs, shown in Tables 15.7 through 15.18, contain a total of 40 measures. We provide a few insights below, drawn from the data presented here as well as the country-specific chapters.

Health: Mortality and morbidity

The results on health (mortality and morbidity) do not follow clear patterns with regard to the type of health care system employed by each country, implying that other factors such as social determinants of health and social support systems are more likely responsible for the findings. No country performed consistently at the top in the eight measures of mortality as listed in Tables 15.7 and 15.8. Switzerland and Australia performed consistently the best in terms of reducing mortality, and the United Kingdom worst, with Germany also performing relatively poorly. With respect to the three indicators of morbidity and measuring safe care, Switzerland again was a high performer along with the Netherlands, and the United States, the worst performer. Unfortunately, data for only one of the three measures was available for Japan. In summary, while some countries appear, on average, to be performing better than others, it is difficult to attribute these differences to the health care systems in place.

Access: Affordability

Across most measures, four countries performed best: Germany, the Netherlands, Sweden, and the United Kingdom. Five performed more poorly (few data were available for Japan): Australia, Canada, France, Switzerland, and the United States. The United States was exceptional in performing most poorly on the majority of measures, and next-to-last in the others. As detailed in Chapter 14, which examined equity, there are several system characteristics that enhance affordability: universal coverage, a comprehensive benefits package, reasonably low cost-sharing requirements, and a smaller role for voluntary health insurance (VHI). While all of the countries except the United States have universal health insurance coverage, the five countries that performed more poorly all lack dental care coverage for the whole population, and one, Canada, does not include prescription drugs in provincial health plans. Switzerland has by far the highest patient cost-sharing requirements, and Australia's are also considerable outside of public hospitals. Canada and Australia rely more on voluntary health insurance than the others. France's affordability problems appear to be largely the result of a system that is finally changing: requiring that patients pay medical bills up front and wait for reimbursement.

It is not surprising that residents of Germany and the United Kingdom are more able to afford care. Both have very comprehensive benefit packages, including coverage for dental care; there is no patient cost sharing for most services; and VHI plays a miniscule role in health care financing. Sweden is similar except that adult dental is less fully covered, resulting in access and affordability problems.

Access: Waiting for care

Four countries show consistently higher waiting times, particularly for specialty care and elective surgery. Canada showed the most problems, with Sweden and the United Kingdom next, with Australia also ranking relatively poorly compared with most other countries. The main characteristic that these countries share is that the public sectors in these countries have single-payer health insurance systems. We hypothesize that single-payer systems are more susceptible to longer waiting times in part because revenue typically is not earmarked to health care. Rather, the health sector needs to compete with all other public priorities that are funded by taxes. In contrast, when there are dedicated revenues in the form of payroll taxes and/or premiums, there is less financial pressure put on the system budgets. While issues with long waits to receive care have been recognized for decades, solutions have been difficult to come by. Some countries such as Sweden and the United Kingdom have legislated explicit maximum wait times but often they are not able to achieve them [20, 21]. Wealthier persons often bypass these long waits in Australia, and to a smaller extent in the United Kingdom and Sweden, but this is not allowed in Canada.[f]

Access: Use of care

As described earlier, it is difficult to judge efficiency by examining the use of care, in large part because it is often not clear whether high or low usage is better. This depends not only on the health of the population but on cultural norms regarding utilization. The Japanese, for example, go to the doctor much more than patients in other countries, but this may be something that they expect from their health care system. Nevertheless, comparative national data can point toward potential inefficiencies—for example, Germany's high hospitalization rate and lengths of stay as well as rates of use for angioplasty, CABG, and hip replacements that exceed those of the other countries. At the same time, the fact that the United Kingdom has lower usage rates for most of the procedures listed in Table 15.15 could very well reflect a strained system that results in underuse.

Another example involves generic drug penetration. In terms of the share of total prescriptions, rates for the United States, United Kingdom, and Germany all exceed 80%, with Canada not far behind. On the other end of the spectrum, rates for Switzerland (23%) and France (30%) are very low by international standards (Table 15.16). When this share is combined with drug prices through examination of the share of generics in terms of money, the United Kingdom and Germany, with rates of 35% or more, far exceed the other countries. Germany success is due to the use of reference prices, some requirements for generic substitution for brand-name drugs, and not rewarding pharmacists with additional fees for filling prescriptions with brand-name drugs. Similarly, the United Kingdom's success is in large part due to various government-enforced methods of controlling prices described in Chapter 3, and by government efforts to encourage physicians to write "open scripts" along with incentives to pharmacists to fill them with generic medications [22].

---

[f] Roosa Tikkanen, personal communication, November 19, 2020.

Satisfaction with health care system

One needs to be careful in putting too much stock in self-reported satisfaction or dissatisfaction with the health care system since views are likely to reflect, in part, cultural norms. This still cannot explain the strong dislike Americans express for their system, however, with less than 20% saying that the system works pretty well and that only minor changes are needed. The three countries that were rated best—Germany, Switzerland, and France—all have social insurance-based systems as opposed to single payer. Whether there is a causal relationship between satisfaction with the system and system type cannot be determined through available data.

Concluding thoughts

Based on the measures of input use and outputs employed in this chapter, an inescapable conclusion is that the US system is highly inefficient. It spends far more but achieves relatively poor performance on most of the health outcomes examined. The United States lagged behind all of the other countries in such indicators as mortality amenable to health care, consumer evaluations regarding the provision of safe care and overall system satisfaction, and nearly all measures of financial access. There are some bright spots that we saw both here and in Chapter 12—cancer screening and outcomes; technical innovations in medical and pharmaceutical research and development; and innovations in health care organization and delivery—but we do not view these as providing sufficient evidence to conclude anything other than that the United States is the least efficient of the 10 health care systems examined in this book.

We are reluctant to make blanket statements about the relative efficiencies of the remaining countries' systems. As noted, input use as measured by spending is about the same in each country after correcting for national wealth, so differences in efficiency are largely the result of different outcomes. But the people in different countries may put different weights on different aspects of outcomes. A good example is the United Kingdom, which had excellent results with regard to affordability but relatively poor ones for the measures of mortality and waiting for care. Switzerland, on the other hand, performed well on mortality but poorly on affordability. The German system is very popular and has almost no waiting for care, but fared poorly in both the measures of mortality and morbidity. Table 15.9 showed that it ranked second in asthma and COPD hospital admissions, and highest in diabetes admissions. Thus, all countries have room for improving the efficiency of their health care systems and can learn a great deal from each other.

References

[1] Cylus J, Papanicolas I, Smith PC. How to make sense of health system efficiency comparisons? Health systems and policy analysis, vol. 27. Copenhagen: WHO Regional Office for Europe; 2017.

[2] Tikkanen R, Gunja MZ, FitzGerald M, Zephyrin L. Maternal mortality and maternity care in the United States compared to 10 other developed countries. The Commonwealth Fund; 2020.

[3] Purchasing Power Parities—Frequently Asked Questions (FAQs). OECD [Internet]. [Accessed 18 November 2020]. Available from: https://www.oecd.org/sdd/prices-ppp/purchasingpowerparities-frequentlyaskedquestionsfaqs.htm.

[4] Himmelstein DU, Campbell T, Woolhandler S. Health care administrative costs in the United States and Canada, 2017. Ann Intern Med 2020;172(2):134–42.

[5] Cubanski J, Neuman T, Freed M. The facts on medicare spending and financing. KFF; 2019.

[6] Papanicolas I, Woskie LR, Jha AK. Health care spending in the United States and other high-income countries. JAMA 2018;319(10):1024–39.

[7] Anderson GF, Reinhardt UE, Hussey PS, Petrosyan V. It's the prices, stupid: why the United States is so different from other countries. HealthAff 2003;22(10):89–105.

[8] About HCCI. Health Care Cost Institute [Internet]. [Accessed 18 November 2020]. Available from: https://healthcostinstitute.org/about-hcci.

[9] Hargraves J, Bloschichak A. International comparisons of health care prices from the 2017 iFHP survey. Health Care Cost Institute; 2019. [News]. [Accessed 18 November 2020]. Available from: https://healthcostinstitute.org/in-the-news/international-comparisons-of-health-care-prices-2017-ifhp-survey.

[10] Wenzl M, Mossialos E. Prices for cardiac implant devices may be up to six times higher in the US than in some European Countries. Health Aff 2018;37(10).

[11] Kang S, DiStefano MJ, Socal MP, Anderson GF. Using external reference pricing in medicare part D to reduce drug price differentials with other countries. Health Aff 2019;38(5):804–11.

[12] Salas-Vega S, Mossialos E. Cancer drugs provide positive value in nine countries, but the United States lags in health gains per dollar spent. Health Aff (Millwood) 2016;35(5):813–23.

[13] Laugesen MJ. Do other countries have a better mix of generalists and specialists? J Health Polit Policy Law 2018;43(5):853–72.

[14] OECD. Health at a glance 2017: OECD indicators. Paris: OECD Publishing; 2017.

[15] Born K, Levinson W. Choosing wisely: An international campaign to combat overuse. The Commonwealth Fund; 2017.

[16] Follow-up Examination Fee. ShiroBon Net [Internet]. [Accessed 24 September 2020]. Available from: http://shirobon.net/30/ika_1_1_2/a001.html.

[17] Anon. Health at a glance 2017. OECD indicators. OECD; 2017. [Chartset]. [Accessed 23 September 2020]. Available from: https://www.oecd.org/els/health-systems/Health-at-a-Glance-2017-Chartset.pdf.

[18] Bödeker B, Remschmidt C, Schmich P, Wichmann O. Why are older adults and individuals with underlying chronic diseases in Germany not vaccinated against flu? A population-based study. BMC Public Health 2015;15:618.

[19] Khan JA, Mahumud RA. Is healthcare a 'Necessity' or 'Luxury'? An empirical evidence from public and private sector analyses of South-East Asian countries? Health Econ Rev 2015;5:3.

[20] Planned specialized care—Operation/Action. Sweden's Municipalities and Regions [Internet]. [Accessed 18 September 2020]. Available from: https://www.vantetider.se/Kontaktkort/Sveriges/SpecialiseradOperation/.

[21] Parkin E. NHS maximum waiting time standards. Commons Library Briefing; 2020 [CBP08846].

[22] Oxera. The supply of generic medicines in the UK. The British Generic Manufacturers Association; 2019.

[23] Cylus J, Thomson S, Evetovits T. Catastrophic health spending in Europe: equity and policy implications of different calculation methods. Bull World Health Organ 2018;96(9):599–609.

Chapter 16

Some insights

It is necessary to tread lightly in drawing lessons. Political challenges often make it extremely difficult for a country to make significant changes to its health care system in general, and to health insurance in particular. Even if politically feasible, what works in one country may not have the same effect as in another or might meet with resistance from the population. Not only might people in different nations prioritize different things, but each country has its own unique historical, governmental, and social contexts [1].

Nevertheless, the overriding purpose of comparing health care systems is to draw lessons—even if very tentative ones—about how countries can improve their own systems. Chapters 14 and 15 presented a great deal of evidence about what factors facilitate better equity and efficiency. In considering the 10 countries we have included, there is one overriding pattern: the United States performed poorly overall in both equity and efficiency, and at the same time, has a health insurance system that is substantially at variance with those in the other countries. Moreover, the evidence is convincing that this appears to be causal; that is, it is the unique features of US health insurance that are responsible for the country's poorer performance in health equity and efficiency. This is also the conclusion of most others who have compared performance across health care systems.

We begin by presenting the health care system rankings of other researchers. Next, we explore the generally poor US performance to glean what the country might be able to learn from the other countries in the area of health insurance. That is followed by a discussion of other lessons that have relevance to all countries.

Health care system rankings

There have been a number of previous attempts to rank the best or most successful health care systems; no rankings are available specifically about health insurance systems. We were able to find five previous efforts, all but the first of which are either recent or regularly updated. They are:

(1) The World Health Organization *World Health Report 2000*
(2) The Commonwealth Fund *Mirror, Mirror 2017* report
(3) Health Consumer Powerhouse *Euro Health Consumer Index 2018*
(4) Ezekiel Emanuel's book, *Which Country Has the World's Best Health Care*, 2020
(5) The Foundation for Research on Equal Opportunity World Index of Healthcare Innovation, 2020

Health Insurance Systems: An International Comparison. https://doi.org/10.1016/B978-0-12-816072-5.00013-4

Except for Emanual, each of these efforts results in an explicit ranking of national health care systems. Another, published by the OECD in 2010, is not included because its findings are not easily summarized across its many measures of mortality, morbidity, and service usage [2]. A final one, the Healthcare Access and Quality index, was discussed in Chapter 15, with the scores achieved by our 10 countries appearing in Table 15.7.

Every ranking system is based on choices made by the researchers on which performance measures should be included and what weights should be applied to each. Some emphasize health outcomes, others access to care and equity, and still others, innovation. While some compare output to spending, others do not. One would therefore not necessarily expect much agreement among the studies—nor is there.

WHO's *World Health Report,* 2000 [3]

The World Health Organization *World Health Report*, 2000 was an unusually ambitious attempt to rank the performance of the health systems of its 191 member states in the year 2000. Performance was based on several categories of indicators: overall level of population health, health inequalities within the population, health system responsiveness, and the distribution of the health system's financial burden within the population. Rankings of the 10 countries discussed in the current book (ranking out of 191 countries in parentheses) were:

1. France (1)
2. Japan (10)
3. Netherlands (17)
4. United Kingdom (18)
5. Switzerland (20)
6. Sweden (23)
7. Germany (25)
8. Canada (30)
9. Australia (32)
10. United States (37)

The United States ranked just behind Costa Rica. Curiously, Italy was ranked 2nd in the world in spite of the fact that only one-fifth of Italians rated their health care system as being satisfactory [4, p. 1595]. Some other countries in the top 10 included San Marino (3rd), Andorra (4th), Malta (5th), and Oman (8th).[a]

While the performance measures would appear to have face validity, many observers felt that the results did not. After the report was published, there were a number of negative critiques published about the methodology employed. Some of the issues cited were failure to control for important international differences other than education levels and health expenditures; the assumption

---

[a] The lowest-ranking country of the 191 was Sierra Leone.

that all differences in outcomes are the result of health system performance; extreme sensitivity of the results to changes in specification of the statistical model[b] as well as how different measures were weighted to come up with a single ranking (a common criticism of most ranking systems); omission of broad classes of important performance measures including satisfaction, health promotion, and preventive care; and the assumption that every country has the same goals for its system [4–7].

The Commonwealth Fund *Mirror, Mirror 2017* [8]

The Commonwealth Fund, a US-based foundation, defines its mission as seeking "to promote a high-performing health care system that achieves better access, improved quality, and greater efficiency, particularly for society's most vulnerable, including low-income people, the uninsured, and people of color" [9]. One of the fund's activities is to conduct population surveys in a number of high-income countries. Eleven countries are now surveyed: 9 of the 10 countries covered in this book (excluding Japan) plus New Zealand and Norway. The surveys are usually conducted annually but with varying population groups sampled. Fielded in 3-year cycles, the sampling frame for the surveys are either all adults aged 18 and older, adults 65 years and older, or primary care physicians. The 2016 survey, which is used here, was based on samples of all adults aged 18 and older in the countries. The survey was conducted by telephone and had sample sizes in each country of at least 1000 respondents, although it was much higher in some countries and exceeded 7000 in Sweden [10]. The 2020 survey was being released at time of writing but because data were collected during the COVID-19 pandemic, this book focuses on the earlier one. Some results from the 2020 survey on the topic of equity were provided in the Appendix of Chapter 14.

The countries were ranked both overall and in five domains: care process (preventive care, safe care, coordinated care, engagement, and patient preferences), access (affordability, timeliness), administrative efficiency, equity (differences between low- and high-income individuals), and health care outcomes (population health, **mortality amenable to health care**, disease-specific health outcomes). In 2016, ratings in each of these domains were based on multiple measures: 72 in all. Most of the measures are from the Commonwealth Fund's country surveys (both patient and physician), plus other measures taken from OECD and other international data sources. The overall rankings of our nine countries were (ranking out of the 11 countries in parentheses):

1. United Kingdom (1)
2. Australia (2)

---

[b] Jamison and Sandbu recalculated the results by adding in just one extra control variable: geography (e.g., whether the country is in a tropical location). The results changed markedly for some countries. Bolivia performed at the 26th percentage in the WHO model, but was at the 52nd percentage level with this simple adjustment [4].

3. Netherlands (3)
4. Sweden (tied) (tied 6th)
5. Switzerland (tied) (tied 6th)
6. Germany (8)
7. Canada (9)
8. France (10)
9. United States (11)

The Commonwealth Fund studies provide a wealth of information not available elsewhere (especially because they are derived in large part from representative population surveys, as well as including countries outside of Europe) and are used heavily in this book. Nevertheless, the results and country rankings are subject to several limitations, which are made clear by the authors. The two most important ones, perhaps, are related: most of the results are based on individuals' subjective assessments, and these assessments can be influenced by each population's expectations [11, p. 14].

Moreover, the overall rankings shown earlier are an average of the rankings of the five domains, with each domain weighed equally. This results in rankings that some might disagree with. In particular, the United Kingdom is ranked first overall, but next to last in health care outcomes. Germany's relatively low standing contrasts with the fact that its citizens (along with the Swiss) viewed their health care system more favorably than people in the other countries. Similarly, France's very low ranking is also in contrast to the system's popularity (see Table 15.18 for ratings about satisfaction with the health care system).

Health Consumer Powerhouse *Euro Health Consumer Index 2018* [12]

Health Consumer Powerhouse has provided information since 2005 that allows for comparisons of health care system performance among about three dozen European countries. It does so by generating general and disease-specific indices "to empower patients and physicians through comparing and reviewing health care provision and policies" [13]. The indicators used to evaluate national health care systems are chosen by experts using a Delphi method.[c] Data are collected from national and international data sources, stakeholder (but not population) surveys, and interviews with stakeholders to devise a score for each performance indicator as being "good," "intermediate," or "not so good." The performance areas are patient rights and information, accessibility (waiting time), outcomes, range and reach of services provided, prevention, and pharmaceuticals, with multiple measures used to evaluate each. In 2018, the overall

---

[c] The Delphi method is used to develop consensus from a group of experts. See Okoli and Pawlowski [44].

rankings of the six European countries covered in this book were (ranking out of 35 countries in parentheses):

1. Switzerland (1)
2. Netherlands (2)
3. Sweden (8)
4. France (11)
5. Germany (12)
6. United Kingdom (16)

The ranking of the United Kingdom is the reverse of that given by the Commonwealth Fund; one reason might be that the index's access measures emphasize waiting times but not affordability. Although Switzerland ranked the highest, in most previous years the Netherlands held the number 1 ranking.

The index has come under criticism. Jonathan Cylus and colleagues note several concerns. One is arbitrariness. A country that scored 69.6% on one measure was given a score of "not so good," while another scoring 70.0% was given an "intermediate" score. A second reason is that the performance measures do not seem to reflect population preferences. Cancer survival and abortion rates, for example, carry the same weight, and cancer survival is less important in the scoring than a measure like having direct access to a specialist. A third is a lack of clarity as to why certain performance measures were chosen. Some measures are defined as changes over time, while others are based on the current time period. Finally, some of the conclusions are hard to reconcile. Switzerland's designation as having a "good" score in health care equity provides such an example in light of the equity findings in Chapter 14.

Ezekiel Emanuel, *Which Country Has the World's Best Health Care?*, 2020 [1]

In 2020, Ezekiel Emanuel, a US health policy analyst, published his book, *Which Country Has the World's Best Health Care?*—in which he examined 11 countries, eight of which are included here. He also included China, Norway, and Taiwan but excluded Japan and Sweden. As is the case with the current book, the analyses were based largely on assessment of the literature and the opinions of national experts. Unlike this book, Emanuel examined not only health insurance, but also health care delivery system.

After describing and evaluating each country in separate chapters, Emanuel chose 22 performance indicators over five domains: coverage, financing, payment, delivery, and pharmaceutical prices. These included:

- *Coverage*: universal coverage, simplicity and ease of obtaining coverage, comprehensiveness of benefits, affordability at point of service
- *Financing*: progressive financing, subsidies for particular low-income groups, dedicated mechanisms for long-term care financing, and limits on total health care spending

- *Payment*: alignment of payment incentives, simplicity for patients and providers, innovation
- *Delivery*: choice of provider; simplicity in obtaining services; excellence in primary care, mental health care, and chronic care coordination; waiting times; innovation
- *Pharmacy prices*: low prices, access to innovative drugs, rigor in pricing drugs

Rather than ranking each country, Emanuel identifies what he determines to be "notably poor-performing countries" as well as the "best-performing countries." If one does a simple count among the 22 indicators used, the countries listed the most times as best performing are, in order, the United Kingdom and the Netherlands. The countries listed most often as poor performing, again in order, are the United States and (although listed much less often) Switzerland. The Netherlands was not listed as performing poorly in any of the 22 indicators and the United Kingdom was listed just once, for waiting times. It may surprise some that Switzerland was ranked poorly in so many areas. Most revolved around financing: low affordability at point of service, few subsidized population groups, high drug prices, high total spending, and regressive financing.

Readers will not be surprised that the single-payer countries generally performed best in coverage, with the exception of Canada, whose benefit package is less comprehensive than the other countries. The Dutch performed well in delivery, and the Australians in pharmaceutical prices. Even though the United States scored poorly on more than half of the measures, it performed well on innovation in both innovation payment and care delivery as well as in chronic care coordination and the quality of mental health care. Overall, perhaps what is most notable is not how well the Netherlands performed, which other studies have found, but the relatively high performance of the United Kingdom and low performance of Switzerland.

The high performance of the Netherlands and the United Kingdom, and low performance of the United States are consistent with the Commonwealth Fund's finding. However, Switzerland's poor showing is the opposite of what was found in the Euro Health Consumer Index. Most measures where Switzerland underperformed are consistent with what was found in Chapter 10 of this book: out-of-pocket (OOP) costs are higher than elsewhere, fewer people are subsidized when purchasing coverage, drug prices are high, and total health care spending is high—although, as was shown in Figs. 15.1 and 15.2, spending is not high when one considers Switzerland's wealth. Switzerland was also downgraded in two aspects of care delivery: chronic care coordination and mental health care.

A limitation of Emanuel's analysis is that his designations into high- vs low-performing countries are subjective and not transparent. One might question designating the United States as being high performing in comprehensiveness of benefits (Chapter 12); scoring Australia poorly in limiting total health care spending (Table 15.3); or failing to list the Netherlands among countries that keep drug prices low (Table 15.5). In addition, the discussion of "Who's the Best" (his answer, appropriately enough, was "None") failed to mention the United Kingdom even though it scored so highly [1, pp. 351–356].

The Foundation for Research on Equal Opportunity's World Index of Healthcare Innovation, 2020 [14]

The Foundation for Research on Equal Opportunity is a US nonprofit think tank "committed to deploying the nation's leading scholars and the tools of individual liberty, free enterprise, and technological innovation to serve this mission" [15]. In 2020, it published its first World Index of Healthcare Innovation, which rated 31 national systems on many measures, focusing mostly but not entirely innovation. The 31 countries include many Asian countries that are often left out of international health system rankings, such as Singapore, Taiwan, Hong Kong, South Korea, and the United Arab Emirates.

The rankings are based on very different criteria from what we have seen. Because the Foundation is examining innovation driven through the private sector, the United States would be expected to do well, and single-payer systems, poorly. The index, best described by the authors,

> *ranks countries not only by traditional measures such as universal affordability and health outcomes, but also by features such as the degree to which patients have the ability to choose their doctor and their insurer; health care-related patents; scientific impact and Nobel Prizes in Chemistry and Physiology or Medicine; access to new treatments; and health digitization. The Index also measures the fiscal sustainability of countries' health care systems: that is, how much ability a given nation has to sustain its public health care spending without punitive taxes or a debt crisis [14].*

Overall rankings are based on the scores in four domains: quality, choice, science and technology, and fiscal sustainability. Each of these is given 25% weight, and within each domain, there are between 3 and 11 performance measures. What makes these rankings unique is their emphasis on innovation. Some of the elements upon which countries are scored include:

- *Science and technology*: Nobel laureates in medicine or chemistry, scientific document citation rates, new drugs approved, patents, research and development expenditures, and adoption of electronic health records
- *Quality*: survival rates for various diseases, waiting, patient assessments of their interactions with providers, doctor, and nurses per capita
- *Choice*: percentage of new drugs "launched for sale" within 1 year of approval, population insurance coverage rates, OOP spending, administrative costs, choice of providers and insurance products
- *Fiscal sustainability*: public health spending and growth over time, debt-to-GDP ratio

While these measures reflect the specific views of these authors as to what is most important in an innovative health care system, the computation methods used to score each country are transparent [16].

The overall rankings of the 10 countries covered in this book were (ranking out of 31 countries in parentheses):

1. Switzerland (1)
2. Germany (2)
3. Netherlands (3)
4. United States (4)
5. Australia (11)
6. United Kingdom (13)
7. Sweden (15)
8. Canada (17)
9. France (28)
10. Japan (31)

One concern is the relevance of the some of the unique performance measures chosen by the researchers. Nobel laureates in science, for example, skew the results in favor of large and wealthy countries and is a very limited gauge of a country's contribution to science and technology. Another concern involves the way the World Index of Healthcare Innovation is calculated: some variables have unusually large influence on the overall score. Even though there are almost 30 variables that go into the score, just two of them—public health spending per capita and debt-to-GDP ratio—are responsible for 20% of a country's total score— and a full 25% when one adds a related variable, the growth in public spending. Indeed, those three variables fully comprise "fiscal sustainability." In contrast, the population insurance coverage rate and OOP spending each contributed less than 2.5% to the total ranking, which highlights the priorities of the authors.

Reflecting the libertarian viewpoint of the authors, high public spending is considered a *bad* thing because countries "may struggle to fund other priorities, have high tax burdens, or both" while less government spending "allow[s] the private sector to develop innovative and cost-effective treatments for patients" [16]. Needless to say, this viewpoint is diametrically opposed to ranking systems that favor strong government involvement in guaranteeing coverage and benefits. This issue is illustrated by Japan's ranking at the very bottom of the list, partly due to its very high government debt, which is largely unrelated to its health care system. As a result, Japan scored 0 points (out of 100) in overall fiscal sustainability, a score no other country approached on any of the other 30 scoring elements. The fact that Japan scored 9th out of 31 countries in quality could not compensate and lift it out of last place, overall.

Summary

It is clear that overall rating systems come up with entirely different rankings with respect to which countries have the most successful health care systems.

All such rankings are driven by the measures of system performance that their authors include and prioritize. Since different studies emphasize different performance measures, the great variation in results is not surprising. The United Kingdom, for example, performs well in rankings that emphasize financial access and expenditure control, but poorly in ones focusing more on quality and outcomes. Switzerland is the opposite. The Netherlands was the only country performing well in all of the studies. The United States and Canada generally were below average across the different studies.

What can the United States learn from other countries?

Based on the material in the country chapters as well as the assessments of equity and efficiency provided in Chapters 14 and 15, we list four lessons for the United States provided by the other countries' health insurance systems.

The systems are built on a bedrock of equitable access to care

It is frequently pointed out that the United States is unique among wealthy countries in not providing guaranteed, universal health insurance coverage to documented residents. Not only are almost 10% of Americans uninsured, but even more face that prospect if they lose their jobs. Because most Americans obtain their health insurance through employment, this means that about half of the population is vulnerable to becoming uninsured. If they become uninsured, they would have to rely on individual **premium** subsidies, or if they become very poor, they would have to rely on Medicaid. Recent experience highlights this risk. It has been estimated that by June of 2020, about 3 months after the COVID-19 pandemic struck the United States, 14.6 million workers and their dependents had lost job-based health insurance although about half were able to retain their coverage [17].

The difference between the United States and other countries goes beyond this, however. All of the other countries included in this book base their health care systems as well as other social institutions, in some fashion, on the concept of *solidarity*: the belief that needed resources such as health care services should be provided to all who need it irrespective of the ability to pay. Although different countries go farther than others in this regard depending on historical, economic, social, and political factors [18], it is a defining characteristic of the world's wealthiest countries—the notable exception being the United States. Although certain programs in the United States do exhibit this trait—for example, the fact that Medicare covers nearly everyone over the age of 65—it is not the case for the population at large.

The United States is exceptional in this regard in a number of ways.[d] Lower-income persons commonly experience financial impediments to receiving

---

[d] Data in support of these statements were provided in Chapters 12, 14, and 15.

needed care. Those with Medicaid often have difficulty getting a doctor who is willing to take them on as patients, having instead to rely on community health centers or hospital emergency rooms. Many experience catastrophic levels of spending and far more face the prospect of doing so if they or a member of their family becomes ill. Medical bankruptcy is a real and not uncommon occurrence in the United States [19], but almost unheard of elsewhere—and often occurs even when a person has health insurance. Deductibles in the United States—averaging over $1600 annually for employer-based single coverage [20] and $4000 among the most commonly purchased individual plans on the Affordable Care Act (ACA) marketplaces [21]—are far beyond the level of savings of a large portion of Americans, and continue to increase rapidly as the cost of health care rises [22].[e]

The countries have a single, publicly mandated system to promote fairness and efficiency

The United States is also unique in having multiple, parallel systems of health insurance. Elsewhere, people are guaranteed coverage based simply on being a resident of the country. Moreover, they are entitled to a set of basic benefits, often generous, which typically are uniform irrespective of factors like age, income, and geographic location. Not surprisingly, there are minor exceptions. For example, a small percentage of Germans obtain their coverage through a private, parallel system. The precise benefits to which Canadian are entitled depend on the province in which they live. A more important caveat is that in most of the countries, many people do augment the benefits in the public system with secondary private insurance, which is not evenly distributed across income and other socioeconomic groups.

In sharp contrast, there is no single source of health insurance in the United States that is shared by all residents. Instead, a myriad of factors affects a person's source of primary coverage, including employment status, age, income, disability status, state of residence, and such things as being or having been in the military or status as an American Indian. From an equity standpoint, this is problematic because each source of insurance has its own benefit package, patient cost-sharing requirements, premiums, and oftentimes network of providers. Moreover, different insurers pay providers different amounts, resulting in preferences to treat patients with one source of insurance over those having a different source.

---

[e] The major reasons that deductibles are so high is that they are a means of controlling overall health care spending. It is unlikely that most employers prefer them for their employees, or that the designers of the ACA marketplaces want their policyholders to face these financial barriers. Substantial reductions in deductibles are likely to come about only if other mechanisms are adopted that successfully control spending. This could occur through incremental changes such as finding ways to lower unit prices, or alternatively, through fundamental policy reforms such as adopting a **single-payer system**.

Fragmentation also diminishes efficiency in numerous ways. Planning for the country's health care needs is undermined. It increases administrative costs on the financing side and reduces coordination of care on the deliver side. Fragmentation also makes it extremely difficult to implement a common set of provider payment rates. It effectively prevents government from exerting macro-level controls over health care spending or influencing the amount of medical technologies that are available.

One other aspects of these countries' insurance systems should be noted: in nearly all cases, when private insurers are used to provide publicly mandated coverage, they operate on a nonprofit basis. Being nonprofit, and often a quasipublic arm of national health systems, they do not have a strong incentive to deny claims or impede patients from receiving care and reimbursement. In stark contrast to their for-profit counterparts, they were originally established to serve workers and the public at large rather than shareholders—and still do.[f]

Governments are actively involved in planning for the supply of health care resources and constraining prices

For the last several decades, the US government has not been actively involved in planning for the supply of the nation's health care resources.[g] Neither federal nor state governments directly control the number of physicians trained or their specialty distribution, the deployment of major capital equipment both in and outside of hospitals, or total expenditures. Instead, this authority, when used, is in the hands of private entities. Medical schools, for example, choose how many students to train; hospitals choose how many medical residents to accept in different specialties[h]; and hospitals and physicians' practices decide which medical technologies to purchase.

---

[f] Ewout van Ginneken, personal communication, October 28, 2020.

[g] This was not always the case. During the 1960s, 1970s, and 1980s, health planning and regulation was much more prevalent in the United States than it is now. It may have reached its apogee in 1974 with enacting of the Health Planning Resources and Development Act, which required states to develop health planning programs. The country was divided into over 200 areas each with its own health system agency. Moreover, states were required to implement Certificate of Need (CON) programs, one role of which was to approve requests for construction and expansion of hospitals and nursing homes as well as purchase of major capital equipment. Research studies at the time found that CON programs did not lower expenditures but changed its composition so that new services and equipment was substituted for inpatient beds [45]. While many states still have some aspects of these programs in place, they are far less influential than they used to be.

[h] The United States does have some programs designed to encourage physicians to practice in designated "shortage areas." The National Health Service Corps provides students with medical schools scholarships who commit to 2 years of subsequent full-time service in providing primary care in areas with a dearth of primary care physicians, for every 1 year of financial support [46]. Another program gives a 10% fee bonus when primary care physicians and psychiatrists provide Medicare services in such areas [47].

In contrast, the other nine countries in this book are actively involved in health care resource planning, regulation, and budgeting. Because this is the norm rather than the exception, there are too many examples to name here. Box 16.1 provides a single example from several countries concerning planning or regulation that, collectively, span the many sorts of activities in which governments engage. Examples of how some of the countries employ budgeting appear in the following section.

The setting and/or regulation of prices provides another example of how the United States differs from the other countries. In the United States,

---

Box 16.1 Examples of resource planning and regulation.

Australia	Uses cost-effectiveness analyses to determine which new pharmaceuticals are included in the public benefits package.
Canada	Provincial Ministries of Health work with provider organizations to set the number of medical students, based in part of the amount of funding provided by the province.
France	A new technology is covered by insurance only after the government assesses it as being more effective than existing technologies, with prices being determined in part by how much of an improvement the new technology provides.
Germany	Nearly all regulations devolve to quasipublic corporatist organizations, which, through negotiations, determine (among other things) which services and technologies are covered, as well as provider fees.
Japan	Government sets the prices of all health care services, medical devices, and pharmaceuticals, and updates them every 2 years.
Switzerland	Government must approve health insurance premiums; they may be denied or result in refunds if they are deemed excessive.
United Kingdom	Generally, new technologies and drugs must be able to achieve, on average, an additional quality-adjusted life year for every 20,000–30,000 British pounds, or else they will not be covered under the National Health Service.

(**Sources:** Blümel M, Spranger A, Achstetter K, Maresso A, Busse R. Germany: health system review. Health Syst Transit 2020;22(6). [in press]. De Pietro C, Camenzind P, Sturny I, Crivelli L, Edwards-Garavoglia S, Spranger A, Wittenbecher F, Quentin W. Switzerland: health system review. Health Syst Transit 2015;17(4):1–288. Chevreul K, Berg Brigham K, Durand-Zaleski I, Hernández-Quevedo C. France: health system review. Health Syst Transit 2015;17(3):1–218. Marchildon GP, Allin S, Merkur S. Canada: health system review. Health Syst Transit 2020;22(3):i– 194. Sakamoto H, Rahman M, Nomura S, Okamoto E, Koike S, Yasunaga H, et al. Japan health system review. vol. 8 no. 1. New Delhi: World Health Organization, Regional Office for SouthEast Asia; 2018.)

government health care programs do set prices for paying for patients in their programs, in most cases through diagnosis-related group (DRGs) for hospital inpatient care and fee schedules for physician care. In contrast, private insurers are subject to few government constraints; the prices they pay to providers tend to be determined by market-based factors such as the relative bargaining power of insurers compared with providers in particular geographic markets. The main exception is that state insurance regulatory agencies sometime exert authority on the premiums charged by insurers to ensure that a sufficient amount of premium dollars is used for paying medical benefits instead of for administrative expenses or profits. Overall, government programs are more effective than private insurers in keeping prices lower. In 2017, Medicare paid physicians an average of only 75% as much as preferred provider organizations operated by private insurers. Medicaid, in turn, paid only 72% of the Medicare rates [23, p. 117].

In the other countries, price setting is the norm; sometimes it is done directly by government (Australia, Japan, Sweden, the United Kingdom), sometimes by government after negotiations with provider groups (France, Canada), and sometimes by quasigovernmental "corporatist" organizations—consortia of insurers and provider groups—but overseen by government (Germany, Switzerland). As shown in Table 15.4, cross-national data show that these fees are far lower than in the United States.

Some of the countries go further than regulating individual fees by also setting limits to aggregate health care payments. These can apply to particular health care sectors or to the health care system as a whole. In the case of sector-specific budgeting, Canadian provinces negotiate annual global budgets with each hospital. In Germany, ambulatory care physicians are paid through fee schedules that are negotiated between consortia of **sickness funds** and providers. These negotiations involve aggregate payments to regional associations that represent physicians in their geographic areas. These regional associations, in turn, pay physicians in their area based on points: a measure of the number of patients served by the physician practice and the number of services provided. If point totals exceed those provided in the previous year, fees are reduced to meet the budget [1]. Similar fee negotiation occurs in France and Japan although government plays a heavier role [24].

England provides an example of national budgeting, where government establishes a global budget that is distributed to local administrative bodies through **capitation** payments. These administrative bodies, called Clinical Commissioning Groups, are responsible for ensuring that patients in their local areas receive the appropriate health care services. In Sweden, health care is largely administered at the regional and local levels, which are required by law both to establish and to meet annual global budgets [25]. The French Parliament establishes an overall health care spending target each year based on government recommendations, which is then allotted to the different sectors (e.g., hospitals, ambulatory care) [26, p. 25].

Cost-effectiveness analyses and pricing tools are used to determine benefits and prices, particularly for pharmaceuticals

With the exception of universal coverage, there is perhaps no sharper contrast between the United States and the other countries than in how they determine what services are covered under their national health systems as well as the prices that are paid, especially for pharmaceuticals. This contrast is best illustrated by the fact that the US Medicare program is forbidden from negotiating prescription drug prices with pharmaceutical manufacturers, nor does it establish federal formularies. Rather, private insurance companies that sell the benefits to Medicare beneficiaries are responsible for negotiations [27]. It has been estimated that if Medicare employed drug formularies and negotiated prices in the same way as the Veterans Administration does, it could save 44% on drugs [28].

Other countries commonly use **reference pricing** systems as part of their pharmaceutical benefits programs. There are two types of reference prices, and they are often used in tandem. External reference prices limit how much a country will pay for particular drugs by setting as a maximum the amount paid by other countries; most countries set their own list of comparison countries. One study found that 36 of 41 European countries were using external reference pricing for some drugs, with 26 relying on it as the only or major mechanism for controlling drug prices [29]. Internal reference pricing is directed at the consumer. Under these systems, if consumers want to choose a drug that costs more than others on the market but does not provide additional benefits, they must pay for the difference out-of-pocket. Internal reference pricing is also the norm in Europe; in 2017, 22 of the 28 European Union countries employed some form of it [29]. While both external and internal reference pricing systems have been proposed in the United States, the latter has been used only on a very limited basis by private insurers, and the former, not at all [30].

The stark differences in drug prices between the United States and several other countries are given in Table 15.5, with selected prices often several times as high. Although the United States is a leader worldwide in use of generic drugs (Table 15.6), this is not enough to keep its spending equal to that of other countries. In 2015, US per-capita pharmaceutical spending exceeded $1000/year, which was 25% higher than the next highest country, Switzerland, and more than double the spending in Sweden, the Netherlands, and the United Kingdom [31]. Pharmaceuticals are not unique in this regard, as per-capita US spending exceeds that in other countries for all types of services.

Other insights

The previous section focused on lessons for the United States from the other nine countries. Here, we examine lessons from the perspective of what all of the countries can learn from each other. It is divided into sections on access and equity, expenditures control, health outcomes, and satisfaction, mirroring the various measures of performance examined in the previous two chapters.

Access and equity

The tables and figures in Chapters 14 and 15 focused on performance measures that can most plausibly be attributed to a country's health care system. Those that are most directly attributed to health insurance involve access and equity. The health insurance system is largely responsible for whether there are economic barriers to receiving care. In addition, the resources devoted to health care directly affect whether people have to wait for treatment.

We concluded that greater equity and access are facilitated by several factors: universal coverage, universal comprehensive benefits, reasonably low cost-sharing requirements, additional financial support for the economically vulnerable and children, and only a modest role for VHI. The UK National Health System is often viewed as the prototypical system that allows excellent financial access to services, with the only (relatively minor) exception being that there are substantial patient cost-sharing requirements for some dental services. The German system meets all of the above-mentioned characteristics, with a caveat: 11% of the population obtain their services through a parallel private insurance system that, some argue, weakens solidarity, results in unequal waiting times (although there is little such waiting in the country even for those opting to stay in the statutory health insurance system), and may incentivize the overprovision of services [32]. Japan also meets most of these characteristics, but unfortunately, comparative performance data on most of the measures of access and equity were not available. Finally, although it might appear that France presents patients with high cost-sharing requirements for adults, many people and diseases are exempted. While having VHI is necessary to cover some of these expenses, it is now almost universally available and fully subsidized for the poorest citizens.

As discussed earlier, other countries have one other tool that is not used in the US arsenal to make access to care more fair: in most cases, all insurers pay the same amount to providers so there is not an economic incentive to treat the patients of any particular insurer. The provider access problem is most acute in the United States for those with Medicaid coverage. Under the program, payment rates are determined by the states, and as a result of budget restrictions, fees are often so low that it is unprofitable for hospitals and office-based physicians to treat Medicaid patients. While it is true that some patients are more valuable than others in some countries, it is not the norm. Exceptions are that private insurance pays more to provider for the 11% of Germans with access to that system, and more to some Australian specialists.

The other aspect of access examined was waiting for services. Four countries have systemically longer waits than the other six: Canada, Sweden, the United Kingdom, and Australia—despite explicit guidelines aimed at preventing long waits. In most cases, these problems have existed for decades. The characteristic they share is that they all have tax-based single-payer systems where revenue is not earmarked for health care. As a result, health spending has to compete against other government priorities and is often chronically underfunded. The situation is somewhat different in Australia, where waits are much shorter for patients who have VHI and who therefore have financial access to private hospital care, which is more lucrative for physicians.

Expenditure control

All of the countries actively pursue expenditure control, but in different ways. Particularly among the European countries, there are a number of avenues by which countries can learn what others are doing through organizations such as the OECD, European Community, World Health Organization, and European Observatory on Health Systems and Policies.

As discussed in the country-specific chapters in this book, nations approach expenditure control in three ways: by controlling prices, utilization of services, labor and capital inputs (e.g., number of specialists or capital purchases like magnetic resonance imaging scanners), and total budgets. Some approaches combine more than one of these. An example is moving away from FFS medicine, which has the potential of both limiting prices and providing incentives to providers to reduce the provision of unnecessary services. In the following section, we list examples of how different countries have successfully pursued expenditure control.

All-payer systems

Many governments set fees either at the national or at the regional level. Direct government control is not necessary, however. Under Germany's statutory insurance system, which serves almost 90% of the population, so-called corporatist organizations—consortia of insurers on one side, and of providers on the other—determine provider fees based on negotiations (see Chapter 9 for more details). While government oversees the process to ensure that national goals of quality, value, and costs containment are met, primary responsibility rests with these nongovernmental, self-regulating bodies—so much so that they are in effect quasipublic organizations that define covered services, prices, and standards [33]. This results in what is sometimes called an "**all-payer system**" because the fees that providers are paid apply to all insurers. One effect of this system is that there is little or no financial incentive to favor treatment of one patient over another. Switzerland employs a similar version of all-payer, while Japan relies more on having government set unit prices that in turn apply to all the care of all patients [34].

Alternatives to fee-for-service

Traditionally, most countries pay their physicians on a FFS basis. The practice is often viewed as problematic because it encourages the overprovision of services, many of which are viewed by experts as unnecessary [35], as well as billing for more lucrative services—even if they are not actually provided (a practice called "upcoding"). But other ways of paying for care have their own shortcomings. As noted by James Robinson, "[S]alary undermines productivity, condones on-the-job leisure, and fosters a bureaucratic mentality in which every procedure is someone else's problem," while "[c]apitation rewards the denial of appropriate services, the dumping of the chronically ill, and a narrow scope of practice that refers out every time-consuming patient" [36, p. 149].

Robinson calls for hybrid systems that blended the best incentives of each payment mechanism. There are different ways of trying to accomplish this, and it needs to be stressed that to date, there is at best only inconsistent evidence about the effectiveness of alternative approaches. Most discussion has been on pay-for-performance systems that reward cost containment and/or quality, usually by targeting particular diseases or services—for example, providing bonuses to providers for the proportion of patients whose cholesterol levels or blood pressure is under control. An alternative approach, advocated by Robert Berenson and this author, is to devise a system that embodies "incentive neutrality" to "support health professionals' intrinsic motivation to act in their patients' best interests to improve overall quality..." [37, p. 2155]. An example that is gaining popularity is bundled payment, in which insurers pay a fee that covers an entire episode of care. This can both provide flexibility to physicians in how they choose to marshal services and tests to best treat patients while at the same time removing the economic incentive for overtreatment. One study reviewed 23 examples of bundled payment models from 8 countries, with the United States exhibiting the most examples, and with most studies showing both cost savings and quality improvement [38].

Pharmaceutical payment

There is probably no area of health policy that has involved more international cooperation than pharmaceutical payment policy. Innovations have occurred in two broad areas: using health technology assessment (HTA) to determine which drugs to cover under national health insurance plans, and the use of both HTA and various pricing tools—particularly external and internal reference pricing—to determine pharmaceutical payment rates.

Two countries that have been leaders in using HTA in deciding which drugs to cover are Australia and the United Kingdom. Australia was the first country that required new pharmaceuticals to be evaluated for cost-effectiveness. This has been carried out since 1992 by its Pharmaceutical Benefits Advisory Committee, based in part on analyses conducted by health economists [39]. It helped to pave the way for other countries, with the most notable example being the National Institute for Health and Care Excellence, or NICE, in the United Kingdom. NICE uses HTA to determine which new services, health technologies, and drugs to be covered and is well-known for employing strict and explicit cost-effectiveness criteria before approving coverage.

External and internal reference pricing systems were discussed earlier in this chapter. In describing innovative practices in this domain, one could point to several countries. France provides a good example. Some of the key aspects of France's procedure for determining the reimbursement rate for outpatient pharmaceuticals include [40, 41]:

- New drugs are evaluated on a five-point scale with regard to their medical benefit compared with existing products or therapies on the market. The five categories are major innovation, important improvement, moderate improvement, minor improvement, and no improvement.
- The price of a new drug is determined by the government after negotiation with the pharmaceutical company, and is based on several factors including the medical benefits conveyed by the product; the price of substitute drugs already on the market; the prices paid by other countries, and in particular, the United Kingdom, Germany, Italy, and Spain; anticipated sales; and cost-effectiveness for drugs granted a major to moderate improvement.
- The percentage of costs paid by the patient is determined by medical benefit. Drugs viewed as irreplaceable, like antiretroviral drugs for HIV/AIDS, are fully paid for by health insurance, as are prescribed drugs for patients with particular chronic diseases. The reimbursement for most other drugs for people without chronic diseases is 65%, but it is as low as 15% for drugs with little medical benefit [26, p. 76].
- Annual price increases after the drug's launch are limited and typically are lowered after 5 years. Moreover, the companies are required to pay rebates if the conditions of use that were initially agreed to (in terms of volume and length of treatment) are not met.

One area in which France has not been successful is in encouraging the use of generic drugs. As was shown in Table 15.16, only 30% of prescriptions were for generics in 2017, compared with over 80% in the United States, Germany, the United Kingdom, and Germany. Generic prescription is high in countries that have strong economic incentives for patients to use generics, provide practice guidelines to physicians to encourage generic use, and do not reward pharmacists for dispensing prescriptions with brand-name drugs.

Health outcomes

Tables 15.7 through 15.9 showed little in the way of consistent patterns across countries with regard to mortality and morbidity. Moreover, even though care was taken to use measures that are influenced by countries' health insurance systems, it is still very difficult to attribute any differences in outcomes solely to insurance system characteristics. Social factors and health behaviors are undoubtedly also responsible, as are countries' health care delivery systems, which are not examined in this book.

The country that performed most consistently highly in measures of both avoidable and hospital mortality was Switzerland (with Japan and the Netherlands also performing well), with the United Kingdom performing among the worst in most measures. Japan performed best across the measures of cancer mortality, with the United Kingdom again performing worst. The fact that the Japan and the United Kingdom's performance indicators were on different sides of the spectrum is noteworthy because they are the 2 countries of the 10 with the lowest average per-capita health care spending. Clearly, how much a country invests in its health care system does not have a strong influence on the outcome measures examined here. That is further exemplified by the fact that the United States spends by far the most, but performed among the worst in avoidable mortality, and was the poorest in measures of safe care. It did, however, perform well in two of the three cancer mortality rates, perhaps implying better success in specialty care rather than primary care outcomes.

Satisfaction

Unlike outcomes, in the measures of satisfaction with health care systems (Table 15.18), there was a clear pattern, with the top three performing countries—Germany, Switzerland, and France—all having **social health insurance** systems. (Data were not available for Japan.) Even here, it is difficult to draw much in the way of conclusions, for at least three reasons: (1) respondents are being asked about the entire health care system, not just health insurance; (2) while France has multiple insurers, people cannot choose among them but rather are assigned based on employment and occupation; and (3) more generally, cultural factors may affect how enthusiastically people express themselves to be about their system. Still, these results do indicate greater satisfaction among those in countries with multiple-payer systems than among those covered by single-payer systems.

The most glaring finding regards the US system, which was far more unpopular than any of the others. There are many likely reasons for this. One centers on the economic insecurity people face not only by the lack of comprehensive benefits, but also by the prospect of being without coverage if they lose their jobs. As noted, this manifested itself during the COVID-19 pandemic.

A second reason for the US system's unpopularity is likely to be its expense, which requires not only considerable patient cost sharing but also high premiums from employers and employees, and considerable taxes to support Medicare and Medicaid. A third and more general reason is that the American people do not share a common view on issues such as health care being a right. In 2020, the Gallup polling service found that 54% of Americans said that it is government's responsibility that all Americans have health care coverage, but 45% opposed this viewpoint. Interestingly, those numbers were almost the reverse between 2013 and 2015 before many Americans became accustomed to the ACA [42, 43].

Final thoughts

There is little agreement about what aspects of health insurance systems are the highest priority for reform. Different researchers reach entirely different conclusions about what are the overall best health care systems. We also see disagreement within countries, where proposals for reform are almost always met by strong opposition.

It would be a mistake, however, to think that it is impossible to make progress. That is made clear by the fact that nine of the 10 countries have, at least broadly speaking, reached similar conclusions about the necessary and desirable underpinnings of their health insurance systems. These include (1) building systems based on the ethic of affordable, equitable access to care, (2) having a single, publicly mandated insurance system to promote fairness and efficiency, (3) using government for health care planning activities involving the supply of resources and constraining prices, and (4) employing economic tools to determine covered benefits and prices, especially for pharmaceutical products. There is a great deal of variety in how each country implements each of these; nevertheless, it would be hard to deny that there is strong international agreement in such critical areas. The United States is a notable exception.

Future challenges will be even greater as populations age, climate change accelerates, and future pandemics loom. Every country faces continuing challenges in finding reforms that are politically feasible, to deal not just with their current problems but also with the prospect of greater ones down the road. Throughout this book, we have seen examples of countries in which care was still unaffordable to many with lower incomes or entailed long waits to receive services, was costly and wasteful, and in which people get sick or die from diseases that should be treatable in a well-operating system. While countries may sometimes find it possible to move forward by working in isolation, there is far more promise through accelerating collaborative efforts with researchers and policy makers *across* countries, discovering and implementing best practices worldwide.

References

[1] Emanuel EJ. Which country has the world's best health care? New York: Public Affairs; 2020.
[2] Joumard I, André C, Nicq C. Health care systems: Efficiency and institutions. OECD Economics Department Working Papers. 769; 2010.
[3] Health Systems: Improving Performance. The World Health Report 2000. Geneva: World Health Organization.
[4] Jamison DT, Sandbu ME. Global health. WHO ranking of health system performance. Science 2001;293(5535):1595–6.
[5] Robbins A. WHO ranking of health systems. Science 2001;294(5548):1832–3.
[6] Mooney G, Wiseman V. World health report 2000: challenging a world view. J Health Serv Res Policy 2000;5(4):198–9.
[7] Oliver A. The folly of cross-country ranking exercises. Health Econ Policy Law 2012;7(1):15–7.

[8]   Schneider EC, Sarnak DO, Squires D, Shah A, Doty MM. Mirror, mirror 2017: International comparison reflects flaws and opportunities for better U.S. health care. Mirror, Mirror: The Commonwealth Fund; 2017.

[9]   About us. The Commonwealth Fund [Internet]. [Accessed 24 November 2020]. Available from: https://www.commonwealthfund.org/about-us.

[10] Anon. 2016 commonwealth fund international health policy survey of adults. The Commonwealth Fund; 2016.

[11] Schneider EC, Sarnak DO, Squires D, Shah A, Doty MM. Mirror, mirror 2017: International comparison reflects flaws and opportunities for better U.S. health care. The Commonwealth Fund; 2017.

[12] Health Consumer Powerhouse. [Internet]. [Accessed 24 November 2020]. Available from: https://healthpowerhouse.com/#.

[13] What we do. Health Consumer Powerhouse [Internet]. [Accessed 24 November 2020]. Available from: https://healthpowerhouse.com/about-us/#what-we-do.

[14] Roy A. Introducing the FREOPP world index of healthcare innovation. The Foundation for Research on Equal Opportunity; 2020. [Internet]. [Accessed 24 November 2020]. Available from https://freopp.org/wihi2020-505b1b60bce6.

[15] Anon. Our mission. The Foundation for Research on Equal Opportunity; 2016. [Internet]. [Accessed 24 November 2020]. Available from: https://freopp.org/our-mission-3b16e8e8c656.

[16] Girvan G. How we compiled the FREOPP world index of healthcare innovation. The Foundation for Research on Equal Opportunity; 2020. [Internet]. [Accessed 24 November 2020]. Available from: https://freopp.org/how-we-compiled-the-world-index-of-healthcare-innovation-4761214447f4.

[17] Fronstin P, Woodbury SA. Update: how many Americans have lost jobs with employer health coverage during the pandemic? The Commonwealth Fund; 2021.

[18] Saltman RB. Health sector solidarity: a core European value but with broadly varying content. Isr J Health Policy Res 2015;4:5.

[19] Hamel L, Norton M, Pollitz K, Levitt L, Claxton G, Brodie M. The burden of medical debt: Results from the Kaiser Family Foundation/New York Times Medical Bills Survey. KFF; 2016.

[20] Claxton G, Rae M, Damico A, Young G, McDermott D, Whitmore H. Employer health benefits. San Francisco, CA: Henry J. Kaiser Family Foundation; 2019.

[21] Coverage Levels: The Metal Tiers. Covered California [Internet]. [Accessed 24 November 2020]. Available from: https://www.coveredca.com/support/before-you-buy/metal-tiers/.

[22] Federal Reserve Board. Dealing with unexpected expenses. In: Durante A, Chen L, editors. Report on the economic well-being of US households in 2018 - May 2019. Washington, DC: Federal Reserve Board's Division of Consumer and Community Affairs (DCCA); 2019.

[23] Anon. Medicare payment policy. Report to the Congress. Washington, DC: The Medicare Payment Advisory Commission (MedPAC); 2019.

[24] Gusmano MK, Laugesen M, Rodwin VG, Brown LD. Getting the price right: how some countries control spending in a fee-for-service system. Health Aff (Millwood) 2020;39(11):1867–74.

[25] Glenngård AH. In: Tikkanen R, Osborn R, Mossialos E, Djordjevic A, Wharton GA, editors. Sweden. International health care system profiles. The Commonwealth Fund; 2020. [Internet]. [Accessed 17 September 2020]. Available from: https://www.commonwealthfund.org/international-health-policy-center/countries/sweden.

[26] Chevreul K, Brigham KB, Durand-Zaleski I, Hernández-Quevedo C. In: Hernández-Quevedo C, Nolte E, Van Ginneken E, editors. France: Health system review. Health systems in transition, vol. 17. Copenhagen: The European Observatory on Health Systems and Policies; 2015.

[27] Lee TT, Gluck AR, Curfman GD. The politics of medicare and drug-price negotiation (updated). Health Affairs; 2016. [Blog]. [Accessed 24 November 2020]. Available from: https://www.healthaffairs.org/do/10.1377/hblog20160919.056632/full/.

[28] Venker B, Stephenson KB, Gellad WF. Assessment of spending in medicare part D if medication prices from the Department of Veterans Affairs were used. JAMA Intern Med 2019;179(3):431–3.

[29] Hoagland GW, Parekh A, Hamm N, Cassling K, Fernekes C. Examining two approaches to U.S. drug pricing: international prices and therapeutic equivalency. Bipartisan Policy Center; 2019.

[30] Robinson JC, Brown TT, Whaley C. Reference pricing changes the 'choice architecture' of health care for consumers. Health Aff (Millwood) 2017;36(3):524–30.

[31] Sarnak DO, Squires D, Kuzmak G. Figures from paying for prescription drugs around the world: Why is the U.S. an outlier? The Commonwealth Fund; 2017.

[32] Anon. Country report Germany 2019: Including an in-depth review on the prevention and correction of macroeconomic imbalances. Brussels: European Commission; 2019.

[33] Busse R, Blümel M. Germany: Health system review. 2nd ed. vol. 16. Copenhagen: Health Systems in Transition; 2014.

[34] Reinhardt UE. The many different prices paid to providers and the flawed theory of cost shifting: is it time for a more rational all-payer system? Health Aff (Millwood) 2011;30(11):2125–33.

[35] Brownlee S, Chalkidou K, Doust J, Elshaug AG, Glasziou P, Heath I, et al. Evidence for overuse of medical services around the world. Lancet 2017;390(10090):156–68.

[36] Robinson JC. Theory and practice in the design of physician payment incentives. Milbank Q 2001;79(2):149–77. III.

[37] Berenson RA, Rice T. Beyond measurement and reward: methods of motivating quality improvement and accountability. Health Serv Res 2015;50(Suppl. 2):2155–86.

[38] Struijs J, De Vries EF, Baan CA, Van Gils PF, Rosenthal MB. Bundled-payment models around the world: How they work and what their impact has been. The Commonwealth Fund; 2020.

[39] Freund DA. Initial development of the Australian Guidelines. Med Care 1996;34(12 Suppl):DS211–215.

[40] Chicoye A, Chhabra A. France - pharmaceuticals: Global health technology assessment road map. ISPOR; 2009.

[41] Rodwin MA. What can the United States learn from pharmaceutical spending controls in France? The Commonwealth Fund; 2019.

[42] Healthcare System. Gallup [News]. [Accessed 24 November 2020]. Available from: https://news.gallup.com/poll/4708/healthcare-system.aspx.

[43] Anon. KFF health tracking poll: The public's views on the ACA. Health Reform; 2020. [Internet]. [Accessed 25 September 2020]. Available from: https://www.kff.org/interactive/kff-health-tracking-poll-the-publics-views-on-the-aca/#?response=Favorable-Unfavorable&aRange=twoYear.

[44] Okoli C, Pawlowski SD. The Delphi method as a research tool: an example, design considerations and applications. Inf Manag 2004;42(1):15–29.

[45] Salkever DS, Bice TW. The impact of certificate-of need controls on hospital investment. Milbank Mem Fund Q Health Soc 1976;54(2):185–214.

[46] Anon. About us. National Health Service Corps (NHSC); 2020. [Internet]. [Accessed 29 November 2020]. Available from: https://nhsc.hrsa.gov/about-us.

[47] Anon. Health professional shortage area physician bonus program. Centers for Medicare & Medicaid Services; 2020. [PDF]. [Accessed 29 November 2020]. Available from: https://www.cms.gov/Outreach-and-Education/Medicare-Learning-Network-MLN/MLNProducts/Downloads/HPSAfctsht.pdf.

Glossary

(Terms in italics are defined elsewhere in the Glossary)

Accountable care organizations (ACOs) Originated in the United States, these are provider groups, which can include hospitals, physicians, or other clinical professionals, that have agreed with insurers to be responsible for the care that they provide to a group of insured persons. They are provided with financial incentives to meet goals of high-quality care and for being prudent users of medical resources.

All-payer system A financing system that applies to the *public or statutory* insurance sector, where all health insurers pay the same fees to providers. In such a system, providers do not have a financial incentive to favor treating the patients of one insurer over those of another.

Balance billing When physicians charge patients amounts in excess of an insurer's fee for providing a service. Typically, these additional fees must be paid either out of pocket by the patient or by private insurance that supplements a person's primary coverage. In some countries, it is referred to as *bulk billing* or *extra billing*.

Beveridge William Beveridge is often given credit for designing the United Kingdom's National Health Service in the 1940s, which serves as a prototype for national health systems with a single public insurer and strong government involvement in both the financing and delivery of healthcare services.

Bismarck The government of Chancellor Otto von Bismarck is often given credit for originating the first social health insurance system, in Germany in the 1880s, which serves as a prototype of national health systems that rely on private (usually nonprofit) insurers or *sickness funds* to provide coverage that is funded jointly by employer and employee contributions.

Brexit In 2016, voters in the United Kingdom voted to leave the European Union by a margin of 52% to 48%. This has been coined as Brexit—the exit of Britain.

Capitation A fixed payment (usually annual) to a provider or provider organization for each patient under their care (see Box 2.3).

Coinsurance The percentage of a medical bill that has to be paid by or on behalf of the patient (see Box 2.2).

Community rating A system in which private insurers are required to charge the same premiums to all enrollees irrespective of factors such as health status. Sometimes community rating is modified to allow different premiums for different age-groups or others (e.g., smokers vs nonsmokers).

Copayment A fixed monetary amount that must be paid by or on behalf of the patient when receiving a service (see Box 2.2).

Corporatism As applied to healthcare systems, this connotes a system largely administered by private organizations representing (certain) societal interests, typically consortia of insurers and consortia of providers, which negotiate with each other over issues such as the benefits that will be covered and the fees that will be paid to providers. While government oversees these activities, typically it is not directly involved.

Deductible The amount of money that has to be paid by or on behalf of the patient during a specified time period before insurance benefits are paid out. Deductibles usually but do not always apply to a calendar year (see Box 2.2).

Diagnosis-related groups (DRGs) A patient classification system used primarily for hospital payment. A country or insurer may use several hundred or even thousands of DRGs, each of which identifies patients with a particular illness or receiving a particular type of service. Insurers pay a fixed amount to hospitals and sometimes physicians for patients in a particular DRG that is not explicitly linked to length of stay or use of resources, providing a strong incentive to discharge patients when they no longer need further hospital care.

Experience rating Under this system, private insurers can charge more to individuals or groups of enrollees (such as employees working for a particular employer) based on factors such as health status and anticipated costs of providing care.

Fee-for-service (FFS) A fixed amount paid to a provider—typically a physician—to provide a single service (see Box 2.3).

Gatekeeping A requirement that a patient receive a referral for hospital and/or specialist care from a primary care physician in order to have the care paid for by the insurer.

Gini coefficient A quantitative measure of equality across a population. It is commonly used in health care to denote whether a financial system is *progressive or regressive.* The Gini coefficient ranges from a value of 0 (perfect equality) to 1 (perfect inequality).

Gross domestic product (GDP) A measure of the total monetary value of all goods and services produced in a country during a calendar year, providing a measure of national wealth.

Horizontal equity The degree to which similar people are treated the same with respect to some characteristic. The term is commonly used in the tax literature and connotes that people with similar incomes and or assets incur the same tax liabilities. In the health economics literature, it usually means equal treatment for those with equal health needs.

Kakwani index A quantitative measure of whether a particular tax is *progressive or regressive.* Positive values indicate progressivity, and negative values, regressivity.

Monopsony When there is only one purchaser of a good (in contrast to a monopoly, when there is only one seller). Single-payer systems are examples of a monopsony in that there is only one purchaser of hospital and physician services, typically national or regional government. Monopsonies provide the purchaser with a great deal of bargaining power in setting or negotiating provider fees.

Mortality amenable to health care Death from a disease or condition (in most cases before the age of 75) that should have been prevented by the effective and timely use of medical care (see Box 15.1).

Out-of-pocket maximum The most a patient is required to pay in cost sharing requirements during a time period (usually a year). After reaching that expenditure level, insurance pays all remaining costs (see Box 2.2).

Pay for performance (P4P) A term that encompasses financial rewards or penalties that provide incentives for providers to perform in the way that a public or private insurer desires. It applies to both hospital and physician payment (see Box 2.3).

Premium A fixed amount of money (often charged monthly) paid to secure health insurance.

Progressive/regressive taxes If a tax is progressive, higher-income people pay a larger proportion of their income, and lower-income people, a smaller proportion. Regressive taxes are the opposite: the burden on lower-income persons as a proportion of income is greater than it is for higher-income persons.

Public/statutory health insurance The primary health insurance program in countries with automatic or mandatory coverage. In most countries, some people supplement this with private, *voluntary health insurance.*

Purchasing power parities (PPPs) A tool used to convert international currencies to a common scale, allowing for cross-national comparisons of *gross domestic product* and other metrics of interest. PPPs are constructed so that it would take the same amount of money in any given country's national currency to purchase a standard basket of goods and services. PPPs are usually tied to US dollars.

Quality-adjusted life year (QALY) A measure of healthcare outcomes that is calculated by summing the expected number of years of life remaining, with each year weighted by a factor that quantifies the quality of life experienced during that year. QALYs are often used in cost-effectiveness analyses to determine the most efficient way to invest societal resources.

Reference pricing (internal and external) Systems to control the price paid by insurers for prescription drugs. Under internal reference pricing, if consumers choose a drug that costs more than others on the market but does not provide additional benefits, they must pay for the difference out of pocket. External reference pricing limits how much a country pays for particular drugs by setting as a maximum the amount paid by other countries.

Sickness funds A name often given to nonprofit health insurers (typically in Europe) that are funded jointly by employers and employees. Their origin was in the middle ages, where workers in guilds banded together to help each other and their families with the financial consequences of illness and death.

Single-payer system A system that applies to the *public or statutory* insurance sector, where there is a single public (national or regional) health insurer that typically sets or negotiates the benefits covered by, fees paid for, and regulation of healthcare services.

Social health insurance Often contrasted with a *single-payer system* and sometimes used as synonymous with a *Bismarck-style system.* These systems rely on private (usually nonprofit) insurers (i.e., *sickness funds*) to provide coverage that is funded jointly by employer and employee contributions.

Solidarity In health, this refers to an ethic whereby everyone is entitled to high-quality health care based solely on medical need and regardless of their ability to pay.

Tendering A system in which specialist services or specialized prescription drugs are put out to bid to competing suppliers.

Value-added tax (VAT) A consumption tax put on the sale of goods and/or services that is levied at each stage of the production process.

Vertical equity The treatment of those with fewer resources more favorably, typically applied to taxation systems. When poorer persons pay a lower percentage of their incomes for a particular tax than do wealthier persons, it is vertically equitable.

Voluntary health insurance (VHI) Private health insurance that often supplements the *public/statutory* system in a country. There are three types: *Substitutive VHI* exists when people can choose a private insurance product instead of the *public/statutory* coverage, as is the case for high-income residents (and some others) in Germany. *Supplemental VHI* provides benefits for services that are not covered by the *public/statutory* system (e.g., dental care, eyeglasses, private hospital rooms). *Complementary VHI* pay for some or all of the remaining costs that are only partly paid for by *public/statutory* systems (e.g., coinsurance).

Welfare state A national system where government is responsible for ensuring that the basic needs of its citizenry are met, particularly for people of limited means. This typically includes old-age pensions and health insurance.

Abbreviations

ACA	Patient Protection and Affordable Care Act (United States)
ACO	accountable care organization (United States)
Ccgs	clinical commissioning groups (United Kingdom)
CEPS	France's economic committee for health products
CHI	complementary health insurance (France)
CHIP	Children's Health Insurance Program (United States)
CMS	Centers for Medicare & Medicaid Services (United States)
CMU	France's social insurance program for health
CON	Certificate of Need (United States)
COPD	chronic obstructive pulmonary disease
DHHS	Department of Health and Human Services (United States)
DPC	Japanese hospital payment system, diagnosis-procedure combination
DRG	diagnosis-related groups
DTP	diphtheria, tetanus, and pertussis
EMTALA	Emergency Medical Treatment & Labor Act (United States)
FFS	fee-for-service
FOPH	Federal Office of Public Health (Switzerland)
GDP	gross domestic product
GP	general practitioner
HA	Health Authority (Canada)
HAQ	Healthcare Access and Quality index
HDHP	high-deductible health plan (United States)
HMO	health maintenance organization (mainly United States)
HSA	health savings account (United States)
HTA	health technology assessment
JHIA	Japan Health Insurance Association
LTC	long-term care
MAS	Mutual Aid Societies (Japan)
MBS	Medicare Benefits Schedule (Australia)
MHI	Mandatory Health Insurance (Switzerland)
MHLW	Ministry of Health, Labor, and Welfare (Japan)
MRI	magnetic resonance imaging
NHS	National Health Service (United Kingdom)
NIC	National Insurance Contribution (United Kingdom)
NICE	National Institute for Heath and Care Excellence (United Kingdom)
OECD	Organization for Economic Co-operation and Development
ONDAM	France's National expenditure target
OOP	out-of-pocket
P4P	pay for performance

PBAC	Pharmaceutical Benefits Advisory Committee (Australia)
PBM	pharmaceutical benefit manager (United States)
PBS	Pharmaceutical Benefits Scheme (Australia)
PHI	Private Health Insurance (Germany)
PMPRB	Patented Medicine Prices Review Board (Canada)
POS	point-of-service plan (United States)
PPO	preferred provider organization (United States)
PPP	purchasing power parities
PBR	Payment by Results (United Kingdom)
QALY	quality-adjusted life-year
SES	socioeconomic status
SF	Swiss franc
SHI	social health insurance
SMS1	Japan's Society-Managed Health Insurance program
T2A	France's hospital payment system, a form of DRGs
VAT	value-added tax
VHA	Veterans Health Administration (United States)
VHI	voluntary health insurance
WHO	World Health Organization

Index

Note: Page numbers followed by *t* indicate tables and *b* indicate boxes.

Printed in the United States
by Baker & Taylor Publisher Services